The First Confederate Soldier

The First Confederate Soldier

*George Washington Lee
and Civil War Atlanta*

ROBERT SCOTT DAVIS

McFarland & Company, Inc., Publishers
Jefferson, North Carolina

ISBN (print) 978-1-4766-9731-4
ISBN (ebook) 978-1-4766-5527-7

Library of Congress cataloging data are available

Library of Congress Control Number 2025043342

© 2026 Robert Scott Davis. All rights reserved

No part of this book may be reproduced or transmitted in any form or by any means, electronic or mechanical, including photocopying or recording, or by any information storage and retrieval system, without permission in writing from the publisher.

Front cover images: Postwar photograph of George W. Lee taken in New York (Lee/Huss Family Papers, AC 69-249, Georgia Archives, Morrow). *Background* Atlanta, Georgia, and its rebel defenses, circa 1864–1865 (Library of Congress).

Printed in the United States of America

*McFarland & Company, Inc., Publishers
Box 611, Jefferson, North Carolina 28640
www.mcfarlandpub.com*

Dedicated to Marion O. Smith, George W. Lee researcher.

And in Memory of Deanna Slappey and in tribute
to everyone like her who does historical research
that is never published or properly recognized.

Acknowledgments

ATTEMPTING TO DO Lee justice when other writers have failed or given up required the help of extraordinary people to whom I give my thanks for help greater than I can even begin to recall, notably Bruce Allardice, the late Carl A. Anderson, Vicki Betts, Dr. Keith Bohannon, James Bullock, Dr. David Carlton, Dr. Stephen Davis, Gerald Flinchum, George Jones, Dr. Jacqueline Jones, Bill Kinsland, David Yoakley Mitchell, Jim Ogden, Mary Palmer Linnemann, Jane Singer, the late Gordon B. Smith, Marion O. Smith, Dr. Larry Stephens, Karen S. Walker, and Greg White.

Ken Denney is extremely generous in allowing me the use of his amazing research on the buildings of Civil War Atlanta and the people who owned them. He is planning to donate his research to the Kenan Research Center of the Atlanta History Center. My brother Gus Welborn made the illustrations one of the important parts of this work.

I want to make more than just an acknowledgment of the help provided by the staff of Southern History of the Birmingham Public Library, one of the greatest places for Southern history that will ever be. Let me say to all of you, "Bob's your uncle."

This book would not have been possible without the genealogy collection at Wallace State Community College in Hanceville, Alabama, a preeminent center for Civil War research, and my co-workers Iman, Betty, Dean, Dalene, and Martha. The collection and the multi-million-dollar six-story library that housed it will likely soon be no more for reasons the college administration refuses to explain. For asking why, I am banned, under threat of arrest, from even coming on campus.[1] Such is today's Alabama.

This book would not be without the resources of that library and its loss would be a tragedy for the students and the public. I built the award-winning nationally recognized Family & Regional History Program there through the foresight and generous support of the late Dr. James C. "Jake" Bailey, president of Wallace State Community College, and with the advice of the late Professor Hollis Royal Laney. Royal wanted a center where his history students could experience research, but especially on their own respective families.

Libraries, like history and literature over political correctness, are victims in our partisan times in a world that in every good way is contracting to something less and less. Archives, books, libraries, and real research are a true lost cause. The internet is responsible. So too is the short-sighted, immoral greed common to our times, not unlike what George W. Lee experienced in his Civil War Atlanta.

Table of Contents

Acknowledgments — vi
Preface — 1
Introduction — 5

One. The First Confederate Soldier — 13
Two. Atlanta, Savannah, Atlanta, Virginia, Atlanta — 29
Three. In the Confederate Special Service in Atlanta — 57
Four. Resistance and Insurrection in North Georgia — 71
Five. Atlanta's Secret Yankees — 92
Six. Sherman (and History) vs. George W. Lee — 107

Appendix A. Rank Held by George Washington Lee — 129
Appendix B. C.C. Hine's Report on Atlanta in 1859 — 131
Appendix C. The Other Great Locomotive Chase — 137
Appendix D. George W. Lee's Prisoner Lists — 142
Appendix E. Civilians Forced to Evacuate Atlanta, September 1864 — 144
Appendix F. Some Civil War Atlantans — 157
Appendix G. Research in Atlanta and the Atlanta Area — 160
Chapter Notes — 171
Bibliography — 199
Index — 209

Preface

"Some people would rather leave that wound [of the Civil War] closed.... Those who do not want to hear the story, those who do not want to tell the story, are part of the problem, not part of the solution."—Joseph McGill, Jr., National Trust for Historic Preservation

I AM SURE THAT the preeminent historian of the South and my friend, the late Dr. E. Merton Coulter, never knew the epic story of Colonel George Washington Lee, the commandant of Civil War Atlanta. He did, however, publish many articles and books on people who deserved more of a note, if not notoriety, in Southern history than they received. Coulter did incredible, seemingly impossible, work for his time bringing such history and lives to light, made the more amazing because of the limited research resources available in his time. Most of these figures remain obscure to public history but are hunted by scholars who seek the reality of the past rather than cherry picking facts for some agenda or repeating legends. If Dr. Coulter had the resources that we enjoy today, he might well have written this book! This esteemed researcher told me that more has appeared in print on the American Civil War than any other topic and that new work on it will continue to appear in print forever as it will always remain relevant to America's changing times. He would have written something to that effect could he have prepared a foreword to this book.

In the 1970s, however, Coulter's claims about the importance of the Civil War seemed to me exaggerated as so much of what was published in those days only repeated standard histories of battles and generals, a problem going back to when the old veterans wrote their memoirs and often filled space by repeating stories they had read. Unlike Coulter, other writers frequently rehashed standard works of writers like Bruce Catton and Douglas Southall Freeman. The public wanted to read the stories told by their grandparents and pushed by the racist "Lost Cause" ideals in the mainstream media in the late 1800s through to almost the present times or its often equally false and racist counterculture successor.

Critics rightly describe such publications on the military history of the time, and sometimes in the present, as viewing the war from 30,000 feet with arrows moving across a map. Today, simplistic, poorly researched regurgitations are sometimes used to publish personal political and social partisan rants under the false guise of scholarly research. Conversely, two readers of this biography of George W. Lee

Preface

Historian Wilbur Kurtz's imaginative rendering of Atlanta on the eve of the Civil War (Kenan Research Center at the Atlanta History Center).

adamantly opposed publishing this book because, in their view, the Civil War's military and social history should not be told together.

In the early 1970s, when I made a special effort to meet Dr. Coulter, I knew I wanted to write the stories of Georgia lost to popular history from a lack of known and used sources. My high school Georgia history teacher was the famed, award-winning, gifted Ted Key. He beguiled his students with stories of French Fort Caroline, Andersonville Confederate prison camp, and so much else. As a student you never knew what to expect in the teaching laboratory that was his classroom. His highly personal teaching could be life-changing experiences and inspiration for the best of future teachers. He required each student to write a 100-page report; my first scholarship—however below his high standards—was my finished product.[1] Even before I met Dr. Coulter, I was Georgia's first history intern in 1974 and, as such, began research and writings that continue to this day to try to recover lost history of the forgotten Revolutionary War Kettle Creek battlefield.[2]

Fort Caroline and then Kettle Creek are where I started as a researcher, but I did not want to write about the Civil War or the institution of slavery. When I started, Southern history consisted largely of those areas, and even that was, and is, too often, rehashing popular public history. I had to overcome many personal and professional obstacles to publish, but I had articles on lost Georgia history in print for 15 years before my first significant work on the Civil War appeared in print.[3] In my writings, I have tried to largely relegate the "Gods and Generals" to the background in order to explore what the great Lincoln assassination expert Dr. James O. Hall complimented me on: the "little people" in the historical shadows who are an overlooked part of the Civil War. Although my research on African American history appeared in print as early as 1980, I only published my first important piece on that fascinating subject in 2007.[4] I hope that I have since made amends.

Advising on, finding, and publishing the forgotten, lost, and suppressed lives of the lost to Georgia history became what I do, and here are the results on George Washington Lee and his likely acquaintances, notably the parallel lives of George W. Ashburn, Robert A. Crawford, and Samuel Dexter Niles. This book is not a *Gone with the Wind* for our times, but a history of the new rapidly expanding Atlanta whose worst qualities were exacerbated by the Civil War. Lee was a part of most of what happened and witnessed all of it.

Unlike most of the people I have researched, Lee has so much material to work with. He has hundreds of references in the official Confederate correspondence and the Atlanta newspapers of his time almost form a memoir of his career, but, unfortunately, without his personal or ideological reflections. The diaries of Cornelius Hanleiter and William Gibbs McAdoo are rich sources of information on Lee.

Civil War researcher Greg White went so far as to say that George Washington Lee may be the last great untold Civil War story. For reasons I can only speculate upon, this Confederate leader was largely forgotten even in the extensively published Atlanta and Civil War histories. He is not mentioned in the great novel *Gone with the Wind*. Other scholars have considered writing a fair and balanced biography of this Confederate provost marshal of Atlanta but found the complexity of the subject too daunting. Credible in depth research only began with the work of Marion O. Smith, a staff member of the *Papers of Andrew Johnson* and explorer of the history of the Confederate Niter Bureau.

Thomas Dyer wrote of Lee in *Secret Yankees*, presenting one image of Lee and the other figures in the text at odds with the sources he explains in his annotation.[5] Some writers have rehashed Dyer's work without serious analysis, one of whom even attacked facts that I presented in my text, as had Dyer in his annotation, as my misguided personal prejudice. Making Lee to be head of some sort of predecessor to the Nazi Gestapo and anyone who writes anything contradictory is apparently thought to sell books.

Famed classicist Emily Wilson talks of exploring such other worlds as Lee and his Atlanta in the Civil War so different from our own as a great adventure. She referred to the Trojan War, but her point is for all times, and a reader can see that in Lee's career. Discovering the history of Atlanta's Confederate provost marshal without judgment and excuses is challenging but necessary even as people of the past are now often judged by applying what are alleged to be our modern standards of morality. Much more, as playwright Eugene O'Neill wrote, might be learned from an honest study of the past to understand the present than from imagination used to support some popular agenda, especially in the conflicted history of the Civil War. Publicly aired misunderstandings do injustice to the past, promote conflict and dishonesty in the present, and prevent us from solving the challenges that create problems for what will be our shared future. The issues of the Antebellum Era, Civil War, and Reconstruction are, however, too complicated for simplistic, undocumented judgments, however politically correct, whether in 1860, 1890, or 2025.

George Washington Lee fully supported the Confederate States of America and is an excellent vehicle for such a study in our times. He was a devoted and effective supporter of the idea of and the nation created by Southern independence, although he and his family lived without enslaved labor or a direct connection with the institution of slavery. I cannot document why. I knew people like the late former Georgia governor Lester Maddox who reportedly held no contempt toward African Americans but supported segregation; that idea troubles me too.

Nothing survives of Lee's views on race and human bondage. Some people would explain Lee's silence about slavery with "cookie cutter" imaginative visions of the past that come from personal agendas rather than the understanding of people within their own time, although he likely represented an entire class of white—and Black—Southerners. The best answer I have is that he and the Atlanta professionals who followed him believed that the Confederate States of America would offer white middle-class entrepreneurs and tradesmen like Lee opportunities not available to them in antebellum America. That idea is completely at odds with the reasons that the slave-owning planter class intended in creating the Southern nation and which proved a false ideal in the more than a century and a half after the Civil War.

I never learned why Lee chose to be the first soldier and almost the last of the Confederate States of America or took the actions that he did in between. He is also controversial because of his treatment and alleged treatment of opposition to the Confederate war effort. He was accused of abusing, threatening, and, in one instance, killing "secret Yankees," Atlanta citizens who supported the United States rather than the Confederate States of America.

More than an adamant supporter of an independent Southern nation, Lee had many reasons to just walk away as so many other Americans, North and South, did. The circumstance of his Atlanta suggests answers, but any definitive explanations are speculative. This work sets out to present the facts but must leave the reader to construe the meaning.

This work comes in a golden age of Civil War scholarship and owes much to that work. Scholars such as Dr. William Bragg, Dr. George W. Lamplugh, Dr. Larry Stephens, and others continued Dr. Coulter's work in uncovering lost Georgia history. Despite the unprecedented availability of research sources, publication, however, opportunities are now in decline, as are the numbers of the reading public and formally trained history scholars. Yet, people of all walks of life and educational background still seek to find and publish lost history, especially in uncovering the important and incredible past of Dr. Hall's "little people." Scholars such as Dr. Francis H. Casstevens, Dr. Gerald Flinchum, Jane Singer, and Dr. Larry Stephens shine a light on these shadows of the Civil War.

Introduction

"It is not the cover of the book but what the book contains is the question. Many a good book has dark covers."—Southern Black Revolutionary War veteran Agrippa Hull

GEORGE WASHINGTON LEE had an epic military career, from Florida to Virginia, but most importantly in Atlanta and Georgia. He served the the South as an independent country steadfastly and effectively, even before the Confederate States of America existed. This first official Confederate soldier served in the Southern nation's darkest hours and successfully led troops in battle, including in defending Macon late in the war for a hopelessly lost cause. His life was often at risk, as he faced assassination attempts, military battles, and bouts of tuberculosis, time and again, when many others would have or did walk away—or, so often, ran!

As the provost marshal of Atlanta, Lee fought bootlegging, counterfeiting, espionage, organized crime, petty thieves, public fear, and saboteurs, important chapters in the lost social history of the Civil War, but not any real insurrection by African Americans. He also played an essential but controversial role in suppressing opposition to the Confederate war effort in Georgia and the Southeast. He earned praise from the highest levels of the Confederate government, but he also made dangerous enemies!

The First Confederate Soldier

The writings about and of Lee fail to explain why he gave so much to a cause that seemingly offered him no benefit. His old Southern family in Atlanta were middle-class clerks; he was a tradesman and failed saloonkeeper, real estate speculator, and millwright. Yet, for all that he experienced and his sacrifices for the Confederate States of America, he and his family had no recorded connection to enslaved labor. Lee's story and that of the Atlanta artisan class who followed him can be seen in the context of the Civil War South in this book, but their reasons for why they marched under him to war remains only speculative. From the silence of these Southerners, they remain an enigma now as they did to Americans then. In other wars, they would be assumed to have volunteered to march off to war to defend their homes and nation from invasion, whatever any other issues. Men fought and died on both

From the post–Civil War painting *Cyclorama of the Battle of Atlanta* (1886), showing an accurate view of wartime Atlanta on the horizon (Kenan Research Center at the Atlanta History Center).

sides without any regard for or in opposition to emancipation and without questioning their opinions on race. Their reasons for fighting have not changed, only modern perceptions.

Lee's extensive official correspondence and diaries of men close to him make no mention of how he felt about African Americans or slavery, even race or immigrant labor, an example of one of the inconvenient paradoxes that remain in the honest discussions of the American Civil War. His silence is especially strange as his antebellum Atlanta had a complicated, conflicted, and controversial history with African American labor, as explained herein. He was not under suspicion by Atlanta's ad hoc committees that saw support for slavery as necessary to support of the Confederacy or the war, however.[1]

George W. Lee's service to the cause of secession began before the war and lasted until the final moments of that struggle. That career had four phases. He rallied the middle-class white artisans of Atlanta to the cause of a new Southern nation and overcame political obstacles to become the first official Confederate soldier at Jefferson Davis's inauguration in Montgomery, Alabama, on February 18, 1862. He and his ad hoc company served in the Confederacy's failed siege of Pensacola. Resigning because of his recurring poor health, and back in Atlanta, Lee enlisted as a private but soon rose to the rank of colonel and commanded enough men at Savannah and Richmond for a brigade and then a division in the second period of his career. With his health failing him again, the colonel resigned and retired to Atlanta where he began a third phase, raising companies for the army, serving as the city's provost marshal, and personally leading entire campaigns against draft evaders, deserters, and all varieties of threats to Atlanta's civilians, and the war effort. Finally, as federal forces overran Georgia, he defended his state, led troops into battle, and saved the state archives. He helped to restore Confederate authority in Atlanta and North Georgia after both armies had abandoned the city and the region.

Lee participated in campaigns and events seldom explored by scholars, parts of the war in Atlanta, Pensacola, the Georgia coast, Virginia, the Appalachian Mountains, and even the Okefenokee Swamp. He headed cooperative state/Confederate campaigns, some with Cherokees, to fight war resistance in North Georgia, East Tennessee, and Western North Carolina. As provost marshal, he no doubt played a role in the logistics of moving Longstreet's divisions through Atlanta to Chickamauga in time to make that 1863 Confederate victory possible. On one occasion, Lee and his home defense battalion defended a bridge where they stood alone as the sole barrier between his city and Sherman's nearby approaching federal armies. This first Confederate soldier likely brought down one of the last of his nation's flags in Atlanta in 1865.

Crippling tuberculosis could have exempted Lee from military service. He resigned when his health would fail, but he always came back, literally to the end of the war. This champion for an independent Southern nation held various positions, sometimes fulfilling the responsibilities of a general without rank. In the "Gate City" of Atlanta, particularly as the provost marshal, Lee experienced much of the Civil War's partisan, political, and social challenges that were *not* directly associated with battlefields. This Confederate officer dealt with all types of social upheaval of the war and the evils that came from it, an understudied part of the story of the South in the Civil War. In this broader struggle, Lee's enemies included bureaucratic failure, class, fear, misconceptions, organized crime, politics, racism, and rumor.

Atlanta's provost marshal had the disadvantage that the Confederate government never defined his authority and responsibilities. Yet, Lee succeeded in dealing with the obvious and present problems in Atlanta, a critical crossroads of the Confederate States of America and the gateway to all that had to be preserved if the Southern nation would survive the war and keep its independence as a nation. The American Revolution was won by waiting out the invader, and supporters of the Confederate nation held out that hope to the end as growing numbers of people on both sides believed that the costs of the war were not justified by abolishing or preserving the institution of slavery—or the original union of states, or the Confederate nation.

Lee succeeded in his responsibilities so well that the Confederate government, critically short on competent administrative personnel, added more tasks but not resources to his workload as the war progressed. He founded the first American secret service for battling counterfeiters, an organization identical to the federal agency that soon followed. The owners of Atlanta's four railroads, all critical to the war effort, unsuccessfully petitioned the Confederate government to have him take over the management of their lines.

George W. Lee made enemies in doing his duty. The book *Secret Yankees*, the only work where Lee is mentioned prominently, tells the story of an apolitical organized crime syndicate of profiteers hiding their crimes after the war with questionable claims of support for the Union. They worked to at least have Lee removed and were later responsible for orders issued against Lee by General Sherman that classified Lee as a war criminal, outlaw, or traitor. The wife of one of these "secret Yankees" even created a faked diary and her sister a novel that promoted this falsehood. General Braxton Bragg worked to remove Lee from his command in Atlanta with false claims that contradict Bragg's earlier praise for this Atlantan. At least three assassination attempts were made on the Atlanta provost marshal's life.

Did Lee merit such treatment? The American Civil War lends itself heavily to biography and metaphorical judgments in public history, in black and white, not narratives complicated by exceptions, facts, shades, and shadows. Individuals who enforce the law and public safety in wartime, such as Lee, create controversy in carrying out their responsibilities. He had the added disadvantage of serving in a highly partisan war with everything from petty crime to profiteering to matters of life and death. Passions and racism also obscured the truth and continue to do so to the present.

Lee had a situation not unlike that of Captain Henry Wirz, a mid-level bureaucrat at the horrific, notorious Andersonville Confederate prison who was executed after the war out of revenge for the circumstances in that compound, not for anything he was proven to have done. Wirz, contrary to the public history then and since, was never commandant of the prison, only the officer most of the prisoners knew and the highest-ranking officer without anyone of influence to save him. He carried their blame for the horrors of the Andersonville.[2]

Conversely, many prominent people endorsed Lee as a competent and honest administrator in a time and place of extraordinary civil unrest. They described him as a devoted Confederate officer defending the home front, not unlike the legendary Roman Horatius Cocles at the Gate (but this time the Gate City), and against enemies outside and within. Lee preferred diplomacy rather than force, perhaps as a necessity borne of too much responsibility and insufficient authority, or because he was a failed businessman whose nature was cooperation and accomplishment rather than anger, fanaticism, and ideology.

A Rebel in the Court of King Cotton

The American Civil War put Atlanta "on the map," making it a place in the public's consciousness and popular history. The Cyclorama of the Battle of Atlanta, *Gone with the Wind*, and the Stone Mountain carving commemorate that legacy. No public relations can make the city's past disappear, no matter how much some people want to build a different Atlanta with a different imaginary, invented past and present. Groups with different views have told Atlanta's history or tried to bury its past as part of their respective agendas rather than the historical reality. Atlanta is a Gate City in many ways, including how much can be learned of the great importance of the objective study of fact while screening out loud ignorance and partisanship.

The story presented in this book is more of a man at the heart of the Confederate States of America who owned no one and whose family owned no one, who fought for that cause without any expressed opinions on race or the institution of slavery that have survived. That void in our knowledge of such Southerners should not be filled with modern speculation. His loyalties surely came from forces beyond the tremendous economic power of cotton and the cheap chattel labor upon which that economy depended. His country, war, and world came from the institutionalization of industrial-scale agriculture, capital, labor, manufacturing, and mining that included enslaved and non-enslaved African Americans. Racism and xenophobia became factors in the competition for work between native-born white male laborers and all other workers, throughout America. Northern economic interests also used contempt for African Americans, immigrants, Roman Catholics, Jews, and all races' poor and middle class to control the work force and to keep employee costs minimal. Famed violent abolitionist the Rev. John Brown opposed the factory's oppressive, dehumanizing working conditions just as he opposed human bondage on plantations, both of which was industrial scale labor, with all of the indifference to the individual that entailed.

Capital and a market for manufacturing were present in the antebellum South, just as in the North, and depended upon skilled independent workers without regard to race. George W. Lee could have met Georgian entrepreneurs Mark Anthony Cooper, Robert Findlay, John T. Milner, John H. Newton, and John G. Winter, who succeeded in making manufacturing at least appear to succeed in the largely plantation-economy Southern states. Innovative planter Thomas Spalding and slave trader Ephraim Ponder allowed skilled enslaved African Americans to work almost as independent contractors, accommodating all but free Black labor to a degree in the changing America and South. Ponder ran a factory in Atlanta that used an independent labor force that was officially in bondage.[3]

Manufacturing and non-agricultural pursuits in the South, however, had to compete with the image of the plantation economy and the social status that went with it. Families were encouraged to acquire enslaved workers as a responsible and justified means of economic security in a time and place where people could be allowed to starve to death or die from exposure from want of shelter.[4]

Some scholars argue that manufacturing, even in the South, offered a higher return on investment and, considering the difference in population, the South was not that far below the North in industrial development and railroads, especially factoring in the notorious lack of waterpower in the Southern states. Still, Robert Seymour Symmes Tharin in Wetumpka, Alabama, found himself disdained by his neighbors for even suggesting profitable small-scale mills and farms instead of large plantations with low wages or enslaved labor.⁵ Engineer John T. Milner called for removing all African Americans from Alabama to fulfill his vision of the state as a paradise for a white middle class that owned relatively small independent farms, manufactories, and mines worked by free white labor. Milner described Alabama as one of the richest states in the Union, but he opposed developing that wealth with large operations that used mass labor that dehumanized and cheapened any people. He might have written something similar about other areas of the South, then and since. The low-cost labor on large plantations just in Alabama, however, grew cotton as over 13 percent of the nation's exports and 21 percent of the cotton produced in America overall in 1860.⁶

This Cotton Kingdom created struggles of conscience far more complicated than a Black and white, North and South, plantation South in increasingly industrial America, and in all ways. Robert E. Lee and George W. Lee were unrelated by blood or class, but each served the Confederate States of America to the end of the Civil War. These two Lees, however, had decidedly different visions of the change that had become so apparent in the 1850s and for the future of their South.

Robert E. Lee, of Virginia's upper class, eventually came to fight a war to defend his Virginia only for honor, but that still meant defending human bondage, an institution that he and many plantation owners agreed was morally reprehensible.⁷ Lee and the *Richmond Examiner* referred to the American conflict from 1861 to 1865 as the "Civil War."⁸ He saw that term as accurate as he wanted to resist the change to the South's caste-based cavalier society, even for the white citizens, to keep the Old South he knew frozen in place with a new government that would shut out the capitalist industrial change and related social upheaval. Unfortunately, that vision remained a reality with the South up to modern times.

George W. Lee, however, had no reason to support Robert E. Lee's Old South caste system or the enslavement of anyone who might compete with him or his class of white workmen for employment and opportunity. He and his other Atlantans of the professional class were not oblivious to the reality that the Confederate States of America was created to protect and expand the wealth from enslaved people and cotton, but they could fail to recognize that the new Southern nation was also intended to shut out from power any of the South's middle and lower classes, of any race. Middle-class tradesmen like Lee and the men he led, however, could argue that Northern interests exploited all labor in the South, of which the institution of slavery was only the most obvious example, and took the profits to the North, keeping this wealth from the South where it could benefit all the region's people as capital for agricultural, industrial, and all other economic development.

Under George Washington Lee's leadership, white Southern artisans and small-scale entrepreneurs in Atlanta formed a Masonic lodge, military companies, and political demonstrations within an all but a formally organized labor movement. In the newspapers of their time, North and South, such native-born white workers expressed that they wanted no competition for the wages by which they supported their families. Finding work in this American society with no social safety net always proved challenging, especially daunting during the national economic downturns of 1857 and 1859 that immediately preceded the American Civil War and highlighted how the United States' national economic situation affected Atlanta and the South.

Robert E. Lee, thus, fought a rebellion to preserve a past that offered Southerners like George Washington Lee nothing, while the latter led a rebellion for a new independent Southern nation with expanded opportunities for at least the entrepreneur and skilled worker class of white population. The men the two Lees led and even the soldiers they fought from the North all likely shared fears of change brought on by the industrialization of the 1850s that could steadily reduce most American labor to peonage.

Race did play a significant role in those fears, even if that went unacknowledged by George W. Lee. In all areas of the United States, the economic elite used ethnicity and race as valuable tools to keep their labor force loyal and willing to die for an economy that often exploited its workers. That strategy continues in the present. The United States Supreme Court, in its 1857 Dred Scott decision, arguably ended prohibitions on the institution of slavery throughout the United States, threatening to diminish the cost and value of immigrant and white labor across the country. This ruling consequently sparked the national Panic of 1857 that brought on severe unemployment for skilled workers like Lee in Atlanta.[9]

Federal commanders resisted returning the escaped enslaved to owners, but the United States government never had a relatively peaceful organized effort to bring down the Confederacy by ending slavery, at least until the seceding states declined Lincoln's offer to return to the Union with their institution of slavery intact in 1863. Even Lincoln stood with the many Americans who did not want competition with Black labor (or immigrants). He was a Southerner from an even lower social class of Americans than George W. Lee. City ordinances in Atlanta and state laws in Georgia and elsewhere outlawed or restricted skilled Black free labor to protect jobs for white men like Lee and Lincoln.[10]

The wealth of the South and the United States, however, largely came from this enslaved labor of the cotton, rice, and sugar plantations that the non-slave-owning classes could resent. In a Southern nation free from the North, that profit could remain in the South. Lee and his free white artisan class could believe their livelihoods were held back in the Old South that Robert E. Lee wanted to save but would prosper in a new Southern nation.

Before, during, and after the war, George W. Lee believed in Atlanta and his chances for financial success, but he had an incredibly long list of failures. A mechanic and millwright, he had a reputation of being untrustworthy that likely had more to do with bad luck, incompetence, and poor choices in partners. Lee may have blamed the wealthy Northern interest that owned Atlanta for his lack of success. After the war, however, he continued to fail as a businessman.

The economic boom of the 1850s that created Atlanta's success did not benefit everyone. Even prominent leaders in the new age of industry often failed in finance, and sometimes used less than ethical practices to keep them from losing all they had.

Lee's acquaintance Robert A. Crawford lost at least four fortunes in a long career in peddling alleged opportunities in Southern manufacturing, mining, railroads, and finance. Crawford, like Lee, only knew real success when the war came, but, with Crawford, through the operation of Atlanta's first and reportedly what became the Confederacy's largest market for enslaved persons. His nationally infamous Atlanta pen specialized in selling skilled Black workers, the very people Lee and his class did not wish to compete with. Crawford claimed to have been involved in managing chattel labor since he was a boy.

Similarly, New Hampshire–born classics teacher Samuel D. Niles, like Lee, owned no enslaved people and was a small-scale speculator in Atlanta real estate. During the war, however, Sara Huff remembered that she saw 300 African Americans, the most she had seen in one place, on Niles plantation, but that one day she found that they were gone, their cabins empty. She understood that they had been sent out of the country for resale in places where human bondage would remain legal if it were abolished in the United States. Niles' would return to the North in 1864 a wealthy man and died in 1907, a wealthy revered citizen.[11]

The Roman historian Plutarch argued that understanding history requires a thorough view of the character of participants like Crawford, Lee, and Niles. This book consequently reveals a dark side of Civil War Atlanta that does not spare some of its citizens like Crawford who had outlived the truth and died as respected founding fathers. Ironic, as today as we live in an America of such intolerance that even the long dead are narrowly classed as either metaphorically being on the cross or driving in the nails. People today could form very different opinions of someone like Lee, even if based on his actions instead of imagined 21st-century political correctness.

One interpretation would exclude the idea that a man without a connection to the institution of slavery **could not** make sacrifices for the Confederate States of America, whose founders created that nation through enslavement and racism. Proponents of that view could envision him as a murderous fanatic of opponents of the new Southern nation. Other Americans do not want his or any other history published of their sacred Confederacy remembered in the context of administrative incompetence, criminal conspiracies, enslaved people, madness, petty politics, and racism.

Chapter One

The First Confederate Soldier

A REVOLUTION DOES NOT begin with the dreams of one person but rather when economic and social change finds leaders who, from their backgrounds, will become its avatars and icons, men and women who can have remarkably different personalities and backgrounds.[1] George Washington Lee of Atlanta was a leader found by the revolutions within the United States created by the Confederate States of America and the Civil War. He was officially the new Southern nation's first soldier, and among its last. Lee would serve his new country with distinction from Pensacola to Richmond, and in many ways, including on battlefields and creating whole companies of infantry. As Atlanta's provost marshal, he fought counterfeiters, epidemics, profiteers, saboteurs, and spies. Among the other responsibilities given him, the Colonel led expeditions against draft evaders, deserters, and other resistance to the Southern war effort.

Lee, however, had recurring, near fatal bouts of tuberculosis that would have allowed him to honorably walk away from the war. He could have joined in the incredible level of profiteering in Civil War Atlanta. Attempts were made to murder him, and conspiracies were concocted to remove him from service. General Sherman ordered him, if captured, to be arrested (or worse) as a bandit and a traitor, not as a prisoner of war.

Yet, Lee kept coming back, even more unlikely because he and the members of his family had no direct connection to cotton or enslaved labor. They owned no one. Nonetheless, he repeatedly risked his life and his family's future effectively and efficiently serving in this revolution for a nation founded to protect the enslavement of African American labor but which also discriminated against the white working classes that included Lee!

George W. Lee was a sometime mechanic, millwright, and saloon keeper but a full-time entrepreneur who believed obsessively in the future of Atlanta and the new Southern nation. He was a leader of a middle class of almost all white, skilled workers of Atlanta whom he led off to a war fought over cotton agriculture. Lee left no account of his political, racial, or social views, only documentations of his actions, circumstances, and struggles.

George Washington Lee, no known relation to George Washington or Robert E. Lee, started on his path to becoming a local leader in in Civil War Atlanta with his birth.² A son of Barney Drury (or "Barnaby Drewry") and Cynthia Jordan Lee, he began life in Gwinnett County, Georgia, on September 25, 1831, during Georgia's last days as a true frontier and on the eve of becoming "the Empire State of the South" as celebrated in books of the time by Adiel Sherwood and George White.³

His grandparents Barnett and Sarah Lee had moved from South Carolina to the Franklin County, Georgia, frontier by 1813 and west to Gwinnett County by 1824. Their neighbors fought in the battle of Shepherd's Plantation on June 9, 1836, in the last Creek Indian War. In Gwinnett and DeKalb Counties, the Lees lived on the gateway to the Cherokee Nation until that tribe's removal to the West in 1838.⁴

During those years, the Lees successfully adapted to their new home. Barney Drury Lee became a commissioner of New Gibraltar in 1839. After the town had been renamed Stone Mountain, he had enough local political pull to receive a federal appointment as its postmaster from 1846 to 1847. George W. Lee married Nancy Catherine Dean (daughter of blacksmith Hiram Hornbuckle and Sarah Hudson Dean) in DeKalb County, Georgia, on September 28, 1851. The new city of Atlanta, where they settled, became the county seat of Fulton County, created on December 20, 1853, from DeKalb County. Within a few years, they had a daughter they gave the then-popular name of Indiana.⁵

This place in the forest where the Lees settled began as a proposed location for a railroad junction in 1837, with the first railroad arriving in 1845. At that time, this settlement was hardly more than Thomas Kile's grocery, a cabin home, a tavern, and a blacksmith shop at a rural intersection of five roads, the origin of the area's Five Points, and where only one family lived. The neighborhood had a population of 100 people. Hardly a decade before then, it had been a Creek-Cherokee community and an abandoned War of 1812 fort called Standing Peachtree, from which modern Atlanta's many Peachtree streets are named. Even in 1847, one resident described it as only a shanty town in the woods without a city government but to where the locals already talked of moving the state capital and where they, including George Washington Lee, would stake their future!⁶

On December 29, 1847, however, this community created in the wake of the railroads of the new age of steam became incorporated as Atlanta, a name invented by railroad superintendent J. Edgar Thomson (later a national transportation czar) from the Western & Atlantic Railroad that made this "Gate City" possible. This railroad went neither to the West nor the Atlantic (feminine "Atlanta"), a tradition of confusion in naming continued in the city government for streets for generations to come. This intersection for the iron horse joined Georgia's railroad network with the Midwest transportation web of rivers and tracks through Chattanooga, Tennessee. Local people told stories for naming the city that included the story of Greek goddess Atalanta and her race for three golden apples, for Governor Joseph Lumpkin's daughter Martha Atalanta Lumpkin (the city initially had been named Marthasville for said daughter); and even the lost continent of Atlantis.⁷

By then, this city had three grocery stores, at least one tavern, two hotels, a butcher, a banker, and a bookseller, not unlike Chicago, whose growth in transportation would parallel Atlanta in many ways, even today. Chicago, however, would have the advantages of immigrants, New England innovation, and investment capital in a city already a major transportation center in the industrial North. Atlanta developed as one of several cities, from Pittsburg to Dallas, in the nation's true Mid-West, created and expanded from the steam technology of the 19th century, the first truly new age of transportation in thousands of years. The Gate City's future lay with that technology, although from Mobile to Minnesota, the region's economy and culture also developed around the labor of industrial managed and organized systems of plantation agriculture, with all the class, labor, and race issues exacerbated by this expansion.

George Washington Lee (1831–1879) in a pre–Civil War uniform, likely of Atlanta's Gate City Guards (Lee/Huss Family Papers, AC 69-249, Georgia Archives, Morrow).

With the union of four railroads—the Western & Atlantic (connecting to Tennessee's expanding national transportation network), the Macon & Western (connecting to Macon and from there by cotton railroads to Albany and Savannah, Georgia), the Georgia Railroad (connecting to Athens and Augusta), and the Atlanta & West Point Railroad/Western Railway of Alabama (connecting to Montgomery, Opelika, and Selma, Alabama), Atlanta developed into the fastest growing inland city in the Deep South. In this shallow river region, this urban area was the first major city without direct access to a navigable waterway from which cotton and other products could float to the sea.

Reportedly, 19 stores went up in Atlanta in 1858, with an equal number planned for the following year, despite much of the city's skilled labor of both races being out of work from the national economic downturn of 1857. So much business went on in Atlanta that the situation at times became absurd, such as in 1859 at H.G. Kuhrt's building where, among other businesses, a post office, a printing shop, two barbers, a bookbinder, a clothier, a bank, a lottery office, and a restaurant all shared space. A visitor in 1862 observed:

> Business seems to be the keynote of all, and the point of sight in the picture of daily life. Horses are driven furiously through the streets; men dash along the pavements as if fearful of losing a customer, and even the women are "swift of foot," like ATLANTA [sic, Atalanta, the mythical Greek huntress who ran a race for three golden apples], and hurry on as if the terrible gadfly of Jo were after them.[8]

Boosters claimed that the city had a population of 6,025 in 1850 and had grown to 11,500 people by the state census in 1859. (The 1860 federal census, however, only credited the Gate City with a population of 7,741.) By then, Atlanta had passed the older Fall Line cities of Columbus and Macon to become Georgia's third largest city after the Savannah River cotton ports of Savannah and Augusta, respectively. By contrast, the nearby twin cities, Chattanooga and Dalton, the northern terminus of the Western & Atlantic Railroad, also had rapidly expanding populations of 5,000 each.[9]

Geography and topography gave Atlanta an advantage. Its location on a steep hill or plateau stood on a geographic divide that allowed the railroads from the south that eventually linked up with the W&A to need few bridges, unlike the WA&A itself that had to bridge streams, rivers, mountain passes, and other obstacles, to reach Chattanooga. The terrain prevented the tracks from going north from nearby Decatur in DeKalb County along the route known as the Federal Road of North Georgia, a primary route since 1804. DeKalb County's small farmers, including the Lees, and planters appreciated that they could access this railroad network.

On the eve of the Civil War, Atlantans invested heavily in the Air Line railroad that, after the war, would connect the city through Northeast Georgia to markets in Virginia and beyond. Plans moved forward for another line that would have connected the city, by way of its link to Macon, to the Gulf Coast.

An antebellum version of the Biblical "bright and shining city on a hill," Atlanta did have criminal and disorderly elements. Still, anything other than petty brigands existed more in rumors than reality. Far from being a large metropolis, even by the standards of the largely rural Old South, in this Gate City, the destitute, wealthy, criminal, respected, enslaved, and free were all close neighbors. Even in death, Atlantans of all classes and races remained together, the rich and poor, in the city cemetery, near the junction of the railroads and the connected factories, foundries, machine shops, stores, and warehouses from which the different classes and races of its people made their livings and sometimes their fortunes.

Judge William Gibbs McAdoo of Knoxville, Tennessee, first saw Atlanta on

February 1, 1862. Leaving the Trout House hotel, he stepped out and tried to see Atlanta, but "I could not learn that there is any particular quarter where any particular feature is exclusive to other features can be seen—such as nice residences, fine retail stores, or the anything in short. It is all confusion, and patchwork, and bears unmistakable evidence of the vulgarity of a mere trading mart where rogues live by cheating each other."[10]

One early writer humorously suggested a steam train to carry the busy citizens through the city's still narrow boundaries. That correspondent wrote, "We are a monstrous fast people in Atlanta ... energetic, powerful, and wonderfully New Yorkish in our notions."[11] Atlanta's Gate City Rolling Mill, the major industrial complex and which manufactured machinery and refurbished railroad tracks, well represented the city. It was owned by Yankees and built with Northern capital, with 100 white employees. The complex, however, also used 100 Black workers in bondage.[12]

Built by enslaved labor and rapidly growing from transportation of the South's cotton, Atlanta was created by Northern interests with Northern capital that bypassed the Southern banks. This cosmopolitan city's residents boasted of enslaved labor as minimal in their "Yankee" city, reflecting its Northern roots. In 1847, William N. White claimed that the new city did not have 100 enslaved people and that "white men black their own shoes, as independently as in the North."[13]

In 1850, the city did have 139 white persons listed in the census as owning African Americans, but only two of them, the city's hotelkeepers, had more than 20 enslaved each, the common standard for a "planter." (Hotels used these people as nurses and servants for the white only guests.) Ten years later, the number of owners had grown to 373, although the owners of Atlanta's notoriously second-rate white-only hotels still possessed the largest number of enslaved people, and surely as domestic servants.[14]

Such examples perpetuated a false image of the Gate City. African Americans built this first Atlanta and would rebuild it after the war. This city that Lee knew as a young entrepreneur had a complex history of bondage, class, and labor that could encourage people like him to support or denounce the Confederate States of America, based on protecting the institution of slavery, even though Lee had no direct connection to institution of slavery. Georgia leader Alexander H. Stephens publicly proclaimed the Confederacy as the first country founded in racism. He neglected to say, however, that the new Southern nation would leave only the wealthy planter in power, over all other Americans, even men like Lee in the white middle class.

Historian Ralph Singer wrote that enslaved labor "contributed enormously to the city's growth and prosperity," from manual labor and domestic servitude to artisans contracted to do "skilled tasks including iron forging, cabinet making, carpentry, and bricklaying."[15] Oakland, the city's cemetery, had African American burials.

The cotton produced by enslaved labor on farms and plantations outside the city fueled its rapid growth. William Kay, the city's leading bookseller, advertised for sale copies of Joseph C. Stiles' *Modern Reform Examined*, an 1857 book that attacked reformers in general but particularly people committed to the abolition of human bondage. Stiles described the latter as arrogant, belligerent, and impractical. New Yorker D.S. Newcomb lost his job and felt compelled to leave Atlanta after toasting to the memory of John Brown, an abolitionist who famously tried to start a national rebellion of enslaved persons at Harper's Ferry, Virginia, in 1859. Atlanta enslaved African American, but likely an independent cobbler, Harrison Berry wrote *Slavery and Abolition*, a defense of slavery that attacked Brown and the abolitionists.[16]

Atlanta, this economic engine on the new boundaries of the Cotton Kingdom during cotton's boom years of the 1850s, had many such fiscal, political, and social secrets worth knowing. So many cotton bales passed through the city, and at such a rate, that by 1859, the Georgia Railroad alone annually sent some 3,000 cars empty to the city for cotton despite the amount of the product consumed by the area's large and profitable textile factories. This disparity in cargo did not make the transportation of goods to the city cheaper, however, as the railroads kept freight rates artificially high.

Mule-drawn wagons from across North Georgia brought their cotton and produce to Atlanta's prosperous market and would continue to do so for decades into the 20th century. These small farmers also bought goods such as coffee and salt brought to the city by train from as far as St. Louis and beyond. The teamsters stayed in parks set aside for them, but they also spent money on entertainment in the city, conveniently located near where they kept their wagons in the mule yards on Decatur Street.

Northern capital invested in and profited from Atlanta and the Cotton Kingdom to the extent that New York Mayor Fernando Wood warned newly elected President Abraham Lincoln that secession of the cotton-rich Southern states threatened to end New York's financial superiority over the whole country. Atlanta merchants, however, traded directly with New York City. They thus gave local farmers, manufacturers, merchants, and ranchers direct access to Northern capital that bypassed the politically and economically powerful planter-owned banks in the South to reach Northern finance. This situation gave Atlanta some, but far from complete, immunity from the effects of the national panics of 1857 and 1859.[17]

George Washington Lee joined in this grand pursuit of opportunity and profit, the legendary golden apples, in Atlanta and, in doing so, created a reputation as a consistent business failure. As with many money managers, he always seemed to find money when needed for starting a factory, buying a hotel, raising a company for Southern secession, etc., yet his financial ventures still failed in a city that prospered. In the 1857 tax digest for Fulton County, Lee paid taxes on only $400 worth of real estate and only $800 worth of land and in Stone Mountain in 1858.

The pre-war city directory listed him as the proprietor, with L.A. Guild, of the Senate Saloon on Atlanta's notorious Decatur Street that served the vices of visiting waggoneers. Guild used his wife's money to start the business but then sold out and left Atlanta in 1859, leaving his partner broke and unable to pay the saloon's debts. Lee made some small profits in real estate, but his partnership with grocer Twiggs V.W. Rhodes dissolved the following year. They had also jointly owned an extensive steam sawmill, but after Lee bought out Rhodes's interest and then sold the whole operation, Rhodes unsuccessfully sued Lee over the income and debts of the mill.[18]

By 1860, Lee and his little family lived with his parents and several younger siblings in a house next to the Atlanta jail. While his father and his three brothers worked as clerks, he had a job in a sawmill, and, in 1861, he and his new partner, B.F. Wiggin, offered services in setting up and repairing sawmill machinery. An anonymous critic later described him as ignorant, corrupt, and incompetent. His lack of success likely contributed to the contempt later shown by some of the city's successful entrepreneurial and financial elite. He represented what could happen to any of them from even just one bad decision or partnership in what had been a rapidly growing but was now a volatile American economy of the late antebellum years.[19]

Leadership in revolutions, like all that the American Civil War entailed, has a tradition of coming from a middle class of perennial personal business failures, unsuccessful opportunists like Lee. In that, he stood in good company with such famous historical figures as Samuel Adams, Button Gwinnett, Thomas Paine, and Robespierre. Nothing found suggests that Lee's failures as a businessman did or did not have anything to do with his not owning enslaved people.

Business opportunities and politics in the new city became conspiracies in the war that followed. Former temporary mayor William Markham made money building and, after the war, rebuilding Atlanta and from supplying the Confederate war effort. During the Civil War, this Yankee and other wealthy Atlantans, Northerners and Southerners, would lead a smuggling scheme, illegal in both warring nations, as a "secret Yankee" while conspiring against Colonel George Washington Lee for trying to expose their criminal syndicate. After Atlanta fell, these people claimed to have been "secret Yankees" who were oppressed, restricted, and threatened by Lee for supporting the Union cause. Markham would persuade General Sherman to issue orders for Lee and others to be arrested as bandits and traitors. Following the war, however, Markham and his descendants failed to obtain compensation for property he claimed to have lost from the federal military occupation of Atlanta, in part due to testimony provided by George W. Lee![20]

Antebellum Atlantans knew about conspiracies. They even believed, falsely, that their city was the victim of antebellum organized crime.[21] Elites like Markham tended to belong to the Native American "Know Nothing" Party. Members of this secret political party railed against the waves of Roman Catholic immigrants in the late 1840s and the 1850s and opposed immigrants as competition to white American labor. The class of skilled white workers like Lee tended to be Democrats and opposed to competition for jobs and land by any African Americans.[22]

Mercenary military organizations also had followings in Atlanta and across Georgia. Atlanta Mayor Allison Nelson resigned his office to join 150 other North Georgians in what they claimed was an expedition to the California gold fields. Instead, they joined Narcisco López's ill-fated mercenary "filibuster" invasion of Cuba in 1850–1851. Atlantans belonged to the Knights of the Golden Circle. This secret political movement sought to expand human bondage with at least the economic conquest of the islands and the countries along the rim of the Caribbean, the "Golden Circle." This organization first proposed the United States annexation of the Caribbean lands to guarantee the dominance of the Southern slave states in Congress.

After 1857, the Knights called for secession to create a nation of only states that allowed African American bondage. The organization excluded from membership abolitionists, African Americans, convicts, drunks, felons, foreigners, gamblers, the mentally incompetent, and Native Americans but did include boys as young as between the ages of eight and sixteen as soldiers.

George W.L. Bickley of Virginia had organized the first "castle" of the Knights of the Golden Cross (a.k.a. Knights of the Golden Circle, Knights of the Golden Horseshoe, etc.) in 1854. In 1859, he toured the South promoting an invasion of Mexico to restore African American bondage to that country by supporting Mexico's government of Benito Juarez against a French-sponsored invasion. Bickley held a meeting in Atlanta on March 20, 1860, wherein he claimed that the United States government promised not to intervene in this scheme, that he had $700,00 raised for the campaign, and that 12,000 men had already enlisted from whom 5,000 were already chosen.

Three of Atlanta's four newspapers supported the KGC and Robert A. Crawford, then living in nearby Griffin, raised a Georgia regiment as a major and later a colonel for this Mexican expedition. Men from other KGC groups from across the South joined with Crawford's regiment to gather on the Mexican border only to learn that the whole plan came from Bickley's delusions. The recruitment of these men did help in forming the Confederate army soon after.[23]

Few names of participants in these ventures survive. George Washington Lee does not appear among these soldiers of fortune, participating in the California gold rush, or serving in the United States war with Mexico, 1846–1848.[24] He did live in the right place and time to participate in any or of these schemes, such as the campaigns by William Walker of Tennessee to invade Central America. Often, such ventures began among members of the Masonic lodges, although the Masons prohibited politics in their meetings. Lee had membership in Atlanta's Lodge 59 of the Freemasons. When he openly worked to win his city for secession to create a new Southern nation, he formed a military company from his Masonic Lodge.

George Washington Lee became a significant leader of Atlanta's white middle class skilled labor, men who saw any African American labor as a threat in the earliest days of the newly independent state of Georgia and the subsequent Confederate

States of America. Many people and groups across America supported progressive and even liberal social causes, like Abraham Lincoln, but still did not support native-born white working classes having to compete with African Americans in an age where the families of the unemployed could starve to death. In 1856, striking white dock workers in Savannah were replaced by African Americans, seen as threatening white labor elsewhere. "Free," enslaved, or only officially enslaved, Black Americans as skilled labor grew in numbers across America, likely outnumbered their white counterparts, and faced growing resistance from white labor.[25]

The city of Atlanta, as in most parts of America, discouraged any African American labor from challenging white workers for employment. In 1859 Atlanta, a city ordinance compelled the African Americans not in bondage to pay an initial $200 cash fee for residence. They already had to pay an annual state tax of five dollars, and a city tax of $25. Each "free person of color" also had to have a white guardian.

That same year, the city passed, but likely never enforced, an ordinance requiring each African American not in bondage to pay $1,000 for the privilege of living in the city. On April 13, 1860, an ordinance forbade African Americans from purchasing or selling any product, including food, in Atlanta. The city also prohibited anyone Black from alcohol, playing cards, riding in carriages, carrying canes/walking sticks, having firearms, possessing poisons, or even smoking a pipe in the city's streets.

On January 4, 1861, Atlanta's city government considered but failed to pass an ordinance requiring a $100 fee on any Black mechanic [skilled laborer] in the city whose owner lived outside of Atlanta. Historian Franklin Garrett believed that this motion specifically targeted the skilled workers of Ephraim G. Ponder's Atlanta factory. Ponder erected a spectacular mansion and gardens in Atlanta and built a factory, likely more like a machine shop, where his almost completely independent 65 skilled artisans, technically in bondage, used him as their agent. By officially remaining enslaved, these otherwise at-liberty Black Atlantans avoided the fees and taxes imposed by Atlanta's city government on the non-enslaved persons of their race.[26] Operations like the Ponder factory could encourage men like Lee, who did not own anyone, to support the coming war where, some believed, a Southern nation would protect white livelihoods from competition with African Americans, convict labor, factories, immigrants, machines, and anyone or anything else.[27]

Atlanta did not exist with human bondage long enough to see if its strict measures at keeping out the employment of African Americans would have worked or failed as it had in every other city of the Cotton Kingdom. Emancipated African Americans, however, could find community and even a growing degree of liberty in cities, as opposed to the countryside, as did the families in bondage.[28] Historian Wendy Hamand Venet noted that any of the enslaved, even those who lived and worked at liberty and as independent contractors, such as the officially enslaved in Ponder's Atlanta factory and the famous "conductor on the underground railroad" who helped enslaved persons to escape to the North Harriet Tubman, could still find themselves abused, killed, or sold.[29]

Thomas Sims of Savannah, one of the "enslaved" living independently achieved national notoriety because, like Henry Long of Atlanta, he became one of the first escaped African Americans apprehended under the Fugitive Slave Act of 1850. He had escaped to Boston despite his independence as a bricklayer, and under public pressure, his owner was forced to bring him back to Savannah and have him sold at the slave market in Charleston, South Carolina. Sims ended up in Mississippi with a master who allowed him trips back to Savannah to visit his family.[30]

Historian Edgar T. Thompson wrote that an enslaved-worked plantation resembled a frontier mining camp, with all its relative problems of supply, labor, and transportation. By that standard, Lee's Atlanta became the equivalent of a boomtown during a gold rush, where its merchants grew rich off the labor of those workers in the surrounding "mines" and where eventually the small operations came to be owned by a few large distant investment syndicates. This new city of such economic promise did have some "rags to riches" stories. Investors, Northern and Southern, however, brought money and bought up Atlanta's opportunities as they acquired its property. According to historian James Michael Russell, in 1850, only 0.5 percent of the adult citizenry owned 43 percent of the real estate, and 80 percent of the population owned no property. By 1858, only 1.6 percent of the population held 55 percent of the real estate.[31] The skilled white workers could see the Civil War as not about saving the Union or freeing the enslaved as much as the North and South to reducing all American labor and immigrants to a peonage class. Resentment by white labor grew in the North and the South. In 1860, African Americans had to document their emancipation to avoid seizure and sale.[32]

Mechanics and professional men like Lee had difficulty finding work during the Panic of 1857, the sharpest economic drop in American history. This collapse came about, in part, from the potential for the Dred Scott decision of the United States Supreme Court on March 6, 1857, in allowing enslaved workers to compete for white labor throughout the country and by the sinking of a shipload of California gold off the coast at Savannah that threatened the credit of the entire nation. War fears brought on the Panic of 1859 that almost immediately followed. Fears of further economic downturns were fueled by the concerns of Northern banks and financiers that they would lose the money loaned to the merchants and planters of the South. Half of the families in the United States suffered severely.[33]

Lee must have supported secession because he believed that a new Southern nation offered men like him opportunities that the United States he knew did not. He also likely believed that new Southern states would be free from the increasing economic troubles of the United States that killed opportunity for his professional class. The antebellum South had various organized labor movements and surely Atlanta had one that included the Masonic Lodge and militia companies where Lee became a member before the Civil War, which taught him how to lead civilians and soldiers in Atlanta during the years that followed. Southerners like Lee could believe that if the wealth generated by the South's industrial-scale plantation economy, 61 percent of America's exports in 1860, remained in the South, the United States Panic of 1857 would not have killed growth and jobs across the region.

Supporters of Southern secession, however, had greater dreams, of a cotton empire of enslaved labor stretching from Maryland to California, and even into Mexico and the Caribbean! Seeing the "Cotton Kingdom" as an economic entity beyond national boundaries, attempts were made to replicate the South's cotton economics in India.[34]

No state that seceded from the Union did so with a mandate of its voters, as echoed in Abraham Lincoln's Emancipation Proclamation and his remarks on democracy in his Gettysburg Address. Georgia was no exception. Similarly, no one publicly called for Americans to risk their lives to preserve the Union only in order to protect Northern interests in enslaved labor-produced commodities or to keep the port of New Orleans open for export of upper Mid-West produce.[35] In Atlanta, English-born Samuel Richards, however, recorded in his diary that the loudest voices in Atlanta for secession came from young professionals, men like George W. Lee, a class with little or no property to lose from the war, and pro-slavery politicians inflaming voters.[36]

Lee was prepared for war. His Atlanta neighbors elected him as a major of the 101st Infantry Militia Battalion in DeKalb County, by which he received his commission on March 6, 1852, before his 101st District became part of Fulton County. As a major of the militia, Lee found himself holding the responsibilities of a colonel and asking the governor to call for an election to fill his acting position. Elihu P. Watkins of Atlanta wrote to Georgia Governor Joseph E. Brown to urge that the major instead immediately receive a grade commensurate with his new duties, describing Lee as "a gentleman of integrity worthy [of] your confidence ... [who] would serve his county efficiently in any post."[37]

On October 30, 1860, George W. Lee joined many of his neighbors at the armory of the Atlanta Grays, a local militia unit, to form a combination of political association and a quasi-military unit called the "Minute Men of Fulton County" to support the cause of Southern independence. Initially led by the prominent Dr. Willis Foreman Westmoreland, they swore to defend by lawful means the right of a state to secede from the federal United States (what at that moment they ironically termed as the "Confederacy").

Lee's group grew to more than 200 members in the following months. With speeches, parades, revolutionary cockades, and torchlight processions, they managed to change an Atlanta with a small majority of the electorate in favor of waiting on events into a city where "submissionists" and "cooperatists" did not even appear on the city ballot, and where the pro-secession delegates to the state convention of 1861 received two-thirds of the city's votes. Later that year, Lee traveled to the then–state capital of Milledgeville to request arms and equipment for the newly formed

Fulton Dragoons, a volunteer military unit in which he served, despite his tuberculosis, as a trumpeter. On February 6, 1861, he was commissioned captain of the 1026th Georgia militia district.[38]

For whatever else to which others would assume or write about George W. Lee, circumstances made him the first Confederate soldier. A millwright and mechanic by trade, he organized his own independent company, "Lee's Volunteers," for the cause of Georgia's secession on February 15, 1861. Other members included Elihu Watkins and Green Foreacre, men who would later become involved with Lee's Confederate career, and many members of Atlanta Masonic Lodge No. 59, of which Lee was a member.

With recommendations from some of Atlanta's most prominent men and the city council, Lee sought acceptance of his unit into the state's military by Governor Joseph E. Brown so that his men, whom he described as poor, might be paid. Michael Johnston Kenan, who knew the governor, wrote of him as a vain, mediocre intelligence and a corrupt but successful politician. Brown supported secession but declined to accept Lee's company. Even before the war, Georgians argued over moving the state capital from the isolated village of Milledgeville to Atlanta or Macon, a reflection of the political conflict between the rural and the urban in the state that continues today. Accepting an Atlanta company at that moment could have had negative political consequences for the governor.[39]

Brown likely ignored "Lee's Volunteers" or the "Georgia Volunteers" company only because the state had met its quota of companies for the provisional Southern army. Atlanta already had six commissioned volunteer militia companies. Supplying even the troops already accepted strained the state's resources. More units risked reducing the situation to anarchy.[40] The governor may have also confused Lee with another Major Lee of Atlanta, a swindler who claimed to be an army drillmaster seeking troops for an Indian war in Florida. The latter may be a confusion with the previously mentioned George W.L. Bickley and his Mexico scheme. George Washington Lee believed that the governor mistakenly saw him as a future competitor for the governorship or a potential candidate for president of a new independent Southern nation.[41]

Despite this setback, Lee took his company to Montgomery, Alabama, for the inauguration of Jefferson Davis and to enlist his volunteers as the first company of the newly created army of the Confederate States of America. Thus, at the inauguration, he became the first Confederate soldier. During the trip back to Atlanta, women accompanying the company acquired material in Grantville and made what became the first Confederate flag in Georgia.[42]

George Washington Lee subsequently had one of the most unusual and varied careers of any officer in the Civil War. Ironically, while some writers have at length described every criticism made against Lee to make him an icon for Confederate political repression, no one has explored how he stood in the shadows of so many very different military events. Pensacola would be such an episode in Lee's long, important, and now largely forgotten career.

The inauguration of Jefferson Davis as the first president of the Confederate States of America in Montgomery, Alabama. The soldiers on the left may be Lee and his company with their flag (*Frank Leslie's Illustrated Magazine*, March 24, 1861, Library of Congress).

At that moment, United States troops still occupied forts in the Confederate states of Florida, South Carolina, and Virginia. On March 7, 1861, President Davis ordered Lee's company to Charleston to aid in the siege of the federal troops at Fort Sumter. Before Lee's company could leave Atlanta, however, Governor Brown was asked to send a regiment to join in the effort against federal Fort Pickens at Pensacola. He sent Lee and his company of 105 Atlanta engineers, mechanics, and machinists.

Governor Joseph E. Brown of Georgia had urged the seizure of the Pensacola forts, even if by Alabama militia. Although the town had no railroad connection, it did have a deep harbor, a naval base, and four forts. Capturing Fort Pickens would deny the federal military this established military base on the Gulf of Mexico and raise Southern morale. The new Confederacy wanted Pensacola as a gateway to trade in the Caribbean, and no doubt some supporters of enslaved labor hoped for conquest in Latin America. Famed engineer John T. Milner worked to finish the railroad he had begun before the war to reach Pensacola. If federal Fort Pickens fell, Pensacola could add to the South's few ports and become an entry for ships that successfully ran the tightening federal blockade and would provide the Southern military with naval artillery. Whether the Civil War finally began in Charleston or Pensacola depended on which besieged garrison the Lincoln administration tried to save first.[43]

George W. Lee (thin man in the center) and members of his Atlanta company at Pensacola, Florida, stand around the mortar that fired the first shot against Fort Sumter (*Photographic History of the Civil War*, 1911).

Before their journey, Lee and his company received a new national flag, only the second one made in Georgia, with a formal presentation in Atlanta. On March 19, as crowds cheered and cannons roared in salute, these volunteers set out on the Atlanta & West Point Railroad to Montgomery before traveling to Florida via Mobile. People gathered to meet them with gifts of food at Hogansville and LaGrange.

In Pensacola, Lee's now 113 skilled artisans proved useful in building the batteries and other works for attacking Fort Pickens. They had responsibility for some 100 pieces of heavy artillery at the Confederate-occupied Fort McRee, including a mortar brought in from Charleston that reportedly fired the first shot at Fort Sumter and, therefore, of the Civil War. Lee's Atlantans labored until their clothes became rags. They dined on food sent from friends in Atlanta while supplementing their diet with the local fish, oysters, and crabs. Lee answered directly to the overall commander, General Braxton Bragg, for whom he had only compliments. The general, in turn, gave the Atlanta engineers company and its captain public praise.[44]

Eventually, Georgia's Governor Joseph E. Brown would send 3,000 soldiers to the siege of Fort Pickens near Pensacola. He allowed Lee's Atlantans to join the Confederate army as 12-month volunteers. By excluding them from Georgia's official

Top & above: photographs of Confederates camped at Pensacola in 1861 (Library of Congress).

quota, however, he spared the state from having to pay or supply them. Lee had to spend at least $800, likely borrowed, on his men and asked the Confederate government to provide them with at least cheap uniforms and to accept them into the engineers (or any other service) so that they might, at the least, be paid, especially as his men were poor and had families to support. Augustus Romaldus Wright, a Georgia member of the Confederate Congress, unsuccessfully tried to introduce a special act to allow the regular army to accept Lee's men as a unit. A bill in the Georgia Senate to reimburse Lee for his expenses also failed. Eventually renamed the Atlanta Advance Guards, his company became part of the newly created First Independent

Georgia Volunteer Infantry Battalion. When the battalion's Major Leary resigned, Lee narrowly defeated several contenders to win the election as its commander.

The Confederates failed to take Fort Pickens by assault, siege, or yellow fever, and in May 1862, the Confederates finally abandoned their siege. Pensacola became a major base for federal operations and a threat to Mobile, the South's last open port in the Gulf of Mexico east of the Mississippi River after New Orleans fell to federal forces in late April 1862. In the summer of 1864, the federal garrison at Fort Pickens only numbered some 100 men, and a plan was hatched in Mobile to take it by small boat warfare. The plan was not implemented because of the failure of the Confederate military bureaucracy.[45]

Bragg had thus commanded one of the Confederacy's first major defeats, the beginning of a career his modern critics have called his success at consistently snatching defeat from the jaws of victory. He would seek scapegoats. Observers claimed that the new Southern nation had wasted its limited resources in a failed effort to capture a port it did not need and would have been better expended in defending New Orleans, the Confederacy's largest city and greatest port. The failure of Braxton Bragg to take Fort Pickens began a series of Southern failures that exposed the geographic and military weaknesses of the Southern nation.

Before the failed assault on Fort Pickens, Lee had moved on. He suffered from the ravages of tuberculosis, the notorious ailment that allowed such persons as Lee's younger Georgia contemporary, John Henry "Doc" Holliday, to suffer but still function for decades despite relapses brought on by stress and overwork. It proved to be the great American killer well into the 1900s, and Lee struggled with it while playing a major role in the Civil War.[46]

On March 25, 1861, Lee offered his resignation due to his poor health. General Bragg accepted it only on August 6. Retiring to Atlanta, the now former Major Lee helped organize ten full companies for the Confederate army despite growing public animosity towards enlistment officers. An anonymous writer urged that he form an entire legion. His former company remained in Pensacola for a time and suffered at least six men killed and 38 wounded in the Confederate defeat at the battle of Santa Rosa Island on October 9, 1861.[47]

Chapter Two

Atlanta, Savannah, Atlanta, Virginia, Atlanta

AFTER GEORGE W. LEE's health improved, he enlisted as a private in Company M of Augustus R. Wright's Confederate Legion on September 26, 1861. With Lewis J. Parr, he raised ten companies for the new unit and earned election as a company's captain. Lee also contracted for the light arms needed for the whole command.

This unit combined artillery and infantry in an unusual way. Wright's Legion had two artillery batteries, including four revolutionary breech-loading Sumner rifled guns made by the Rushton Company in Atlanta for Confederate Ordnance Bureau chief Josiah Gorgas. Lee conducted a successful trial of these heavy guns at nearby Stone Mountain, and Wright wrote that he wanted the captain to demonstrate these weapons before national government officials in Virginia. The Legion also had four batteries of rifled artillery fired from tripods, an idea that evolved from such weapons as the swivel guns of the American Revolution and would foretell the coming of 20th-century shoulder-fired missiles. Other innovations included 400 spring-saber lances and 400 Enfield rifles. Wright envisioned expanding his legion into a special artillery/infantry brigade akin to a modern armored unit. Although Atlanta's newspapers hailed these achievements, the Confederate government, besieged with ideas for new tactics and weapons, went on to fight the war without those innovations.[1]

Lee came to see the divisiveness and contradictions of Civil War–era politics in his dealings with Wright, a situation not fully appreciated in later histories. An adamant Unionist opposed to the war, A.R. Wright still raised his legion for the Southern Army and served in the Confederate Congress while four of his sons served in the army. Wright's motives and true politics, confusing at the time, remain so even to his modern biographer.[2]

Within less than one month of joining Wright's Legion, Lee received election as its major and was then promoted to lieutenant colonel. In November 1861, he received orders to rush Wright's Legion to Manassas, Virginia, to defend Richmond, the city that had recently beaten out Atlanta to become the capital of the new Southern nation. Before he could move his troops to that front, however, orders arrived for the Legion to travel to Savannah to help defend the Georgia coast from assault from the sea. Twenty train cars, including four just for the horses, pulled out of Atlanta on November 16, carrying the Legion's ten infantry and two artillery companies of more than 1,000 men. Wright and Lee rode on a later train that carried the artillery. In Savannah, Lee took acting command of Wright's Legion and called for more volunteers.[3]

The time that Wright's Legion spent as part of the garrison on Skidway Island near Savannah had little to recommend it as chronicled by Atlanta newspaperman, native Savannahian, and Legion battery commander Captain Cornelius Hanleiter in his diaries. Captain George Anderson Mercer described Lee's men as the best armed, drilled, and disciplined in their brigade and, along with the other men, defending Savannah:

> I see them every day marching from their camp for miles to labor there all day under the boiling sun, and then returning late in the evening soiled wet and weary; theirs is no holiday task; little of the poetry and romance of war do they ever experience. Poorly armed, fed and clothed, and hard worked, they are still cheerful and patriotic, exhibiting beneath their rough garb, and uncouth appearance and manners, a genuine patriotism, and a simple child-like confidence and spirit that is worthy of all praise. No Spartan could have borne his wounds with greater equanimity, or died with more calm courage than is exhibited by our soldiers every day.[4]

The highlight of the stay in coastal Georgia came when the men witnessed the later famous General Robert E. Lee travel from Savannah to Wassaw Island to view the gathering number of federal ships. Several soldiers died from disease, but the Legion had only one loss from gunfire; one man accidentally died from being shot by another. They did kill a federal officer while he tried to land a boatload of his soldiers.

The Legion served in the newly formed First Brigade of Brigadier General William Duncan Smith that, with Brigadier General Hugh Weeden Mercer's Second Brigade, served under Brigadier General Alexander Robert Lawton. Wives and children accompanied the officers, including Lee's wife Nancy and their child Indiana "Anna," who joined their husbands and fathers. They helped in such tasks as making cartridge sacks for the artillery. While urging ordinary soldiers to work like enslaved forced laborers, the officers spent their time politicking for election to higher grades.

Sickness and drunkenness became rampant in the camp. The government failed to issue the men uniforms or even work clothes. Dissension broke out everywhere. Misinformation caused alarms that resulted in orders for the men to prepare to march, march, and countermarch to where they had begun for no discernable purpose. Twice petitions passed through Hanleiter's company to have Hanleiter replaced and twice he faced a court-martial for incompetence. In the two trials, Lee testified as Hanleiter's sole witness and, in both instances, the newspaperman survived without serious harm to his position.[5]

Hanleiter's complaints, however, included criticism of his frequent companion, Lieutenant Colonel George W. Lee. He wrote that he hoped that Major Lewis J. Parr,

Georgia soldiers in Virginia. Note the state flag (*Battles and Leaders of the Civil War*, 1887–1888).

formerly captain of his company, would replace Lee as second in command because the major had a better idea of his duties, more "*esprit de corps*," "presence of mind," and "decisiveness of character."[6] Hanleiter wrote of Lee, who occasionally became "indisposed" from his recurring bouts of tuberculosis, that "it is constitutional with him to prefer ease and security to danger."[7]

After the Legion moved to the Isle of Hope, its members complained that Lee, rather than their often-absent Colonel Wright, led them. They requested a new election for their commander. Wright resigned in January, on February 14, on February 18, or April 23, 1862, according to different records, respectively, to keep his seat in the Confederate Congress. On February 16, 1862, Lee officially became colonel of the Legion as the field officers each "ranked up" one position to fill the void created by Wright's leaving.

General Mercer, now commanding Savannah, began removing the artillery from the Legion over the protests of Hanleiter and the other gunners. Lee tried to keep the men by offering to reform their two companies as infantry. When orders arrived for the ten existing infantry companies in the Legion to move to Virginia, the two artillery units had to stay in Savannah until the infantry companies returned. The latter, however, would remain in Virginia as the 38th Georgia Infantry Regiment, while the artillery stayed in Savannah as the Chestatee Artillery (from Dawson County in North Georgia) and the Jo. Thompson Battery (from Atlanta).[8]

The Confederate States that Lee and his men served faced numerous threats just one year into the war and at the end of the only months in which the Southern nation remained largely intact and relatively at peace. Savannah seemed doomed as

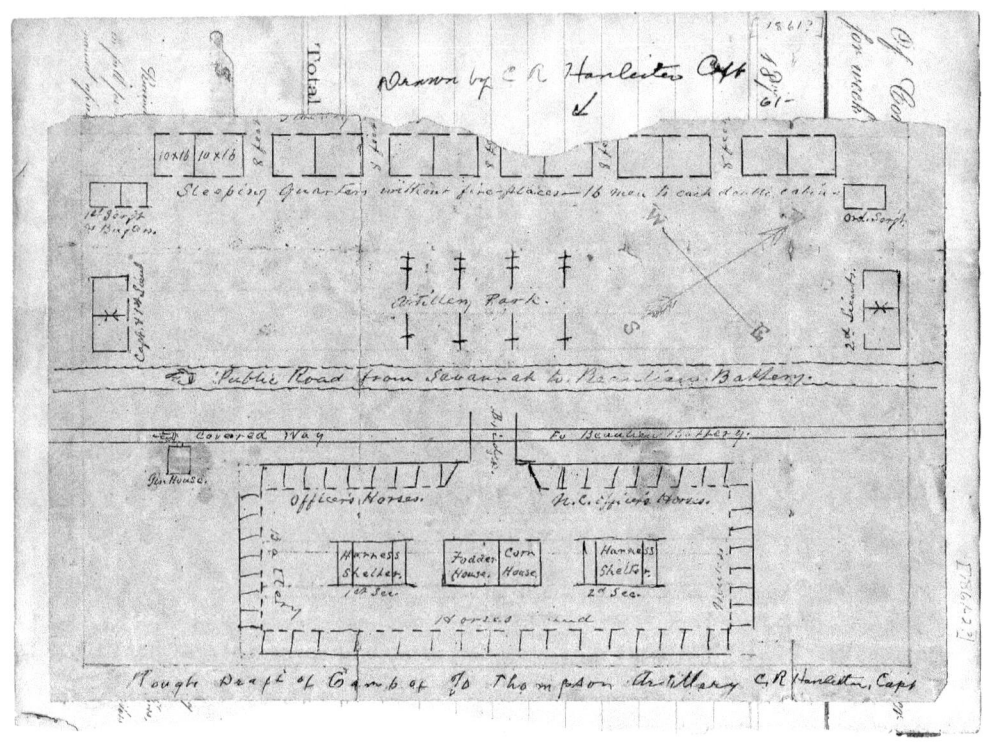

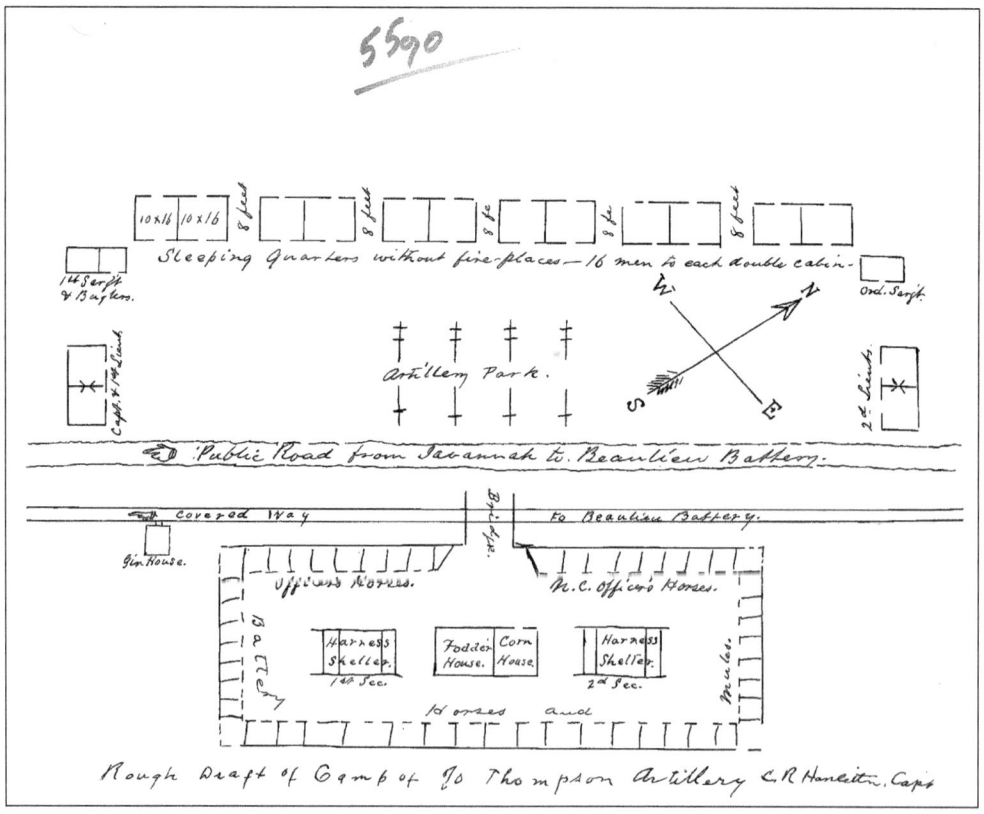

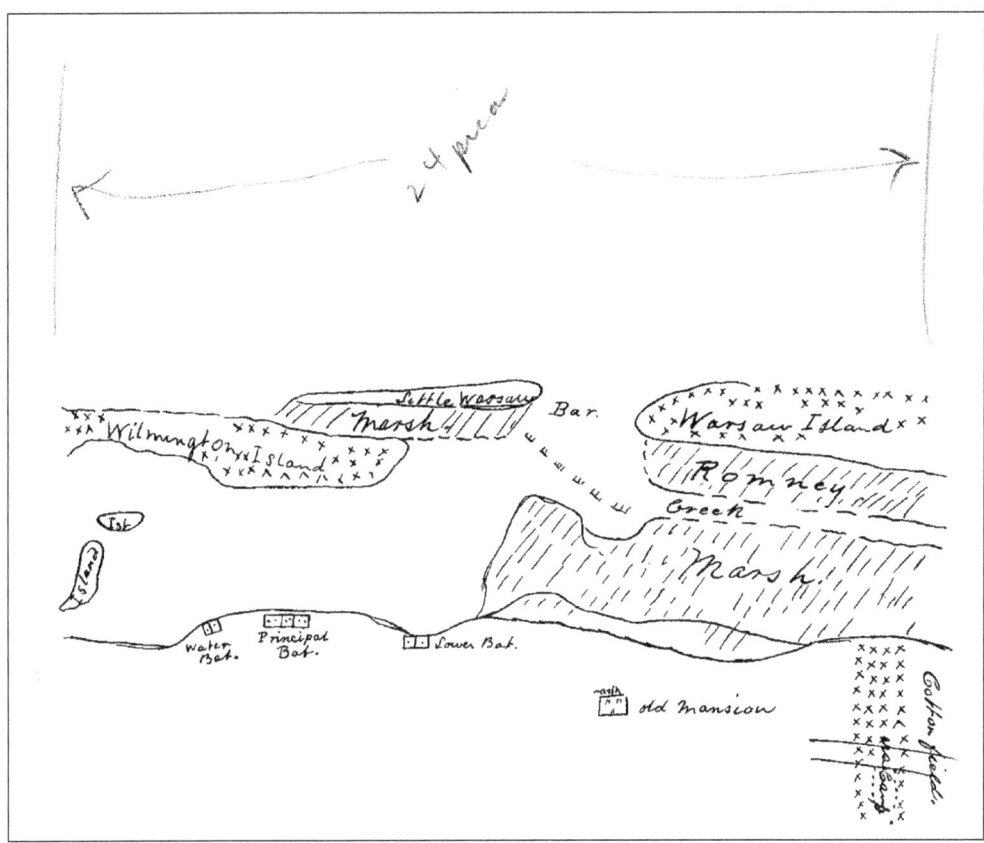

Opposite & above: **Cornelius Hanleiter's drawings of the Georgia coast and the camp of the Jo Thompson Artillery (Kenan Research Center at the Atlanta History Center).**

nearby Beaufort, South Carolina, fell to federal forces on November 7, 1861, and even closer, Fort Pulaski fell to the enemy on April 12, 1862. Confederate surrenders in North Carolina and Tennessee in February resulted in the loss of thousands of men. Reports of Southern successes proved to be false.

The wartime economy often failed to meet even its most elementary needs, such as salt for meat preservation and saltpeter for gunpowder.[9] Weapons proved to be in short supply everywhere. Efforts to fill gaps in the often-segmented "cotton-fields to the sea" oriented railroad network failed to meet the new nation's needs for transportation. The Confederate war effort required hundreds of miles of more tracks that were largely never built. Railroad crossroads, like Atlanta, became critical for what goods and men the trains could transport.

To run the railroads and all else, the new government had to create a nationwide bureaucracy almost without any model or national experience in such management beyond the pre-war postal service. Bureaucratic incompetence, inexperience, fraud, and waste also existed in the North on a massive scale, but those states had relatively unlimited credit and resources, while the United States' war effort fueled its economy instead of nearly depleting it. Captain Mercer compared the two sides:

> Our greatest defect in the South is a want of method and system and an indifference to details; we go into battle without even knowing whether our ammunition will fit our guns; this actually occurred at Port Royal and New Orleans. We certainly lack the systematic organization of the Yankees; our Quarter Master, Commissary and Medical Department are very inferior to theirs; they possess a splendidly organized medical & infirmary corps, corps of sharp shooters with telescopic rifles, engineer corps, corps of sappers & miners &c. &c. In fact the Yankees are eminently a business people, and pay great attention to detail.[10]

Both the Northern and the Southern governments achieved greater efficiency later in the war, but only as each side faced new problems, such as the number of men willing to enlist or even serve as forced conscripts dwindling down to almost none. General Robert E. Lee would win many victories but, early in the war, realized that he could lose the war because he could not replace the men he lost as casualties. For all the writings on the war's strategies and battle plans, critics often saw it as simply economics, transportation, and manpower.

Ironically, men like Lee could fight the war not to preserve the institution of slavery but because they believed that the wealth created by the plantation economy would be better saved for the region where it was produced. Now they learned through the depredations of war how much the new nation created to achieve that end had depended upon Northern manufactures and foreign trade. The South did not, in proportion to its population, lag in the industry compared to the North, but the region's manufacturing, as with its agriculture, was inadequate to supply the wartime demands of these men and the civilian population but existed almost exclusively to supply cotton to the economy. Cloth and iron manufactured in the South before the war sometimes had even gone to customers in the North, from a Southern contempt for Southern manufacturers, even though these products might then be resold at a markup in the markets back in the South on the false presumption of being Northern-made products! An extensive Charleston shoe factory, for example, went bankrupt from a lack of regional patronage.

Eventually, as a means of survival, the Confederate military developed two separate organizations, one for the military commissary and the other for arms/munitions manufacture, each based upon the plantation economic system that the South had developed for cotton. These efforts would have achieved more if combined; if transportation had been coordinated around the growing seasons; and if the Confederate government had completely taken over the business of cotton and the no less lucrative naval stores (turpentine and pinewood) exports. Whatever the new nation did, however, it faced the often-insurmountable problem of staying within its avowed principles of state sovereignty; autonomy for its business; and the plantation economy's interests.[11]

By April 1862, threats back in Atlanta became all too apparent. Confederate authorities arrested three suspected enemy agents in the city that month, two of whom they released for lack of evidence but were later taken back into custody in Alabama. The third man went as a prisoner to Richmond with evidence of a conspiracy. Reports soon after reached the Confederate capital that Yankees had taken over Atlanta on May 12 and, with the help of a rebellion of the enslaved, had started a riot before commencing to burn the city to the ground. Commander of the District of Georgia Brigadier General Alexander Robert Lawton placed Lee temporarily in charge of Atlanta and ordered him to take four companies from Savannah to the city's rescue. An angry Hanleiter resented that the colonel passed on taking his artillery company.[12]

The panic proved unwarranted, for the moment, although it did bring to the surface fears about the city's safety. One warehouse had burned and had set afire some adjoining structures. The city's *Daily Intelligencer* believed that the fire had been the result of carelessness rather than arson, all likely an accident by boys seen smoking cigars on the roof earlier in the day. Even before the war, Atlanta frequently had such fires, and the war, with its growing stockpiles of cotton and supplies, made the city even more combustible.[13]

Lee came home to a very different community, one without cheering crowds but instead enveloped in fear. Atlanta and its environs, North Georgia, and employees of the city's vital Western & Atlantic Railroad all had known outspoken supporters of the Union and resistance to the war. The Union army threatened to capture Chattanooga and to begin a campaign to take Atlanta.

General Don Carlos Buell had sent a force of saboteurs, known as the Andrews raiders, and disguised as civilians, to burn the bridges on the Western & Atlantic Railroad, the one rail connection between Atlanta and the Confederate corps in Tennessee. Almost regular collisions on this state road frequently closed the line, even in peacetime. Reports abounded that Yankee sympathizers, spies, and incendiaries now operated in the city and potentially received aid from the Andrews Raiders, some of whom the public mistakenly believed still hid among the general population. Governor Joseph E. Brown ended cotton collecting at railheads like Atlanta, where thieves could steal the bales or saboteurs use them to set fires.[14]

In any war, the struggle becomes the war itself as much as the military threat, as this manmade event acquires all the attributes of natural disasters, including damage, death, profiteering, refugees, shortages, and suffering along with bigotry, martial law, paranoia, and political pandering-pontificating. A war may or may not begin as a corporate conspiracy, but it ends as a matter of financial gain, legitimate and criminal, including debt and reparations for private profit.

As the war wrecked Atlanta's economy for the average person, the city was filled with desperate refugees of both races who exercised more liberties than the law allowed. Sentries appeared on street corners to maintain order and to check for the identification papers of strangers. In October 1863, Mayor Calhoun closed the Athenaeum, the city's theater, because of the rowdiness of the crowds. It reverted solely to its other uses as a stable and warehouse for auctions.[15]

The newcomers accelerated the city's problems. As a major railroad junction and commercial center. Atlanta always had a significant transient, non-native population, but these arrivals included thieves, smallpox victims, and spies. Federal forces moving into Tennessee and those threatening Savannah added refugees to the people of all classes, including characters who had come to this Gate City to benefit from the war by any means. The city's population grew to over 15,000, most of whom had arrived as strangers since 1860. As early as May 1861, a local newspaper writer asked how many arsonists and spies operated among the city's new beggars and other strangers. The city also acquired banknotes, bread, gold, and meat speculators. Twenty Atlantans made fortunes of $100,000 or more. The city's culture and George W. Lee were products of this true American Mid-West, and, as with much of the South, had traditional Mid-Western prejudices against abolitionists, Jews, and Eastern financial conspiracies. Lee wrote:

> [Atlanta] has been since the Commencement of the revolution—a point of rendezvous of traitors, Swindlers, extortioners [sic], and Counterfeiters. The population has a predominant element is a mixture of Jews, New England Yankees, and of refugees shirking military duties.[16]

Lee had a serious problem with federal spies in Atlanta from then to the end of the war. Without national intelligence agencies existing on either side, individual officers and government officials like federal General George H. Thomas conducted the espionage operations. They acted so independently that generals would unintentionally capture spies operating for other officers of the same army. When an adamant Southern secessionist later falsely claimed to have been a private spy for the then deceased President Lincoln, he was paid by the federal government. Often, the records of covert information, when they survive, are only fragmentary materials relating to specific individuals.

The relatively extensive records for Thomas and his Army of the Cumberland, however, show that he employed a variety of people for several different intelligence services and paid them well ($100 to $150 per month per agent). Detectives worked within federal camps like Chattanooga and even from within military units for counterintelligence and undercover police work. Scouts, recruited from the army or civilians, observed enemy movements, often in disguise. Spies attempted to obtain information while posing as civilians, smugglers, soldiers, and even as spies for the other side. Thomas also sought information from sympathetic civilians, refugees, rebel deserters, escaped prisoners of war, and slaves. By the war's end, he had gathered intelligence from more than 650 people.[17]

Credible information survives on only a tiny fraction of the total number of such informants. Some of them were professional actors such as Henry Thomas Harrison of Gettysburg fame and Pauline Cushman who penetrated Confederate General Braxton Bragg's headquarters and successfully made away with important plans.[18] Their number included adventurers seeking fame and fortune, such as the man who called himself James Andrews and English born James George Brown of Dalton, Georgia. Northerners who had lived in the South before the war and had personal reasons, such as family members left behind in "rebeldom," had reason to return and could work as spies behind enemy lines. Native Southerners

Top & above: Southern refugees (*The Great Book of 1866*, broadside, BRO1866G7, Broadside Collection, mss4299, Hargrett Rare Book and Manuscript Library, University of Georgia Libraries).

who supported the Union but in East Tennessee and North Georgia made loyal and locally connected operatives for Thomas. The federal army supplied bold young men as scouts.[19]

Detectives, scouts, spies, and everyone interviewed by Thomas's officers received detailed debriefing. The men conducting the interrogations had the results recorded on loose paper in a standard format. Copies of these depositions were then sent to all affected commands and the Provost Marshal Office in Washington, D.C. Depositions in Thomas's files provide information on several of the people he used as spies. Carrie King, for example, passed through the Confederate lines to her family in Columbus, Georgia, and back again, returning with extensive information on the situation in Alabama and Georgia. In Rome, Georgia, Confederates mistakenly arrested her as a Mrs. Polin, an expected federal spy, before she took her leave from them.[20]

Samuel Wilson had been a Yankee mining engineer in North Georgia before leaving for Colorado. General Grant allowed him to return to Georgia to look after his family, but only as part of a plot to burn enemy bridges. Wilson found his objectives too wet and too well-guarded to incinerate, however. He did travel about North Georgia gathering information and even rode through the defenses of Lee's Atlanta unimpeded. Wilson returned through Thomas' lines and the general paid him $100.[21] Dr. Mary Walker, the only female doctor in the Civil War army, also received pay for her intelligence work while helping poor white civilians. These adventures resulted in her capture twice, once by the notorious rebel partisan Champ Ferguson (he had her released) and her imprisonment in the notorious Castle Thunder prison in Richmond.[22]

Native Frenchman Emile Bourlier of Louisville, Kentucky, used his ethnicity to pass himself off as a French national attempting to return to his homeland while he worked to obtain intelligence for several generals. Already identified as a spy, he still risked a journey behind the rebel lines that produced critical information that might have prevented the battle of Chickamauga, but Bourlier had failed to find a way back into federal territory on his journey from Mobile to Richmond.[23]

Some scouts and spies returned with less than valuable data. James C. Moore made several trips into the Confederacy by working as a rebel spy for a Colonel Hill, Confederate General Braxton Bragg's provost marshal (the man responsible for catching spies). Moore usually provided Thomas with erroneous information, however. Because of Thomas' insistence on recording how each agent obtained his or her "facts," researchers know that Moore failed because he depended upon second and third-hand gossip repeated in the rebel camps, not upon documents and what he had witnessed, valuable information for historians today on what the Confederate military knew.[24]

Thomas usually used a spy for only one mission. His widespread dispersal of the reports, with no attempt at concealing names, discouraged operatives from taking more than one assignment. Confederate agents might obtain copies of the depositions and report Thomas' agents' identities. James George Brown sought to avoid detection by using the codename "Letty," after his late wife, in his letters to Thomas. Grenville Dodge, General Grant's spymaster in the West, declined to reveal the names of his spies to anyone, even long after the war.[25]

Historian Edwin Fishel believed that no Civil War executions occurred as punishment for espionage, but contemporary Southern newspapers reported otherwise.[26] In one celebrated case, a one-armed fiddler in Dalton, Georgia, died in jail while awaiting execution as a federal spy.[27] John William "W.J." Lawton and Bradford Hendricks waited too long to retire as scouts. They died at the hands of pro–Confederate guerrillas.[28] Pennsylvanian Samuel W. Kenny went to the gallows as a spy at Tullahoma, Tennessee, on February 13, 1863.[29]

The operatives who served undercover for Generals Rosecrans and Thomas certainly believed that they risked their lives. John Fitch wrote of a double agent who, by acting as a personal spy for General Bragg, really worked for Rosecrans and the Union. Leaving on a final mission:

> Our spy was a brave man; yet during the last three days of his service he was most sensible of his peril. To pass between hostile lines in the lone hours of the night,-for he did not wait for daylight,—to be halted by guerrillas and scouts and pickets, with guns aimed at him, and, finally, to meet and satisfy the anxious, keen-eyed, heart searching rebel officers as well as our own, was a mental as well as physical demand that could not long be sustained. While proceeding upon his last expedition, the author met the nameless one upon a by-road. We halted our horses, drew near and conversed a few seconds in private, while our attendants and companies moved on. He was greatly exhausted and soiled in appearance,—his clothing having been rained upon and splashed by muddy water, caused by hard riding, and which had dried upon him. He said he was about to try it once more, and, though he had been so often and so successfully, yet he feared detection and its sure result, the bullet or the halter. He had been unable, amid the hurry and excitement, to make some final disposition of his affairs. He gave us a last message to send to his wife and children in case it became necessary; and he also desired a promise—most freely given—that we would attend to the settlement of his account with our general for services recently rendered. Thus concluding, he wrung our hand most earnestly, and, putting spurs to his fresh and spirited animal, dashed off upon his mission.[30]

Fortunately, after 20 hours, the spy returned safely to the federal lines with the needed information. He had survived to complete his last spy mission.

Almost two years later, John Milton Glass of Walker County, Georgia, faced the same dilemma. He succeeded in his many trips behind the rebel lines because the Confederates believed he worked for their provost marshal in Atlanta! Despite the suspicions of some rebel officers, Glass went on another mission, even after his partner abandoned him. Historian Wilbur Kurtz speculated that Glass' reports ended abruptly because the spy was the corpse that federal soldiers later found hanging outside Atlanta. He had, however, given up his career as a spy and would live to die in Arkansas in 1891. The federal government turned down his claim for payment for his services due to his failure to prove that he had done secret work![31]

Atlanta has always drawn a class of characters, dreamers, grifters, swindlers, and combinations of all, many of whose identities, like those of spies, were false then and are now lost to time. In the era when Lee lived, society pressured the individual to live by unrealistic standards of "hypocrisy" with the promise of respect and success. Persons who failed, like Lee, could earn disdain while swindlers appeared as respectable people they were not, even as literally the first individuals identified as confidence criminals. "Confidence" was a magical commodity of that age that allowed people to achieve positive notoriety in the arts, business, innovation, religion, and even the supernatural. This quality could be used for fraud, but sometimes for people wanting only to escape one life for another by taking on a completely new identity, and even sex.[32]

This commodity of the age was "an invisible, ineffable aura" of "black magic, good fortune, and hard cash combined" that "could turn worthless paper into glittering gold, cow towns into cities, empty lots into bustling businesses, losers into winners, paupers into millionaires."[33] As Mark Twain would write, it heralded the next modern marvel of "shoddy." Confidence had turned a broken-down tavern into the city and great economic engine of Atlanta, at least because of the arrival of railroads.

Lee's acquaintance Robert A. Crawford was one of these opportunists and extensive records of his activities survive. Both men were failed entrepreneurs, but unlike Lee who was honest, Crawford somehow avoided credit reports and his past catching up to him. (He should not be confused with Lee's friend Robert C. Crawford, a city councilman.)[34] As William Aduston Rogers Crawford, he was born in Gloucester County, Virginia, on February 11, 1812.[35] His father, Samuel, was a highly respected Free Mason, surveyor, and former newspaper

Hanging (*The Great Book of 1866*, broadside, BRO1866G7, Broadside Collection, mss4299, Hargrett Rare Book and Manuscript Library, University of Georgia Libraries).

editor who lost everything to the bankruptcy of his store, even to the point that the family was living under the open sky for years. William A.R. Crawford likely had an apprenticeship as a grifter that is undiscovered before he found himself in New Orleans in 1835. Crawford subsequently became a nationally noted swindler from New Orleans, Louisiana, to Wheeling, West Virginia, along the Mississippi and Ohio rivers. He was sentenced to five years in prison in Louisville, Kentucky, on December 17, 1838. Five years later, he was released, having finished his sentence. Even then, he is recorded in his prison records under the stolen identity of A.C. Wood of Nashville, Tennessee.[36]

Robert A. Crawford (1812–1892) in Confederate colonel's uniform near the end of the war (author's collection).

This grifter learned from his experience not to do anything that would result in criminal prosecution. He became, as novelist David Cornwell ("John Le Carré"), wrote of his own father, an unscrupulous confidence artist who "could bankrupt himself in one town, and next day raise credit in another fifty miles away."[37] As Robert A. Crawford, he appears in Butts County, Georgia, in 1849 where he began a series of schemes built on the credit and the private assets of his various wives (the majority of whom died from complications of childbirth), that included a coach and buggy factory in Auburn, Alabama, that his employees reportedly burned down; and a hotel-quality merchants flour mill in Houston County, Georgia, that bankrupted. He also formed a state militia company and tried to start a newspaper; organized a regiment for an unsuccessful expedition to Mexico; and became a newspaper editor and plantation owner in Griffin, Georgia, before he arrived in Atlanta just before the Civil War.[38] He became editor of Atlanta's *Southern Confederacy* newspaper but left it to hold various positions as an officer in the Confederate and Georgia forces.[39]

Like Lee, Crawford was an adamant supporter of the Confederate States of America, and to the day he died, even to being buried in the uniform he had worn in an invented military career as a colonel of a fictional "Third Georgia" regiment.[40] His last wife claimed that he served in the 53rd Georgia during the nearby battle of New Hope Church in late May 1864, and a newspaper reported that Confederate General Alexander Welch Reynolds fell wounded in that battle while riding with Crawford. The Confederate 53rd records Robert A. Crawford enlisting and immediately deserting, but he did not serve in the Atlanta Campaign. Atlanta's R.A. Crawford might have been in the 53rd Militia Regiment. He served as a pallbearer for bringing to Atlanta the body of Confederate General Leonidas Polk, who died at Pine Mountain June 14. He, like, Lee worked to raise whole companies for the Confederate army, for which his career as a swindler likely proved an asset and he raised funds for the Confederate hospitals in Atlanta that Lee managed.[41]

Crawford had learned, however, that no matter how he swindled people and unethical was his conduct, he could not be prosecuted if he technically committed no crime. Only once did someone, and then anonymously, question his character. He would open Atlanta's first real market/pen for holding and selling enslaved people, earning him nationally a negative notoriety but which would become the subject of one of the most often reproduced photographs of the Civil War. After the war, he pursued various schemes in Georgia and New York, even achieving a false national reputation as a successful entrepreneur to his death on a business trip in Atlanta in 1892.[42]

In the spring of 1862, however, Colonel George W. Lee brought calm to Atlanta's threatened and frightened populace. He made his Captain William H. Battey the provost marshal, while he took de facto command of the hospitals, the quartermaster stores, conscripts, and seemingly all other aspects of the Confederate government establishment in the city. In what has then and since been incorrectly described as declaring martial law, Lee made Atlanta a military post and issued a string of orders for protecting the more than 60 million dollars of government stores in the city. Atlanta had become a major depot for the Confederate army and navy. Lee stopped the sale of alcohol. Under his orders, the city was closed to any officer or soldier without a permit.

Beginning with General Order No. 1, Lee ordered that all persons, including officers and soldiers, passing through the city had to have passes, and he threatened to incarcerate any African American after the legally imposed curfew of 9:00 p.m. without a pass or an owner present. With the latter, he only extended the spirit, if not the letter, of both old and new Georgia laws that reflected the public's fear of racial insurrections. Nothing survives in his writings on how he felt about African Americans, but he did draw criticism for being too liberal in providing passes to the city's Black population.[43]

The undoing of Lee's efforts always came from unexpected directions and unforeseen circumstances. He had only been back in Atlanta for a few days when, in early June, an Atlanta newspaper announced that he and his "well-drilled and well-seasoned troops" would be dispatched again. He received urgent orders from his appreciative superiors to leave his grateful city and return to Savannah as quickly as possible. Colonel Elihu P. Watkins and his regiment from nearby Camp McDonald would replace Lee and his men. In the interim, the government ordered Brigadier General Lawton to Virginia. Lee's Legion band serenaded Lawton on leaving Savannah with a rendition of *Dixie* as the men saluted in his honor.

Brigadier General Smith's transfer to a new command in South Carolina reorganized the command in Georgia. Battalions had enlarged into regiments, but all merged into one command under Brigadier General Hugh W. Mercer. On May 26, 1862, the government sent Mercer to Charleston as commander of the Second District of South Carolina to replace General Roswell Sabine Ripley, who had been transferred to Virginia.

The Confederate Secretary of War would months later write that George W. Lee received his appointment as provost marshal in Atlanta from General Robert E. Lee, a statement that seems an error as General Lee (no relation to George W. Lee) had left the Georgia coast for Virginia in March 1862 long before George W. Lee became provost marshal of Atlanta. R.E. Lee likely did send G.W. Lee to Atlanta but at the end of a very complicated piece of lost history.[44]

In his home state of Virginia, General Robert E. Lee found himself "reduced to the functions of an expeditor" of General Joseph E. Johnston's demands in a confused, failing command system that had lost its way in the fog of war. General Lee, sometimes using "behind-the-scenes manipulation," called upon the eastern departments of the upper Confederacy for troops to defend Richmond. Aside from being already greatly outnumbered, the troops Johnston had available lacked training and anything like adequate arms and supplies.[45]

The Confederate States of America was notorious for favoritism in promoting certain officers to the grade of general while some deserving, capable men received too little consideration, such as George W. Lee. With all the generals sent to other threatened areas, Confederate officials ordered Lee, still in Atlanta but also the senior colonel of the troops in Savannah, to rush his six best regiments by train from the latter to Virginia. On the way to Richmond, he had a relapse of his tuberculosis. By the middle of June, Lee had his command in Petersburg, Virginia, with orders to send each regiment, as it arrived, to General Thomas Jackson in the Valley of Virginia. Before he could carry out that plan, the Confederate command formed his regiments into a brigade almost the size of a division. Commanded again by Brigadier General Lawton, this new unit would earn renown as the Lawton-Gordon-Evans Brigade, but it entered the war under the command of Colonel George Washington Lee of Atlanta. It immediately became engaged in the Seven Days Campaign to drive the federal forces back from Richmond.

Lee, however, did not participate in that fight but returned to Atlanta gravely ill. He soon returned to Virginia in command of his regiment. An Atlanta newspaper announced that he and his men would likely be needed to "make peace with the Yankees." At the battles of Gaines Mill and Malvern Hill, he would write that his 38th Georgia suffered "dreadfully" but acted "nobly." Captain William H. Battey commanded the regiment most of that time as Lee remained ill, Lieutenant Colonel Parr lost his left arm to enemy fire early on and acting Major James D. Mathews received a wound so bad that Atlanta newspapers mistakenly reported him as dead. Of the 1,050 men of the 38th Regiment whom Lee had brought to Virginia in several train cars in June, by the end of the Battle of Antietam on September 17, fewer than 35 of them could still stand. In the first six months of the war, as few as 20 men died in both armies combined from the fighting (although many more surely died from the diseases that swept through the camps). Now Atlanta newspapers, for the first time, printed entire pages filled with lists of casualties.[46]

With lung hemorrhages rendering him unfit for field service, Lee resigned his commission as colonel of the 38th Georgia on July 15, 1862, and returned to Atlanta. Eight days later, the Confederate Secretary of War gave him the position of provost marshal and assistant adjutant general in the city with the rank of captain in the Department of East Tennessee. The government did him no favors with these new responsibilities. A newspaper in Mobile, Alabama, offered an opinion of the provost marshals in general:

> There has been no part of the machinery of our military administration quite so distasteful to our people—none which has so sorely tried the public patience, as that of the provost system. It has happened not infrequently that inexperienced, rude, and thoughtless men have been put in these offices; men, who seemed to regard themselves as invested with senseless rudeness, and exercised arbitrary and capricious authority.—In some cases, we doubt not, there has been corruption and favoritism on one hand, and oppression, if not persecution, on the other. In the main, however, it is believed these officials have discharged their difficult and delicate trusts with tolerable fidelity, and possibly with some advantage to the public service.[47]

The command structure in Atlanta, since Lee had been away, essentially ceased to function. Colonel Elihu P. Watkins, Major Austin Leyden, and Colonel Winburn J. Lawton had each succeeded Lee as post commander in just the few weeks since he had left.[48] Watkins had appointed Green Jones Foreacre as provost marshal. This Ohio Yankee, railroad agent, and disabled Confederate veteran had a local reputation as a swindler even before the war, especially as an insurance agent. He had recently been involved in a scheme to sell wooden bowls to the army for thousands of dollars. Leyden claimed that he still commanded the post at Atlanta and refused to give up command of the small local guard unit. Foreacre did report to the government that there were hundreds of men, many of them officers, who roamed the city without papers or with forged documents. While he tried to keep his job with the support of Atlanta's various illicit whiskey rings, he also declared himself powerless to do anything about the mounting crisis in the city.

The situation also proved beyond the control of Atlanta's 20-man police force. Founded in the late 1850s, this law enforcement agency had received praise for its service, but as the war continued, it became a part of the crime problem and was corrupt to the point that even dismissals and prosecutions failed to reform it. Robert C. Crawford (not Lee's local swindler Robert A. Crawford, although the two men have been confused with each other) in applying unsuccessfully for command in Atlanta, painted a grim picture in the newspaper and a letter to the Confederate government. He wrote of profiteering, illegal trade, illicit dealings by Yankee civilians, treason, inflation, and deteriorating security.[49]

Lee began his new job with the first of several unsuccessful attempts to learn the limits of his authority from the national government in far-off Richmond. Without waiting for an answer that never came, he stationed men at the railroad stations to arrest suspicious persons while ordering ticket agents and hotels to refuse to accommodate anyone without proper papers. All hotels, each day, had to send him lists of guests.

Atlanta, even before the war, had its share of economic, political, and social scandals, real and rumored, from thugs to revolts by the enslaved labor to bands of filibusters (mercenaries) with dreams of foreign conquests. The Civil War made matters so much worse, and across Georgia, from common brigands to organized armed gangs like that of John Gatewood to draft evaders to insurrectionaries of all types to wholesale profiteering and smuggling that broke the laws of both warring nations. These problems seemed insurmountable, but until the return of George Washington Lee to Atlanta, no one even tried to deal with the problems in the Gate City.[50]

Lee also, with so many transient people, had to act against an epidemic reminiscent of modern pandemics but in an age with so little knowledge of how diseases spread. He began by ordering proof from strangers of having avoided areas with smallpox outbreaks. The press panicked over the latter, an especially deadly disease for children. Large gatherings of people and strangers passing through Atlanta spread the disease. When a case finally appeared in Atlanta, Lee kept the patient's name out of the press but quarantined him.

Following nearby outbreaks in July and August 1862, the provost marshal ordered all soldiers vaccinated. By the following January, the city council required the same for all residents. When an epidemic broke out in nearby Stone Mountain, he asked Governor Joseph E. Brown to override DeKalb County officials and implement a quarantine. Lee ordered the sick in the city's military hospitals to provide passes from physicians or remain at a secure contagious disease hospital that he set up for civilians and soldiers on William Markham's 155-acre Davis plantation on October 1, 1862. Markham, formerly the temporary Atlanta mayor, unsuccessfully sued for damages and the return of his property.

The Fulton County Inferior Court took charge of the smallpox hospital from Lee in January 1863. At least one of the enslaved people there died working as an attendant. If a patient in the smallpox hospital escaped, he would find little to do in Atlanta. Lee ordered the billiard halls, saloons, and gaming establishments closed. He had cotton and other combustibles moved to places of safety.[51]

Atlanta's new provost marshal also built a new command from scratch, a task made easier by exemptions from the Confederate draft offered by various home guard units. His position included the authority to raise one provost (police) company for local security. Somehow, he also obtained the services of a company of Echol's battery that he used as cavalry.

Enlistment officers would still seize Lee's men. Others of his command resigned to take payment to join the army as substitutes for men drafted. Soon, his command consisted of only some 100 members of a home guard unit, but even they were threatened with enrollment in the regular army. Lee had promised them bounty enlistment pay, only to later learn that he held no such authority.

On June 25, 1863, the Confederate military approved Lee creating the 25th Infantry Battalion (Provost Guard) with Lee as its major and commander. This battalion of 12 cavalry and infantry companies usually had 600 to 700 members total, but, at its peak, consisted of at least 1,156 old men, boys, convalescents, and other citizens exempt from the national draft into the regular army. Because of its size, it could have counted at least as a regiment with Lee as a colonel. The Confederate Secretary of War eventually allowed a transfer of survivors from Lee's original 1861 company, who had been serving in Mississippi and had reenlisted in the Confederate service, to company A of his new provost battalion and under his younger brother Captain Marcus D. Lee. Company E was created as mounted infantry specifically to pursue deserters and draft evaders in Northeast Georgia, while Company F consisted of boys under 18 and for which required each member had to obtain permission from a parent to serve.[52] Captain James Spurlock Hargrove wrote of the men of his Company D, "Lee's Rangers" (formerly Hardee's Company) at Camp Preston, Lee's base two miles from the city, that they were boys and men of

> good moral and military character, quiet, orderly, and well behaved, not given to drinking, frolicking, or anything of the kind. They were all young men—all except one or two entered on the roll as under eighteen years of age—and for merit as soldiers, they were, for young men, exceptions in Major Lee's camp.[53]
>
> The battalion even had a popular brass band.[54]

Even Lee himself described his troops generally as disrespectful and obnoxious in carrying out their duties, however, but soldiers largely drawn from railroad workers and adolescent males would hardly have made the most disciplined or sophisticated soldiers. When Lee sent out a detachment to hunt escaped prisoners in October 1862, his boys and old men bought whiskey from a dealer in Marietta and became embroiled in a drunken brawl that left one man dead and two wounded. A minister serving as a chaplain in the Dahlonega campaign in 1863 wrote that the morals in Lee's battalion were far from satisfactory.[55]

In February 1863, the now Major Lee had to order the arrest of three of his men for breaking into and looting Thomas F. Lowe's store on Peachtree Street. Lee had stored confiscated contraband whiskey there. A year later, the provost marshal sent out a company that raided Wesley G. Collier's house. They acted on reports of a gang of thieves operating in the Buckhead settlement north of Atlanta. The county's superior court, later upheld by the State Supreme Court, would convict Lee's soldiers of riot for the ensuing brawl.[56]

Lee's civil guards had many responsibilities and the tasks included fighting this Civil War equivalent of a war on illegal substances. Controlling whiskey-related problems, including violence and theft, became the most persistent and widespread problem for the Confederacy's provost marshals. He had seen the discipline problems caused by alcohol among the men of Wright's Legion in Savannah. Drunken soldiers would molest civilians and damage private property. Governor Brown received reports, but especially from drought-stricken North Georgia, that the corn producers there refused to sell their crops as food to starving families, even those with men gone to the war, as the farmers profited more from making illegal whiskey.

Lee found that soldiers passing through Atlanta had no problems with obtaining alcohol from the employees of the Atlanta & West Point and the Western & Atlantic railroads. Starting with his first general order on May 14, 1862, Lee banned the sale of alcohol to soldiers and ordered the arrest of anyone found drunk in the streets. He later extended these orders to troops stationed in outlying areas.

Several people smuggled in homebrew, however, often under the pretense of providing medical supplies for the hospitals. Lee had been a saloonkeeper before the war and knew that some of the product was potentially toxic. Bootleggers traditionally sometimes use toxic substances such as wood alcohol as a filler to supplement the volume of the whiskey. One Atlantan commented that the local illicit brew came in two varieties, one of which tasted like swallowing a cat and the other like pulling it back out by the tail. As early as April 1862, Cornelius Hanleiter saw such "split scull," "rifle," "knock knee," "O.B. Joyful," "knock in the head," "sure shot," and "rot gut" as common in the city.[57]

In August 1862, Governor Brown received a complaint that a squad of Lee's men had broken up a still operating under a government contract, became drunk, and abused the African Americans of Mr. Vaughn, the distillery owner. When J.J. Hall of Butts County complained of the destruction of his still by Lee's orders, a state official asked Hall if the offender even understood that making alcohol when the state's civilians needed the corn for food violated the law?

Dr. Anderson L. Scott, an Atlanta Unionist, had drawn attention for comforting the Andrews raiders, the Union soldier saboteurs captured while trying to destroy bridges on the Western & Atlantic Railroad. Incarcerated for bootleg alcohol, Scott told Lee that friends would get him released, although Lee believed sufficient evidence had turned up for a conviction. While Scott sat with filthy soldiers in the Confederate barracks, the provost marshal's men searched his office without any concern for the damage that they did.

The following October, a similar incident occurred. Men who had paid substitutes to serve for them in the army had joined Lee's Provost Guard and started trouble over alcohol in Marietta, the popular place to get liquor after Lee had outlawed it in Atlanta. Under Lieutenant M.D. Lee, a detachment had set out to find some of the "bridge burners" (members of the Andrews raiders who had escaped custody in Atlanta) when four of their number decided to frequent the dram shops in Marietta. They boarded a train and recklessly fired their weapons, wounding three people and killing a fourth. Upon learning of the situation, George W. Lee took over an old locomotive and, acting as engineer, set out for Marietta. He soon had three of the culprits in custody, but the ringleader, Elisha Crawford, "a regular desperado" according to the Atlanta police, escaped.[58]

Actions such as enforcing the prohibition on alcohol made Lee powerful enemies, especially among Atlanta's ambitious financial elite. Some of those individuals and their lawyers began a campaign against the seizure of alcohol. As with any prohibition involving a popular vice, enforcers, officials, and politicians took bribes. At least one of the officers in the Atlanta Provost Guard found himself under arrest for accepting brandy from a farmer. Lee took a risk when he "washed" Peachtree Street with the "spiritual" T.O. Kyle's 12 whiskey barrels, for the smuggler's brother sat on the city council. Marvel J. Camden of Chattanooga operated the state of Georgia's Western & Atlantic Railroad and used his position to illegally smuggle whiskey into Atlanta. In the spring of 1863, Lee confiscated the alcohol, but Governor Brown pressured him to buy the contraband for use by the state or to send it back to Camden, at the maximum freight rate and with a bill for the shipping. The governor eased the restrictions on whiskey production to provide for necessary purchases by the Confederate hospitals in Richmond. He discovered too late, however, that he unintentionally sanctioned a highly placed whiskey ring that took in $120,000 in profits. In April 1863, General John K. Jackson ordered the Atlanta provost marshal to stop the campaign against alcohol. General Braxton Bragg reinstated the prohibition, however, when he later proclaimed martial law.

Lee had acted, as usual, with tact. For example, a woman named Harrington in Augusta shipped whiskey to her sister, another war widow in Atlanta, allegedly for the hospitals. The provost marshal believed that they lied about the intent, but he still paid for the alcohol and had it turned over to the medical department. He had to arrest Joseph Harford six or seven times for running a small dram shop and selling "his miserable poisonous concoction which he has been in the habit of calling Spirits" at the train station to soldiers, convalescing Irishmen, and almost anyone else. Harford concealed his "stuff" in a carpet sack. Lee's men also caught him bringing it into the city in barrels, nailed and secreted among other goods, as he "endeavored in a thousand ways to evade the law."[59]

George W. Lee succeeded in Atlanta because of his competence and tact, and because exaggerations and fears about the crisis in Atlanta made him look good. The provost marshal of Atlanta did have to deal with many kinds of desperate characters, including bushwhackers, counterfeiters, deserters, murderers, and thieves. He had the most serious of these offenders transferred to Richmond, although he often assigned that duty to his boys under the age of 18 in most instances the first real adventure and responsibility of their lives!

The problems of crime in Civil War Atlanta only grew, however. A man named George from Athens, Georgia, for example, conned his way into the highest circles of the Confederate government in Richmond just by wearing an officer's uniform. When he tried his schemes in Atlanta, Lee had him arrested twice and sent to General Braxton Bragg's headquarters. Each time, "Gentleman George" conned the general into letting him go. This character could likely, at the least, have encouraged Bragg's later animus against Lee.

An Atlanta quartermaster who ordered shoes for Bragg's army from those made in the state penitentiary then rejected them only as a means of then profitably selling the shoes to the public in Atlanta. Similarly, in a nationally reported incident, Lee and his men arrested soldiers selling five wagonloads of military supplies, some $60,000 to $75,000 worth of goods, just outside of the city. A man from Alabama passed through Atlanta selling 200 government blankets he had recovered from the battlefields in Virginia.[60]

Confederate provost marshals like Lee were also primarily responsible for apprehending deserters and draft evaders. Men and boys joined the Southern military for such reasons as to defend their families, for adventure, racism, or fear of conscription. Some soldiers in both armies chose not to suffer from the war's dangers over someone else's right to own anyone or to expand a class of free African Americans to compete with white Americans for jobs, land, and opportunity. White Southern men could flee the Confederacy to avoid the South's draft. They were exempt from the federal conscription, unlike African American boys and men, but they might obtain good paying jobs in Northern factories or join the regiments of "Galvanized Yankees," volunteers who largely served in the Union army in West defending settlements against bands of Native American warriors.

Even firebrand supporters of Southern secession had limits. Men like Reconstruction era serial killer Milton Malone and the Lincoln assassin John Wilkes Booth could murder for that cause even as they refrained from fighting in the trenches and otherwise suffering the deprecations of military service. Frank N. Graves of Stewart County remembered such voices speaking of drinking blood and of fighting in the first to the last trench but never making an appearance in either.[61]

Early in the war, businessman Sidney Root of Atlanta attended a gathering of Georgians in the hotel room of Alexander H. Stephens, a Georgian and the new Confederate vice president, in Montgomery. The group had come to hear Abraham Lincoln's inauguration speech as it was telegraphed. They agreed that the Confederacy would only need 50,000 men to defend itself from the United States. The reality of the war eventually set in, however, and the Confederate states' government passed a national conscription law on April 26, 1862.[62] That law made all able-bodied men aged 18 to 35 eligible for three years of military service, and another law, on September 7, 1862, raised the maximum age to 45. The final draft act made the age range 17 to 50. Each state had a quota. An act of December 28, 1862, ended the practice of hiring substitutes for service, although the act of October 11, 1862, granted an exemption for every overseer of twenty or more people enslaved, and to various professions to try to meet the blockaded Confederacy's desperate need for the services of skilled workers.[63]

Almost any other physically able white male in the legal age range for the draft became fair game, even if he traveled from out of his state. Names of some 1.4 million individuals appear in the Confederate military service records that survive today in the National Archives and Records Administration, although scholars argue that number would be a quarter higher, if all the service records survived and despite some one-third of the South's manpower opposed to the war. Aside from the estimated 260,000 men who died in service, likely as many Southerners followed the example of Private Samuel Clements (aka Mark Twain) and left the ranks before the war ended. Consequently, the gray legions likely never numbered more than a few hundred thousand men ready to fight, but even they were too often scattered to the wrong places at the wrong time, waiting for orders, pay, supplies and transportation never provided.

At the same time, federal raiders, such as in Mississippi in 1863 and Georgia in 1864, could move quickly and largely unopposed, destroying railroad tracks and supplies, increasingly with help from local war dissenters and draft evaders. Lee reported how doctors and surgeons in areas of North Georgia like Pickens County protected able-bodied men opposed to the war with medical deferments. Consequently, he established his own board for determining fitness for conscription for any man found passing through the city. On June 19, 1863, state Adjutant General Henry C. Wayne ordered all deserters captured by the state troops sent to Lee.[64]

The provost marshal had a challenging time enforcing the draft laws because Governor Joseph E. Brown granted exemptions to more than 5,000 local politicians and others he deemed as holding essential offices and occupations, men cynically referred to as "Joe Brown's pets."[65] For as long as he could, Brown also tried to keep some form of state army in the field to exclusively protect Georgia. Critics claimed that the governor, with his exemptions, ignored pleas by poor families seeking the release of their men from prison or military service. Draft evasion became rampant when the Confederate government ended the exemptions, as well as ending the policy of allowing individuals to hire substitutes to go to the war in 1864. Governor Brown allowed the creation of home guard local defense companies made up, at least in part, of the increasing numbers of deserters and draft evaders. Ironically, they had the responsibility of arresting other men trying to escape military service.[66]

Atlanta had a form of draft evasion through the claims of essential service. Employees of the Gate City's newspapers, growing in number due to the arrival of refuge presses, served in the Atlanta Press Guards, a home defense company that included Samuel D. Niles. As a newspaper of the time could have fifty or more employees, this unit could have substantial numbers. It also offered membership to anyone willing to pay $500. An observer noted that another 3,000 well-connected men used "service" in Atlanta's non–steam powered fire companies as a dodge to avoid military service. They included 30 to 35 northern-born opportunists and profiteers who, after the war, claimed to have supported the Union throughout the conflict.

A newspaper writer urged the fire companies to be abolished, with their responsibilities given to Lee's 25th Provost Guard Battalion. As a home defense unit, the fire companies put on a good parade—bright armor, flying banners, and marital music. The men of the fire companies elected Lee as lieutenant colonel of their "Atlanta Fire Battalion," in August 1863. They briefly became part of the Third Battalion, Georgia State Guards Cavalry Battalion, a unit created on August 3, 1863, to defend Fulton County for a maximum of six months of duty during a threat of invasion by federal armies and with Lee as major and then lieutenant colonel as their commander. This sometime infantry battalion was disbanded on February 4, 1863.[67]

Lee's command had other shirkers. Critics claimed that the provost marshal sold draft exemptions he officially issued to persons needed to maintain the city's railroads and other vital services, but an investigation exonerated him. When General John K. Jackson arrived from the Army of Tennessee to collect any deserters from the 58th Georgia, however, he found that the provost companies in Atlanta included many men he deemed fit for the army. Jackson took them back with him as conscripts, reducing Lee's garrison to almost nonexistent. The men taken felt betrayed. They were likely the survivors of Lee's original who had been allowed to return to again serve under him, So many of Lee's men had been taken from his command that he doubted he could now find more than 100 men for a defense force.

To his superiors, Lee wrote that, although his city had become the Confederacy's supply depot, including for the Navy, in the case of another panic Atlanta, with less than 100 men, might face a threat from as many as 5,000 enemy soldiers. Even 500 Yankee raiders could take his city upon a hill, he warned, and render this southern terminal of the vital Western & Atlantic Railroad useless to the Confederate armies in Tennessee. In September 1863, on the eve of the battle of Chickamauga, Lee published an impassioned plea for men to join the Confederate army to fight against the approaching invaders.[68]

In May of 1863, when federal Colonel Abel Streight's raid in Alabama threatened Georgia, Lee moved to protect Rome with his few remaining men and two pieces of artillery. He soon announced to Atlanta that General Nathan Bedford Forrest had captured the Yankee force. Lee had the prisoners transferred from Rome to the Confederate prisons in Richmond.[69]

By the spring of 1863, the deteriorating Confederate military situation in Mississippi brought on a flood of deserters who headed east through Georgia, traveling back to their respective homes. A few months later, Confederate soldiers from the surrender of Vicksburg showed up in Atlanta as mobs—hungry, nearly naked, barefoot, sick, and without money—a forewarning of the times to come. General Grant had paroled them on the condition that they would not return to the Confederate army until exchanged for the federal soldiers being held in Richmond. Concern arose that these men, if not given help, would just take what they needed. Disillusioned and feeling abandoned by their nation, they announced that they would refuse to return to their units even if they were officially exchanged.

Reports appeared that even before Vicksburg fell, Confederate authorities executed soldiers who wished for the war to end, even if it meant a northern victory. Whole regiments conspired to desert, reportedly influenced by the anti-war Peace Society. People across the South had mistakenly thought that the Confederacy was winning at Port Hudson and Vicksburg until the arrival of the citizen and soldier victims of the Mississippi River campaign staggered into places like Atlanta, physically proving otherwise.

Lee and Atlanta's civilians did what they could for these soldiers. The Atlanta Ladies Hospital Association, for example, gave 1,000 of these veterans a dinner. The Confederate government ordered that as the Georgia soldiers received official exchange, they would leave their homes for Atlanta en route back to the army.

Confederate disasters in the Gettysburg, Jackson, Middle Tennessee, Port Hudson, and Vicksburg campaigns happened in July 1863, as did the end of the prisoner exchange, making the cause of the independence of the Southern nation even more hopeless. The Southern nation's hopes now rested on using its outnumbered, poorly supplied, and ineptly managed military to block the divided, often delayed, and poorly coordinated federal advance. General Ulysses S. Grant's victory at Chattanooga, November 23–26, 1863, concentrated the western armies of the United States for a campaign to take Atlanta, Georgia, and, ultimately, the Carolinas out of the war. Many Georgians intended to cooperate rather than oppose the pending federal advance into Georgia, including profiteers. Sherman even had a map of Macon color-coded with the politics of individual residents.

The disintegration of the Confederate armies continued to accelerate from further losses of the living, not just the dead. Wives had to obtain passes to visit their soldier husbands, or the men had to receive leave, just as African Americans had to do on plantations. Food, labor, and living conditions in Confederate camps, even without considering the disease and fighting, fell below that of what was typically Black labor in bondage. Officers treated soldiers like the enslaved, and the Confederate soldiers received little or no pay. Slave owners demanded better treatment of their people impressed into working in the Confederate military, which depended upon enslaved labor to continue.

In 1864, General Ulysses S. Grant allowed Confederate prisoners of war to return to their homes in federally occupied areas upon taking an oath to the United States, the beginning of the repatriation of the states that had seceded from the Union. As the federal armies prepared to invade Georgia, Confederate soldiers also deserted to protect their homes, to put in crops to feed their starving families, or because they saw the Confederacy's demise as inevitable or, at least not dying for.

At that same time, off the coast of North Carolina, the United States Navy enjoyed unprecedented success in capturing blockade runners and further shutting the Confederacy off from the outside world. Ships that did get through were not large pre-war freighters filled with needed goods for the starving nation, but vessels designed for speed. They carried less cargo per trip and often luxury goods for the wealthy, through harbors kept open by the sacrifices of the general population. The Confederate government, however, had to allow these risky private ventures to be profitable.[70]

Legal sales of cotton to the United States did bring food and other goods into the Confederacy, officially for humanitarian reasons, into the Southern nation that federal officials knew fed Southern soldiers! Even General Robert E. Lee saw this system as hypocrisy, but his army would not have survived without it or enslaved labor. An observer in London noted, in an article published in an Atlanta soldiers' publication, that 130,000 bales of cotton had gotten through the federal blockade to Europe and the North, for the enrichment of private individuals and to pay for luxury goods rather than the necessities that the average civilian in the South had to purchase at increasingly inflated prices. Had the Confederate government sold those exports, it would have met its military needs at the lowest prices and without taking on debt.

Wars of any duration have profiteers from whom the general population suffers. Even the American Revolution had loyalty for money, profiteering, and usury on all levels, and all sides. Operating a "black market," however, can also be the only means of survival for individuals and families. Loreta Janeta Velásquez, for example, claimed that she so supported the Confederate cause that she dressed as a man to enlist. As the war progressed, however, she saw fraud, profiteering, and usury all around her to the point that by the end of the war she was working as a spy for the highest bidder. Ambrose Spencer in his time and forever as a character in the play *Andersonville Trial*, appears in the play as a "Southern planter" appalled by the horrors of the Confederate prison popularly known as Andersonville. A Yankee swindler and a perennial failure in business, he really worked during the war as a Confederate claims agent and even offered to raise an artillery battery for the Southern army![71]

Two years into the war, a refugee wrote of witnessing how strangers in Atlanta were all but ignored as the cotton commerce and speculation seemed to go on at an even more frenzied pace than before the war on the cities' main thoroughfares of Alabama, Decatur, Peachtree, and Whitehall Streets. The population swelled with refugees and wounded, however, and that changed the culture into a patchwork mixture of societies. Until 1863, for example, Atlanta's white puritanical society would have prohibited dancing but afterwards, balls and soirees became common. By the time of the siege of Atlanta, reports circulated about the widespread sex trade. People seemed obsessed with making a fortune as they cried out "gold, gold, gold!"[72]

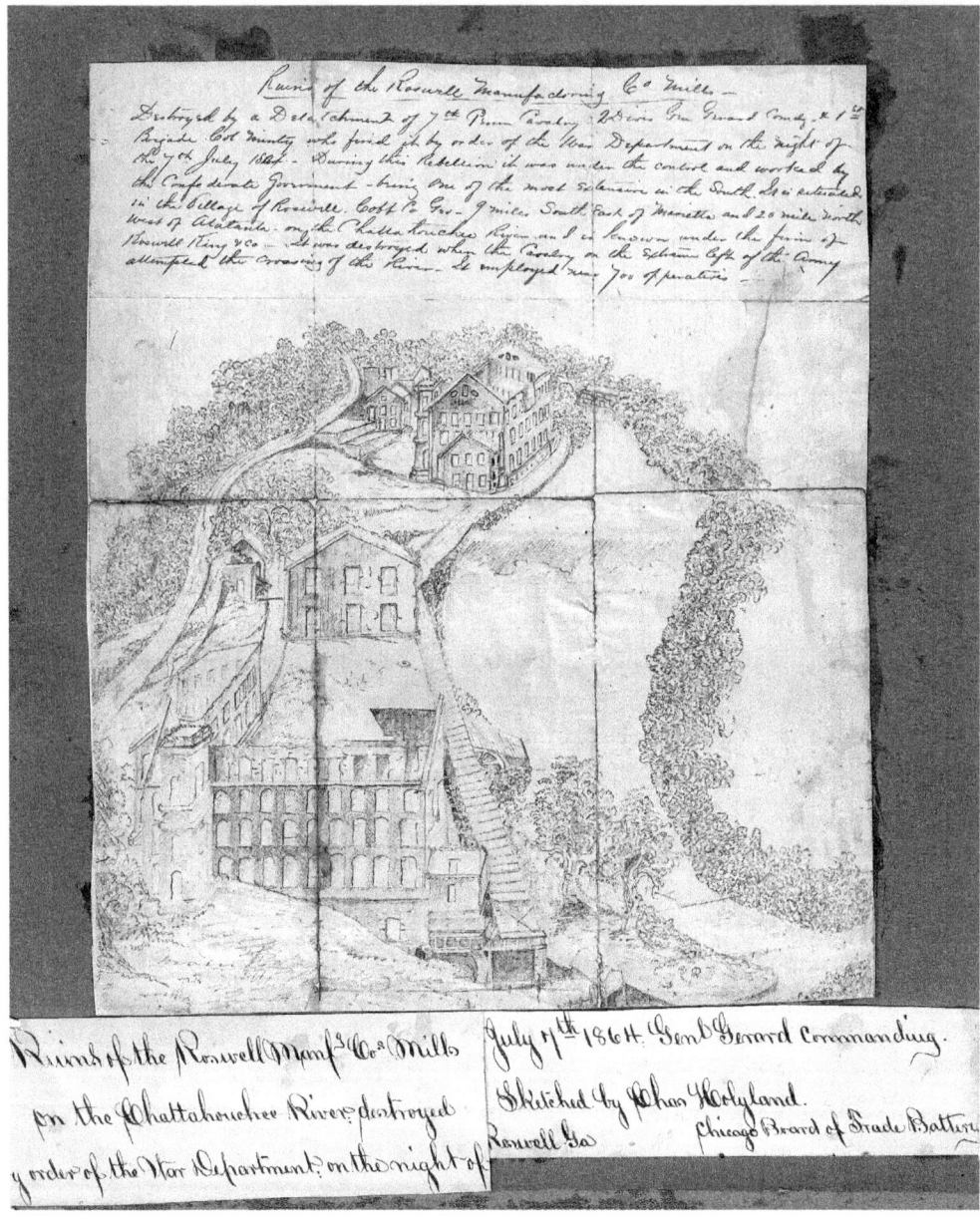

Union Private Charles Holyland of the Chicago Board Regiment drew this sketch of the ruins of the Roswell Manufacturing Company near Atlanta in 1864. His brother served in the Confederate army (Roswell Historical Society).

William McAdoo discovered that the nearby Roswell textile factory claimed to sell its products at fair prices and that it gave away cloth to the poor. He believed that the company traded with local farmers for food at the lowest cost and then sold the provisions at a significant markup to its employees. The owners also sold textiles secretly at top dollar to select merchants who re-sold the cloth for as much as the market would bear, thus hiding the factory owners from public view as profiteers.

Such speculation and gouging of the suffering public went on across Georgia. An Atlanta newspaper, however, announced that the Roswell company had given away 1,000 bunches of cotton yarn worth $4,000 to the poor in ten counties.[73]

Critics charged that jobs created by the war went to men and women based upon political connections or social status. The poor and middle-class families began resisting impressments of property by producing cotton instead of food as a means of avoiding having their food crops taken as taxes or impressed by the army that was fighting to defend this nation of plantations and forced labor.

Atlanta became a center for the desperate effort to supply the Confederate military, producing 90,000 garments per month and 500 pairs of shoes daily.[74] Federal Colonel Edward J. Wood, while stationed at nearby Cartersville, wrote of how Southerners who before the war would only have worn cloth manufactured in the North now made their own cotton clothes. He believed that the Southern civilians had developed an economic defense to the war by moving towards self-sufficiency, a goal long advocated by promoters of the plantation South.[75]

A visitor to Macon on March 3, 1864, found a situation that must have been the same in Atlanta and the other Confederate cities. The citizens wore homespun cotton jeans and wooden shoes covered in cloth. Half of the businesses were closed and empty. A quarter of the other stores only served as warehouses for cotton and tobacco, with real estate as the only remaining safe investment. Even that property often belonged to Northern and foreign investors who believed that their nationalities protected them from property loss to the coming victorious federal army. Women and children in Atlanta starved, and women reportedly would walk 16 miles for a meal. Robert A. Crawford's Atlanta auction house primarily traded with enslaved people but later offered gold and silver for bacon and traded in hogs.[76]

This new economy took many strange turns. Confederate families famously dug up floors of smokehouses for salt, and soldiers did whatever they had to do to find food. Local substitutes were used for coffee, meat, fresh vegetables, etc. Cornelius Hanleiter, in the winter of 1861–1862, saw the government setting up a boiler for a salt works near Savannah. Southerners came to make lubricants by crushing cottonseeds. Cottonseed husks—but not the toxic seeds—could also feed livestock and people.

Newspapers published how Captain James Henderson of Jasper County used his dairy cattle to pull his plow. He pronounced the experiment successful, with the cows even giving more milk than before! Georgia's State Commissary called for county conventions to discuss price controls. Howell Cobb attended such a meeting and found the planters unanimous in following whatever prices were set to sell their surplus.[77]

Atlanta started a particular form of populist resistance to the wartime shortages. Rioting, like terrorism and voting, is a means of democratic social protest with a long history. On March 18, 1863, a group of 15 to 20 women in Atlanta marched into a grocery in the merchant district of Whitehall Street. Outraged at the high

Confederate women rioting over the price of food (*Frank Leslie's Illustrated Newspaper*, May 23, 1863, p. 141).

price of bacon, the mob leader pulled a naval revolver from her bosom and held the shop owner at bay while her associates looted the store. Before leaving, the women explained that aside from a bit of cornbread, their families had not eaten in days.

Women would emulate the ensuing Atlanta riot across the South but most famously in Richmond, where President Jefferson Davis had to confront a mob that may have numbered 5,000. In August, eleven women in Pickens County, Georgia, proclaimed themselves Yankees and announced that their families would stop working to take whatever they needed to live as they claimed other people did. In 1864, women across South Georgia stole cattle.[78]

Aside from the refugees, sick, and wounded crowded into the cities, there was also the growing problem of orphans and widows left destitute by the war. They left few memoirs, but like future President Woodrow Wilson, then a child in Augusta, they become traumatized as they suffered the most while understanding the least in their confusing world of war. Sidney Root offered his 50-acre former racetrack property to the Georgia Baptist Convention for an orphanage in 1863 that he offered $75,000. The GBC declined the offer. Ironically, the federal Fort McPherson, named for the federal general killed in the Battle of Atlanta, was erected there after the war. Starting in 1866, the Masonic Orphans Home Lottery attempted to help the 50,000 Georgia children left fatherless by the war and 10,000 other young people with no parents. The beneficiaries lived in Fulton County, in or around Atlanta.[79]

Chapter Three

In the Confederate Special Service in Atlanta

George Washington Lee did the seemingly impossible job of securing Atlanta. The Confederate States of America would have done well to have had more administrators like him. His various and growing number of tasks even included hiring two enslaved men to repair the depot at West Point to obtaining wood for coffins. Lee would physically supervise such work and fill out the forms required for reimbursement. His tasks were not made easier by the paperwork of the different George W. Lees becoming jumbled together in Richmond.[1]

With his success as an administrator, Lee also acquired the problem of attracting problems needing solutions and then drawing criticism for succeeding! For example, he found himself responsible for battling counterfeiters. That crime traditionally becomes common in places and times of inflation and shortage, such as in the Civil War in America. So much privately printed paper money in the antebellum economy had well-established the means and methods for that crime.

During the Civil War, fake paper money improved buying power in the face of the shrinking value of the legitimate currency that corresponded with the rise in commodity prices that encouraged further inflation. People escaping from North Georgia for the Northern states reported that average families could no longer afford necessities such as salt for meat preservation. Companies like Crawford, Frazer & Co. of Atlanta encouraged costs to rise by exchanging so much money to battle the hyperinflation of the Confederate currency. The company sold anything available, including livestock and people, for bonds and cash.[2]

Counterfeiting was a relatively poor use of increasingly scarce and valuable printing resources, however. Lee did issue an order reminding the citizens and merchants to come forward with any counterfeited currency on August 26, 1863, and the Marietta Paper Mill, outside of Atlanta, made the paper for the Southern nation's bonds and currency. A story circulated that detection of counterfeit Southern currency made in the North became possible because the fakes had better quality than the legitimate paper money printed in the South, even though the plates that produced the legitimate Confederate money came from the North and were smuggled into the South!

Samuel C. Upham and other printers in the North printed copies of the

Southern currency to sell to federal soldiers and blockade-runners. Those notes used the counterfeit money to buy cotton and naval stores in the Confederate ports where these commodities were then smuggled to the North in violation of the laws of both nations. The United States government did not recognize the existence of the Confederate States of America, and therefore did not consider fake printing of the money of a country that did not officially exist as a crime![3]

As early as July 1862, Simon Stern of Columbus, Georgia, and his brother-in-law were arrested for buying over 100 bales of cotton with counterfeit notes. Most of the phony currency seemed to have been centered in that city, but in Atlanta the following September, Lee ordered $50 and $100 Confederate bills brought to him for examination. Jabez Richards of Atlanta had discovered $1,200 in bogus bills in his store's receipts. By November, the *Southern Confederacy* listed the only banknotes it would accept as payment for advertising and subscriptions. Lee, however, insisted that legitimate Confederate notes had to be accepted by businesses.[4]

The Secretary of the Treasury placed Lee in charge of a small detective force, what amounted to a Confederate version of the later United States Secret Service, to fight counterfeiting across the whole Southern nation. A G.H. Gilbert worked undercover for the provost marshal in a hunt for such miscreants in Atlanta, Chattanooga, and southwest Georgia. His investigations found a few phony notes among innocent civilians, although considerable amounts of this script turned up on captured Union soldiers. Lee had at least two people found with bogus notes under lock and key by 1863. One prisoner escaped but he soon found himself back in custody with the help of the young son of Dr. Stephen T. Biggors. The fugitive had tried to befriend the boy, but the youngster helped Lee's guards set a trap for the man.[5] Capturing such miscreants required help from everyone from professional detectives like Gilbert to small boys like Biggors. Lee would exempt George McGinnely, proprietor of the Trout House hotel, from military conscription for use as a spy, for he could read a person's character and knew everyone. With McGinnely's help, Lee captured spy Martin Hinton.

The provost marshal organized a network of operatives for his pioneer secret service, including Atlanta detective James Gettys McGready Ramsey from Knoxville, Tennessee. By late 1862, the provost marshal of Atlanta used three investigators, and by April 1863, his secret service included seven full-time and four temporary agents. Their investigations of counterfeiting, espionage, theft, etc., always led to finding perpetrators of other crimes, as with work done by Captain James A. Burton. He had been working for the Confederate Treasury Department west of the Mississippi River. While he worked in Georgia and South Carolina, Vicksburg fell, and he found himself unable to return to his usual hunting grounds. Burton then went to work for Lee and eventually caught one Yankee spy, one extortionist, one forger of passports, one forger of army papers, one forger of all types, four deserters, and one man who took money under false pretenses.[6]

Lee also found himself involved with foreign affairs. He was responsible for

Captain David R. Brown (20th Connecticut Infantry Regiment) created this engraving of Atlanta in 1864, including the Atlanta Rolling Mill in the distance (Kenan Research Center at the Atlanta History Center).

checking the credentials of alleged aliens and answering queries from consulates in Atlanta. Foreign nationals were exempt from military service, and a provost marshal could issue passports that allowed individuals exempt from conscription and of proven loyalty to the Confederacy to leave for countries other than the United States. He also helped his government to arrange for international currency exchanges even though none of those nations recognized the official existence of the Confederate States of America.[7]

While George W. Lee dealt with these daily responsibilities, the official war occasionally interfered with his routine duties. In May 1863, he had to ship a coffin to Tennessee for the body of the famous Confederate General Earl Van Dorn, killed in a duel with a husband he had wronged. Early one morning in December, while on a routine inspection tour, Lee came upon Confederate President Jefferson Davis and General Joseph E. Johnston. The Richmond government had tried to telegraph their pending arrival, but the lines were down. These two Confederate leaders found themselves in Atlanta, and unable to proceed to Tennessee.

Lee ordered a passenger car added to a freight train to send them to Chattanooga in good spirits. General Johnston also had a private conversation with Lee.[8] The war brought cavalryman General John H. Morgan to Atlanta on February 6, 1864, after he had famously escaped from the Ohio state penitentiary. The citizens threw, for him and his wife, the biggest parade and public gathering in the city to that date. He subsequently made Atlanta his headquarters, and Lee helped him to recruit men.[9]

Atlantan Cornelius Hanleiter wrote that in the early months of the war,

Georgia's medical facilities were so inadequate that the sick in Savannah were shipped across the state for medical care.[10] Undoubtedly, many men were sent home to recover, and would inadvertently spread or return to the army with sickness. The battles of Stones River in 1862 and Chickamauga (fought less than 120 miles from Atlanta in 1863) flooded the city with wounded, as the fairgrounds became a massive hospital. When it filled up, Lee had to beg civilians to take in the wounded. Eventually, this Gate City would be second only to Richmond in hospital patients, with an estimated 80,000 Confederate and 25,000 Union soldiers spending time in Atlanta receiving medical care by the war's end. By 1863, the city had 23 hospitals.[11]

The wounded and sick physically brought the human costs of the war to the city's general population in ways that could not be ignored. Civilian and government efforts to ease the suffering never matched the needs, as generations later depicted in the movie *Gone with the Wind*. Citizens walked blocks to avoid just the smell from the wounded at the train yards where they lay in the open waiting for doctors to decide whose chances of survival determined who went to the hospital and often private homes or would stay there in the open until ready for removal to Oakland Cemetery for burial.

In November 1863, a visitor from Augusta found the crowding and noise in the city overwhelming and that he could go nowhere in Atlanta without being confronted by the wounded.[12] Men would send their wives and daughters to work in the hospitals to avoid risking the lives of their enslaved workers from contagious disease. Wounded soldiers would survive but at the cost of becoming alcoholics and drug addicts. The hospitals had supply shortages, and the doctors practiced the widespread medical incompetence that was common at the time.[13] When some of the Atlanta women would provide aid to Confederate sick and wounded in the hospitals but not to the Union soldiers, the Confederate soldiers in the hospitals would then share with their "enemy."[14]

Several organizations and individuals offered to help with the hospitals. The provost marshal became an agent for receiving various donations of goods and money for the patients from individuals and charitable groups of both races. Lee created a committee of six men to oversee charity work for the hospitals to supplement the work done by women's societies to help. That aid included proceeds from concerts and theater performances, cloth goods from Upson County, and straw that Lee himself sent from Stone Mountain in June 1864. Lee had to provide for the wounded in different ways. Guards were needed for the medical stores and the 2,000 or more patients in Atlanta hospitals at most times. He posted sentries to prevent sick soldiers from escaping to the city and spreading disease to civilians.[15]

Robert A. Crawford, owner of an auction house and Atlanta's first and most infamous slave pen, began the Soldiers Executive Aid Association to raise funds for the Confederate Army of Tennessee hospitals and help refugees. He even arranged to clean up the grounds around the hospitals to save the female volunteers from wading through the garbage, gore, and waste. Falsely claiming to be colonel of an imaginary Third Georgia Regiment and visiting Georgia's battles as a tourist as they happened, he donated $1,000 of his company's profits to the hospitals and briefly closed the business when the Committee asked Atlantans to tend to the arriving wounded from the battle of Chickamauga in September 1863.

Crawford and his committee pleaded with the citizens "to send their carriages and their servants to assist in removing the wounded to the several hospitals, by night as well as by day, and that the servants receive (for themselves) suitable compensation for the same." Enslaved people were thus sent to move sick and wounded soldiers of a nation created to defend the institution of slavery from a war that only eventually became about emancipation, to hospitals funded by a partnership that sold enslaved African Americans but was closed to help move these wounded! Crawford served on a committee to prepare a "statement of the deficiency of ambulance accommodation and urge that steps be taken to supply that deficiency."[16] He modestly declined the honor of having a hospital named for him. In 1865, an Atlanta writer reported that Crawford, over the previous two years, had acted "with the energy and zeal no one could have excelled, for the sick and wounded soldiers, and to refugees his hospitality bounteous[ly]."[17]

With the fall of Vicksburg, Mississippi, in July 1863, Atlanta also became a gateway to what remained of the Western Confederacy, even as if it were the Southern nation's auxiliary capital created by geographic circumstances. On September 1, 1863, Georgia's state Adjutant and Inspector General Henry C. Wayne warned Lee to have his battalion ready to march because General Bragg had warned him of a coming federal invasion of Georgia. Within two weeks, Wayne reported that 21,000 Confederate soldiers would arrive shortly from Mississippi and Virginia to reinforce General Bragg's army. Two divisions of General James Longstreet's First Corps of the Army of Northern Virginia passed through the city on September 17, 1863. No records survive of any part George W. Lee had in moving these men, with their equipment and horses through Atlanta in time to join the battle of Chickamauga, September 18–20, a great Southern victory.[18]

Considering his position and known competence, Lee surely played a major role in the herculean effort to move these men, and all that they brought with them, for the final leg on the South's inadequate, fragile, and declining railroad system. Like agriculture, finance, and manufacturing in the South, transportation principally serviced the Cotton Kingdom. Soldiers came by every type of rolling stock; many needed supplies from Atlanta's military stores and warehouses, everything from shoes to horses to artillery. Efforts were necessary to prevent men from wandering off between changing trains and even deserting.[19]

Lee proved himself repeatedly to be an efficient manager of people and materials. Many Atlantans wanted George Washington Lee to take on even more responsibilities. Historians have described the Confederacy's railroads as operated by corrupt civilians for profit to the treasonable detriment of the new nation. Critics have then and since blamed the Confederate defeat on the new nation's inability to adequately move men and supplies except under the pressure of an immediate crisis. The superintendents of Atlanta's four railroads unsuccessfully petitioned the national government to take over their worn-out lines and place Lee in charge of all railroad operations! Jefferson Davis's administration, however, had no interest in government takeover of the railroads despite the government's interference in railroad operations as wartime necessities required.

Lee could have made a difference in the day-to-day use of the Confederacy's limited railroad rolling stock and transportation of supplies for civilians, prisoners, and soldiers. An Atlanta newspaper editor estimated that Georgia alone, through the national tax in kind, could provide every soldier in the Southern army with one-third pound of pork per day for four months. He did not explain how the provisions might reach the army, however.[20] In the infamous march across Georgia to the sea, Sherman's army would feed on mountains of supplies waiting at railroad sidings to be shipped to the Confederate armies on trains that never came.

Lee's successes must also be considered within the context of the problems around him that he was not asked to solve. This provost marshal fought to save his city and his new nation in a bizarre new world of unforeseen domestic challenges. Among starving people, with a tax in kind imposed upon farmers to try to feed the army through the South's inadequate transportation system and poor government administration, the real currency became cotton, the value of which to both sides had contributed to bringing on the war, regardless of who planted and picked it. Railroads were needed to transport supplies to cities like Atlanta, but the railroad agents made greater profits shipping cotton. Even as people went hungry and despite pressure from the government, planters produced more cotton and less food, a hunger crisis made worse by a wartime drought in North Georgia and the Confederacy's tax in kind on farm produce.[21]

This consumption of labor, physical resources, and even public support by the armies that served the preservation of the enslaved worked plantation economy extended to its cities, but especially Atlanta as a major manufacturing and transportation center. Increasingly, the Confederate army needed tradesmen even more than soldiers; cobblers and other craftsmen were transferred from the military to the factories and shops in Atlanta in a desperate effort to make what the army needed to function. What remained after the defeat at Cumberland Gap of the 55th Georgia Confederate Infantry, for example, had to give up its cobblers to Atlanta to make shoes for the army. At the same time, however, tradesmen holding local, critical positions needed by the civilians, such as blacksmiths, were still drafted into the military as soldiers.

The local trade in human beings also developed in a strange and particularly twisted way in Civil War Atlanta. Although George W. Lee had no known part in it, he witnessed it all. In 1859, the first Atlanta city directory listed only three auction houses that sold the enslaved. Georgia implemented and then retracted, only to bring back, laws preventing the sale of human beings in the state from 1798 to 1856.

In 1849, the state again made this business legal, and in the summer of 1850, Atlanta entrepreneur, saloonkeeper, and vintner Hancke C. Mühlenbrinck built the city's first slave market–pen, likely to chiefly provide accommodations for the servants owned by white guests of the nearby Atlanta Hotel.[22]

Before this market opened, Atlanta newspaper editor Cornelius Redding Hanleiter, using the *nom de plume* "Gabriel," wrote a piece in which he claimed that two-thirds of the city's citizens opposed it. Atlanta was built by enslaved labor and prospered on the shipment of cotton produced by chattel workers, but the city's Northern financiers and backers promoted a false image of a Southern city with minimal ties to slavery. Nothing came of the Gabriel article in Atlanta, but 90 miles south in Macon, the *Georgia Citizen* reprinted the piece on its correspondence page. Macon's economy and extensive manufacturing served Georgia's enslaved-worked cotton plantations. The city's Findlay Iron Works, for example, opened branches in Albany, Atlanta, and Griffin to supply plantations with everything from plows and cotton presses to steam engines and boilers. A committee of vigilantes demanded that the slave-owning Kentucky-born ex–Universalist Minister and spiritualist Dr. Lewis Feuilleteau Wilson Andrews shut down this newspaper, reveal the identity of Gabriel, and leave Macon forever, just for reprinting the letter that they interpreted as sympathetic with abolishing slavery. Andrews responded by publishing personal attacks on the mob's ringleaders and he continued to publish the *Citizen*, even after a mob attacked his newspaper office. Many prominent Macon residents came to his defense.[23]

Mühlenbrinck's building did not serve as a slave market before the Civil War, however. The resistance in Atlanta to such an openly public symbol of slavery and the Georgia legislature again prohibiting the importing and selling of enslaved people in 1852 likely kept it closed.[24]

When made legal in Georgia for the last time after 1856, sales of Black labor and their families became part of Atlanta's auctioneering trade, but especially with Clarke & Grubbs. North Carolina–born Robert M. Clarke of that partnership even described himself as a slave trader in the 1860 federal census. In October 1862, he advertised the sale of 150 enslaved people, including 25 men ages 17 to 26, to a railroad for $35,725, an average of $1,429 per person, in the largest such sale to that time or likely ever in the city. Prominent Atlanta businessman George W. Adair purchased his people in bondage from that extensive slave business of Nathan Bedford Forrest, whose reputation later became attached to atrocities against African Americans during and after the Civil War.[25]

Ironically, a war that would destroy much of Atlanta and eventually brought about emancipation became responsible for the city's first real slave market. Robert A. Crawford finally opened Mühlenbrinck's building as Atlanta's first slave market at the beginning of 1863, with partners Addison D. Frazer and son Thomas Lafayette Frazer to form Crawford, Frazer & Company. They operated a fully functioning market for selling chattel labor, and their children, as attested by receipts found

today in numerous archives. Northern newspapers would use this business advertising as an argument for ending that trade. The partnership sought to buy 100 or more people at a time. Families were sometimes broken up to sell as individuals, and in exchange for "Bonds, Unremittent Funds, and Exchange," Crawford and the Frasers also offered for sale African Americans as whole families, as presumably family members were less likely to escape if doing so meant leaving relatives behind.

Historian Steven Deyle wrote of the often-reproduced photograph of the Crawford and Frazer market that "such businesses were a common sight in the commercial districts of all southern towns."[26] In 1859, the first Atlanta city directory identified only three of the city's auction houses as selling African Americans, however. The city, unlike Columbus and nearby Macon, only had specific buildings for warehousing and selling enslaved people after the Civil War began and so briefly in its history that little specific information on them is available; no general study of the

Top & above: These 1864 photographs of the slave market of Crawford, Frazer & Company in Atlanta are among the most often reproduced photographs of the Civil War. By the time that these photographs were made in late 1864, however, it had been abandoned and in disrepair for several months. The building down the street is the Georgia Railroad Bank building, also later destroyed by Sherman's troops (Library of Congress).

The Atlanta slave market photograph reproduced at the actual size of the building at the Atlanta History Center (author's photo).

pens mentions the markets in the Gate City. Other pens for enslaved people followed Crawford, Frazer & Company, however.

In September 1863, the firm of Thomas E. Whitaker & Winguit H. Turner opened their operation abutting the east side of Washington Hall, and the firm of Field, Gresham & Company had a slave market "in an elevated and healthy locality" on Peachtree Street outside of the business district. Robert M. Clarke opened a slave yard on the west side of Whitehall Street on October 2, 1863. His business would account for the most significant number of slave burials in the city, all from disease, including children.[27]

Researcher Ken Denney, in his block-by-block research of the city during the Civil War identified several Atlanta auction houses that sold chattel workers, including William K. Bagby on the east side of Cooper between Whitehall and Jones; M.C. Cayce, the Arcade on Whitehall Street; Robert M. Clarke and Thomas F. Grubb, wholesale grocers at 35 Whitehall Street; S.H. Griffin at No. 5 Whitehall; Jacobe D. Mayer & Company in Beach's & Root's on Whitehall between Alabama and Hunter streets; Inman & Cole on Whitehall; Amos, Ligon & Company on Whitehall and Mitchell; Welborn, Taylor, & Co., Kile's building on Peachtree and Marietta; William Chisholm and George W. Adair on nearby Decatur Street near the Trout House; Solomon Cohen began on Whitehall Street near Mitchell; Fred Gresham & Company on Peachtree Street; S.J. Shackleford, north side of Alabama Street between Whitehall Pryor; and J.L. Winter & Company on Whitehall. John J. Ford and his partner L. Fields offered to trade real estate for enslaved laborers from Ford's business on the corner of Whitehall and Peachtree streets. Historian Wendy Venet also lists W.H. Henderson, A.K. Seago, and B.D. Smith as operating in that trade during the Civil War years.[28]

Samuel Dexter Niles, formerly of New Hampshire and a classics teacher at the Atlanta Female High School, opened a plantation, leased his farm, operated a market for selling enslaved labor, ran a breeding operation, or some combination of these businesses on the former Benjamin Thurman plantation for two years, only three miles from the center of Atlanta. Sara Huff remembered that she saw 300 African Americans, the most she had seen in one place, there, but that one day she found that they were gone, their cabins empty. She understood that they had been sent out of the country for resale where human bondage would remain legal if it should be abolished in the United States.[29] As Niles owned no one in 1860, five enslaved people in 1862/1853, and six in 1864, he likely leased his farm to some trader such as Robert A. Crawford for housing enslaved people awaiting sale.[30]

Grocers, hotels, manufacturers, and other businesses benefited from selling to individuals who came to Atlanta to trade in human beings. "Putting a slave in your pocket" meant selling an enslaved person for cash. War refugees needed easily transported money, feared the approach of the federal armies as liberators, or wanted to avoid losing their human property to some kind of general emancipation after the war.[31] Lemuel C. Butler lived in Civil War Atlanta as a boy and remembered one of these markets as "a one-story frame building with benches around the room on which the slaves were seated" and where "perspective buyers made their selections just as they would have a horse or a mule at a stockyard."[32]

More than two million people were sold in America between 1820 and 1860, one-half to two-thirds of whom were sold locally; all the other people were sold in such formal pens, called markets. Other such institutions were operating in the nearby plantation cities of Columbus and Macon, Georgia, since 1856, as well as in what historian Steven Deyle describes as varying from the "elaborate emporiums" of New Orleans to the "dirty and dark" facilities in Richmond. Auctions were equally diverse from courthouse squares to major public gatherings, although most sales were only one or a few individuals, not large public affairs. Enslaved individuals and families were gathered in pens in Baltimore, Nashville, Norfolk, Richmond, St. Louis, and Washington, all Crawford would have known under his previous identity as William Aduston Rogers Crawford in Petersburg, Virginia. African Americans, purchased or kidnapped, were prepared in those places for transport to pens principally in Charleston, Mobile, Natchez, New Orleans, and Savannah. Financing was through Southern banks. Crawford was in New Orleans by 1835, when he began his now known career as a swindler.[33]

Three. In the Confederate Special Service in Atlanta

Researcher Ken Denney believes that the building with the long porch in this photograph is likely to be the slave market of the firm of Whitaker & Turner near the Washington Hotel (the white building in the photograph; the Trout House Hotel is also shown). This slave market could be the one described by Lemuel C. Butler (Library of Congress).

What was started by Crawford and others in Atlanta in 1863 surely was modeled after older operations. Historian Calvin Schermerhorn wrote of Franklin and Armfield, the greatest of these operations and for which Crawford must have known and could have been employed in the 1830s, "packaged and sold captives offered for field and domestic work, trades, and sexual exploitation."[34] The Atlanta markets, starting with Crawford's shown in the Barnard photograph, must have operated in the same way, as reflected in his advertising. Within this complex, no larger than a house lot as many as 50 to 100 people were housed with barracks, cells, dressing rooms, kitchens, and privies in the same complex. Inmates were not allowed outside of the pen but enslaved boys, called stewards made purchases for them, took care of their baggage, and ran other errands. Men and women were kept separate most of the time, to avoid pregnancy and spreading sexually transmitted diseases, although females had no recourse for justice if raped and the traders felt free to do whatever they wanted with their "property."[35]

Most of the enslaved were sold individually but, in Atlanta, the Athenaeum, the city's theater, was available for large auctions and, conveniently, it was also a stable. The showroom in a slave pen complex, where as many as 100 people might be shown at a time, would be nicely furnished to impress the customers. Enslaved people held and sold there were treated as merchandise and, bizarrely, as if they were job applicants. They sought the best owner they could, and vice versa. Salesmen like Crawford packaged and warehoused human beings as if consumer goods. Many states required sellers to fully disclose all physical defects and damage.

The Five Points Metropolitan Rapid Transit Authority Station on the site of the original Civil War slave market of the Crawford, Frazer & Company (author's photo).

The people held in the pens were washed and made as presentable in their best clothes as possible for viewing, even naked, before potential buyers. The interviews were often friendly, although typically the customers judged darker people as healthier for field work and saw scars from whippings as an indication of rebelliousness. Troublesome enslaved people commonly found themselves sent in coffles for sale in the distant pens. Women for households were chosen because of the lightness of their skin. Any of the females were subject to being undressed for examination. Salesmen like Crawford offered to refund money to unsatisfied customers. John White of Richmond claimed that he had 2 to 4 percent returns but, in 1851, he had 15 percent. The market was volatile, and the pen operators would allow enslaved persons sold on a trial basis.[36]

Advertising supplies some information for comparison between the standard market or pen to what Atlanta had after the Civil War began. Slaves with skills brought higher prices and could make money for owners who rented out their services. Crawford, Frazer & Company offered clerks, cobblers, cooks, coopers, domestics, office boys, plowboys, shoemakers, tanners, and waiters. In January 1864, Crawford needed a slave engineer to operate a stationary steam engine. "For a special friend," he wanted "a Trusty Negro 35 to 40 years of age" as a gardener. The company also offered for sale "a number of young girls, from 10 to 14 years of age, such as have been raised in good families, and are likely and spritely." Their competitor on Peachtree Street, Fields & Gresham offered as specials "a good tanner and shoemaker, a good plantation blacksmith, and a fancy girl and child." Fancy girls or "Fancy Maids," were young slave women of mixed race who commanded higher prices because white plantation owners sought them for mistresses.[37]

Because of the need for financing, owners of slave markets were bankers and offered generous terms as part of their sales. Crawford, Frazer & Company advanced money to agents in the field and John Calhoun Crawford, Robert's son, made street loans, what today would be called loan sharking. The company's "Old trusty" porters Andrew and Anthony met arrivals at Atlanta's train depots. The "lockup," where visiting owners could also house their slaves, had a large, fenced yard in the rear, described as "both safe and comfortable." Crawford and the Frazers knew how "to handle the Negro property" "since our boyhood." A city booster bragged in March 1863 of Crawford, Frazer & Company, from the demand for slaves rising, brought in the "tallest kind of figures." The company even sold to planters in Virginia, the famed pre-war source of enslaved people.[38]

Often the purchases were on a trial basis and some sales proved to be not final. J.A. Turner, editor of the *Countryman* and mentor to the later famous Joel Chandler Harris, bought a slave from Crawford in early 1865 and left a detailed account of the experience. He described the purchase as a Tom, "No. 1 body servant cook, and dining room servant" whom he bought for $6,000 in Confederate money. Crawford assured Turner that young man would not escape to Sherman's approaching army as he had several opportunities to do so but had remained. Turner quoted Colonel Crawford as describing the cook as "quite a gentlemanly nigger and sported more fine clothes than he [the colonel] and myself both put together" "overflowing with hats, boots, and store clothes of every variety." The editor's winter wardrobe, by contrast, was only one old gray homemade suit. Tom, however, escaped and left with the federal soldiers anyway.[39]

Similarly, S.F. Power of West Point, Georgia, purchased Ann, "stout built, copper colored," "and likely an old runaway, and smart enough to live and be harbored in cities." She had been living as if an independent contractor but belonged to Shropshire & Thomas of Macon, which had bought her from Crawford, Frazer & Company. Ann came to Power's family highly recommended but, within a few days, she allegedly attempted to poison his wife, child, and child's nurse "without any cause or provocation." She left dressed as a man and Power believed her to be living with a white man.[40]

The Civil War drastically expanded Atlanta's trade in human trafficking because of the growing population of wartime refugees who needed money and feared the approach of the federal armies as liberators. Lee, having responsibility for Atlanta's security, must have been concerned. During the war, boosters proclaimed that the Gate City now challenged Richmond as the South's great market for human beings. Advertisements even appeared seeking to buy laborers from Atlanta to work in the war industries in Columbus, Georgia; Raleigh, North Carolina; and the Tredegar Iron Works in Richmond, Virginia.

Bringing the enslaved for sale in urban areas such as Atlanta and Macon gave African Americans the means of escaping and, with the help of sympathetic residents, disappear into the Black population and, from there, if they chose, finding the means to reach freedom behind the federal lines. Atlanta newspapers had only seven notices of escaped slaves in 1861 but 36 in 1862 and 81 in 1863, and, according to historian Paul D. Luck, "assumed catastrophic proportions" afterwards.[41]

Crawford, Frazer & Company, on Whitehall Street, operated the most infamous market for enslaved labor in Atlanta. After moving to number 10 Peachtree Street, their pen sometimes held 100 or more people in their pen.[42]

Chapter Four

Resistance and Insurrection in North Georgia

Many people in Georgia, referred to by a modern scholar as "Sherman's Fifth Column," did not file any claim, show up in surviving military records, or leave any other record identifying their opposition to Secession, the Confederacy, the War or all three. Even Jefferson Davis and Robert E. Lee had opposed secession and Abraham Lincoln was correct in his argument that none of the states that seceded did so with the approval of a majority of the electorate, or of the people, given the restrictions on voting. He alluded to this fact in his Gettysburg Address in speaking of government "by the people" instead of the powerful few.

Violent resistance by Southerners to the Confederate States of America most often came from the people of the Appalachian Mountains in the north or the swamps and barren plains of the southern counties, where enslaved labor plantations had the least impact and where the institution of slavery found resentment before the war because of its competition with small white farmers for land and work. Peace societies were active from the beginning of the war.[1]

George Washington Lee was a leader in suppressing resistance to the Confederate States of America, in any form in Atlanta, across Georgia, and the Appalachian Mountains of the Southeastern states. Many of the Southerners that Lee should have feared came from a class of small farmers and ranchers, landowning and tenant, and, like him, without a direct connection to the class-oriented, cotton-enslaved, labor-based economy that brought about secession and the war.

The planter society, members of which could come from the rags to riches, encouraged the other white Southerners to invest in human bondage as a means of security for their families. Conversely, stopping the growing demands for economic and political power by the antebellum middle-class, including men like Lee, became for many wealthy planters for secession and for continuing the war, even at such terrible cost.[2]

Antebellum plantations drove down the cost of labor, inflated prices, and absorbed land, enslaved labor, and political power. Even outside of the practical transportation network for cotton, large ranches and truck farms produced crops, livestock, and enslaved persons for the plantations on a scale to which smaller operations could not compete. The average Southerner could even fear and oppose internal improvements that would bring this plantation imperialism closer to their communities, through railroads expanding the enslaved-based economy.

Members of the lower classes often moved upward to become successful planters, but members of the upper classes could also fall rapidly, even from the status of small farmers. Planters also increasingly leased their enslaved for the skilled work otherwise hired out to white workers like Lee. The dispossessed white Southerner would have failed to appreciate slavery propagandist George Fitzhugh's vision of their future in new America as factory labor and manual workers as a caste that historian Eugene Genovese defined as white slaves.[3]

Some families had, since even before the American Revolution and often while in the process of fleeing debt, developed lands for later resale to the planters. Each such land opening resulted in speculators and wealthy developers driving up the value of land to the extent that the small farmers often had to sell out and move on, beginning their lives anew. The politically powerful planter also protected his land values by opposing proposed homestead laws that would have given the small farmers and ranchers opportunities to what remained of the worthwhile federal lands not already taken by the planters and the speculators who even included the so-called champion of the average Southern, President Andrew Jackson.

The Confederate States of America never opened a land office but left any land granting to individual states. The Homestead Act of 1862, an opportunity made possible when Congressional members from the slave states left Washington as their states seceded, gave free federal land in the federal land states of Alabama, Arkansas, Florida, Louisiana, Mississippi,

Raiders burning a house (*The Great Book of 1866*, broadside, BRO1866G7, Broadside Collection, mss4299, Hargrett Rare Book and Manuscript Library, University of Georgia Libraries).

and elsewhere. Starting in 1875, even Confederate families could claim free federal Homestead land—overall, a huge opportunity for the African Americans, middle class white, poor families, and women.[4]

Lee, who had no enslaved people (nor did his family) or any direct connection to cotton, might have appeared a candidate for the resistance or to have chosen to have stayed out of the war. Federal propaganda called for liberating the South and, while that concept referred to the enslaved, it also came to include the region's middle class and poor whites, rural and urban, who passed through the federal lines to jobs in the factories north of the Ohio River, to military service in the federal army, or employment in the racially segregated contraband refugee camps that provided the advancing federal armies with labor and provisions.

Confederate soldiers taken prisoner had these same options, if they took an oath of allegiance to the United States. They could even return to their homes in the South if in federally occupied territory. White Southern refugees were exempt from federal conscription. After the war, the Bureau of Refugees, Freedmen, and Abandoned Lands would serve them as well as African Americans.

Southerners and transplanted Northerners who profited from the Cotton Kingdom of the Confederate States of America crushed any kind and all opposition to their new nation that would protect their institution of slavery and protect them from any demands of the lower classes of white Southerners. Unrestrained, the plantation economy consumed all resources, including the lives of both the willing and the unwilling in the mountains, plains, and swamps who suffered rather than benefited from the slavery.[5]

As the Southern nation steadily lost and its economy failed, the Confederate government did what it could to supply the military and defeat resistance to the war, making no effort to win hearts and minds. King Cotton's war made poverty, fear, subversion, and, by the Confederate definition, treason, growth industries in urban manufacturing, mercantile, and transportation centers. Severe hardships came to Atlanta from a wartime economy of unrestricted pursuit of profit that would prove impractical and self-destructive.

Southerners from all classes and places, including some plantation owners, opposed secession, the war, or both, and from the beginning of this so-called "Second American Revolution" that sought to protect the South status quo as far as plantation economics. An argument can be made that the United States military did not win the war because of the difference in population with the Confederate States but because draft evasion and desertion were more extensive in the Southern military. Ironically, much of the resentment today by white Southerners of some modern views of the Civil War goes back to ancestors who did not support secession or the war but suffered from its consequences. They not only did not fight a war to preserve the right of other people to enslave others, but they even preferred to avoid secession with compromise.[6] The federal government faced the same resistance to the war effort in many places, particularly Midwestern states such as Indiana and urban-immigrant centers such as Chicago and New York.[7]

With the passage of the Confederate Conscription Act of 1862, protests of the war became proactive, with men refusing to serve in the army, threatening to burn the bridges of the militarily important Western & Atlantic Railroad, helping Union soldiers to escape from the Confederacy, hiding deserters from both armies, and plundering plantations of the families who supported the Southern cause. They even fired on passing soldiers.[8] At least 100,000 white Southerners eventually served in the Union Army and more than 200,00 African American soldiers and sailors served in the United States military. Even as Lee took command in Atlanta, an ad hoc prison in nearby Madison, Georgia, held hundreds of East Tennessee civilian men arrested for aiding the Union by trying to burn militarily critical railroad bridges.[9]

A truly pro-union county in the Deep South, made up of many men willing to openly oppose the new Southern nation, did not exist however, except in Confederate paranoia and myth. As in the North, few areas even had organized opposition groups opposed to the war. They became most notable for having an active resistance at all! The federal military consequently found itself in the same position as the British in the American Revolution and the United States later in Afghanistan, Vietnam, and elsewhere, enticed by the illusion that an opposition group could become a widespread populist movement. Most people who oppose a war, however, only seek security from their government and neighbors, not the opportunity to sacrifice themselves for a cause.

Such resistance to the war, or often just to change, found a voice with local leadership, such as in Calhoun, Coosa, Macon (now Lee), Pike, Randolph, Talladega, and Tallapoosa counties, an area in East Alabama but within Atlanta's economic region or metropole.[10] One panicked official in Randolph County reported that two-thirds of the men there belonged to the Peace Society, an organization dedicated to violent resistance to and overthrowing the Confederate government. Members credited their group with having so infiltrated the Confederate army that they took responsibility for the Confederate surrender of Vicksburg and the defeat at Missionary Ridge that broke the Confederate siege of federally occupied Chattanooga and thus opened Georgia to a new invasion.[11]

Appalachia had few plantations and African Americans, skilled or otherwise. In the North and the South, this isolated population had a fear of exploitation that threatened them with further impoverishment and cultural disintegration. They did not see change as necessarily progress if railroads and other internal improvements spread an industrial scale agricultural economy to drive up their land values and compete for what market they had. Railroads also brought mining and, with it, environmental degradation, as already was occurring in Fannin County, Georgia.

The white population feared that the war would eventually share with the formerly enslaved what little that they mountains had, including a privileged racial identity.[12] Observers wrote that the South's mountain people, however, had a noted

Southerners taking the oath of allegiance to the United States (*The Great Book of 1866*, broadside, BRO1866G7, Broadside Collection, mss4299, Hargrett Rare Book and Manuscript Library, University of Georgia Libraries).

tendency to treat their few enslaved people with a level of familiarity, even equality. Emily Burke, a Georgia resident in the 1840s, wrote of the North Georgians who camped in markets like Atlanta with their wagons and baying mules:

> They have no idea of style and refinement in living. A great many of them own slaves, and they all work in the field together, white men and black men, white women and black women without distinction. I have been told it is not an uncommon occurrence to see a white woman holding the plough. When the morning's work is done, they all repair to the house, both masters and slaves, where a pot of hominy has been prepared for dinner, then all sit down on the floor and help themselves out of the same dish.[13]

Georgia had a secession convention that voted the state from the Union, as would other states that formed the Confederate States of America. States leaving the Union came from the political maneuverings of the powerful special interests that wanted to preserve and expand cotton and its existing chattel labor system. The secession movement succeeded, when it did, on the local level against the majority that wanted to wait, the sheer intimidating pressure of the political will of an influential, loud, and powerful minority.

Conversely, in north and west Georgia, anti-secession rallies occurred in Chattooga, Fayette, Gordon, Meriwether, and Talbot counties. James Aiken wrote to Governor Joseph E. Brown that 2,500 men in North Georgia were ready to bear arms to stay in the Union. In Pickens County, citizens raised a United States flag to protest the secession convention. Even the people in Augusta reportedly showed no interest in secession or war.[14] Judge William Gibbs McAdoo of Knoxville, Tennessee, first met George W. Lee in Atlanta on November 17, 1862; he kept him informed of the activities of men like W.P. Washburn, Colonel Blake, Colonel Boyd Byrd of Roane County, North Carolina, and others in East Tennessee who had formed a renegade pro–Union regiment that had drilled since 1861.[15]

In Tennessee, coastal Georgia, and North Georgia, the federal army recruited, at the least, 3,486 Georgians who escaped from bondage as laborers and who later served soldiers for the federal army, sometimes by almost evangelical processions of wagons with recruiting agents from both races. One observer saw 17 wagons accompanied by 150 to 200 soldiers. Sometimes, these African Americans found their circumstances hardly any different in federal camps from enslaved labor on plantations, however. From their number came such units as the 44th United States Colored Troops (also called the First Georgia) that fought for the Union at Dalton and Nashville. Another 2,500 white Georgians joined the Union military in various states, although the state had only one formerly accepted white federal unit, an oversized company designated as the First Georgia Infantry Battalion.[16]

Politics divided families. The sons of Jesse Hammontree of Pickens County, Georgia, were a prime example. Sam and Stephen joined Company E of the 23rd Georgia Infantry, one of five companies in that Appalachian County where observers feared that the Confederate army would not be able to raise any companies. (The United States army also recruited at least parts of three companies from there, one of which was a Confederate cavalry company that defected to the Union army!) Stephen died beside Sam during the battle of Chancellorsville. Their brother Sylvester escaped to north of the Ohio River to stay out of the war while the youngest son William Nelson T. Hammontree joined the First United States Infantry Battalion before deserting, claiming to have returned home to protect his elderly parents from the local home guard. Sam would be celebrated as one of the last Civil War veterans, but his brothers Nels and Vester were held in distain within their family.[17]

In the same county, Edmund Jackson served in the 16th Georgia Confederate Infantry Regiment, while his brothers John and Avery joined in the 10th Tennessee Cavalry, United States Army. Well-to-do Isaac Burleson petitioned for a pardon for being a Confederate postmaster. No military service records have been found for two of his three sons, although a family story has them dying during the war and outside of the state. The other son, William Washington Burleson, served first in the same Confederate company as his neighbors Sam and Stephen Hammontree; then he deserted and joined James G. Brown's Union's First Georgia Cavalry; before ending the war in the First Georgia Infantry Battalion, United States Army.[18]

Lee had a comparable situation in his family. Another George W. Lee, his first cousin once removed in Rome, Georgia, enlisted with his father and brother in the 20th Georgia Confederate Infantry Regiment in 1861. He was wounded in the battle of Fredericksburg and was captured at the battles of Gettysburg and Fayetteville. On September 23, 1864, however, this other George W. Lee joined the First Alabama Cavalry Regiment, United States Army, likely influenced by his first cousin Charles Christopher Columbus Sheats of Winston County, Alabama, a legendary firebrand who famously argued against secession at the Alabama Secession Convention and who recruited for the First Alabama Regiment.[19] Even then, however, he deserted on November 10, 1864, at a time when North Georgia was in a murderous partisan turmoil over the politics of the war.

Federal soldiers, even deserters, would remember the help they received from residents of all races in escaping the steadily shrinking Southern nation and of armed white men "in the woods and hollows" of the South who would never join the Confederate service from opposition to the planter class, secession, racism, or fear of competition for land if the emancipation of African Americans came about from the war. They would be careful, after the war, to not publish the names of the Southerners who had helped them, Black or white. People who resisted the Confederate government became known as "Tories" for the moniker of Revolutionary War Americans who remained loyal to the King. The federal army allowed Confederate deserters and prisoners of war to return to their homes to organize resistance. Southern sympathizers also called these men, from their hiding in caves "mossbacks" and "hogbacks."[20]

The Confederate draft further encouraged resistance across its remaining

William Washington Burleson (1845–1919) in uniform as a member of the First Georgia Infantry Battalion, United States Army (author's collection).

territory. Arresting draft evaders had a benefit of created a system that discouraged desertions from men already in the army, an even bigger problem, and who could inspire resistance to the war if they returned to their homes. On September 24, 1864, even after Atlanta had fallen to Sherman, President Jefferson Davis gave a speech in nearby Macon pleading that the South could still win the war if only two-thirds of the men absent from the Southern army would return. The Confederate and Union drafts, for of the class conflict and social upheaval they caused, sent relatively few men to the war.[21]

Soldiers would desert, even if they still supported Southern independence or the Union. Hunger from an absence of farm labor to the war, made worse in Georgia by drought in Appalachia, encouraged soldiers to abandon the army to protect their farms and put in crops to feed their families. In the South, the resistance stole food from plantations and fought attempts by Confederate officials to seize livestock, supplies, and wagons, in part of the nation's 10 percent tax in kind that would not accept the Confederate currency that continued to decline in value. Lee arranged for shipments of corn from southwest Georgia to Atlanta by October 5, 1863.[22]

Men also deserted from the federal armies, marching through Georgia, becoming bandits, helping the Confederate military, or joining the resistance to the war effort. Southerners encouraged them. Confederate deserter John Gatewood of Tennessee, for example, formed a company of federal deserters who protected pro–Confederate families in North Georgia and defended his private fiefdom in Cherokee

Civil War town under attack, as happened to Cassville and Canton, Georgia (*Harper's Weekly*, August 21, 1863).

County in northeast Alabama in cooperation with local elected officials! His critics regarded him as just another of the region's growing bandit leaders operating on the fringes of both armies.[23]

Georgia Governor Joseph E. Brown responded to the problem of resistance to the draft by giving North Georgia companies preference in the state's contribution to the most distant armies and placing severe restrictions on conscription and impressments in the region. When prisoners J.M. Gout, L.D. McClellend, and L.C. Laxley failed to arrive in Atlanta, George Washington Lee blamed the Fannin County Committee of Safety. He warned the Confederate Secretary of War that many counties had such resistance organizations. As early as October 1862, reports had some one-half of the Confederate soldiers from Northeast Georgia as having deserted. More men left the army after blood baths like Chickamauga in September 1863, which was fought in the mountains of Appalachian Georgia and less than 120 miles from Atlanta. More soldiers, and on each side, did not want to die for any cause, least of all the right of the privileged to own enslaved persons.[24]

Georgia Governor Joseph E. Brown (Hargrett Rare Book and Manuscript Library, University of Georgia).

Georgians like Unionist George W. Ashburn and the notorious federal spy James George Brown took advantage of this dissent to lead resistance behind and in front of the federal lines as they also sought personal gain. Brown, an English-born Murray County lawyer, even recruited a battalion of North Georgians for the federal army and created a district organization for detecting and resisting Confederate raids. In 1864, he went as far as to falsely announce to his followers that Abraham Lincoln had appointed him governor of a new state of North Georgia, with Atlanta soon to be made its capital! In late 1864, he helped federal troops in the destruction of Canton, which, with Cassville, was destroyed in retaliation for the deaths of federal soldiers at the hands of Confederate guerrillas.[25]

Brown was the kind of perennial failure in civilian life from which radical populist leaders in revolutions, such as George W. Lee, frequently arose. Governor Joseph E. Brown (no relation to the federal spy James George Brown) must have recognized the threat of such men when, earlier in the war, he likely saw Lee as a political threat. Most persons who commented on the provost marshal of Atlanta described Lee as an honest man; James G. Brown and George W. Ashburn, however, had complicated, controversial lives from before the war. Ashburn, born in North Carolina ca. 1818, was a failed hotelier and merchant in Columbus, Forsyth, Macon, Marietta, Oglethorpe, and Thomaston, Georgia. During the war, he served in the federal army, and for his supporting Reconstruction, he was killed in Columbus, Georgia, in the first act of Ku Klux Klan violence outside of Tennessee.[26] Governor Brown differed from these partisan leaders in that as a young man, he had gotten help to become a success, politically and financially, and would continue to do so after the war by twice changing his politics with the times.[27] His statue is on the grounds of the Georgia State Capital building.

Little has appeared on the guerrilla war that subsequently occurred within the Confederate States but even less about Lee's campaign against the war resistance in Appalachia. As early as January 13, 1863, the then Major George W. Lee wrote to Jefferson Davis to ask for the authority to raise a cavalry corps of non-conscripts against the deserters in Appalachian North Georgia. Lee had reports of a W.A. Edwards organizing a plot to use gunpowder in canteens to burn down Atlanta and the bridges of the W&A. Stories reached the press of robberies and murders committed by members of the war resistance.[28]

Governor Brown famously clashed with the national Confederate government over having a national draft and the usurping of state authority. William McAdoo witnessed such a speech given by the governor at the Walton Spring in the center of Atlanta. Brown now asked George W. Lee to lead an expedition into the mountains to stop the war resistance. When the major replied that he lacked the men, the governor arranged with the Secretary of War for Lee to obtain 150 cavalrymen from Chattanooga. When Lee unexpectedly took over complete command of the whole expedition, the often obstructionist Governor Brown immediately yielded and ordered his 52-year-old Captain Edward M. Galt and the 150-man state company that guarded the nine Western & Atlantic Railroad bridges to comply. Lee also obtained four companies of the 16th Georgia Partisan Rangers and a local company of 500 men. Concurrently, the governor offered amnesty for draft evaders and deserters who surrendered peacefully.[29]

On January 24, 1863, Lee arrived in Dahlonega, in nearby mountain Lumpkin County, followed one day later by fifty of his convalescent "cripples" (disabled veterans of the Virginia campaigns or "broken leg" men) infantry soldiers and a supply train in bitterly cold weather. The people of Dahlonega welcomed Lee's men to stay in their homes and churches. Local women even prepared a feast. Some of the citizens felt they could manage their own affairs, but the Lumpkin County Superior

The 1836 Lumpkin County courthouse, now the Dahlonega Gold Museum (author's photo).

Court had just released two of the leaders of the resistance and two men accused of harboring African Americans fleeing bondage before it shut down altogether.

Historian Jonathan Sarris has described the situation surrounding Lumpkin County as near anarchy. Often, the war resistance morphed into gangs of brigands that raided towns and villages. To impede the arrest of draft evaders and deserters, the Unionists staged a prison break in an adjoining county, and they would eventually burn down the jails in the region. When this resistance tried to assault the public buildings in Dahlonega, however, the townspeople armed themselves and, led by local officials, successfully defended their town.[30]

The combined expeditionary force, with the local militia, spread into nearby counties to search for bandits, Unionists, and men who should have been in the army. These troops had orders to forage from the property of and to make retribution on civilians disloyal to the Confederacy. Lee dispatched a company to hunt for draft evaders and resistance around Fannin County, where Nathanial Mangum lived. He ordered that "in no case will he [the commander of the company] spare the life of a traitor or deserter when they may try to escape."[31]

Captain Edward M. Galt of the state troops arrived before Lee's troops and resented the supplanting of his authority. The two officers, however, quickly gained respect for one another. Within a week, Lee left all his troops in Galt's charge and had Gault breveted to major. Lee supplemented the state troops left behind to protect the Western & Atlantic Railroad bridges. Major Galt wrote that he wished every Confederate officer acted like Lee, as a gentleman with common sense. Similarly, Lieutenant Ryland F. Holmes, serving with Lee, described him as "a courteous gentleman, clear-headed, judicious leader, and an agreeable companion."

The campaign lasted only a few days longer, resulting in as many as 1,000 men returning to their commands and between 150 to 200 men sent to Atlanta in chains. The latter included 53 civilians deemed guilty of suborning treason, including resistance leader Jeff Anderson who found himself in custody for helping deserters, draft evaders, and African Americans fleeing bondage. He would later escape from the Atlanta jail with the Union soldier-saboteurs known as the Andrews Raiders. Two other captives, D.L. Maldin and J.T. Fagin, were Confederate soldiers released from the federal prison camps to return home to encourage desertions. They had taken oaths not to aid the Southern cause again under pain of death. The *Southern Confederacy* newspaper praised the good conduct of Lee's men in Dahlonega and the hospitality of the townspeople.[32]

Some North Georgians criticized the expedition after Lee had left, claiming that the soldiers consumed too much of the drought-stricken area's food and that the prisoners marched to Atlanta received severe beatings. Other mountain people claimed that families suffered harassment for not supporting the war or for helping neighbors resist. Some of the draft evaders argued that they would have come out of hiding if offered the same exemptions from service that Governor Brown gave to his allies or if they could serve only in their local home guard units. H.H. Walker, however, complained about civilians released after falsely pleading loyalty to the Confederacy.

Lee drew criticism for claiming that the desertions had more to do with the officers of the volunteers than the problems and politics of the enlisted men. Northern newspapers held up the expedition as proof of the declining fortunes of the Confederacy and wrote of Lee's men meeting violent opposition near Dahlonega. Governor Brown, however, beyond his official congratulations, wrote personally to Lee: "I highly approve of your course and thank you for the wise and judicious policies you have pursued in the delicate command to which you are assigned. The promptness and energy displayed by you and all under your command have I think quelled the troubles in N.E. Georgia."[33]

Significantly, Lee's captives included Baptist preacher William Tate of Lumpkin County. While preachers in the plantation region of central Georgia proclaimed that slavery was a blessing from heaven, a minority of Georgia's Baptists had spoken out against the institution of slavery since the American Revolution when Baptists were part of a frontier social movement that challenged the wealth and power of the plantation-owning coastal elites. They belonged to a notably small number of Americans who opposed human bondage purely as a moral issue, not for economic reasons. Baptist congregations are independent; most accepted or even supported slavery, although Abraham Lincoln's family did not. This opposition to the war did, however, reflect on how Appalachian people feared that the war would result in enslaved people being freed to compete with them for land and jobs.

Aside from winning hearts and minds in their Appalachian communities, preachers could hide subversive activities within their ministerial duties, including taking information and people, Black and white, through enemy lines. Baptist leaders who declared opposition to secession included state representative the Rev. Elias W. Allred of Pickens County, arrested in 1864 but earned release because of his brother Lemuel's connections to Governor Joseph E. Brown. Allred was accused of forming a pro–Union company or posse in Pickens County in support of General Sherman, although more likely to protect the local people from the depredations of the Confederate home guard. A newspaper reported that he was to be appointed by Abraham Lincoln to Congress for James G. Brown's new state of North Georgia. Minister Peter Walker of Union County served as a captain in the Union forces. Captain Benjamin F. Jordan, the son of a Pickens County Baptist minister captured and allegedly later hanged by the Union army, had the Rev. John Richards of Cherokee County executed in 1864, allegedly for preaching against secession.[34]

Confederate officials took the threat of such resistance seriously. Atlanta and its Western & Atlantic Railroad, the city's connection to armies in Tennessee as a supply line, remained under threat from federal raids aided by Georgians opposed to secession, African Americans, the war, its lack of maintenance, or any combination thereof. Atlanta's Mayor James M. Calhoun promised that Lee would supply arms and provisions to anyone coming to the city's defense. General Braxton Bragg warned Governor Brown of the danger of a raid on the bridge over the Chattahoochee River in early September 1863, which proved to be a false alarm.

Lee, however, had already determined to conduct another campaign against the resistance in North Georgia, and beyond. Only a month after the Dahlonega Campaign, Governor Brown received a plea for another expedition against the Unionists. Lee persuaded McAdoo to accept a commission to serve in a vague position as Lee's legal advisor on July 12, 1863. At the urging of Governor Brown and Colonel Lee, McAdoo then traveled to Richmond, Virginia, to meet with President Jefferson Davis to receive approval for Lee's plan for another joint campaign of Confederate and Georgia state troops to stop the resistance to the war. He learned of the high regard the top government officials held for Lee.[35]

McAdoo's mission succeeded, and Lee received new orders to lead another expedition into the mountain counties in search of "deserters, stragglers, and conscripts" to answer a "disgrace" "in this hour of the Southern country's need." His forces sought a rumored 600 men organized by Colonel Busty [Goldman Bryson? David C. Beatty?], "notorious for his daring outrages." Lee's command arrived in Dahlonega on September 12, where he divided his 500 men of the 25th Georgia Provost Battalion and other units, into one wing commanded by him and the other by Captain John C. Hendrix. The column then marched through Morganton, Ellijay,

Civil War cavalry battle (*The Great Book of 1866*, broadside, BRO1866G7, Broadside Collection, mss4299, Hargrett Rare Book and Manuscript Library, University of Georgia Libraries).

and Blairsville to North Carolina and Tennessee. Lieutenant Ryland F. Holmes wrote that "the people in the villages were generally friendly to the mission" and rendered Lee every assistance.[36]

On September 15, some 15 miles from Morganton, Georgia, Lee and Holmes decided to reconnoiter after laying aside their uniforms and disguising themselves as civilians. They fell in with a group of some 100 armed Unionists who were trying to flee, led by two federal recruiting officers. Returning to their camp, the two Confederate officers set out in pursuit with their troops. In the ensuing battle, Lee's men killed four Unionists and wounded others; a federal officer and a local preacher were among the 30 to 40 men captured. Captain John C. Hendrix and Lieutenant Eli Tellinger Hunnicutt, commanding the "broken leg" company (Company E "Hendrix's Cavalry," disabled veterans from the Virginia campaign), prevented the notorious Unionist Goldman Bryson from stealing 250 cattle belonging to the Confederate government.

Hendrix's company also defeated a band of men under Jacob V. Ferguson in White County. Captain R.P. Eberhart's Company G captured 25 of Bryson's men.[37] Captain Henderson, with a company from Elbert County, Georgia, captured 25 and killed three of the outlier's band there, but the rest of the Unionists escaped with their leader. Henderson's men took 50 prisoners, including two federal recruiting officers, and 75 head of cattle. Lee pursued Bryson as far as Loudon, Tennessee.[38]

The Atlanta provost marshal continued his campaign as a raid across state lines. Unionists in the mountains of East Tennessee had direct access to support from the federal army and the opportunity to raid plantations, even in neighboring North Carolina. Union sympathizers like David C. Beatty, James G. Brown, and Goldman Bryson encouraged entire families to desert the Confederacy for the North, where they could work for better pay than they had ever known before the war. William McAdoo heard that the federals paid in gold, including men joining the Union ranks. The United States government also set up segregated contraband work camps for white and African American families who escaped the Confederate-occupied areas. They grew cotton and food under tight federal control for the war effort. The Union military, however, only, exempted white refugees from the Confederacy from any but voluntary service.[39]

If the resistance in the two states united, the shrinking Confederacy would have a war on a new front. Lee led 200 men into Cherokee County, North Carolina, across steep mountains (sometimes by moonlight), magnificent vistas, and dark, almost uninhabited forests. Lieutenant Holmes wrote that "freebooters, outlaws, deserters, and tories [Southerners opposed to the Confederacy or the war], dwelt in every valley" and that he found the town of Murphy, North Carolina, "nearly deserted on account of the thieving raids of the bushwhackers."[40] Lee's expedition reportedly captured Colonel Busty. Lee also sent detachments into the Ducktown area of Tennessee. Overall, this campaign resulted in the arrest of 300 to 400 men. Lee was presented to President Jefferson Davis by General George Washington Custis Lee (General Robert E. Lee's son and Davis's aide de camp) for his success in the campaign.[41]

Governor Zebulon Vance, North Carolina's famously pro-state rights leader, disapproved of Lee's raid. He made an official complaint that Lee's Georgians seized some of his citizens too old for conscription, chained them together, and marched the group to a prison in Atlanta, where they remained in confinement until they agreed to enlist in the army. Vance would, however, order similar expeditions against North Carolina Unionists in 1862–1864.[42]

Hunting local resistance leaders became a hallmark of Lee's campaigns, although sometimes he failed to apprehend them. In the spring of 1863, he attempted to have resistance leader William C. Fain arrested. Fain escaped to federal lines, but his family later charged Lee's men with trespassing! The worst offender, Goldman Bryson, from Cherokee County, North Carolina, but an opposition leader in three states, held a commission in the federal army and had a reputation among the Confederate population as a horse thief and a serial killer. He contended that he and his men protected Southern families from losing what little they had to Confederate impressment.

Informants reported that Bryson had assembled an ad hoc regiment of Southerners opposed to the Confederacy at Murphy, North Carolina, to seize the gold and other assets transferred to the Dahlonega's mint from the New Orleans mint when

Post-Civil War photograph of the Dahlonega mint. The building was destroyed by a fire in 1878 (University of North Georgia).

that city fell to federal forces in 1862. Panic ensued in official circles when the treasure did not make the planned transfer to Augusta. News then arrived that Lee had sent Captain Tiller's artillery company to Dahlonega, who brought the gold safely to the Georgia Railroad Bank in Atlanta. Reports arrived in Atlanta that Bryson had learned that his prize had moved to Athens, Georgia.[43]

Atlanta Provost Marshal George W. Lee dispatched two of his best scouts, John H. "Coote" and H. Blount Rhea, to guide 300 members of the Provost Battalion to the Tellico Plains of Tennessee in pursuit of this Unionist. Lee offered a $500 reward for Bryson's capture. William Axe and Elena Rattle, members of General John Crawford Vaughn's command and with 100 Cherokee warriors of Colonel William Holland Thomas' "Legion of Indians and Highlanders," set out to arrest the Unionist leader.

Public history writes of how the Native Americans in today's Oklahoma supported the Confederacy only because their leaders owned enslaved labor. That excuse does not explain Thomas' Legion with its 2,000 Eastern Cherokee and their allies, which fought for the new Southern nation despite white regional prejudices against their race that continue to this day. Like Lee and his white Atlanta workmen, these small farmers owned no one and surely did not fight for the rights of the wealthy planters.

Left behind in the Cherokee Removal to the West in 1838, 800 Cherokees and 100 Catawba had formed a land company, reportedly claiming 72,000 acres, called the Qualla Boundary. They achieved this success through the efforts of their chief merchant, William Holland Thomas, adopted by these Cherokees when he was a boy. On that land, Charles Lanman observed that these Indians had created a new, highly literate society. They had made a life for their families in the then-modern world. Thomas had voted for secession for North Carolina at the state's secession convention. He organized his battalion of Cherokees and Catawba to fight for the Confederate States of America.[44]

In 1863 and below Murphy, North Carolina, Lee's men joined Vaughn's Native Americans in attacking Goldman Bryson's men at dinner time, capturing a captain and 17 men while killing four more on November 8, 1863. The Confederates also hanged 34 of Bryson's men. Lee's mixed-race Confederate detachment came through the battle unscathed.[45]

Atlanta's Georgia Railroad Bank (right) held Confederate gold from Dahlonega and elsewhere (Library of Congress).

The Eastern Cherokees, left behind because they cooperated with the United States Army in rounding up their neighbors during the Indian removal of 1838, now hunted white men, including some like Bryson, who had served in the Cherokee removal to the West in 1838. The federal captain escaped, however, and rode 14 miles to his home. While attempting to capture Bryson, the Cherokee scouts Axe and Rattle killed him. Lee wanted them to be paid the bounty. Bryson reportedly had led a mob that murdered Cherokee John Timson in 1856, and he had committed other atrocities against the Indians during the war, making this act likely a revenge killing. Cherokees paraded through the streets of Murphy wearing parts of Bryson's bloody uniform.[46]

The Civil War was the greatest era of Native American (Indian) conflict in United States history, but it resulted in even worse treatment of the descendants of the original Americans. Despite having supported the Confederacy the people of the Qualla Boundary kept 50,000 acres of their land and, in 1868, gained independence from the Western Cherokees, who had also supported the soldiers to the Confederacy!

Resistance to the Confederacy continued and worsened as different forms of dissent, exploitation, and speculation merged into one problem of growing mass discontent that encouraged organized brigands who challenged Confederate authority. Months later, the *Memphis Daily Appeal*, by then a refugee Confederate newspaper published in Atlanta, reprinted an article from a Northern newspaper of Union soldiers who had escaped from a train between Augusta and Macon and reached the federal army in Chattanooga, a common occurrence. They "confirm all previous accounts of the kindness extended to escaping prisoners of by the negroes on their route, and report the woods and hollows in North Georgia full of [white] citizens, who are well armed, and vow they will not join the rebel service. They shoot those who attempt to arrest them."[47]

The threat of Southerners willing to aid the Union army in winning the war only came closer to Atlanta. In June 1863, George W. Lee requested help stopping bandits and guerrillas in counties around Atlanta. Captain John R. Patrick's company of the 1st Regiment of Georgia State Troops in Fairburn, Campbell County, immediately southwest of Atlanta, responded. As Patrick's company passed Dan Dobson's farm on Dry Creek, deserters opened fire. Several of the desperados and one of Patrick's men fell wounded. The captain took 10 men as prisoners and later captured 30 more, some who gave themselves up, for a total haul of 43 men. Patrick received orders to, in the future, immediately hang any such men caught firing on his troops.

Lee also organized a company in Forsyth County and took over the state's troops in Dawson County for use against the local resistance. Governor Brown accepted his recommendation for creating a local defense company in White County to deal with anti-war partisans.[48] State Adjutant General Henry C. Wayne wanted Lee to send another expedition to Dahlonega in January 1864. Still later in the war, Congressman Hiram P. Bell urged the government again to give Lee the troops to make a sweeping arrest of deserters in North Georgia.[49]

Even before Lee could launch more expeditions, orders from Richmond came to transfer spies and other prisoners from such posts in Chattanooga, Selma, and Tuscaloosa to secure incarceration in Atlanta. Any federal surgeons and chaplains found among them would receive transportation under a flag of truce to Huntsville, Alabama, for release as prisoners of war on parole. Lee's garrison had to escort the most serious prisoners to Richmond for imprisonment in Castle Thunder, a converted tobacco factory used as a Confederate prison for civilians, spies, and resistance members of both sexes.[50]

Atlantans also had reason to be concerned about an uprising by the enslaved. Georgia had among the most restrictive laws, even in the states of the South, applied to African Americans in or out of bondage, starting in 1783 with a special tax on free persons of any African descent. Before, during, and after the American Revolution, African Americans set themselves free by forming communities in the swamps and frontier wilderness. Whites were suspected of aiding in these escapes, and some African Americans escaped by passing themselves off as white. Many of these self-emancipated remained in the states with bondage by falsely claiming to be free or persuading white friends to pretend to be their owners. In labor strapped Atlanta, opportunities for African Americans out of and even in bondage for independence and prosperity increased even before the approach of the federal army gave opportunities for emancipation.[51]

Curiously, despite the South's fear of African American insurrections, Lee would see nothing of the sort in his long and varied career in combating insurrection and conspiracy within the Confederacy. As African Americans did even in colonial times, however, they usually avoided open confrontation that would end so disastrously for white resistance to the Confederate States of America. They emancipated themselves in other ways, such as escaping to the federal lines, refusing to take instructions, demanding pay, work slowdowns, sabotaging machinery, and ignoring restrictions on their gatherings and travel. They even aided white resistance groups that helped deserters from the Confederate army and draft evaders.[52]

In 1863, stories appeared in Macon newspapers, reprinted across the country, of the arrest in Atlanta of a man claiming to be a major general in a resistance organization of 10,000 African Americans centered in East Georgia. He allegedly planned to take his army to the Gate City after it fell to Union General William S. Rosecrans. The insurrectionists would then start a systematic campaign of rapine and murder of white Southern families. Promoting this tale allowed Secessionists to rally support for continuing the war and, in the North, for not making the war about emancipation.

Officials in Hancock County, Georgia, however, discovered that this conspiracy consisted of only a few dozen African American artisans who would meet secretly at night to drink wine, occasionally drill, and talk of emancipation. After they shot at a planter, thirty of their number suffered arrest and a whipping; two of their ringleaders were hanged. Ironically, in the bigger picture, they came to join a struggle for survival against King Cotton that had gradually come to include most of the white citizens and even the Confederate government itself on a level beyond just the war but later against the United States and its military.[53]

Whatever Lee thought of reports of uprisings by the enslaved, in the public panic created by the failing Confederacy, he had reason to act against Union sympathizers in Atlanta. Oliver H. Jones and Lieutenant E.T. Hunnicutt followed any suspected Unionists. In August 1862, Lee held five men and three women brought to him for interrogation about conspiracies against the government. Someone had allegedly tried to set fire to the Atlanta munitions works. Government officials held trials for six Atlantans for treasonable activities, including espionage. All the defendants obtained release. Robert Bezley was arrested in Atlanta for giving fraudulent passes to African Americans. By contrast, Confederate officials held more than 100 people for sedition in Gainesville, Texas, and hanged at least 42 on October 1, 1862.[54]

Lee had people detained and interrogated about conspiracies against the Confederate government and its white society, although, by all credible reports, he conducted his inquisitions fairly and with respect. For example, he questioned Cyrena Stone, an avowed white Union sympathizer whose modern biographer believed aided escaped African Americans, federal prisoners of war, and enemy spies. She sat before Lee in a crudely furnished hotel room but in an interrogation attended by several witnesses, including a newspaper reporter. With no Bible available, Lee allowed her to testify without swearing an oath. Cyrena later only complained in her fake diary that she "saw" in all his features a hatred of Yankees. In a version of the meeting used later in a novel, her sister described the provost character as a tall man with small pinched-up eyes and a coarse suit conducting a reign of terror. Lee, however, released Cyrena after only a few questions about Unionist meetings and an alleged plot of 300 Atlanta Union sympathizers to organize an uprising of the enslaved.[55]

Lee carried out his duties with patience and tact. Enslaved but largely independent merchant Robert Webster, for example, helped a federal colonel from East Tennessee to escape, and he ran a currency exchange between federal prisoners with United States script to trade for Confederate money. Although he claimed to fear Lee hanging him, he only spent a short time incarcerated. Similarly, Lee raided a "tiger" (card game) run by professional gamblers where one of the prominent men present lost $20,000 that Lee initially believed came from Confederate government funds. He quickly released all the parties when he discovered otherwise.

Criticism appeared in print for Lee's lenient treatment of federal soldiers held as prisoners. The provost marshal published a statement that, contrary to rumor, he did not allow the prisoners of war to walk the streets of Atlanta, doing as they pleased. Men captured from Colonel Abel Streight's Raid had thousands of dollars on them that Lee declined to confiscate despite his belief that they had stolen the money. He did investigate crimes alleged to have been committed by some of the raiders. (Other Confederate soldiers would remove valuables from prisoners even without official sanction.)[56]

The provost marshal of Atlanta even showed courtesy to the notorious Andrews raiders. These federal soldiers, led by civilian spy and smuggler James Andrews, had stolen the locomotive *General* in a failed effort to cut the Confederacy's vital Western & Atlantic Railroad by burning its bridges in what became known as the Great Locomotive Chase. In 1862, ten of the captured saboteurs suffered severe torture before Lee took command. Confederate guerrilla Ned Edwards had his feet whipped until the skin burst. Under orders from General Edmund Kirby Smith, then Atlanta Provost Marshal Green Foreacre hanged eight of their party, including Andrews, an action that Lee learned of only after returning to Atlanta and which he found appalling. Richmond officials wanted to know why Lee did not hang the others, however. The remaining raiders would remember Lee's kindness and that he risked his career to speak with them, but they also saw a change in his questions over time that implied to them that he expected to receive orders to resume the executions. When the city jailer ignored Lee's instructions to always enter the cell armed, the prisoners jumped the jailer and escaped. The fleeing men quickly (and suspiciously) immediately obtained pistols and horses.

Lee quickly dispatched scouts and cavalry after the fugitives and recaptured some of them. Prisoner William Pittenger claimed that the provost marshal shouted to his men to take no prisoners alive and to leave the bodies in the woods. Reports appeared in the press that the guards killed three of the 13 men who fled. A Mrs. Nancy Vaughn of nearby Decatur captured another escapee. Five of their number raided a farm near Palmetto, Georgia. The owner and his African American workers unsuccessfully tried to fight them off. Eight of the Andrews Raiders eventually escaped to the federal lines.

Provost Marshal Lee, however, eventually had his remaining six saboteurs reclassified as regular prisoners of war to save them from execution as

The escape of the Andrews Raiders from the Atlanta jail (from William Pittenger, *Daring and Suffering*, 1863).

spies. He also removed them to better but more secure accommodations in the Confederate barracks and ended the access to all prisoners by citizens with Unionist sympathies, including in the hospitals. Later, he had the remaining Andrews Raiders transferred to the prisons in Richmond.[57] An anonymous observer, however, wrote that the prisoners housed in the city could still hear conversations and observe what went on in the streets. They defiantly sang out the *Star Spangled Banner*, *Hail Columbia*, and *Columbia Gem of the Ocean* for all, including the city's secret so-called Unionist community, to hear. By contrast, federal officials at Camp Chase, Ohio, did not allow Confederate prisoners to sing.[58]

Chapter Five

Atlanta's Secret Yankees

WHETHER SHERMAN'S ADVANCING ARMY came to Georgia as conquerors or liberators depended upon point of view as more and more people on all sides just wanted the war to end, whatever the consequences. Corruption and fraud, prevalent on both sides, was bringing down the entire economy, and in different ways. America would not recover from the effects of the Civil War until the 1880s, when, ironically Republican politicians wanted to spend that windfall on expanding federal Civil War pensions to what had been dubious claims and Democrats wanted to see the funds used to pay down the government debt left from the war! George W. Lee's acquaintance Robert A. Crawford wanted, at the least, for individual states to be allowed to reimburse individuals for the Confederate debts left over from the war as an economic boost to the South.[1]

In what remained of the shrinking Confederate nation in 1864, want became a particularly formidable enemy, created by profiteering, the federal blockade, the declining railroad network, and the army's needs for the decreasing available provisions, labor, livestock, wagons, and rail transportation. Southerners of all races increasingly tried to escape to the federal lines to obtain transportation to security and good-paying jobs north of the Ohio River. They enlisted in the United States military and thus added still more bodies to the federal war effort while further depriving the Confederate nation of soldiers and civilian workers, regardless of race. Northern soldiers could come to the South, eventually with the added purpose of liberating the enslaved, but they also freed the poor and the growing-poorer white population. Another argument has the Civil War replacing slavery only with apartheid/racial segregation and even more widespread poverty.[2]

During this growing crisis, Mayor James M. Calhoun, Atlanta's press, and prominent city citizens praised Provost Marshal Major George W. Lee. Local officials told his superiors how his command worked harmoniously with local authorities. Lee transferred civilians arrested by the military to the city authorities while he took into custody soldiers apprehended by the city police. Governor Joseph E. Lee Brown requested that Lee receive a promotion in the Confederate army to a grade compatible with his numerous and growing responsibilities. The editors of the *Southern Confederacy* echoed the sentiments of other men who knew him: "...there is not a more faithful and energetic officer in the service of the Confederate States."[3]

Civil War engraving of Southern refugees (*Harper's Weekly*, November 5, 1864, p. 708).

H.L. Hubbard (William L. Hubbard?) described Atlanta's provost marshal to the Confederate Secretary of War as: "a man whom, we all honor for and esteem for his many good qualities, and who is denounced by no one but a miserable set of whiskey sellers, and speculators, who employ little pettifogging Lawyers to write letters to your Honor."[4]

Other people who knew Lee felt differently. The mercurial Georgia Adjutant General Henry C. Wayne would make numerous complaints about the provost marshal over the years, likely because Wayne perceived the Atlantan as a challenge to his own authority, starting with the claim that while good supplies of flour existed in Atlanta's storehouses what Lee had shared with the state troops had gone bad. An anonymous critic made broad and vague accusations about Lee but with only one specific claim, that the major had a financial interest in a newspaper that charged the government exorbitant prices for printing. (Lee did become a partner in the *Southern Confederacy*, but only after he had resigned as post commander in Atlanta, and he had moved the newspaper to Augusta.)[5]

Newspapers reported on three attempts made on the life of George W. Lee, details of which are lacking. In August 1862, Private John Kershaw allegedly tried to cut the throat of the provost marshal in his tent while he slept. Lee awoke to strike a blow against his assailant and call for help. For whatever reasons, no one pressed charges against the Private. Two years later, a bushwhacker slightly wounded Lee in the head near Roswell. In the last days of the Civil War, two men called him out of the house where he stayed and struck him with a slug shot. Lee pulled out a gun and shot one of his fleeing assailants.⁶ The Dean Merchants Mill in Newnan, Coweta County, owned by Lee, Captain J.C. Hendrix, and others, went up in flames in October 1863. Arson was suspected but not proven.⁷

The Atlanta provost marshal had other enemies and of a different sort. General Braxton Bragg, now commanding the Army of Tennessee from Chattanooga, became George W. Lee's most prominent critic. He had crossed Georgia Governor Brown in the spring of 1862 by threatening to seize the state-owned Western & Atlantic Railroad because he claimed that the railroad would not transport ordnance to his army. On August 12, 1862, without the required legal authority of President Davis, Bragg declared Atlanta and its environs under martial law and went on to order the mayor to appoint a military governor of the area, an act that left Calhoun conflicted with what he could legally do and as he had excellent relations with Provost Marshal Lee, whose authority he did not want to supplant.

Politicians of the new Southern nation famously guarded civil liberties on all levels, including in cases where state and local government expressed blatant disregard for Confederate law. Bragg's action consequently created a public uproar that went far beyond any complaints about Lee's earlier general orders when he took command of the city. Confederate Vice President Alexander H. Stephens famously wrote that Bragg had no more of a right to subvert local authority in Atlanta than did any prostitute. During this controversy, the *Southern Confederacy* newspaper felt the need to defend Lee and to contrast him with General Bragg:

Brigadier General Henry Constantine Wayne (1815–1883) (Library of Congress).

> He is bound to take notice of and regard all orders and *instructions that are officially sent to him*, and no others. He is well known in the community, having resided here for a number of years, and many of our citizens have known him from childhood. Everybody knows that he is not a tyrant, and is not disposed to usurp any authority.⁸

George W. Lee, by all indications, obeyed directives and orders from Bragg without question, although by the spring of 1863, the general had decided to replace him. Bragg made this matter personal and claimed that, as an officer earlier in Pensacola, Lee had been arrested for stealing clothing funds entrusted to him by his men and that the captain only escaped prosecution by resigning his commission. Bragg described him as a man so notorious that Georgia's governor had refused to accept a company he had initially raised and that, while in Atlanta, he had spent government funds lavishly, had citizens imprisoned for months without charges, and had men in his non-conscript companies who should have been serving in the army. Bragg described Lee as a man of "misrepresentation and downright falsehood."

The government in Richmond and Atlanta's most respected citizens came to the provost marshal's defense. The Confederate Secretary of War wrote, mistakenly, that General Robert E. Lee had endorsed the provost marshal. Bragg employed a more reasoned tone in the face of such resistance, but he still claimed that, from his first meeting with Lee in Pensacola, he had been unable to find any merit in the Atlantan. He argued that Lee had to go if only because any officers the General sent to Atlanta must outrank him. That the provost marshal had a grade of major, at that time, makes the General's point confusing and countering his argument that Lee held too much authority.[9]

Colonel Moses H. Wright, commander of the post in Atlanta and no relation to Augustus R. Wright, now suddenly began to complain that he could learn nothing from the provost marshal and that the troops in the city, including Lee's railroad guard company, annoyed respectable travelers while allowing "villains" to pass. He had placed Lee in charge of the city so that he could devote his full time to moving a Confederate arsenal from Nashville to Atlanta and then expanding it into one of the most extensive munitions operations in the South.

Wright asked if he had the authority to replace Lee and his men. At the same time, Bragg threatened to have all his army's hospitals removed from Atlanta, an impractical solution to where no problem existed. Finally, the General sent Colonel John Q. Loomis of the 25th Alabama Infantry to take command of security of all of the city's military medical facilities, at great expense and in redundancy with the efforts of Lee's headquarters. The colonel went further. He all but officially took over responsibility for the security of the city. Lee acquiesced, but as he had tried before, he unsuccessfully attempted to get clarification of his duties from Richmond. Conversely, Lee now had orders from General Bragg, sent by the Secretary of War, on July 25, 1863, retaining him in command of the post.[10]

Surviving records belie most of Bragg's charges and fail to support the rest, reflecting the General's reputation for irrational behavior and inefficient management that lost him battles and, arguably, the Confederacy in war. Although Governor Brown had initially declined to accept Lee's original company, he did so without questioning anyone's character or motives. In 1861, Bragg had issued an order in which he referred to it as "an admirable company" and Lee as being "in high estimation," to which the Atlanta papers added that Lee had become one of Bragg's favorites. The government subsequently accepted 40 other companies into the army that Lee had helped to raise. The provost marshal had led his successful campaigns against the deserters, draft dodgers, and Unionists in 1863 while technically under the command of General Bragg.[11]

The provost marshal's surviving letters contradict the General's often-published remark to General Joseph Johnston that anyone could see Lee's illiteracy because he had someone else to sign his name. Being unable to read and write was common in both armies among enlisted men. Frances Thomas Howard even found three federal sentries she conversed with near her home who could not read or write. Whole companies of the Confederate army had almost no soldiers who could as much as write their names. George W. Lee, coming from a family of professional clerks, however, had a consistent signature and writing that showed better penmanship than that of the mayor of Atlanta and attorney James M. Calhoun![12]

Bragg may have acted vindictively against the captain because, earlier in Pensacola, Lee agreed to step aside to allow John B. Villepigue to win the election to command the Georgia Battalion. The enlisted men, however, refused to go along with the change in commanders. A scuffle afterward resulted in Lee's brief arrest for only being in the area. Bragg also misrepresented the money incident. Lee had entrusted the funds to his successor, Jabez R. Rhodes. When the new captain misappropriated the money, Lee insisted on the repayment of the funds to the troops.

The emotionally troubled and chronically ill Bragg likely confused these two men, although Rhodes still served under the general but was now in the Army of Tennessee.

Rhodes continued as captain until a court-martial finding had him executed by a firing squad on September 3, 1863, as one of the few and possibly the only officer executed in the Civil War for desertion. He had been cited for bravery at Pensacola, but he had since been charged with making false returns that showed deserters as still being present, being drunk on duty, encouraging his men to desert, embezzling money paid to substitutes for drafted soldiers, and splitting enlistment bounty money with men who had deserted.

Congressman Augustus R. Wright tried and failed to persuade Bragg and other Confederate officials to accept the resignation of Rhodes, instead of executing him. According to Wright, Rhodes had been the best captain in his regiment, helped to raise two companies, and held a great deal of influence among working men in Atlanta. Even officers had to spend all their money just to get enough to eat and fraud became a necessity for survival. Just before his execution, Rhodes confessed to what he had done without apologies.[13]

The story of Lee at Pensacola, however, has another version not easily explained. An anonymous person claiming to belong to the Georgia Battalion wrote to Georgia Gov. Brown from Pensacola on October 4, 1861:

Capt. G.W. Lee who came to this place as commander of the com called Lees vols., was charged & under arrest at this place "for leaving his qeurs [quarters?] without leave of the proper officers & for Gambling, drinking & riotous conduct" and he resigned & left the service the day before the court martial convened. He is also accused of selling & appropriating to his own use & not accounting to the Company the Rations for the same probably to the amt. of $200 at one time I refer you to Lieut Col. John B. Villepigue & Capt. J R Rhodes or any members of the company.[14]

This letter raises many questions. Why did this person write to Governor Brown when Lee's company belonged to the Confederate and not the state government? What purpose did it serve since Lee had resigned and gone home? If these charges were true, why did Bragg fail to mention them in his scathing attacks on Lee? Why did this complainant write anonymously? Was Rhodes or Villepigue the writer?

At Pensacola and throughout his military career, Braxton Bragg had complex motives for his mercurial actions that remain hard to understand beyond speculation about his emotional health. Often, leaders who perceive themselves as under siege with intractable problems will choose, out of frustration, to fight unrelated and unnecessary battles with imagined enemies. The famously troubled Bragg had difficulties with seemingly all his subordinates, a problem that dated to before the war and became legend. General Ulysses S. Grant would remember that Bragg, while serving in the old Army, even tried to bring up charges against Bragg! By 1863, Bragg even joined his officers in writing to President Davis to call for his own removal for the sake of the army. With a deserved reputation as an effective and uncompromising disciplinarian, he certainly resented sharing any authority, more so with an amateur soldier like Lee who had earned the type of respect that Bragg would never know from so many people.[15]

An Atlantan with a personal agenda must have compiled Bragg's long and detailed—and misrepresented—charges against George W. Lee. The general repeated them without conducting his own investigation. A conman named George whom Lee twice sent in custody to Bragg only to see him released both times by the general, may have been the source of the complaints. Sympathetic Atlantans argued that Lee's problems came from the city's entrepreneurial class.[16] In mercantile Atlanta, a repeated failure in business like Lee could receive disdain from those people and remind them of how close they had been, and remained, to disaster, even to being replaced by someone like him!

The survival of the Confederate States of America depended on the middle class and poor whites of the South, but the new Southern nation proved anything but egalitarian. That seems particularly odd as some of the planter and financial elite descended from families that had been of at least as low a social status as that of George W. Lee, including Jefferson Davis and Joseph E. Brown. Throughout the Confederacy, the important and the self-important could resent any authority given to lower-class men and adolescent boys who served under commanders like Lee. As a target of social prejudice, George W. Lee joined such notable Confederates as Nathan Bedford Forrest, Patrick Cleburne, Thomas J. "Stonewall" Jackson, and Varina Howell Davis in being a victim of coming from no better than the South's middle class. A provost marshal risked a great deal using his authority to take decisive but provocative actions that raised the ire of politically connected people and the Confederacy's uninhibited press.[17]

George W. Lee, however, blamed his problems with Bragg upon the "Union Circle," a community of what one Atlanta refugee claimed consisted of 75 to 100 Northerners who had remained in Atlanta and included some of its leading citizens. An Atlantan wrote of them long after the war:

> There were several hundred citizens of northern and foreign birth who were known to be union sympathizers. These persons were closely watched, and any indiscretion on their part would have led to unpleasant consequences, but the majority of them were sensible, well-mannered persons who were on good terms with their southern neighbors and while they were opposed to secession, they did not want to see the South oppressed or injured. As a rule, these people attended quietly to their business and gave no offense to anybody. They were not molested and a few thought it necessary to go elsewhere to insure their personal safety.[18]

Bragg's charges against Lee bear a striking similarity to those made after the war in a postwar memoir, written as if a diary, by Atlanta Yankee Cyrena Stone likely to protect her husband, a member of a not so "secret Yankee" conspiracy of an Atlanta crime syndicate of wealthy Northerners and Southerners to make profits over any political loyalty. When it benefited them to do so financially, chiefly after the United States won the war, the Yankee members would claim to have been oppressed and suffering supporters of the Union throughout the conflict.

General Braxton Bragg (1817–1876) (Library of Congress).

Reality makes them appear more as apolitical opportunists who proved that in Atlanta even patriotism was a commodity.

Lee counted William O. Markham, a former acting Atlanta mayor who had built much of the city, as the most dangerous of the Yankee conspirators. The provost marshal had received a fine of $10 for harassing him. Markham had a partnership in one of the few rolling mills for refurbing worn railroad tracks in the South, which also profitably made machinery and produced iron plating for all or almost all the Confederate ironclad warships including, according to legend, the *Merrimac* (aka, the CSA *Virginia*). Markham rented much of his property, including the space used by Lee as an office, to the Confederate government. After the war, he would claim that he only did business with the Southern nation under pressure from Provost Marshal Lee.[19]

Lee may have only followed orders when he investigated Markham. Colonel Moses Hannibal Wright, commander of the Atlanta Arsenal, repeatedly ordered civilian companies such as Irishman James Dunning's Atlanta Machine Works to take government contracts. In retaliation for federal legislation seizing all property used in the war against the United States, the Confederate Congress passed the Sequestration Act of May 21, 1861, that confiscated and sold all property of "enemy aliens." The Confederate States court in Marietta, Georgia, near Atlanta, subsequently issued orders of garnishment. Even Lee became involved in a suit over confiscation when he served as trustee for railroad and bank stock held by Charlotte Smith that Confederate officials claimed belonged to her husband Horace Smith, Sr., an enemy alien. The court awarded possession of the assets to her son.[20]

The Confederate court never actually confiscated the Gate City Rolling Mill of William O. Markham or the Atlanta Machine Works of James L. Dunning. Researcher Ken Denney believes that their claims of confiscation otherwise originated with Dunning after the war as his falsehoods about Confederate oppression due to loyalty to the Union. After the war, Markham attempted to receive compensation for cotton and other property allegedly lost to Sherman's occupation of Atlanta to the amount of $114,000. He used claims of harassment by Lee and sequestration as proof of his loyalty to the Union. The government refused his claim, and another filed by his descendants in the early 1900s, in part because he not only admitted to serving in the state militia and profitably supplying the military of the State of Georgia but also for his deliberately concealing other unspecified "important facts" in the case. On February 5, 1868, Lee testified in the federal proceedings that dismissed Markham's claim for compensation for property loss.[21]

When Sherman's army occupied Atlanta, Markham called himself a Union loyalist, even though he had been a Confederate collaborator. He provided names of men he accused of having persecuted Unionists. Sherman subsequently declared that Colonel George W. Lee, Colonel Alex M. Wallace, Captain G. Whit Anderson, and Lieutenant [Eli Tellinger] Hunnicutt were to be treated as outlaws and traitors, instead of as prisoners of war. At that time, Lee responded from Macon that he had

Markham and others arrested or reported to the Confederate government. He went on to write that if the government in Richmond had followed his advice these persons would now be unable to aid Sherman in the occupation of Atlanta and persecution of loyal Confederates. Lee might have added that, if killed, the secrets he knew about the real "patriotism" of Markham and the other so-called "secret Yankees" being engaged in treasonable profiteering, even against the laws of the United States, would go to the grave with him. He could have added the charity and kindness that he showed to his prisoners and that he had helped to save the last of the federal Andrews raiders in Confederate custody from execution. The United States government did nothing to investigate, arrest, or prosecute George W. Lee for anything during or after the war. He does not appear on the list of prisoners held in federally occupied Atlanta, 1865–1866.[22]

Early on George W. Lee clashed with Markham's "Jacobin Club" (slang for a conspiracy for seizing power) as Lee called it. He arrested one-member, successful dry goods merchant and bootlegger Michael Myers, who subsequently died in his custody. Over a long period, the provost marshal had received complaints about Myers refusing to accept Confederate currency, of passing counterfeit bills, and of violating the liquor laws. The bootlegger Joseph Harford wrote the Irishman's eulogy. Rumors spread that Lee had ordered Myers hit in the head with a rifle butt, a blow from which the Irishman died. In fact, the provost marshal summoned doctors when he learned of the Irishman having a seizure, who died at home while receiving medical care. An official autopsy determined that he had suffered a stroke and died from natural causes brought on by his notorious alcoholism. That formal inquiry exonerated Lee but, by early 1863, the Confederate government ended his investigations and had his remaining prisoners released.[23]

In January 1864, Lee believed that a conspiracy of special interests stopped his efforts when he came very near to exposing criminal conspiracies involving Amherst W. Stone, the husband of Cyrena. A Northern born attorney who owned African American laborers, and sometimes outspoken supporter, even in the North, of Secession, this Yankee operated a successful Atlanta law practice built upon helping the Confederacy to confiscate and sequester the property of Unionists.[24] With his associates, Stone planned to smuggle cotton out of the South in violation of the laws of the two warring nations. As a provost marshal, Lee started an undercover investigation of this scheme with his former legal advisor and a refugee from Knoxville, Tennessee, Judge William Gibbs McAdoo. Lee failed to learn the full details of Stone's plan until Lee's transfer to the Florida border late in the war.[25]

An ailing Lee intended to prepare a full report that would have named all the persons involved in the criminal enterprise of Atlanta's "secret Yankees." The war ended before he could submit it. Federal authorities had already exposed these plots and had Amherst Stone, as treasurer for the Wyly-Markham Company, and Jonathan Norcross, as agent for the Fulton Importing and Exporting Company, imprisoned when they returned to the North. The U.S. Navy's blockade fleet sunk a steam blockade-runner owned by Norcross, bought and outfitted at the cost of $26,000 to $27,000 in gold, off the coast of Florida.[26] Stone's arrest likely inspired his wife Cyrena to write her memoir, made to look like a diary, of Civil War Atlanta to try to excuse Amherst's support for the Confederate activities although writing mock diaries and letters was used as a literary device for discussing and explaining past events, going back to at least the time of the American Revolution. Her sister would use this memoir as a basis for her postwar novel about oppressed Unionists.[27]

Atlantans had several similar private ventures to operate blockade-runners, ships that slipped past the federal blockade to bring in goods to the Confederacy. Auction houses, what often also served as markets for enslaved African Americans, such as that of Robert A. Crawford, offered for sale whole shiploads of goods that ran the blockade. The United States Navy's closing of Southern ports drastically reduced the tonnage brought into the Southern nation, but speculators made this situation worse by loading the ships that did get through with luxury goods and charging exorbitant prices.

From the cargoes of these ships, Crawford, Frazer & Company, and other auction houses sold bicarbonate of soda, breeding cattle, brogan shoes, cambric handkerchiefs, cigars, claret, coffee, corn meal, Epson salts, French brandy, furniture, harnesses, hogs, Holland gin, horses, liquor, matches, mules, needles, note paper, pocketknives, salt, shoe thread, stock peas, sugar, tallow, tanned hides, tanner's oil, tea, and whiskey.[28]

Lee discovered that what one modern scholar has termed as secret Yankees in Atlanta, including Jonathan Norcross, William Markham, and Amherst Stone, shipped cotton through the federal blockade, against the laws of the United States, with false papers that claimed Europe as the destination but while intending to sell their cargoes in New York, in defiance of the Confederate States' law. In turn, these profiteers smuggled in commodities whereby they sometimes took advantage of desperate people through inflated prices.

Largely Northern entrepreneurial families traveled wherever pursuit of opportunity took them in the South, before, during, and after the war. They included such notables as the Connecticut Tift family of Albany, Georgia, the German Straus, and French Rothschild families of Columbus, Georgia. Nelson Tift advocated reopening the African trade in human beings and built warships for the Confederate navy, however. Many members of this merchant class would join the "Confederate carpetbaggers," people from the South who rebuilt their fortunes in the North after the war.

The Straus family, for example, would use their wealth from cotton speculation and selling Confederate bonds in Europe to build a mercantile empire that would include the famed Macy's department store. Isidor Straus remembered that their former neighbors in Talbotton, Georgia, held him and his family in high regard even while joining in the traditional Southern condemnation of Jewish merchants as speculators.[29]

Atlanta's entrepreneurial class did enjoy a bonanza. This cotton war widened divisions in the city's wealth-based class system and financed the blatant excess of a conspicuous wealthy few that caused a further decline in public morale. As early as 1862, the Atlanta City Council passed resolutions to arrest anyone who questioned Atlanta's loyalty to the Confederacy. One writer who escaped from the city reported:

> While many have thus been laboring, others, in Atlanta in particular, have been riding in their four thousand dollar carriages, dressed in thousand dollar silks and two thousand dollar cloaks, and at night attending the theater or joining in the dance for John Morgan or some other hero.[30]

In June 1864, as Sherman's legions approached Atlanta, a visitor attended a party in Atlanta where he noted that the difference between the trenches he had just left, and the wealthy Atlantans in the rear proved to be as great as between "dark whiskey" and champagne. While most of the city's population starved, panicked, and worried over the fate of themselves and their absent loved ones, the guest had a very different experience:

> To be invited out to dine, where there are a brace of beauties full of music, love, and sympathy, and a service of silver; to reside in a saloon with a carpet which melts like water under your tread, rosewood furniture and marble statues, and mirrors which reflect your satisfaction from every wall; to sit at a table with roasts and fricassees, and wines and sweetmeats....[31]

Most of the population of Atlanta had a different experience, but some horrors were universal. The wartime residents lived with the smells of the downtown from the slaughterhouses, hospitals, and stables. Everywhere filth and garbage overflowed. The constant passage of steam locomotives filled the rather compact city with smoke and noise. Atlanta's population tripled to more than 22,000 people, largely consisting of desperate refugees. What would become the Five Points, in the center of the city, was notorious for its brothels, gambling dens, and saloons that were set up to specifically accommodate the soldiers. Citizens blamed the army and the refugees for the increased thefts and for the smallpox that became rampant. A resident wrote as early as November 1862 that the city had plenty of food but at such inflated prices that many people could not afford it.[32]

This desperate situation existed in all the South's remaining cities. In nearby Macon, for example, almost all the city's manufacturing, except for that contracted to the government, had ceased. The city had an overall run down and dirty appearance. The hotels, now filthy and largely used as hospitals, offered visitors little more than bad beef, corn bread, butter, and various local substitutes for coffee. Ragged refugees from throughout the South who survived on only what the State of Georgia provided for soldiers' families filled the streets. William Whipple had escaped from Macon by July 26, 1864. The people he left there, he claimed, looked for the arrival of William T. Sherman's federal troops as liberators.[33] Ironically, Macon did not surrender to federal forces until the end of the war, while Lee's reoccupied Confederate Atlanta did not submit until even later.

Atlanta had become the same, and with the perceived effect that the rush for money from the expansion of the cotton economy and the wartime deprivations rendered government ineffective on all levels, the Confederacy had come to serve no greater good than depleting all its resources, including human labor and lives, for no better end than giving a few people wealth that, in the long term, hardly existed except on paper.

The city's enslaved population, including those bought and sold, had a place in this history, too. People in bondage fled Atlanta and elsewhere in the hope of emancipation with the approach of the federal army, even by going to work for the Confederate military! Georgia planters sent their enslaved to deep South Georgia and even Texas to prevent their escape to the approaching Union armies. People in Atlanta and elsewhere in the Confederacy sold whatever (or whomever) they could. Desperate owners broke up African American families, as did the slave markets that sometimes had stayed together for generations. In post-emancipation America, these people formerly in bondage had added to their other struggles trying to reunite with family members.[34]

Plantations like those of the Tennessee Valley of Alabama had even begun as offshoots of plantations in Virginia and had established new operations in states like Arkansas and Louisiana before the war. African American life was always about uprooting individuals and breaking up families, often over great distances as reflected in the popularity, and sometimes the origins, of such songs as *Carry Me Back to Ole Virginny*, *Deep River*, *Dixie*, *My Old Kentucky Home*, *Old Black Joe*, *Shenandoah*, *Wayfaring Stranger*, and others. Moving the African Americans to distant locations would not have been a new experience.[35]

The new Southern nation lost more than the plantation labor in its great commodities economy to this greatest mass escape in American history, however. Confederate armies also could not function without African American workers in bondage. Robert E. Lee's Army of Northern Virginia would not have survived without its Black laborers, such as blacksmiths and teamsters, just as it would have been starved out of existence without plantation-produced cotton legally sold to the North for food on the false pretense that only goods for humanitarian civilian needs were purchased in return.[36] In his "Emancipation Proclamation," Abraham Lincoln threatened emancipation anywhere the white population continued to fight for secession but, when those areas failed to return to the Union, Lincoln also formally allowed the enlistment of Black soldiers. More than 200,000 African Americans, most from the 500,000 African Americans who had escaped from bondage during the war, joined the federal army.[37]

The ideal of personal independence, with its risks, however, frightened many enslaved persons and an African American could support their respective white household, the Confederacy, or even slavery (in some forms), but other African Americans abandoned their servitude without needing an act, amendment, proclamation, or other inducement beyond opportunity. Wherever the federal army passed, African Americans would leave their past status behind in hope for an imagined better future. The exodus of so many desperate but determined people created even more security problems for provost marshals such as Lee. These Americans might flee to Atlanta and hide within the population from whom they could escape to independence in the Confederate or Union armies. Conversely, they could find themselves kidnapped and sold back into slavery by unscrupulous traders. Georgia had a long history with such "transactions," despite sales of people in bondage being illegal in the state almost for whole period of 1798 to 1856, that the common name for such interstate human trafficking was called a "Georgia trader."[38]

Civil War Atlanta's trade in human beings grew so extensive with so many such markets and traders in that business that boosters claimed that the Gate City would overtake Richmond in the great human trafficking of the period. Sara Huff remembered that enslaved people were shipped out of the South to "overseas" countries where human bondage continued, out of the fear that Confederate defeat might end that institution in the United States. Persons in bondage from this Crawford's Atlanta market even went the opposite of "sold South" to become exports to Virginia, which had previously served as the great source of enforced labor for the Deep South. They even became workers in Confederate munition works in Raleigh, North Carolina, and Richmond, Virginia, that supplied the armies fighting to keep them in bondage. Months after Atlanta fell to the Union, the same local newspapers that reported the surrenders of the Confederate armies and the capture of Confederate President Jefferson Davis continued to carry advertising offering African Americans for sale.[39]

Residents and refugees needed to convert their inflated currency into commodities such as enslaved people and gold. Crawford, Frazer & Company, as an auction house whose primary offering was enslaved people, came to sell seemingly everything except groceries and munitions. The company's offerings even included medicines and fully furnished mansions, and livestock, on the hoof and butchered.

Lee had to procure food for the garrison and its munitions workers, presumably as an officer of the Quartermaster Corps, amidst the shortages in the overcrowded city and the failing transportation network. Atlanta had a problem with area farmers and ranchers not bringing in their products from fear of seizure by the government and even of impressment of wagons and the conscription of the farmers into the army, what with inadequate and mismanaged railroads making the situation worse. In February 1863, Crawford briefly found himself arrested for cattle rustling. Unable to supply the Confederate hospitals with beef as per his company's contract, he had seized cattle for the government under the orders of George W. Lee, who had even provided Crawford with an armed escort. In March, the Fulton County court had the case dismissed.[40]

Historian Steven M. Stowe wrote of this "warfare's two twins, loss and possibility."[41] The common soldiers serving on both sides knew the former well. Many of their number, including Lee's company, marched off to war for a world where they imagined that they were creating a new nation where, among other advantages, they would not have to compete with African Americans for land and jobs. Many of them wanted no part of dehumanizing institutionalized labor whether factory or plantation. Their societal struggle would continue in all parts of America to the present. They often lost their land because of the problems caused by the war and often became sharecroppers, another form of bondage labor. Ironically, some of the former enslaved acquired land, including under the 1862 Homestead Act dispersing federal lands, even in several of the former Confederate states such as Alabama, Florida, and Mississippi, while the 1862 federal Homestead law did not allow Confederate families essentially free grants to this public land until late 1875.[42]

Confederate officers, government officials, and persons falling into certain other categories were also declared by Congress as insurrectionaries under the new Fourteenth Amendment and could not vote without obtaining pardons from their respective governors. They were not insurrectionists, however, as, whatever else defines the Confederate States of America, it was not an effort to subvert the Constitution or overthrow the government of the United States. The seceding states did not form any conspiracy until after they had left the United States, which the Constitution did not forbid. Ironically, opposing an individual state's secession would have been an insurrection against the state government. George W. Lee did not apply for a pardon, likely because he had no political ambitions. President Andrew Johnson, by proclamation of December 25, 1868, restored the rights of Lee and almost all the former Confederate officers and officials.

The enthusiasts of the independent Southern nation also marched off to war with dreams of a traditional, short, heroic war. Beginning with the battle of Shiloh, where more Americans died in two days in battle than in all the nation's previous wars, this conflict became a modern industrial-scale slaughter of hundreds of thousands of human beings, turning individual adventure into fear and a horror of unimaginable size that included becoming forgotten in the greater horror.

Where war had been heroic, now it was reduced to modern war as chiefly a sanitation problem and statistics, as happened to Lee's 38th Georgia and so many other regiments on battle. Historian Peter S. Carmichael wrote of the soldiers' failure to find moral certitude in the war. "Acts deemed criminal in the civilian world suddenly seemed just, necessary, and essential to survival."[43] The randomness of death challenged faith in God.

The Confederate disasters in the Gettysburg, Jackson, Middle Tennessee, Port Hudson, and Vicksburg campaigns happened in July 1863, as did the end of the prisoner exchange, making the cause of the independence of the Southern nation seem even more hopeless.

The Confederate military's hopes rested on using its outnumbered, poorly supplied, and often ineptly managed forces to block the divided, often delayed, and poorly coordinated federal advance. Chattanooga had been the key, as unlike

Atlanta, Nashville, and Vicksburg, under Confederate control it was not easily cut off or besieged. Confederate General Braxton Bragg gave it up, however, without a fight. After the battle of Chickamauga, he besieged the federal forces there, but General Ulysses S. Grant broke Bragg's forces on November 23–26, 1863. The western armies of the United States could now concentrate for a campaign to take Atlanta, Georgia, and, ultimately, the Carolinas out of the war, essentially all that the Confederate States of America had left. Many Georgians intended to cooperate rather than oppose the pending federal advance, including profiteer supporters of the Union. Sherman had a map of Macon color-coded with the politics of individual residents.

The disintegration of the Confederate armies continued to accelerate from further losses of the living, not just the dead. Wives had to obtain passes to visit their soldier husbands, or the men had to receive leave, just as African Americans had to do on plantations. Food, labor, and living conditions in the Confederate army, even without considering the disease and fighting, fell below the conditions typical of that of African American labor in bondage. Officers treated soldiers as if they were enslaved African Americans, and the Confederate soldiers also received little or no pay.

The plantation economy consumed the lives and property of the South to lose a war that it financed. After the Confederate armies and government finally disappeared, federal soldiers spread across the South to seize cotton to help to pay the cost of war to end the slavery that produced that all-important crop. As a system of political and social power, however, cotton survived to become so powerful as to be the most valuable United States export until 1937. The cotton economy which created a war to protect its cheap labor and the wealth it generated, would become the last survivor of that conflict.[44]

Chapter Six

Sherman (and History) vs. George W. Lee

PROVOST MARSHAL MAJOR George W. Lee, partly because of cuts to his staff, finally resigned from his position(s) in Atlanta in the summer of 1863. He had to make difficult decisions about his future at a time when Confederate Georgia needed him most, but also as his cause for an independent Southern nation truly became lost. In Atlanta, a newspaper editor wrote that he regretted that Lee had left his command in Atlanta where "by his uniform courtesy he has made a host of friends."[1] Without Lee and his men, crime in Atlanta soared with help from miscreants on the city's small police force. One former resident would celebrate the city's fall to Sherman as the end to the rampant corruption, speculation, and thievery.[2]

Colonel Moses Wright was now in complete command but without Lee and his troops. Overwhelmed by the situation, he pleaded for the transfer of his new, expanded, responsibilities to someone else.[3] An editor of Atlanta's *Southern Confederacy* wrote that Lee had been replaced with two provost marshals and their job largely consisted of writing permits for special friends to sell bad liquor. The city's defenders, its "fighting population," now consisted only of officers living at the hotels, enlisted men in the hospitals, enrolling/enlistment officers, and 14 quartermasters. Officials shot at each other, "died game," and were quickly forgotten.[4]

Because of the circumstances that led to his resignation, and his poor health, George Washington Lee had every reason just to walk away from the war as hundreds of thousands of Americans, found on all sides, had already done, inside or outside of the law. He could do so legally because of his tuberculosis. Despite all that he had been through and the fact that he owned no one, Lee had remained loyal to the Confederate nation in action and spirit, and he had served it faithfully despite threats of different kinds to his health and life. Writer Henry David Thoreau famously wrote of people in his time living lives of quiet desperation and, in 1860, Americans had two great fears, death and not being able to support their families. Millions of men, like those who followed George W. Lee, marched off to war, however, where they risked both.

Lee and anyone else who could read a map could see the fate of Atlanta and the Confederate States of America. The city's only real defense was distance and that now crumbled. The federal capture of Chattanooga allowed for invasion from Tennessee

Federal Provost Marshal issuing passes to persons evacuating Atlanta (*Frank Leslie's Illustrated Newspaper*, October 29, 1864).

on the north with large forces that could maneuver past Rocky Face Ridge (Georgia's "Gibraltar") and Dalton near Chattanooga. Capturing the Western & Atlantic Railroad as a supply line as they marched, allowed Sherman's armies to reach the Gate City of Atlanta and to pass through it to all that remained of the Southern nation, ending even hopes of a victory from Union war weariness. The United States Military Railroad repaired and maintained railroads for the federal advance, even at times building its own locomotives! Lee must have been envious.[5]

Confederate failure at Pensacola and Shiloh contributed to the federal success at New Orleans and later Vicksburg, recovering the Mississippi Valley for trade to the world in Midwestern food and Southern cotton for the United States. The seceding states still might have won the war through the Northern ballot box with the destruction of a federal army at Chickamauga, Manassas, Gettysburg, Perryville, or Stone's River, by that the South could sustain its war effort indefinitely by defeating the expensive armies paid for by the United States taxpayer to the profit of big Northern capitalists. Abraham Lincoln believed, on the eve of the presidential election of 1864, that he would be voted out of office, even without a great Confederate success.

Such a complete Southern victory never came, dashing the hopes of even the staunchest supporters of the Confederate States of America. Federal successes opened the way to Chattanooga and Atlanta, on the way to final federal victory. General Robert E. Lee and his ragged, long-suffering, starving soldiers would defend Richmond until little else remained of the Confederate States of America, but to no avail when Atlanta fell and most of the interior was overrun. Jefferson Davis failed to successfully replace Bragg as commander in the West with a successful alternative.

In the spring and summer of 1864, Sherman's armies fought and marched past that last real obstacle at Dalton. The Union military had seemingly endless resources and advanced relentlessly, if sometimes blindly and ineptly, as in the Chickamauga, Red River, and Stone's River campaigns.[6] The Confederacy made the classic mistake of a nation needing to fight a hit-and-run war, forced but trying to hold undefendable places like Atlanta, Dalton, and Vicksburg against overwhelming might with fixed defenses.

Support for the Confederate nation and the war continued to decline. Many Southerners, even whites, could see the federal army as liberators, rather than invaders, from the negative effects of a war most of them never supported. After the first 18 months, both armies had serious problems replacing men in what European observers called mass slaughter by armed mobs. Draft evaders and deserters would organize and, by whatever means, try to survive by avoiding military service.

Fighting this erosion of the military's manpower became a way for the ailing George W. Lee to stay in the war. On September 8, 1863, he joined the Conscript Bureau and announced that he and his remaining men would set out to restore order across South Georgia by arresting deserters and stopping insurrection wherever he found it. To that end, he had the full support of the Confederate and the state government. Lee created 20 home guard companies of non-conscript boys and men otherwise found unfit for field service. Such units originated both in the traditional homeland security in times of war and in the pre-war patrols and urban night watch that hunted African Americans who violated curfews or tried to escape to the "free" states in the North, or to Canada or Mexico.

Some scholars also credit the slave patrols as the structural foundation of the post–Civil War Ku Klux Klan. (Lee made no statement about African Americans, although he was criticized for his leniency for Black Atlantans concerning the city's curfew.) The Confederate Conscript Bureau would use such locally raised existing units or officers.[7] The last Confederate draft law, February 17, 1864, allowed men 17 to 18 and 45 to 50 to serve in state defense forces who could enforce the draft law and arrest deserters. These units were supplemented by partisan ranger units created by the Confederate Act of 1862 that allowed soldiers to enlist to serve only within their respective states.[8]

The home guard military units had a reputation for brutality and robbery. Critics described these "soldiers" as deserters, murderers, and thieves whose actions Governor Brown sanctioned because he needed someone to arrest the other deserters and draft evaders. They seized cattle, horses, mules, supplies, and wagons officially for the Confederate government, although these confiscated goods sometimes, reportedly, either did not reach the army because of the inefficiency of the government bureaucracy or because of theft by members of the home guard themselves. Sherman's federal soldiers would march across Georgia supplied from Confederate stockpiles at local railroad stations that waited for trains which never came.[9]

Lee's new command likely included, for Georgia, the one company created in each respective congressional district for the Confederate Conscript Bureau to arrest draft evaders and deserters while impressing horses and other property for the military. Complete records for those men have not survived. The company of Captain Benjamin F. Jordan, who operated in Cherokee, Gilmer, and Pickens counties, had a reputation for murder and robbery and for success in partisan warfare. Jordan reportedly kept a book containing the names of 125 men he killed or had killed.[10]

Lee now had to avert another civil war within the greater conflict. As early as 1862, reports appeared that a Worth County lynch mob, including a local sheriff, hanged an old man with sons in the service and the man's 13-year-old son for harboring deserters. In the anti-war violence on the Florida border, draft resisters reportedly decapitated a conscript officer and left his corpse for the vultures.[11] By the end of 1863, approximately 1,000 to 1,500 deserters hid in fortified compounds on Blackjack Island and elsewhere in the vast natural refuge of the Okefenokee Swamp, in southeast Georgia and on the Florida border, that had once protected Seminole Indians from removal to the West. Some observers decried such reports as paranoia and more a plea for military expenditures in one of the poorest parts of the South. By February 1865, however, the same gang had raided the town of Blackshear, near the swamp, seven times.

Lee still commanded the 12 companies (683 men) remaining in his 25th Georgia Provost Guard Battalion until it was officially disbanded on June 24, 1864. In November 1863, Lee began a four-month campaign with his Provost Battalion through the South Georgia counties of Appling, Coffee, Houston, Irwin, Telfair, Ware, and Wilcox that netted only between 50 and 100 Confederate deserters, and no escaped African Americans or federal deserters. Overall, Lee and his men found only 20 fugitives from the army in the great swamp, although they did kill three men in a skirmish. By contrast, his North Georgia campaigns had netted 600 deserters, 53 men charged as collaborators, and 500 new "volunteers" for the army.[12]

Lee's lack of success in South Georgia may have come from exaggerated numbers of miscreants or the ease with which draft evaders and deserters could escape to the federal navy along the coast. He moved his battalion to the Florida border to defend Georgia against a threatened federal invasion that failed to materialize. Such a raid, if it had taken place and had reached the Confederate Prison Camp Sumter, near Americus, Georgia, better known as Andersonville, could have released more than 30,000 desperate prisoners of war deep inside Georgia. Brigadier General John H. Winder, commandant of the prison, believed that even the local people conspired to release the prisoners, in the belief that if they helped in the escape the Union civilians, sailors, and soldiers there would not harm their families and property. Lee took advantage of his time in South Georgia to sweep the region for men avoiding military service.[13]

Reports continued of crisis in Florida, however. In August 1864, rumors had 500 deserters, draft dodgers, self-liberated African Americans, and unionists banded together in central Florida to march on that state's Gainesville to gather deserters and escaped African Americans in the swamps and woods of several Florida counties. Similar bands also roamed the northern half of Alabama, encouraged by the federal occupation of the Tennessee River Valley.[14]

Lee led his soldiers when, as with everything else, hope seemed in short supply within the declining Confederacy. General Sherman, in leading his invasion of Georgia, ordered his men to give preference to seizing horses, mules, and wagons from the wealthy. He wrongly imagined that the collective impressment of animals, food, and supplies of the great majority of the poorer farmers would lead to public pressure to take Georgia out of the war. These people had proven unable to stop Georgia from leaving the Union and now suffered collective punishment for having no means of taking it out of the war! More Georgians deserted from the army or opposed the war but to no avail.

Nations have long used starvation as a weapon against the public since civilization began. That strategy fails because the enemy government and its military go on despite the sufferings of the general population. The army, the cause, the nation, etc., become oblivious to the opinions and sacrifices of the people, even without a rational hope of victory.[15]

In Atlanta, during the record cold winter of 1863–1864, even firewood had become a scarce commodity because of the incessant needs of the factories and foundries. Wealthy citizens brought livestock into their homes to protect the animals from the weather and their hungry neighbors.

In Georgia, overall, Confederate impressments took far more property from the public than was done later by federal forces, including even that pillaged by the famed "bummers" (vandals) of Sherman's army. Farmers ceased bringing food into the city to keep it from being seized by the military for possible eventual payment in worthless Confederate currency. Atlanta's pre-war economy had depended, in part, upon these teamsters and their truck farming, and would again after the war well into the 20th century.[16]

Despite the desperate circumstances, George W. Lee withdrew again from field service because of his recurring health problems. He delayed leaving because he had struggled so long to keep a command together. On June 3, 1864, while in Atlanta, he gave up his last field commission in the Confederate army. Three weeks later, Secretary of War Seddon ordered his 25th Georgia Provost Guard Battalion disbanded, with the men, according to age, transferred to the 5th Georgia Confederate Infantry Regiment, the 1st Georgia Infantry Battalion, and the state reserves.

As early as December 1862, a report from the Conscript Bureau had described Lee's men as unfit for service due to old wounds. Company A and, sometimes, the whole battalion had come to be known as "broken-legged" because so many of these men had been permanently crippled in the regular service during the Virginia campaigns earlier in the war. Contrary to critics' claims, these men, led by the constantly ill Lee, had given their full share to the cause of secession, and then returned to give the Confederate nation more even though their nation steadily slid into oblivion.[17]

Lee returned soon after, however, and he finally led men in battle against the Union army! Since the spring of 1863, he had published pronouncements that called for the public to prepare for repelling a federal invasion. At that time, he had the responsibility for gathering all unassigned arms in Atlanta and elsewhere. As early as late December 1863, Georgia conducted a census of all males who could still serve in a militia against the approaching enemy armies.[18] Even women formed a militia company called the Nancy Harts for defense.[19]

Plans to fortify Atlanta began in earnest after Streight's raid in nearby Alabama in May 1863. (Lee held Colonel Abel D. Streight and his officers as prisoners in Atlanta until he transferred them to Richmond.)[20] By October 30, 1863, Maine-born Atlantan Captain Lemuel P. Grant of the Confederate engineers used enslaved labor to build 17 redoubts and 12 miles of trenches to defend Atlanta, part of the Confederacy's plans to fortify its remaining cities following the fall of Vicksburg on July 4, 1863. This effort symbolized the Confederacy's declining military fortunes as that meant that the Southern nation might have no better options left than expending more lives and resources in a hopeless defense of its besieged cities as it starved into surrender.[21]

Atlanta and Georgia had geography and modern communications as a defense, however. Mississippi had a railroad network in the Confederacy second only to Virginia. That state and Tennessee had been the war in the West, with Mississippi ravaged by both armies. Alabama had then become a barrier that protected Georgia from the west, as had the fighting in Tennessee to the North because the state's transportation network could not support a huge federal war effort. Alabama had the most extensive river network in America, but the rivers there went contrary to federal military needs, and Mobile blocked any use of most of the rivers for purposes of invasion.

Federal victories in the Civil War West and growing resources of all types, however, made a successful, fully supplied invasion of Georgia from Chattanooga possible with Atlanta as the primary target but only with a single long supply line, the Western & Atlantic Railroad. Starting in May 1864, federal armies in Tennessee marched on the Gate City of Atlanta as the population swelled with even more frightened and desperate refugees. Sherman's armies consumed 100 railroad cars of supplies per day but the people of North Georgia and in the Atlanta area, long-suffering from Confederate impressments and tax-in-kind during a devastating drought, now found themselves robbed of what little they had left by men from both armies. Federal officers complained that while they ordered men to help and protect only civilians, their soldiers even robbed their own army![22]

Historian James Robertson wrote that Atlanta became the turning point of the war because Jefferson Davis believed that the Confederacy would survive if it kept the fighting confined to somewhere to the North and West of the Gate City. Davis believed that the Confederacy could wait out the war in some rump version of its original nation if that city and the great industrial center of Richmond remained in Confederate hands. Fearing the horrors of bombardment and siege as had happened to Vicksburg, most of Atlanta's resettled refugees and residents fled. Some 1,000 families of 4,000 desperate people who had nowhere to go remained behind, however, fed and otherwise supported by the besieged Confederate army, and with all supplied by the city's remaining east, south, and west railroad connections that were not cut.[23]

A writer for an Atlanta newspaper believed that George W. Lee would now receive a commission as a brigadier general to command one of the two brigades of state troops and militia. On April 4, 1864, Governor Brown only made him a colonel and aide-de-camp. State Adjutant General Henry Wayne, however, referred to Lee only as a major who could call out the cadets from the Georgia Military Institute in an emergency. At Roswell, Georgia, just north of Atlanta, in fact, Lee commanded 400 militiamen and scouts at Island Ford and Shallowford on the Chattahoochee River. With four pieces of artillery, these boys, crippled veterans, and old men acted like the legendary Horiatis at the gate in Ancient Rome as they guarded a single bridge that would have given the federal army an otherwise unimpeded march into Atlanta. Any defense, even Lee's small band, made a difference just by their presence as the federal army of tens of thousands of men moved against the city. (Historian Albert Castel counted six times the federal armies could have taken Atlanta by just continuing to push forward.) An estimated federal force of 2,000 cavalrymen, passed through nearby Pickens County and stopped at Ball Ground, presumably intending to destroy the textile mills in nearby Roswell.[24]

The governor ordered the Georgia militia to gather at Camp Rescue, established near Macon. From there, Colonel George W. Lee dispatched 6,550 men to help defend Atlanta. When enemy cavalry threatened central Georgia, Lee gathered 500 men, with arms but no ammunition, whom he dispatched to protect the State Capitol of Milledgeville. He sent 445 armed men fit for duty, each armed and carrying fifteen rounds, to relieve the guards watching the federal officers held as prisoners at Camp Oglethorpe in Macon following escapes from that former fairground turned prison.

Before that time, Lee had just missed leading troops into battle against the federal armies but he now, finally, had his chance to do just that. Under General Howell Cobb, he commanded four militia regiments to defend Macon on July 30, 1864. On that day, he took two regiments east of the Ocmulgee Indian Mounds and southeast of Fort Hawkins, on the Garrison Road east of the Ocmulgee River from Macon. He led these men from the front line in repulsing federal General George Stoneman's cavalry charges. The press specifically cited his bravery amidst the danger and heat.[25]

Lee again came under suspicion, however. Adjutant General Wayne criticized him for leaving Milledgeville without Wayne's permission, to which he replied that he left by order of the governor to deal with a sudden emergency. Claims flew that Lee issued fraudulent passes to militiamen during the crisis. Despite the deteriorating military situation in the state at that time, he received a lengthy trial with numerous witnesses. On September 18, 1864, the court found that the illegal sale of exemptions from service had occurred, but it acquitted Lee and his subordinates of any involvement in that fraud.[26]

George W. Lee continued to work for the state of Georgia in other positions. On November 19, as enemy armies moved across the state's interior, Lee became the engineer for the train that carried Georgia's archives and other state property from Milledgeville to safety in Columbia, South Carolina. Unfortunately, the records of the Georgia military that had gone to Macon burned with the building that housed them two days after the federal occupation of that city in April 1865.

Lee received orders from Governor Brown on November 19 to call in and organize the Georgia militia east of the Oconee River at Augusta. Before he could publish the general orders, President of the State Senate in absentia and acting Major General Ambrose Ransom Wright arrived in Georgia with orders from the Confederate government to take command of the state. He announced that he would command the militia and threatened to arrest Lee. Governor Brown denounced Wright as making an unconstitutional usurpation of power. Before this conflict came to a head, Sherman's armies proceeded to Savannah, cutting Georgia in half.[27]

Upon reaching Augusta with his train, Lee had orders to organize the militia Governor Brown intended to call out. He also had orders to move food stores from Macon to supply the people left by Sherman in the ruined city of Atlanta and victims of the devastation by Sherman's March to the Sea. The colonel acted as the governor's emissary to federal General James H. Wilson in Macon in arranging to have state stores of grain in North Georgia released to starving civilians. Also, for Governor Brown, Lee inspected what remained of the state-owned Western & Atlantic Railroad, now abandoned by the advancing federal armies and for which he filed a detailed report. Brown asked him to prepare a roster of the troops that Georgia had contributed to the Confederate cause, a task that the end of the war prevented him from carrying out.[28]

After a series of bloody battles, Atlanta finally fell to Sherman's troops on September 1, 1864, and the great legends of the Gate City of the Civil War began. The city's fall likely did not itself save the Lincoln presidency, as he would have won the electoral college even had he lost the popular vote. Also contrary to popular legend,

Sherman did not burn down the entire city. The federal bombardment and the destruction of militarily valuable buildings contributed to the damage already done by both armies when soldiers tore down buildings for fortifications. What happened reportedly was severe: "The fire is represented by those who beheld it, to have been terrific and sublime. The city from centre to circumference was enveloped in a sheet of flame, which in the opinion of those who witnessed it, was to have consumed all or nearly all the buildings in the city."[29]

Reportedly 40 percent of the city remained, including one in three houses. The city lost five-sixths of its value in real estate. In the decades that followed, what of antebellum Atlanta that survived fell victim to other fires and, as late as the 1950s, the city's historic buildings of the period were demolished for urban renewal; even the site of the Battle of Atlanta is gone.[30]

Atlanta's population had been largely evacuated north and south, both voluntarily and involuntarily, resulting in some families traveling north of the Ohio River and even abandoning the city forever. Sherman's armies had routinely evacuated or moved civilians north as they progressed across North Georgia. When the textile factories at Roswell and Sweetwater were captured, the workers, including women and children, were sent to a federal prison camp in Louisville, Kentucky. Many people, notably the famous "Roswell women" textile workers never returned home.[31] Among the population sent south to what remained of Confederate Georgia by Sherman, six adult women and 13 children of Lee's extended family left with their belongings packed in one wagon pulled by a single old horse. Sherman and his armies would abandon the ruins of Atlanta and northwest Georgia, leaving its people to become victims of the bandits and the local Confederate home guards and guerrillas.[32]

Federal General George H. Thomas authorized General Steedman to accept the surrender of members of the Confederate home guard, guerrilla, and partisan units, and threatened to make Georgia a wilderness if they did not surrender. When offered captured guerrillas in exchange for Union soldiers in rebel hands, however, Confederate General Nathan Forrest stated that the federals would do him a favor if they would hang any guerrillas they captured.[33] The Georgia Home Guard units largely surrendered at Kingston, Georgia, on March 12, 1865, although their parole records disappeared before the War Department began compiling the Confederate records into personal records. A Confederate soldier described the men of all types, including deserters from the Confederate army, who gave up:

> I saw the moteliest crew I have ever seen before or since. These so-called scouts were strutting around with broad brimmed hats, long hair and jingling spurs. You could see the old "moss back" who had crept out of his cave. You would find groups of sad looking men who had followed Lee, Jackson, Johnston, and Wheeler through the war. Some of them carried the mud and dust of 5 or 6 states on their old clothes.[34]

The last page of General George Thomas's headquarters diary, May 25, 1865, announced that all amnesties to Confederate soldiers and citizens since December

The Atlanta Rolling Mill as depicted in the *Cyclorama of the Battle of Atlanta* (1886) (Kenan Research Center at the Atlanta History Center).

15, 1864, were repudiated and annulled, which may explain why the Kingston paroles have not survived.[35]

General Sherman, in explaining his forced evacuation of civilians from Atlanta and what destruction his army did to the city, justified his orders by arguing that the sooner the war ended, then peace would return and the suffering Atlantans could return to their homes and resume their lives.

Confederate officials, including George W. Lee, did not wait that long. With Sherman's armies gone, Colonel Luther Glenn resumed his position as commandant of Atlanta and, under orders from Major General Howell Cobb, arrested collaborators and Confederate deserters left behind by Sherman. Judge E.A. Nesbit tried people "under suspicion of treason." Lee returned to Atlanta by December 20, 1864, as one of the first people to reach the devastated city. Sherman had erected a fort from the city's ruins on the city's high ground, large enough to defend an occupation garrison of 10,000 men. The general ultimately decided to abandon the fort. Without its all-important railroads supplying the Confederate military, Atlanta had nothing left to defend but ruins.[36]

Sherman's legions had marched to Savannah and the Carolinas or returned to Tennessee, proving that the Confederate armies in the West had all but ceased to exist as any effective military force. Like the Confederacy, Atlanta had passed

Ruins of the Atlanta Rolling Mill, destroyed during the Confederate retreat from Atlanta (depicted in the movie *Gone with the Wind*) (Library of Congress).

from a state of war, to siege, to an extreme victim of violence, as four major battles had raged around the city. Lee helped restore order during this second Confederate occupation of his city as the flag of the Southern nation came down everywhere else. George W. Lee, the first Confederate soldier, became one of the last.

Modern author and journalist Chris Hedges has pointed out, "Von Clausewitz is wrong; war is not the continuation of politics by other means; war is about the destruction of all living systems—economics, living, familial, social, communal."[37] Reconstruction, however, often is not building back something better, rather for the entire United States, the war would continue to be a drag on the nation until the 1880s, and to some extent well into the 20th century. The Southern defeat came to make the sacrifices of Lee and many other Southerners in vain as the people of the South went from being a new nation to only individuals and families, of both races, fighting for survival. Governor Brown ordered him and his last command to set out to recover the lost and stolen property of the Western & Atlantic Railroad "with his accustomed energy."

Lee discovered that the local people had stolen anything they could, including metal. He worked with Captain Henry P. Farrow of the Niter and Mining Bureau to restore the Western & Atlantic Railroad to aid the starving families in North Georgia. Farrow used the opportunity to trade provisions to the local people on behalf of the Confederate government in exchange for the tons of lead, iron, and copper that littered the region's many battlefields. (Likely accounting for so much metal missing from the battlefields today.) Colonel Luther J. Glenn rounded up Atlanta's previously exempt railroad workers, now without jobs, and anyone else who might qualify to serve in a Confederate army that would soon, altogether, cease to exist.[38]

The people in Atlanta, too poor to leave, not forced out under General Sherman's evacuation order, or who chose not to go, formed an unofficial provisional government and vigilante police force. Ironically, many of these citizens now lived in the homes of and pillaged the abandoned property of the absent entrepreneurs who had taken advantage of them throughout the war.

Selling civilian and public property from the ruins became a vast and profitable new business in Atlanta. Some of these *ad hoc* entrepreneurs hobbled together pieces of wrecked houses to rent as residences on property they did not own. Residents and people from the countryside, including children, took the opportunity of the change in armies of occupation to load up and take away hundreds of wagonloads of anything of value, such as scrap metal.[39]

In the last days of the Civil War, the federal armies occupied the South and struggled to end civil violence and crime. The soldiers seized hundreds of bales of cotton, for which the owners seldom, if ever, received compensation. Until 1869, the federal government continued to tax cotton produced to pay for the war.[40]

The Confederate States of America had become only its armies and by April 1865, only one army mattered, that of Robert E. Lee in Virginia. When it surrendered, the Southern nation spun off into legend. Many people, however, believed that the surrenders of the armies in the spring of 1865 were only an agreement to end the war, not an end to the Southern nation, emancipation, or the relationship of the states that had seceded from how they were before the war. They could envision that they had won the right to guarantee the pre–1860 status quo. This mistaken idea became the basis for the later "Lost Cause" and the "South was Right" mentality and myth.[41]

The same Atlanta newspapers that announced the surrenders of Confederate armies and the capture of Jefferson Davis still carried advertisements for sales of African Americans. Human bondage continued and only ended when the United States Army's occupation forces allowed African Americans to kill it, and with the final ratification of the Thirteenth Amendment in 1868. Even after general emancipation, the formerly enslaved could still find themselves held in bondage or kidnapped and transported to in other lands that still had slavery.[42]

When the truth finally set in, many Southerners could not bear the defeat. Edward Ruffin of Virginia, a public advocate for slavery and the Southern nation who claimed to have fired the first shot of the war, for example, wrapped himself in a Confederate flag and committed suicide by bullet. Other whites from the South moved to England or the Northern states to become "Confederate carpetbaggers" or *ex parte* from the Old South. Some southerners moved to Brazil, Cuba, Honduras, or elsewhere.[43]

Lee sought opportunities closer to home, although his Gate City was in ruins.

Visitors to Atlanta's burned-out business district used such words as "demoralized," "cheerless," "mean-looking," and "cheap looking" to describe the city and its inhabitants. The cost of coal had forced the shutdown of the city's gas streetlights in April 1864. They did not burn again until 1866. Vandals had even destroyed fences and torn up shrubbery. Rumors circulated in Atlanta that criminals roamed the streets at night, murdering and robbing visitors.[44]

If anyone saw Atlanta's destruction as a Biblical judgment against its past connections to cotton and bondage, its entrepreneurial class failed to get that message. Business soon boomed on every level as the city ceased wasting its assets on the war. The fighting left Atlanta in ruins, but, like the genies in *1,001 Arabian Nights*, the city's economy acted like a demon that could suffer containment for a time but not death. Travel writer Sidney Andrews, among others, noted that in 1866 Atlanta already did more business than Augusta and Macon combined and had 30 percent more commerce immediately after than it did before the war. Visitors found navigating the piles of building materials and new construction more of a problem than the ruins. Atlanta developed a serious problem with brick thieves. Georgians gathered the bones of animals killed in the area's numerous battles for sale as fertilizer.[45]

Historian Martin Ruef has described postwar Atlanta as the prototype of the city of a New South, quadrupling its population in just a few years and with an increasingly diversified economy that supported 300 businesses in 1870 and 900 in 1880. A city comparable to the urban growth of other American cities in the Mid-West and West. George W. Lee proved a part of a successful revolution—not the Confederacy, but an Atlanta dominated by his middle class of entrepreneurs, although that came after his death.[46]

This dynamic economic growth would continue into the present as symbolized not only by the city's phoenix symbol replacing a locomotive, its motto "resurges," the Atlanta Compromise, and the claim of being too busy to hate, but also by the ironic loss of almost all that remained of Civil War Atlanta to expansion and urban renewal in the century that followed.

The people connected to George Washington Lee's story led as complicated lives after the war as during it. Joseph E. Brown, for example, would join the Republican Party. With the failure of Reconstruction, he returned to the Democratic Party and ruled Georgia as a member of the "Bourbon Triumvirate" for 18 years. As with Crawford and Lee, he worked to develop opportunities for North Georgia. Spy James George Brown lived Gilmer County in North Georgia after the war but died in 1867 while failing to obtain money he claimed, likely falsely, to have been owed to him for his intelligence work. A mob murdered the previously mentioned Georgia Unionist George W. Ashburn in Columbus, Georgia, as the first such victim of Ku Klux Klan violence in Georgia on March 30, 1868. He very actively and vocally supported African American rights. Restricted African American labor moved to a form of Apartheid and did not begin to end until the post–World II mechanization of cotton, sugar, and other plantation crops. Ending the related racist Jim Crow laws would follow in the decades afterwards.⁴⁷

Lee's acquaintance, conman and slave trader Robert A. Crawford, tried to work with the federal Bureau of Refugees, Freedmen, and Abandoned Lands to continue to control the African Americans he still held, he said for their benefit. He did apply for a pardon, claiming to need one not because he had been a lieutenant in the Confederate army (true) but because, he had been a colonel of a Third Georgia (false). His widow would later be unable to prove his service to receive a pension from the state of Georgia because she did not have the correct information, only his delusions and lies.

Crawford became one of the "Confederate carpetbaggers," people from the South trying to succeed in the postwar United States.⁴⁸ He became associated with the greatest dubious characters of prominence in Georgia, and he sold shares in railroads in Georgia and New York where he represented himself as president of railroads that, in fact, only existed on paper. Self-promoting himself as a lawyer and minerologist, he also peddled mining interests in an era of fraud that has since been called the "Era of Good Stealing" and "Gilded Age" that contributed to the United States' economic Panic of 1873.

Nationally he drew attention for calling for reparations for the Confederate debts as a means of rebuilding the South and by his supporting President U.S. Grant's failed attempt to be elected to a third term as president, while falsely claiming to have lost various plantations during the war.⁴⁹ He died a much-respected promoter of North Georgia while on a business trip in Atlanta on April 14, 1892. His descendants heard stories of his better days, of lavish wine parties and a chest of gold coins, but he left his last wife and several children impoverished.⁵⁰

Post-war photograph of George W. Lee taken in New York (Lee/Huss Family Papers, AC 69-249, Georgia Archives, Morrow).

George Washington Lee stayed in Georgia, except for one largely unknown trip to New York. No matter how often he failed at it, he never stopped chasing success as an entrepreneur. He weaved his way through Reconstruction and the New South much as he had before the war as a dreamer who went from one failure to the next in a world where cheap labor, cotton, and race mattered no less than before the war. A eulogy of Lee recalled that he "retained pleasant recollections of the friendships formed during the dark days of the War Between the States."[51] He undoubtedly used those connections to try to rebuild his life in the same ways—and with the same lack of success—as before the war in emerging Atlanta as the Gate City in Reconstruction again became a grand dream of a bright future.

Lee took advantage of any opportunity. He presided over a committee of fellow lumbermen who attempted to stabilize local wood prices. A credit reporter wrote that Lee had extensive real estate acquired during the war, and his buildings had survived, providing him the capital to open two stores from which he lived off the rent.[52]

The former first Confederate did invest in Reconstruction Atlanta, but gambles defeated him. G.W. Lee & Company took over a foundry from B. Schofield and purchased lot 79 on Marietta Street in 1863 for $23,000. The company became Atlanta's Gate City Foundry, Car Manufacturing, and Machine Works late in 1865. A year later, a new partner bought into the company for $10,000. As the Empire Manufacturing Company, it set out to meet the growing need for railroad rolling stock. When the partners sold the property in 1868, however, it brought only $220.[53]

Lee hunted for success across Northwest Georgia but did not find it. In 1866, he operated the Orme Hall, a theater in Atlanta, before moving back to Stone Mountain to become a partner in a distillery. In 1867, creditors foreclosed on the property in Atlanta that he still held and that of his brother Mark. In 1866–1867, he resided in Stone Mountain, although he frequently stayed at the American Hotel while doing business in the new city, reconstructed in more than one way. Later, he lived in Rome, where he helped to organize the city's fire department. He moved to Cartersville, where he and his partners leased the Cartersville Foundry and Machine Shop and the Bartow House Hotel. There he would have at least become reacquainted with Robert A. Crawford and, likely, shared business ventures.[54]

With his associates, Lee filed a patent for the Lee, Fontaine, & Harris railroad switch in 1870. Asa L. Harris, a Vermont-born "carpetbagger" from Ohio but now the Georgia House of Representatives clerk under Reconstruction, fraudulently sold the rights to the invention to the Western & Atlantic Railroad for $2,760 without his partners' knowledge. A government investigation revealed that Lee made no money from the "Harris Railway Switch Swindle." Martin H. Dooly, an employee of the line and associate with Governor Brown, testified of the switch "that any experienced railroad mechanic could see it was worthless." The auditors rejected Lee's claim for $1,400 for a steam engine but did allow him $625 for building a pump. That money, however, likely went to his creditor, the Georgia Loan & Trust Company.[55]

Also in 1870, a census taker found Lee in Bartow County and recorded him as a railroad engineer for a new line, with real estate worth $1,000 and personal belongings valued at $300. By then, he and his wife had taken in a blind African American woman and her 15-year-old daughter as servants. That year for the Lee family. At least one of his parents died. That April, his daughter and only child, Indiana "Anna" F. Lee, married Joseph Robert Rawlins in Bartow County. Rawlins had served under Lee in the 25th Georgia Provost Battalion. The Rawlinses had at least five children. Through their daughters, Kathron Stewart (later Mrs. William K. Howard) and Myrtle Burkett (later Mrs. Arthur Johnson), Colonel Lee has descendants today.[56]

During the 1870s, George W. Lee traveled to New York, likely involving the sale of Georgia railroad bonds promoted on Wall Street by people like Robert A. Crawford then, and had his photograph made. In Atlanta by 1872, he became a partner in the Steam Road Wagon Company, a business that built steam-powered vehicles for public roads. In 1873, however, Atlanta gave him $20.25 as a destitute citizen. Three years later, an Atlanta newspaper described him as an earnest and successful entrepreneur in Stone Mountain. By 1878, however, he had lost most, if not all, of his property, and he managed only a third rate-boarding house in Atlanta.[57]

Not everyone did badly in early Atlanta. Samuel Dexter Niles, an Atlantan even less remembered than Lee, makes for a relevant comparison as he had a parallel but different experience. He was born in Auburn, New Hampshire, on October 22, 1829, but was a resident of Orford. He moved to "Ironton," Georgia, by December 1854 and Indian Springs by 1857.[58] By 1860, he taught the classics in a school for young women in Atlanta. His home and school burned in 1861. Niles was also an agent for the Southern Insurance Agency and, in 1862, a partner in Gaar, Niles & Company, that dealt in general merchandise and real estate, and later in Niles & Brother. Both Lee and Niles each owned little property in 1860 but, while Lee was consistent business failure, Niles was described as an "honorable Christian gentleman."[59]

Niles owned five slaves in 1862 and six in 1864, while Sara Huff remembered that he held 300 enslaved people on his plantation for two years that supposedly were shipped to a foreign land such as Brazil or Cuba that still had the institution of slavery. [Lee and his family owned no one, however.] This Yankee was considered "unsound," by a committee on the issue of slavery, but he was not a Unionist and, in his daily newspaper the *Reveille*, he offered hope that the South could still win the war despite the fall of Chattanooga in September 1863. When Georgia was threatened with invasion by federal armies, he was required to serve in Captain S.P. Bassett's Atlanta Press Guards Company of the Third Georgia State Guards Cavalry/Infantry Battalion in Fulton County, under Lieutenant Colonel George Washington Lee, on August 3, 1863. The unit was created for six months duty but was mustered out of existence on February 4, 1864.[60]

Atlanta's post–Civil War rolling mill (*Pioneer Citizens' History of Atlanta*, 1889).

Niles and his wife and daughter were reportedly in Atlanta when it surrendered and burned in the autumn of 1864, but his home was the headquarters of General Joseph E. Johnston on July 7, 1864, when Johnston was relieved of command of the Confederate armies in the West. The house was likely destroyed in the subsequent fighting as it was between the lines of the two besieging armies and under heavy fire.[61] He and his family moved to Reading, Massachusetts, where he was a real estate broker in 1865. Niles made ornamental brackets in 1870, but he had $27,000 in real estate and $10,000 in personal property.[62] He and his family moved back to Atlanta by 1881 and he initially worked as a travel agent. Retired as a member of the firm of Langley & Niles, contractors, he died in Atlanta on November 12, 1907, a well-to-do and much-respected citizen.[63]

The complicated and controversial Atlanta adventure that was the life of George Washington Lee ended on April 3, 1879, in Rome, Georgia. At only age 47, and after months of suffering, George W. Lee finally succumbed to tuberculosis, having survived assassination attempts, battle, and disease during the war. The Methodist Church conducted his funeral, and the local Masonic lodge performed the graveside services. Newspapers at the time across the state reported his passing but made no mention of his wife's surviving him. Remarkably, despite his years of battling tuberculosis, he had outlived almost all his potential critics, including Cyrena Stone (died 1868), James L. Dunning (died 1874), and Braxton Bragg (died 1876).

William Markham, however, lived and only passed away on November 9, 1890, no doubt helping to account for his eulogist's claim that he died without an enemy in the world. (He had outlived most of the people of his generation.) He prospered, as did many of his class of Northern born "carpetbaggers," in rebuilding the city he had claimed to have originally built during the same years when Lee continued to go from one financial embarrassment to another. Despite those spectacular years of fraud, including of the taxpayers, what has been termed nationally as the "era of good stealings," Markham failed to obtain anything from the United States for his claimed losses except for cotton seized after the fighting. He even charged the government $3,750 for General Sherman and his officers occupying his 150-room Washington Hall hotel. He billed the government at the rate of $1,500 per month. Markham's heirs unsuccessfully continued his claims against the United States government, although they did get was a congressional investigation. Federal officials questioned compensation for the property Markham allegedly lost in Civil War Atlanta when he had profited so much from the Confederacy.[64]

George W. Lee lies today in Rome's Myrtle Hill Cemetery with no family members but an infant grandson. Through the efforts of Atlanta history enthusiast David Mitchell, he received a monument in 2012. Because of his being a Confederate soldier and modern political correctness, the grave monument acknowledges little more than he saved the state archives of Georgia. That stone could have recorded so much more.[65]

Just after the war ended, George W. Lee had waited upon former Confederate Vice President Alexander H. Stephens as he passed through Atlanta as a federal prisoner. The guards allowed only minimal conversation. Were Stephens allowed to speak freely, he surely would have reminisced on how he had unintentionally written a eulogy for the Confederate States of America before the new nation even began on November 25, 1860: "revolutions are much easier started than controlled, and the men who begin them, even for the best purposes and objects, seldom end them. The selfish, the ambitious, and the bad will generally take the lead."[66]

Lee, the former provost marshal of Atlanta, would have understood that sentiment better than most. Revolutions begin as conservative movements that become radical under threat, before becoming conservative again as the conflicting forces achieve reconciliation. The Civil War had been what the Southerners rightly called "the Second American Revolution," from 1860 to 1876. Both conflicted governments adopted radical views on race, including emancipation, as a survival tactic. Ultimately, the different states compromised to continue as one nation, including still denying millions of its people many civil rights, and continuing the wealth produced by cotton exports that went to a few in the North and South, the bottom-line issue of the Civil War.

In the aftermath of the war, an argument could be made that the labor issue of the Civil War transcended race. Lee's middle class of white tradesmen was replaced with a homogenized peon labor force of all ages, immigrants, races, sexes, etc., on an industrial scale, all working in the factories, fields, mines, etc., of the whole nation, and not just with discrimination and segregation in the Southern states. Sharecroppers, of all races, after the war experienced that brutal form of "economic

Six. Sherman (and History) vs. George W. Lee

equality." For African Americans their enslavement as individuals became, some critics would argue, replaced with an apartheid enslavement of their race.

According to this argument, the white Southern oligarchs won much of what they sought in the formal war of 1861–1865, except for the preservation of outright human bondage, with race mattered civil violence after the surrender at Appomattox that raged from 1865 to 1876. Their victory came at the cost in blood and property of the poor and middle classes of men like George Lee, whose pre-war ambitions they also defeated. With

Above & right: Site of George W. Lee's grave at Myrtle Hill Cemetery in Rome, Georgia (David Y. Mitchell).

race freed from bondage to become a separate issue, even more whites came to support suppressing African Americans than had supported the Confederate States of America. The distinctions of race moved from a matter of local perception or some genealogical fraction to one drop of "African" blood.

An economic system is an artificial intelligence, not a human intelligence with empathy, foresight, or restraint. The society created by the cotton economy would remain powerful in the South until after 1927 with its traditional suppression of labor rights, violent racism, massive debt, lack of economic innovation, limited educational opportunities, and poverty to serve its narrow ends. King Cotton created a war to protect human bondage and would, with cheap labor, become one of the last survivors of that conflict. The United States fought the war to keep its cotton exports and to supply that material to its factories, regardless of the laborers who produced it.[67]

Yet, some descendants of the Civil War celebrate that conflict for emancipation while others eulogize the Lost Cause and the lost city of Atlanta as "the South was Right!"[68]

In reviewing the time and place in which George Washington Lee lived, a reader can ask if he was a monster, whose actions became more reprehensible as the Confederate war effort failed and the Southern nation became more paranoid and repressive, or did he only do his duty compassionately, fairly, and honestly? Was he complicit, a victim, or both? Whatever conclusion might be reached about him, his career represents support and opposition to the Confederate States of America and the Cotton Kingdom behind it, in black, blue, gray, red, and white.

Modern studies argue that the South lost its bid for national independence and effort to preserve the institution of slavery simply from needing more will to win. Sacrifices by men like this "first Confederate soldier," who with his family owned no one, challenge that claim although the opposition he suppressed spoke otherwise. Despite his recurring consumption, critics, and bureaucratic obstacles that would have proven too daunting and discouraging for other men, Lee fought on. Controversy swirled around him, however, even as many Southerners praised his efforts.

Claims by his critics, especially those made by General Bragg, have received notice while Lee, as often the case with people who saw little need to justify their actions, only offered as much of a defense as the time and when required. In the late 20th century, the rediscovery of the highly partisan and suspect Cyrena Stone "memoir," misrepresented as a diary, resulted in works that have created an impression of George W. Lee as an illiterate, ignorant, Yankee-hating fanatic held in low regard by his superiors. Modern authors questioned, ignored, or made minimal other views of the provost marshal. Lee left little defense for his actions as he could hardly have expected that generations after his death, writers would use a partisan memoir created for a private agenda of hiding fraud and questionable contemporary partisan critics to raise doubts about his actions as a metaphor for some harsh treatment of dissent by typical authoritarian regimes facing defeat.

The ruins of Civil War Atlanta (*Harper's Weekly*, January 7, 1865).

Some scholars have explored doing an honest study of George W. Lee's experiences through a balanced examination of his career, not what Truman Capote would have described as a "non-fiction novel" aimed for political correctness. They found the material too daunting. What can be brought together now explains how ruthless individuals would not allow a man to remain in power when he became an obstacle to their ambitions to profit in a once-in-a-lifetime war. In that environment, Lee could successfully battle crime, dissension, subversion, espionage, and the enemy army, only to lose to jealousies, class, and self-serving opportunists. His fragile health alone provided all the excuse that anyone would have needed to abandon the failing Southern nation. Instead, he continued to the war's end until he remained almost alone in the Confederate States of America.

That George Washington Lee, a member of the Old South's still under-appreciated professional middle class, held no one in bondage but gave so much to the Confederacy rather than opposing it, came from his environment. He and the Atlanta professionals who followed him must have believed that the Confederate States of America would offer white middle-class entrepreneurs and tradesmen like him opportunity not available to them in antebellum America. That idea is completely at odds with the reasons that the enslaved owning planter class intended in creating the Southern nation and which proved a false ideal in the more than a century and a half after the Civil War.

In that context, Lee spent his adult life being a part of, however often unsuccessfully, in the grand entrepreneurial adventure of Atlanta that would continue to seduce and obsess to the modern day, as reflected in its great novels such as Margaret Mitchell's *Gone with the Wind* and Tom Wolfe's *A Man in Full*. He believed that his own, his family's, and his neighbors' future would be tied to the fate of his city and whichever nation it would serve as an economic engine.

Lee and his fellow Atlantans would not make that decision, however. From the peripheral boundaries of the Southern nation, the so-called real "enemy" marched in as the final arbitrator of victory and defeat—and liberation—in the South's great forgotten internal struggle as part of the all-demanding King Cotton against the Southern nation it created.[69]

Appendix A

Rank Held by George Washington Lee

THE INFORMATION GIVEN below is incomplete. Documentation is in the text.

- Gate City Guards, photograph of Lee in uniform as a sergeant, no date
- Fulton Dragoons, trumpeter, May 1860
- Minute Men of Fulton County, member, October 30, 1860
- The 1026th Militia Company, captain, February 6, 1861
- Lee's Volunteers (later the Atlanta Advanced Guards), captain, February 15, 1861
- Company D, First Confederate Infantry Regiment, captain, March 25–August 6, 1861/First Independent Georgia Volunteer Infantry Battalion, major and commander, Spring-Summer 1861
- The 101st Militia Battalion, DeKalb and Fulton Counties, major, March 6, 1862
- The online site Ancestry.com/Ancestrylibrary.com has DeKalb County, Georgia, U.S., Confederate Enlistment Index, 1861–1863, DeKalb County History Center, Decatur, Georgia, and that shows a George W. Lee enlisting in the 8th Georgia Regiment as a private, no date given. The DeKalb County History Center has no such record.
- The 38th Georgia Infantry Regiment (Wright's Legion), private, captain (Company M), major, lieutenant colonel, and colonel, Autumn 1861 through July 15, 1862
- Provost marshal of Atlanta and Assistant Adjutant General, captain, July 23, 1862
- The 25th Georgia Provost Battalion, major and commander, June 25, 1863–June 24, 1864
- Atlanta Fire Battalion, lieutenant colonel, August 1863
- Transferred to the Conscript Bureau, September 8, 1863. He likely commanded and even created local home guard units for the State of Georgia and independent companies of home guards for the Confederate Conscription Bureau.

- The 3rd Infantry Battalion State Georgia State Guards (Six Month Men, same as Atlanta Fire Battalion), major and lieutenant colonel, September 1863–February 1864
- Aide de Camp to Governor Joseph E. Brown, colonel, April 4, 1864

Appendix B

C.C. Hine's Report on Atlanta in 1859

Traveling insurance auditor Charles Cole Hines (1825–1897) of the then Aetna Insurance Company (now part of ACE Property and Casualty Insurance Company), of Hartford, Connecticut, visited Atlanta in late 1859. Reproduced below is his report on the city and his company's business there, reproduced with permission of the ACE Group, 436 Walnut Street WA01C, Philadelphia, PA 19106.

This material was first published as part of "Georgia Cities on the Eve of the Civil War: The Insurance Reports of C.C. Hine," *Atlanta History* 31 (Spring-Summer 1987): 22–38. For related information on the city at that time see *Williams' Atlanta Directory, City, Guide, or Business Mirror* (Atlanta, GA, 1859), available on the Internet, *https://babel.hathitrust.org/cgi/pt?id=emu.10002331152&seq=1*, accessed May 24, 2024; or "Residents of Atlanta, Georgia, 1859–1860," *Georgia Genealogical Magazine* 36 (4) (1996): 285–293. Other such sources include the Fulton County credit reports, Georgia, vol. 13, R.G. Dun & Co. credit report volumes, Baker Library, Harvard Graduate School of Business Administration, Cambridge; "Alien Atlantans in 1864," *Georgia Genealogical Society Quarterly* 24 (Spring 1988): 110; and the 1860 federal census of Fulton County, Georgia, *Eighth Census of the United States (1860)* (National Archives microfilm M653, roll 122), Records of the Bureau of the Census, Record Group (hereafter RG) 29, National Archives and Records Administration, Washington, D.C., on the Internet as part of Familysearch.org, *https://www.familysearch.org/en/united-states/*, accessed May 24, 2024.

Hines found the Atlanta agent, Dr. N.L. Anglin, "energetic and shrewd" and the company doing well. Aetna, however, added a war clause to its policies days after the firing on Fort Sumter and, one month later, closed its operations in the Confederate States of America. Ironically, Hine had compiled a fire insurance report on a city that a few years later would famously burn!

The report uses these abbreviations:

- A or First Class. A building externally fireproof in all particulars. BRICK OR STONE BUILDINGS. Side walls 12 inches at least in thickness, and rising above the roof, without doors, windows or openings therein. Roof of tile, slate or metal; gutters and cornices of brick, stone or metal. Doors and shutters front and rear, covered with metal.

- B or Second Class. Nearly externally fireproof. BRICK OR STONE BUILDINGS. Side walls 12 inches at least in thickness and rising above the roof, without doors, windows or openings therein. Roof of tile, slate or metal. Doors and shutters front and rear, not covered with metal.
- C or Third Class. Ordinary description of brick buildings. BRICK OR STONE BUILDINGS. Cornices and gutters, wood; roof, shingle or composition.
- D or Fourth Class. WOODEN BUILDINGS.

ATLANTA, 5 December 1859.

Population about 11,000 & increasing. *Town thriving* 18 fine business houses and about 100 Dwellings—some fine ones—erected this year. *Streets* narrow, usually 60 ft. Some business sts 40 & 45. *Buildings* above an average grade in appearance, mostly brick with fair proportion of slate & metal roofs & in business blocks some reliable fire walls. *Detached dwellings*, a fair showing. *Frame ranges*, only one on business streets & that is a *hard* one. Nine business stands, with offices and families upstairs ad libitum. *Special Hazards*, 1 steam tannery, 1 Distillery, 2 steam flour mills, 2 steam planning mills, 1 Rolling Mill, 2 Foundries, 1 steam Printing. *Fuel*, wood chiefly, consumption of coal increasing. Winter winds, west & northwest mainly. *Fires*, In 1855 a brick block consisting of a Hotel & 4 stores also 5 wooden stores. In 1857 Frame block of 5 stores. The recent fires of November 1859 you are probably posted concerning. *Fire organization*, 3 good Engines with Companies of say 50 members each. Three Hose Cos. A Hook & Ladder about organizing. Supply of Hose scanty but $700 recently appropriated for replenishing. *Water*, supply deficient for size of town, good many public cisterns, but not well filled. *Competition*, Hartford, Phoenix, Connecticut, City of Hartford, Merchants, N. American, Girard & Southern Mutual all in hands of Dr. Angier. Continental, Security, Citizens, Market, Springfield, Charter Oak, Knickerbocker, Quaker City, Alabama, Augusta & State. 19. The Cos. underbid scandalously. *Cargo insurance*, frequent inquiry *but no Co. doing it!* We could probably secure a good business. I would recommend that an inland outfit & instructions be sent on at once.

List of Policy holders, 17 December 1859.

Berch & Root, class B, stock dry goods, stock in lower story of very fine 3 & 1 sty. Bg. Occupied upstairs for Office, Millinery, Daguerreotypist &c

W. Herring & Son, class B, stock clothing, other half of Berch & Root bg. & similarly occupied overhead. Fire walls.

Ramson, Gilbert & Burr, class B, stock hardware, reliable fire walls on both sides, some tin work done in the rear.

D. Meyer, class D, stock clothing, B stores either side no frame exposers.

L.W. Smith, class B, building 3 sty. B. exposed by 2 sty. B. row of 3 stores, and [D. Meyer], no fire walls.

A.W. Hammond, class B, law library, in second story of [L.W. Smith]

D.S. Myer & C0., class B, stock dry goods, corner store of 3. 2 sty. B.

H.G. Kuhrt, class B, stock liquors, in a building *very full* of occupants, P.O., Pr. Ofs., 2 Barbers, Book binder, Clothier, Banking, Lottery, Restaurant, Saloon, Etc.

J. & J. Lynch, class B, building & stock groceries, corner building, fire wall, very good, stock rather low.

T.R. Ripley, class C, stock crockery & glass, exposed by a pretty hard wooden community our [W. Kidd and Tomlinson & Barnes] among them.

W. Kidd, class D, buildings, tin shop, bookshop, rather tough customers & worth all we will get for them.

Tomlinson & Barnes, class D, tinner's stk & tools [in building covered by W. Kidd, separated by 15 feet from Kidd.]

Barnes & Campbell, class B, auction & consignees stock, good except liability of such stock to fluctuate in value.

Jno. Lynch trustee, class B, building; corner building, Drugs & Clothing down, Offices & Concert Hall upstairs.

J.H. Flinn, class B, building, carriage depository between [Jno. Lynch, Berry & Wood, and Healey & Berry], fire wall one side.

Berry & Wood, class C, building, 1 of a Block of 3 stores inside of five walls, occupants upstairs, campo roof.

Healy & Berry, class C, 2 Buildings, the other two of the same 3. [of Berry & Wood.]

J.C. Davies, class D, fancy & grocer stock, wooden corner bg. beside fire wall of brick row beyond.

Jones & McLandon, class B, sk. gro. & liquors, in a block of 6 3 sty. B wholesale warehouses, fine fire walls between each, should call them elegant risks. These are the ones the Phoenix was scolding about! Wouldn't I feel cheap if they were the first to burn?!

F.A. Williams, class B, furniture & upholstery, [same as for Jones & McLendon].

Clark & Lewis, class B, hardware & iron, [same as for Jones & McLendon].

A. Austell, class B, hotel building, "*Trout* House" (Item. *Name* suggests good living—illusionary!) All the Hotels are at exceedingly low rates.

J.J. Trasher, class D & B, hotel building, [see A. Austell above.]

Jackson & Bro., class B, stock groceries, one of 4 2 sty. B. stores, all grocers.

McNaughr Ormon & Co., class B, a very handsome new B. block of 3 stories 2 of which they occupy themselves. Division walls not whole. Outer walls reliable. Exposed opp. By frame range. Upstairs many wooden & plaster subdivisions, will be variously occupied for Offices &c. Sky lights, halls, stairways, 3d sty. Water closet &c. All very genteel.

McNaught Ormond & Co., class B, sk. Hdware, paints, gro.; stock in basement & first floor of above building. Elegant store, fine stock.

Salmans Mathews & Co., class B, stock dry goods, in adjoining row to [McNaughr Ormond & Co.] Fine store & stock

Goodman Shields & Co., class B, stock goods, second store beyond, in same row.

J.H. Johnson, class B, building, building containing [Salmans Mathews & Co. and Goodman Shields & Co.] Fine new B. 3 sty. Block of 4 stores. Outer walls reliable, division walls "no count." Finishing off for Hotel occupancy upstairs.

M.J. Johnson, class D, building; wooden dwelling, exposed by carpenter shop.

W.W. Roark, class C & D, sk. general mdse., stock sold & removed.

J.R. & C.H. Wallace, class B, buildings, 1 sty. warehouse & B. storage sheds fronting inward on hollow square.

George N. Barnard's photograph of the Trout House during the federal occupation of Atlanta, October 1864 (Library of Congress).

W.H. Lester, class C & B, undivided ½ of Bg., 3 sty. block of 2 C. stores, with 1 sty. B. rear, 100 ft. deep, outer walls reliable fire walls. 2d & 3d stys. boarding house, little frame kitchen perched on roof of rear bg. looks like a "varmint"!

M. Myers, class D, dwelg., smokehouse, kit.; little concerns in rear of store.

J. Ryan, class C, stock of dry goods, in row of 4 C. stores flanked by 4 frames.

L. Valentino, class D, confections & fancy sk., 3 doors from [J. Ryan]. Row is respectively occupied.

Lamshee & Purell, class B, clothing & fixtures, in row of 3 B. stores, outer walls reliable. Fair risk.

Appendix B. C.C. Hine's Report on Atlanta in 1859

1. African Methodist Church
2. Aaron Alexander residence
3. Angier House
4. Arsenal
5. Atheneum
6. Atlanta Hotel
7. Atlanta Machine Shop
8. Atlanta Medical College
9. Boutell Residence
10. James Calhoun residence
11. Calico House
12. Car Shed
13. Central Presbyterian Church
14. Christian Church
15. City Hall
16. City Hall Park
17. City Hotel
18. City Park
19. T.M. Clarke Hardware
20. Confederate States Commissary
21. Crew residence
22. Empire House No. 2
23. Judge William Ezzard residence
24. Female Seminary
25. First Methodist Church
26. Ga. RR Freight warehouse
27. GARR Locomotive House
28. Hunnicutt and Taylor drugstore
29. Ivy Homestead
30. LaGrange RR Freight House
31. Er. Lawshe residence
32. Leyden residence
33. Long/Howell residence
34. Patrick Lynch residence
35. Lyons (Neal) House
36. Masonic Hall
37. Mechanics Fire Department No. 2
38. Rice and Mitchell Planing Mill
39. Morrell House
40. Father O'Reilly
41. Peck Residence
42. Peck and Day
43. St. Phillip's Episcopal Church
44. Chapmon Powell residence
45. Second Baptist Church
46. Solomon House
47. Spiller and Burr
48. Trinity Church
49. Trout House
50. Washington Hall
51. Wheat's warehouse
52. James Williams residence
53. Joseph Winship residence

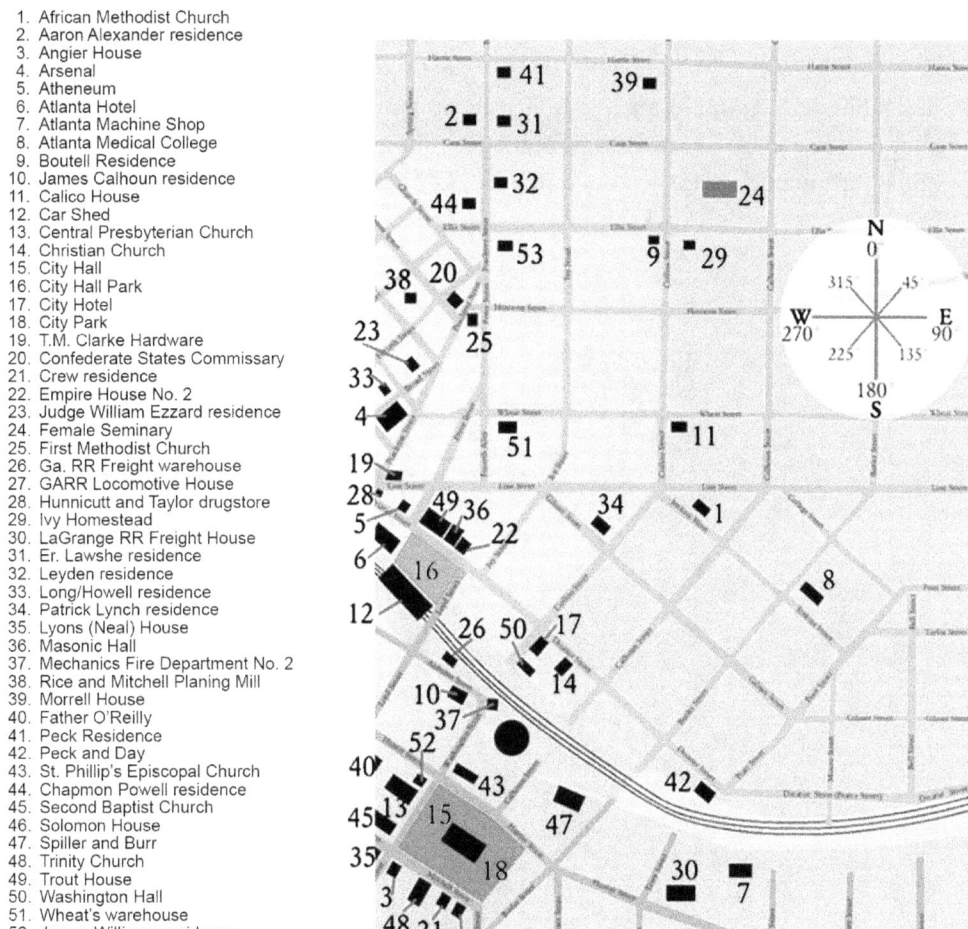

Map of major Atlanta buildings in 1864, research by Ken Denney, enhanced by Gus Welborn (Ken Denney).

P.J. Immell, class C, baker's & confectioner's stock and machinery & engine, family grocer in front, steam bakery in rear. Engine is a small affair. Could not get at ovens to inspect.

McMillen & Fleming, class B, wholesale grocer's stock, two B. stores detached. Printing office & billiard saloon upstairs.

T.C.H. Wilson, class [?], building, pretty tough customer for a little one leans up against big frame 4th [D] class.

Hubbard & Chisolm, class C, banking & stock groceries, tavern—risk occupied as dwelling & grocery. 25 ft. 1 sty. D. Dweig. Only exposure, except across w.

L. Lamshee, class D, building, rather hard & well worth the price, one of 3 in different frames.

Centre & Treadwell, class C & B, wholesale sk. groceries, In bg covered by [W.H. Lester] which description see.

Atlanta Medical College, class B, chemical apparatus & building; elegant, isolated B. building. Did not get an inside inspection. Nice risk.

Blake Scofield & Markham, class D, building machinery; Atlanta Rolling Mill. Very good concern and very well managed. Should call it a good thing of the kind. Stationary ladders to roof & 12 bbls. With buckets always full on roof. No fire comes near woodwork.

Appendix C

The Other Great Locomotive Chase

THE WESTERN & ATLANTIC Railroad played a critical role in the Civil War. Built and still owned but not operated by the state of Georgia, this line first fully opened in 1850, connecting Chattanooga to Atlanta and beyond the Deep South and the sea. During the Civil War, the W&A became the critical supply line to the Confederate armies in the all critical state of Tennessee.[1]

From the beginning of the war, civilians who supported the Union and/or who opposed the war threatened to burn the numerous bridges on the Western & Atlantic and thus cut Tennessee off from the rest of the Confederacy. This situation brought about what came to be known as the "Andrew's Raid," "the Chattanooga Railroad Expedition," and "the Great Locomotive Chase," one of the most celebrated adventures of the Civil War and, eventually, the subject of two very different motion pictures.

In the spring of 1862, a team of saboteurs famously illustrated the railroad's vulnerability. On April 12, federal civilian spy and contraband smuggler James J. Andrews and nineteen Union soldiers disguised as civilians seized the locomotive *General* and three box cars at Big Shanty, near Marietta, Georgia. They planned to burn the railroad's bridges to cut off Chattanooga as a federal division under General Ormsby Macknight Mitchell moved to capture it and Huntsville, Alabama. The saboteurs, however, went into their mission woefully unprepared, especially as the previous night's rainstorm had left everything wet. Without tools, weapons, explosives, or combustibles, they failed to ignite any of the bridges.

The *General*'s conductor, William Allen Fuller, and the foreman of the railroad's wood supply, Anthony Murphy, pursued the raiders for eighty-seven miles on foot, with a hand car, aboard the locomotive *Yonah*, using the locomotive *William R. Smith*, and finally, in the locomotive *Texas* while traveling in reverse. Other men joined them in various stages of the chase. The two locomotives sometimes traveled at more than 60 miles per hour. To maintain speed, anything that would burn went into their respective fires.

Reinforced by armed Confederate recruits and track hands, the pursuers riding on the *Texas* finally caught up with the *General* for the last time two miles north of Ringgold, Georgia. With their engine out of steam, the raiders abandoned it. They had failed to damage even one bridge and were all in custody within a few days. Confederate officials eventually hanged James Andrews and seven of his men in Atlanta.²

Men involved in pursuing the *General* became celebrated heroes of this affair even before the Civil War ended.³ This great adventure captivated the public's memory then and since. The *General* would be in Chattanooga as a historical relic from 1962 to 1970, and today, it is on display in the Southern Museum of Civil War and Locomotive History in Kennesaw (Big Shanty), Georgia, where this Great Locomotive Chase began. The restored *Texas* can be seen today at the Atlanta History Center.⁴

In his later years, however, Fuller actively campaigned against sharing credit with Anthony Murphy, or anyone else, in rescuing the *General* and the Western & Atlantic Railroad bridges.⁵ William Allen Fuller (born Henry County, Georgia, April 15, 1836, son of William Alexander and Marthenia Allen Fuller) also claimed that he was the hero of a forgotten but spectacular second Great Locomotive Chase that occurred on an epic scale.⁶

William Allen Fuller (1836–1905) (Kenan Research Center at the Atlanta History Center).

Around 1903, as part of his effort to win sole credit for thwarting the Andrews Raid, Fuller published an account wherein he claimed that in 1864–1865:

> He rendered services of great value during Sherman's advance upon Atlanta, collecting at the latter city the rolling stock of the road, comprising forty seven locomotives, forty-nine passenger and baggage coaches, and 580 freight cars, as well as the office property, which he took thence to Macon, Savannah Charleston, Columbia, Augusta, and back to Atlanta, avoiding the Federal armies, and losing but seventeen freight cars.
>
> This service, performed so successfully in a period of great confusion and demoralization, is worthy of communication.⁷

In a letter of April 20, 1903, Fuller essentially made the same claim but added that

Georgia Governor Joseph E. Brown had placed him in charge of this grand railroad expedition and that it also lost one passenger coach and one baggage car, that he saved the movable state property from the state capital in Milledgeville.[8]

The image of vast trains, unlike anything previously seen in Georgia and stretching for miles as they escaped destruction by racing ahead of Sherman's legions, makes even stopping the Andrews Raiders seem minor by comparison. Such an odyssey should be remembered as one of the Civil War's great adventures. But why did someone like Fuller, who worked so hard on how he would be remembered, wait so long to mention this other momentous Great Locomotive Chase?[9]

Information on the escape of the remains of the Western & Atlantic's rolling stock has survived without mentioning Fuller or the scale and drama of his account. The W&A evacuated Chattanooga in September 1863 and steadily lost its tracks to the advance of the federal army during the Atlanta Campaign of the following spring. What rolling stock of its railroad that the state still controlled evacuated Atlanta on August 30, 1864, by way of Jonesboro, Georgia.

Similarly, state Quartermaster General Ira R. Foster wrote a report of the subsequent removal of the state property from the then capitol of Milledgeville, but he described it as leaving on only one train. Governor Brown informed the Georgia legislature on November 3, 1864, that seventeen of the W&A's passenger cars had been destroyed, along with thirty freight cars. A single entity, carrying the property of the Western & Atlantic and of the state of Georgia with maybe three engines and enough cars to stretch for a mile, did hold up between Macon and Milledgeville as the nearby battle at Griswoldville took place on November 22, 1864.[10] Four other locomotives suffered damage in that battle, including three engines (including the *General*) and eighteen cars left with the Confederate army in Atlanta and were subsequently destroyed.

The remaining rolling stock moved state property from Milledgeville to safety but went into service on different lines, removing state-owned cotton and freight for the army. A list of the locomotives of the W&A shows that it had, in total, up to December 6, 1864, only forty-three engines, including those destroyed, captured, and serving with other railroads. At the end of the Civil War, the line had only eight passenger and baggage cars and 351 freight cars. The United States government returned the railroad's line between Chattanooga and Atlanta to the control of the state of Georgia on September 25, 1865. An 1871 report on the Western & Atlantic Railroad implies that it had, to that time, only acquired some 500 cars, including those purchased since the war and those lost before the evacuation of Atlanta.[11]

Martin H. Dooley, the true roadmaster for the railroad's rolling stock during its escape from Sherman, would testify in 1867 that what survived of the engines and cars eventually returned to Atlanta by way of Charleston. After the war, Dooley received credit for saving forty engines and 500 cars from Sherman, but not as one train or at one time.[12]

George N. Barnard's photograph of locomotives in the ruins of Atlanta in October 1864 (Library of Congress).

Proving the negative cannot be done, but other documentary evidence further discredits Fuller's account of his second Great Locomotive Chase. He had first gone to work for the W&A on September 8, 1855, but by 1864, he had served no more than as a train conductor. In 1863, the Confederate States of America commissioned him to serve six months as captain of a home guard company of railroad workers. Governor Brown would recreate this "Independent State Guards" Company as state troops for two other periods. In a 1902 account, Fuller only claimed to have commanded his company three times and organized the white railroad workers who moved the state property to safety by train.

On May 30, 1904, Fuller wrote to Wilbur Kurtz that, at the end of August 1864, he and his men prepared to evacuate Atlanta but with only seven or eight locomotives of the W&A. The *General* then had to be abandoned because it had been damaged when the Confederate army detonated its ammunition cars as it prepared to withdraw from the city. Pay records of his service in commanding his company as part of Major George Hillyer's Railroad Battalion survive for the period he claimed to have been leading the trains across Georgia, but he did not draw pay as an employee of the railroad during that time.[13]

The lack of mention of Fuller in other sources also raises questions about his version of events. Judge William G. McAdoo witnessed some of the evacuation from

Milledgeville and claimed that Major George Washington Lee commanded the train that carried the state property.[14] The records of the transportation branch of the United States Army, the United States Military Railroad (USMRR), survive in the National Archives and Records Administration. Although even the most mundane matters received notice in its communications from Atlanta, no mention appears in those records of Fuller or of any return of the rolling stock of the W&A. For the whole of the Confederate States of America, the USMRR only captured or received thirty-five locomotives and 393 cars in 1865 and none in 1866.[15]

Throughout these months of crisis, Governor Joseph E. Brown found no reason to officially correspond with Fuller or to mention him in government letters, an odd fact if that railroad conductor and home guard company captain had responsibility for the surviving rolling stock and movable property of the state of Georgia and its Western & Atlantic Railroad.

Fuller deserved credit for a role in saving his railroad from damage by the Andrews Raid in 1862, but as he worked so hard to describe as minimal the participation of others in that event, he grossly exaggerated the part he played, if any, in the later escape of the W&A rolling stock from Atlanta under Major George Washington Lee and others. He likely did witness something of the initial evacuation of the city in late August 1864, although his erroneous account of the damage done to the *General* at that time raises doubts about how much he saw.[16] He and his men could have ridden on the train or trains that left the doomed city that night, but he held no other responsibility than for his men, which answers why no mention of his role survives any of the other accounts of the evacuation of the rolling stock. Additional details of these events in his account must have come from his imagination or what he misunderstood from his comrades who were there. By 1903–1904, he likely concluded that no one still lived who had information to contradict his tale.

William A. Fuller, the legitimate Civil War hero, thus proved that he could spin a fabulous yarn as forgotten history. He died in Atlanta on December 28, 1905, and was buried in Oakland Cemetery, a short distance from where Andrews and his other raiders had hanged. Fuller's tombstone credits his involvement in stopping the Andrews Raid but is rightly silent on his participation in his second "Great Locomotive Chase."

Appendix D

George W. Lee's Prisoner Lists

LEE SENT OTHER prisoners to Richmond, but the lists have not survived.

Prisoner List, Department of Henrico Papers, Mss 3 C7604a, Confederate Military Manuscripts Series A, Section 3, a14-253, microfilm roll 10, frames 788, Virginia Historical Society, Richmond.

Military Prison
Atlanta Ga July 22, 1863
List of Prisoners to be forwarded to Pro. Marl. Richmond Va

1. Thos. L. Duffell	F 13th Ga to be forwarded to their command
2. P. Dority	13th Ga to be forwarded to their command
3. W.H. Thompson	citizen
4. N.C. Burchett	"
5. J Hicks	"
6. C.W. Taylor	"
7. J. Martin	"
8. B. Martin	"
9. F.G. Majors	"
10. Jas Gasaway	"
11. C Sims	"
12. Jas. Shehan	"
13. J.J. Ingram	"
14. W.H. Relly	"
15. W.C. Ligon	"
16. A.J. Heald	"
17. J.H. Berry	"
18. J.W. Bethow	Co "E" 11th Ala to be forwarded to their command
19. Jas Reed	Co "A" 23rd Ga to be forwarded to their command

From the *National Tribune* (Washington, DC), April 2, 1885, p. 2 c. 2

Appendix D. George W. Lee's Prisoner Lists

List of Prisoners sent to Atlanta, GA, June 13, 1862, from Knoxville, TN, under the command of Major General E. Kirby Smith

Court-marshaled and sentenced	Spies
1. Wilson Brown, Ohio	Engine Stealing
2. Marion Ross, Ohio	" "
3. W.H. Campbell, Ohio	" "
4. John Scott, Ohio	" "
5. Perry G. Shadrach, Ohio	" "
6. G.D. Wilson, Ohio	" "
7. Samuel Slavens, Ohio	" "
8. S. Robinson, Ohio	" "
Court-martialed	
9. E.H. Mason, Ohio	" "
10. Wm. Knight, Ohio	" "
11. Robt. Buffins, Ohio	" "
12. Wm. Pettinger, Ohio	" "
13. Capt. David Fry, Green Co., Tenn.	bridge-burning and recruiting for Federal army.
14. G.W. Barlow, Washington Co., Tenn.	obstructing railroad track.
15. Prisoners of War Federal Soldiers. Thos. McCoy, Morgan Co., Tenn.; Peter Pierce, Campbell Co., Tenn.; John Barker, Estill Co., Tenn.; Bennet Powers, Lincoln Co., Tenn.	

Political Prisoners.

Ransom White, Morgan Co., Tenn., Citizen aiding the enemy. Trying to go to Kentucky: John Walls, Blount Co., Tenn.

Rebellion: John Green, Union Co., Tenn.

Rebellion: John Thompkins, Washington Co., Tenn.

Henry Miller, Sullivan Co., Tenn., suspected as a spy

Wm. Thompson, arrested at Bristol, suspected as a spy.

Respectfully submitted by order. Wm. M. Churchwell, Colonel and Provost-Marshal.

List of Prisoners in Atlanta City Jail, September 16, 1862

Engine-stealers—M.J. Hawkins, J. Parrott, W. Bensinger, A. Wilson, E.H. Mason, W. Knight, W. Pettinger, W. Reddick, D.A. Dorsey, J.K. Porter, M. Wood, W.W. Brown, R. Bufman, David Fry, J.J. Barker.

Bridge-burners—T. McCoy, B. Powers, John Green, H. Mills, G.D. Barlow, P. Pierce, John Walls, R. White, J. Tompkins, John Wollam.

Appendix E

Civilians Forced to Evacuate Atlanta, September 1864

THE ORIGINAL OF the following record has not been located. It was published in the special fourth edition of *Memoirs of Gen. W.T. Sherman* (New York: Charles L. Webster & Company, 1892), volume 2: 546–553. This list was brought to my attention by the late Franklin M. Garrett. For more on the evacuation of Atlanta, see Franklin M. Garrett, *Atlanta and Environs: A Chronicle of Its People and Events*, 2 vols. (New York: Lewis Publishing, 1954), 1: 640–643.

Official account of the people sent south, their numbers and baggage, under Special Field Order No. 67, issued by Major-General W.T. Sherman, Atlanta, Georgia, September 4, 1864.

Information is given as Number—Name—Adults, Children, and Servants—Baggage.

SEPTEMBER 10, 1864

1. J.M. Bryant, 3 adults and 6 children, 1 servant, 30 packages
2. Mrs. B. Ogletree, 2 adults and 27 packages
3. Mrs. Bookout, 1 adult and 1 child, 18 packages
4. Mrs. M.R. Thornton, 1 adult, 5 children, and 1 servant, 41 packages
5. Mrs. F. Winkfield, 1 adult and 1 child, 12 packages
6. Mrs. S. Hood, 1 adult and 3 children, 11 packages
7. Mrs. J.P. Brooks, 1 adult and 1 child, 14 packages
8. Mrs. L.C. Kent, 1 adult and 1 child, 10 packages
9. Mrs. J.W. Thurman, 1 adult and 1 child, 6 packages
10. Mrs. N. Eason, 1 adult and 1 child, 5 packages
11. Mrs. M.F. McDuffie, 1 adult and 4 children, 14 packages
12. Mrs. S.E. Bell, 1 adult and 2 children, 12 package
13. Mrs. J.S. Johnson, 1 adult, 5 package
14. Mrs. Blanchard, 1 adult, 2 children, and 1 servant, 40 packages
15. Mrs. C.E. Harris, 1 adult, 2 packages
16. Mrs. M. Struce, 1 adult and 1 child, 11 packages
17. Mrs. G.E. Forrest, 2 adults and 2 children, 11 packages
18. Mrs. C. Grubbs, 1 adult and 2 children, 4 packages

Appendix E. Civilians Forced to Evacuate Atlanta, September 1864

18½. Mrs. M.A.P. Jones, 1 adult, 4 packages
19. Josiah Kent, 2 adults, 15 packages
20. Mrs. M. Higgenbottom, 1 adult, 2 children, 11 packages

SEPTEMBER 11, 1864

21. Mrs. Stafford, 2 adults and 1 child, 14 packages
22. Mrs. M. Blackburn, 2 adults and 3 children, 12 packages
23. B. Evans, 1 adult and 1 child, 18 packages
24. Mrs. B. Thompson, Mrs. E. Lee, Mrs. M. Lee, Mrs. M. Cook, 5 adults and 7 children, 44 packages and 1 old horse and wagon
25. Mrs. S. Lee, 1 adult and 6 children, 17 packages
26. Mrs. S. Abrams, 1 adult, 7 packages
27. Mrs. M. Wright, 1 adult and 1 servant, 17 packages
28. Miss. J. Combs, 1 adult, 14 packages
29. Mrs. Sims and Davis, 2 adults and 1 child, 24 packages
30. John Cassen, 2 adults, 22 packages
31. Mrs. M. Higgens, 1 adult and 2 children, 23 packages
32. Mrs. S.A. Gossett, 1 adult, 15 packages
33. Mrs. E.J. Lofton, 1 adult and 1 child, 14 packages
34. Mrs. M. Johnson, 1 adult and 5 children, 21 packages
35. Mrs. S. McDuffee, Mrs. M.J. Self, 3 adults and 4 children, 20 packages and 1 cow
36. Mrs. E. McGriff. 1 adult and 1 child, 13 packages
37. G.M. Lester, 1 adult and 2 servants, 26 packages
38. Mrs. A. Patterson, 1 adult and 2 children, 15 packages
39. Mrs. M. Ballard, 1 adult and 4 children, 23 packages
40. Mrs. F.C. House, 1 adult and 2 children, 28 packages
41. Mrs. C. Johnson, 1 adult and 6 children, 25 packages
42. Mrs. S. Ellis, 1 adult and 1 child, 13 packages
43. Mrs. M. Wilson, 1 adult and 5 children, 23 packages
44. Mrs. E. Phillips, 4 adults, 17 packages
45. Mrs. G.W. Adair, 2 adults and 4 children, 2 servants, 53 packages, and 2 horses, carriage, cow, and calf
46. Mrs. M. Ball, Mrs. Brooks, 2 adults and 24 children, 35 packages
47. Mrs. C. Johnson, 1 adult and 1 child, 9 packages
48. Mrs. J. Kramer, 1 adult and 3 children, 4 packages
49. Miss L. Miller, 1 adult, 14 packages
50. Mrs. J. Kilby, 1 adult and 5 children, 35 packages
51. J.M. Blackburn, 2 adults, 15 packages
52. Mrs. F. Witcher, 1 adult, 1 child, 18 packages
53. Mrs. S. Freeman, 1 adult, 7 packages
54. Mrs. E.L. Mill, 1 adult, 3 children, and 1 servant, 27 packages and 1 cow

55. Mrs. N. Mayson, 1 adult, 1 child, and 1 servant, 28 packages, cow and calf
56. Mrs. N. McTeer, 1 adult, 8 packages
57. Mrs. A.M. McTeer, 1 adult and 6 children, 27 packages
58. Mrs. S. Mayson, 1 adult and 5 children, 22 packages, and 1 old horse and dray, cow, and calf
59. Mrs. A.J. Mayson, 1 adult, 10 packages
60. Mrs. S.A. Moss, 2 adults and 1 child, 17 packages
61. Mrs. S. Armstrong, 1 adult, 2 children, and 1 servant 19 packages
62. Mrs. J.L. Mayson, 2 adults and 1 servant, 34 packages and horse & dray
63. Mrs. E. Gilham, 1 adult, 10 packages
64. A.H. Webb, 2 adults, 2 children, and 4 servants, 21 packages
65. Mrs. M. Waier, 1 adult, 17 packages
66. Mrs. E. Harper, 1 adult and 5 children, 27 packages
67. Mrs. M. Brady, 1 adult and 2 children, 17 packages
68. Benjamon Gaum, 2 adults and 8 children, 31 packages
69. Mrs. N. Ireland, 1 adult and 4 children, 19 packages
70. Mrs. N. Waddall, 2 adults, 15 packages
71. Mrs. Preckett, 1 adult, 2 children, and 1 servant, 18 packages
72. J. Hawkins, 1 adult, 4 packages
73. R.W.T. Denham, 1 adult, 5 children, 12 packages
74. Mrs. M.A. Franklin, 1 adult and 2 children, 8 packages
75. Mrs. N.M. Franklin, 1 adult and 2 children, 8 packages
76. Mrs. S. Saul, 1 adult, 7 packages
77. Mrs. S. Clownes, 2 adults and 1 servant, 9 packages
78. B. Eustell, 2 adults and 4 children, 41 packages and cow and calf
79. Mrs. F. Crawford, 1 adult, 7 packages
80. Mrs. Makridge, 1 adult and 5 children, 23 packages
81. Mrs. S. Corsey, 1 adult and 3 children, 7 packages
82. Mrs. A.M. Rollo, 1 adult and 10 packages
83. Mrs. L. Smith, 1 adult and 4 children, 12 packages
84. Mrs. J. Sheppard, 1 adult and 5 children, 20 packages
85. Mrs. L. Whitmire, 1 adult and 2 children, 18 packages
86. Mrs. E. Lee, 1 adult, 1 package
87. Miss C. Powers, 1 adult, 1 package

SEPTEMBER 12, 1864

88. Mrs. S. Corsey, 1 adult, 11 packages
89. Mrs. M. Grubbs, 1 adult and 4 children, 15 packages
90. S. Robinson, 2 adults and 2 children2 14 packages
91. Mrs. E. Hill, 1 adult and 1 child, 10 packages
92. Mrs. L. Patterson, 1 adult and 3 children, 24 packages
93. Mrs. P. Jones, 1 adult and 5 packages

Appendix E. Civilians Forced to Evacuate Atlanta, September 1864

94. Mrs. C. Grubbs, 1 adult and 2 children, 11 packages
95. Mrs. E. Cook, 1 adult and 1 child, 12 packages
96. Mrs. M.B. Atkinson, 1 adult and 4 children, 16 packages
97. Mrs. T. Harebrook, 2 adults and 4 children, 18 packages
98. Mrs. A. Hall, 2 adults and 1 child, 1 package
99. Mrs. E. Sears, 1 adult and 4 children, 7 packages
100. Mrs. A. Willard, 1 adult and 3 children, 7 packages
101. J. Haslett, 2 adults, 22 packages
102. R. McCowan, 2 adults and 1 child, 17 packages
103. Mrs. J. Atkins, 1 adult and 1 child, 16 packages
104. Mrs. M. Wing, 1 adult and 1 child, 7 packages
105. R. Knott, 2 adults, 33 packages
106. Mrs. S. Johnson, 1 adult, 1 child, 10 packages
107. J.M. Knott, 2 adults and 1 child, 7 packages
108. Mrs. C. Knott, 1 adult and 1 child, 22 packages
109. B. Thrower, 2 adults and 2 children, 32 packages
110. Mrs. M.E. Sharpe, 1 adult and 4 children, 26 packages
111. Mrs. E. Glenn, 1 adult and 3 children, 31 packages
112. Mrs. L. Wing, 1 adult and 1 child, 21 packages
113. W.H.H. Dorsey, 2 adults and 1 child, 16 packages
114. Mrs. M.A. Gober, 2 adults, 14 packages and cow and calf
115. Mrs. J.L. Shaw, 2 adults and 3 children, 17 packages

SEPTEMBER 13, 1864

116. Mrs. S. Banks, 1 adult and 2 children, 16 packages
117. Mrs. M. Kelly, 2 adults and 4 children, 19 packages
118. Mrs. L. Dean, 1 adult and 3 children, 7 packages
119. Mrs. M. Kelly, 2 adults and 2 children, 14 packages
120. Mrs. E. Bellew, 1 adult, no packages
121. Mrs. J.S. McWaters, 1 adult and 4 children, 81 packages and 1 cow
122. Mrs. N. Reeves, 1 adult and 2 children, 21 packages
123. Mrs. M.L. Holbrook, 1 adult and 3 children, 83 packages
124. Mrs. S Hewitt, 1 adult, 13 packages
125. Mrs. L. Bowls, 1 adult, 2 packages
126. Mrs. A. Blackman, 2 adults and 1 child, 19 packages
127. Mrs. E. Winfield, 1 adult and 2 children, 15 packages
128. Mrs. D. Defoor, 3 adults and 2 children, 22 packages
129. Mrs. E.N. Hilton, 1 adult and 1 child, 12 packages and 1 cow
130. J.B. McDaniel, 1 adult, 2 packages
131. Mrs. C.J. Lamb, 1 adult and 9 children, 21 packages
132. Mrs. P. Campbell, 1 adult, 3 children, and 1 servant, 8 packages
133. Miss G. Timmons, 1 adult, 1 package

134. Mrs. M. Richards, 1 adult, 1 package
135. Mrs. J. Johns, 2 adults and 5 children, 15 packages
136. Mrs. S. Williams, 1 adult and 2 children, 1 package
137. Mrs. C. Jenkins, 1 adult and 2 children, 4 packages
138. Mrs. M. Kilpatrick, 2 adults and 9 children, 12 packages
139. Mrs. M. Teall, 3 adults, 7 packages
140. Mrs. M. Edwards, 1 adult and 1 child, 10 packages
141. Mrs. S. Blalock, 1 adult, 11 packages
142. A. Grist, 4 adults and 3 children, 34 packages
143. Mrs. N.C. White, 1 adult, 22 packages
144. Mrs. M.E. Hutchens, 1 adult and 2 children, 9 packages
145. Mrs. N. Studevant, 1 adult and 1 child, 19 packages
146. Mrs. M.C. Seale, 2 adults and 2 children, 20 packages
147. Mrs. S.P. Baggerly, 1 adult, 4 packages
148. Mrs. P. Rothwell, 1 adult, 6 packages
149. Mrs. C. McHugh, 2 adults and 8 packages
150. W.L. White, 2 adults, 1 package
151. Miss E. Taylor, 1 adult, 5 packages
152. Mrs. J.M. Taylor, 1 adult and 3 children, 15 packages
153. Mrs. M. Wooding, 1 adult and 2 children, 11 packages
154. Thomas Byrne, 1 adult, 1 horse
155. W.G. Gist, 2 adults and 1 child, 28 packages
156. J. Thompson, 3 adults, 18 packages
157. Mrs. M.E. Brace, 1 adult and 2 children, 16 packages
158. Mrs. E. Brace, 1 adult and 3 children, 17 packages
159. Mrs. S.P. Wilson, 1 adult and 4 children, and 2 servants, 87 packages
160. Mrs. J. McLaughlin, 5 adults and 4 children, 7 packages
161. Mrs. L. Loren, 1 adult and 2 children, 18 packages
162. Mrs. A. Gerrett, 1 adult, 7 packages
163. Mrs. P.S. Jenkins, 1 adult and 7 children, 80 packages
164. Joseph Coker, 1 adult, 10 packages
165. Mrs. Mary Harper, 2 adults and 3 children, 19 packages and 1 cow
166. Mrs. L. Knight, 1 adult and 2 children, 11 packages
167. John Bash, W.L. Bash, 4 adults and 4 children, 40 packages

SEPTEMBER 14, 1864

168. Mrs. E. Robinson, 2 adults, 18 packages
169. Mrs. J. Williams, 2 adults, 19 packages
170. Mrs. M. Bell, 3 adults and 7 children, 38 packages and 1 cow
171. Mrs. L. Plummer, 3 adults and 3 children, 13 packages
172. W.D. Crockett, 2 adults, 16 packages
173. Mrs. W.D. Mitchell, 1 adult, 3 children, and 1 servant, 25 packages

Appendix E. Civilians Forced to Evacuate Atlanta, September 1864

174. Miss Drum, 1 adult and 1 child, 8 packages
175. Mrs. S. Smith, 1 adult and 4 children, 26 packages
176. Mrs. N. Johnson, 1 adult and 1 child, 17 packages
177. Miss L. Buffington, 2 adults, 5 packages
178. Mrs. M.A. Miner, 1 adult and 3 children, 25 packages
179. J.G. Mitchell, 2 adults, 1 child, and 2 servants, 40 packages
180. T.H. Wilson, 2 adults, 21 packages and 1 cow
181. Mrs. M. Johnson, 3 adults and 3 children, 18 packages
182. Mrs. E.M. Tweely, 1 adult and 1 child. 20 packages
183. Mrs. A. Robinson, 1 adult, 4 packages
184. J. Wilson, 2 adults, 9 packages
185. Mrs. M. Faulkner, 1 adult, 13 packages
186. Mrs. Oslin, 3 adults, 49 packages
187. W.C. Parker, 2 adults, no packages
188. A.W. Weaver, 2 adults, 4 children, and 2 servants, 30 packages
189. W. Kenodle, 2 adults and 5 children, 18 packages and 1 cow
190. J.L. Mathews, 1 adult, 2 packages
191. Mrs. J. Whatley, 1 adult and 3 children, 38 packages
192. E. Daniel, 2 adults and 6 children, 19 packages
193. Mrs. H.B. Hutcheson, 1 adult, 26 packages
194. Mrs. S. Robinson, 1 adult, 39 packages
195. Mrs. C. Bell, 1 adult and 2 children, 28 packages
196. J. Carmichael, 2 adults, 31 packages
197. W. Whitaker, 3 adults and 5 children, 35 packages
198. George Kidd, 2 adults, 19 packages
199. Debby Wall, 1 adult, 2 children, and 1 servant, 19 packages
200. L.L. Bird, 1 adult and 2 servants, 10 packages
201. P.W. Carter, 1 adult, 8 packages
202. C. Emmet, 1 adult, 25 packages
203. E.D. Graff, 3 adults and 1 child, 26 packages
204. J.A. Timmons, 2 adults and 3 children, 15 packages
205. Daniel Sanders, 2 adults, 5 packages
206. Mary Richards, 1 adult and 2 children, 16 packages
207. Mrs. M. Shields, 2 adults and 2 children, 10 packages
208. Mrs. J. Batterns, 3 adults, 13 packages
209. T.M. Jones, 2 adults, 4 children, and 6 servants, 70 packages
210. Mrs. M. Crawford, 1 adult and 1 child, 19 packages
211. Mrs. M.C. Morris, 1 adult and 6 children, 48 packages
212. M.E. Grey, 1 adult and 2 children, 20 packages
213. E. Carmichael, 1 adult and 5 children, 12 packages
214. J.W. Rucker, 2 adults, 15 packages
215. Mrs. L.V. Rucker, 2 adults, 15 packages

September 14, 1864

216. S.A. Bidwell, 1 adult, 7 packages
217. Mrs. M. Coker, 1 adult and 2 children, 16 packages
218. Henry Buise, 2 adults and 2 children, 27 packages
219. Mrs. W. Rushton, 1 adult and 7 children, 39 packages
220. Mrs. Rose, 1 adult, 2 children, and 1 servant, 4 packages
221. Jos. Herndon, 2 adults and 3 children, 18 packages
222. Mrs. Zimmerman, 2 adults and 1 child, 10 packages
223. J.L. Wilson, 1 adult, 1 package
224. W.C. Nelson, 2 adults and 1 child, 14 packages
225. C. Harden, 2 adults, 20 packages
226. J.C. Reves, 3 adults, 7 packages
227. Mrs. M.J. Corsey, 1 adult and 4 children, 6 packages
228. Alfred Lamb, 5 adults and 1 child, 17 packages
229. Mrs. M. Paine, 3 adults and 7 children, 19 packages
230. Mrs. T.H. Greyson, 1 adult and 4 children, 21 packages
231. Mrs. R. Nichols, 2 adults, 10 packages
232. Mrs. M.G. Wickner, 1 adult and 1 child, 6 packages
233. S. Hopper, 3 adults and 4 children, 43 packages and 1 cow
234. E.T. Hunnecut, 2 adults, 4 children, and 2 servants, 48 packages
235. Mrs. N. Pullent, 1 adult and 1 child, 17 packages
236. Sarah Fry, 1 adult, 2 children, and 1 servant, 17 packages
237. J. Veals, 2 adults, 2 children, and 2 servants, 22 packages
238. C.A. Martin, 1 adult, no packages
239. D.O. Driscoe, 3 adults, 37 packages
240. Jane Lofton, 1 adults, 1 child, 18 packages
241. Mrs. N.A. Bray, 1 adult, 29 packages
242. Mrs. E.J. Frederick, 2 adults and 4 children, 25 packages
243. Mrs. E. Leach, 1 adult and 4 children, 23 packages
244. H.H. Richards, 2 adults, 1 child, and 1 servant, 18 packages
245. J.A. Rush, 2 adults and 4 children, 23 packages
246. James Lester, 2 adults, 22 packages
247. Mrs. N. Christian, 1 adult, 4 packages
247½. Mrs. W.A. Norris, 1 adult, 6 packages
248. Mrs. C.P. O'Keefe, 1 adult, 2 children, and 1 servant, 45 packages
249. J. Caldwell, 5 adults, 50 packages
250. Mrs. B.F. Bennett, 2 adults and 2 children, 40 packages
251. Mrs. E.C. Smith, 1 adult and 4 children, 40 packages
252. G. Stewart, 3 adults and 6 children, 33 packages
253. Mrs. Cook, 1 adult, 2 children, and 2 servants, 47 packages
254. Mrs. N. Simpson, 2 adults, 22 packages
255. Mrs. A. Smith, 2 adults, 3 children, 1 package

Appendix E. Civilians Forced to Evacuate Atlanta, September 1864

256. Wm. Christean, 1 adult, no packages
257. Mrs. W. Adams, 2 adults and 1 child, 10 packages
258. J.C. Rogers, 1 adult, 2 packages
259. Mrs. S.E. Osborne, 1 adult, 4 children, and 1 servant, 13 packages
260. Mrs. Collins, 1 adult and 4 children, 13 packages
261. Miss Reeves, 1 adult, 12 packages
262. J.J. Whitly, 1 adult, 1 package
263. Dr. Biggers, 2 adults and 1 child, 60 packages
264. A.F. Cuming, 2 adults and 1 child, 10 packages
265. G.A. Pilgrim, 8 adults and 2 children, 35 packages
266. W.M. Bryant, 2 adults and 5 children, 25 packages
267. Jas. Coker, 1 adult, 10 packages
268. E.B. Bachus, 3 adults and 6 children, 40 packages
269. Mrs. N. Carroll, 1 adult and 3 children, 20 packages
270. Mrs. E. Grubb, 2 adults and 1 child, 20 packages
271. Mrs. M. Heton, 1 adult and 4 children, 23 packages
272. Mrs. E. Aiken, 1 adult and 1 child, 13 packages
273. Mrs. N.A. Williams, 1 adult and 4 children, 18 packages
274. Mrs. M. Hartman, 1 adult, 7 packages
275. John Ealeman, 2 adults, 1 child, and 1 servant, 37 packages
276. Mrs. L. Taylor, 1 adult, 15 packages
277. Mrs. S.A. Trout, 3 adults and 4 children, 8 packages
278. W.A. Packett, 2 adults, 3 children, and 3 servants, 42 packages
279. Mrs. L. Ford, 1 adult and 6 children, 42 packages
280. McPherson, 2 adults and 4 children, 17 packages
281. H. Wilson, 2 adults and 7 children, 10 packages
282. W. King, 1 adult, 2 packages
283. Mrs. C.C. Rhodes, 1 adult and 3 children, 23 packages
284. Mrs. M. Combs, 1 adult, 12 packages
285. James Kile, 2 adults and 1 child, 19 packages
286. Mrs. A.F. Powers, 1 adult, 16 packages
287. S. Hamilton, 3 adults and 2 children, 16 packages
288. Henry Gaum, 2 adults and 5 children, 25 packages
289. W.F. Simpson, 2 adults and 5 children, 17 packages
290. Mrs. Robinson, 1 adult, 2 children, and 1 servant, 20 packages
291. Mrs. Scruchen, 1 adult, 1 child, and 1 servant, 40 packages
292. Mrs. C.A. Jett, 2 adults and 4 children, 30 packages
293. J.T. Coppage, 2 adults and 5 children, 25 packages
294. J.H. Smith, 2 adults and 2 children, 56 packages
295. Mrs. L. Simpson, 1 adult and 5 children, 24 packages
296. Mrs. L. Williams, 1 adult and 5 children, 16 packages
297. Mrs. J. Berry, 1 adult and 7 children, 20 packages

298. Miss Cole, 4 adults, 18 packages
299. R.J. Maynard, 2 adults and 4 children, 41 packages
300. R. Faulkner, 2 adults, 1 child, and 1 servant, 45 packages and 1 cow
301. D. Howard, 2 adults and 3 children, 30 packages
302. A.H. Bramlett, 1 adult, 1 package
303. T.J. London, 2 adults and 4 children, 26 packages
304. Mrs. E. Green, 2 adults and 2 children, 50 packages
305. W.B. Webb, 4 adult, 3 children, and 1 servant, 35 packages
306. J.E. Webb, 2 adults, 17 packages
307. A.M. Johnson, 3 adults, 87 packages
308. J.A. Jett, 1 adult, 10 packages, wagon & horses
309. Mrs. R. Otto, 2 adults, 10 packages
310. W.R. Venable, 2 adults and 3 children, 25 packages
311. Mrs. L. Pain, 1 adult and 1 child, 10 packages
312. G.W. Croft, 2 adults and 6 children, 52 packages
313. E.W. Marsh, 3 adults, 4 children, and 1 servant, 67 packages
314. Mrs. H. Ward, 1 adult, 3 packages
315. Mrs. General Bowen, Mrs. Joyner, 2 adults, 3 children, and 1 servant
316. Mrs. Darst, 1 adult and 2 children, 5 packages
317. J.R. Crew, 2 adults and 3 servants, 15 packages
318. W.J. Ballard, 1 adult, 1 package
319. P. Broadshaw, 2 adults, 10 packages
320. T.E. Jones, 1 adult and 1 child, 1 package
321. Mrs. E. Grey, 1 adult and 2 packages
322. Mrs. M.A. Hoosins, 1 adult and 1 child, no packages
323. Mrs. E. Skinner, 1 adult and 4 children, 20 packages
324. G.O. Reed, 1 adult, no packages
325. J.C. Johnson, 2 adults and 2 children, 25 packages
326. P.J. McCullough, 1 adult, 2 packages
327. G. Slaton, 2 adults and 4 children, 25 packages
328. Mrs. E. Warrick, 3 adults and 6 children, 32 packages
329. M. Solomen, 2 adults, 35 packages
330. Mrs. E. Buice, 3 adults and 2 children, 50 packages
331. Mrs. M.A. Haygood, 2 adults, 60 packages
332. Mrs. E. Roberts, 1 adult, 2 packages
333. Mrs. M.E. Martin, 1 adult and 5 children, 42 packages
334. F.P. Rice, 2 adults, 3 packages
335. Mrs. M. Denny, 1 adult and 4 children, 23 packages
336. A.J. Ponder, 2 adults and 3 children, 18 packages
337. Mrs. E. Leach, 1 adult and 4 children, 26 packages
338. W.C. Hueghton, 8 adults and 5 children, 40 packages
339. Sam Farrar, 2 adults and 17 children. 17 packages

Appendix E. Civilians Forced to Evacuate Atlanta, September 1864

SEPTEMBER 16, 1864

340. Mrs. E. Sewell, 7 adults and 1 servant, 48 packages and 1 cow
341. J.J. Hunt, 2 adults, 2 packages
342. Mrs. McCormack, 1 adult and 4 children, 11 packages
343. Mrs. M. Davis, 1 adult and 1 servant, 41 packages
344. W.W. Roack, 1 adult and 3 children, 60 packages
345. T.C. Bradbury, 3 adults, 25 packages
346. M.E. Smith, 1 adult and 2 children, 35 packages
347. Mrs. R.P. Reid, 1 adult and 3 children, 30 packages
348. Mrs. L. Underwood, 1 adult, 1 package
349. Mrs. E. Curtis, 1 adult and 6 children, 60 packages
350. Mrs. J. Winship, 1 adult, 54 packages
351. J.L. Smith, 5 adults and 1 servant, 72 packages
352. Mrs. M.J. Johnson, 4 adults, 39 packages
353. P. Maddox, 4 adults, 50 packages
354. Miss Born, 1 adult, 25 packages
355. Mrs. E.C. Trail, 4 adults, 25 packages
356. Mrs. N. Loveless, 1 adult, 30 packages
357. Mrs. T.C. Jackson, 1 adult, 1 child, 39 packages
358. J.C. Rasboy, 2 adults and 6 children, 63(?) packages
359. J.M. Clark, 2 adults and 3 servants, 10 packages
360. J.M. Bramlett, 2 adult, 4 children, and 1 servant, 20 packages
361. W.H. McMillen, 1 adult, 12 packages
362. C. Rinehart, 2 adults and 3 children, 27 packages
363. E.M. Monday, 2 adults and 4 children, 48 packages and horse & buggy
364. Mrs. F.W. Johnson, 1 adult, 5 children, and 2 servants, 35 packages
365. Mrs. E. Phillips, 1 adult and 1 child, 23 packages
366. B. Mullegan, 3 adults, 12 packages
367. Mrs. M. Owens, 2 adults and 6 children, 30 packages and 1 cow
368. Mrs. A.C. Trenhelem, 3 adults and 1 child, 11 packages
369. Wm. Garvin, 2 adults and 4 children, 15 packages
370. Mrs. C.C. Pain, 1 adult and 2 children, 11 packages
371. Mrs. M. Tubb, 1 adult and 1 servant, 10 packages
372. R. Powers, 1 adult and 3 children, 10 packages and "negro."
373. Mrs. J. Wilson, 1 adult, 8 packages
374. Mrs. E. Farr, 1 adult and 5 children, 20 packages
375. B.J. Austn, 2 adults, 1 child, and 1 servant, 40 packages
376. Mrs. J. Hall, 1 adult, 20 packages
377. Mrs. S. Sumerlin, 1 adult and 2 children, 25 packages
378. J.E. Buchanan, 2 adults and 5 children, no packages
379. Mrs. M. Merritt, 1 adult, 10 packages
380. Mrs. Wilson, 1 adult, 5 packages

381. S.N. Biggers, 1 adult, 25 packages
382. Miss M. Burke, 1 adult, 20 packages
383. J. Ormead, 1 adult, 1 package
384. Mrs. S. Ament, 2 adults and 4 children, 20 packages
385. Mrs. Emma Rince, 2 adults and 2 children, 10 packages
386. T.P. Fleming, 3 adults and 3 servants, 30 packages
387. Mrs. N. Ray, 1 adult and 5 servants, 20 packages
388. Mrs. Coleman, 1 adult and 4 children, 25 packages
389. Mrs. A.G. Ware, 1 adult, 2 packages
390. Mrs. F. Glave, 1 adult, 1 package

SEPTEMBER 17, 1864

391. Mrs. J.R. Wilson, 1 adult and 2 packages
392. Mrs. N. Thompson, 2 adults, 20 packages
393. T.S. Denny, 2 adults and 1 child, 30 packages
394. Mrs. A. Manion, 1 adult, 35 packages
395. J.M. Calhoun, 1 adult, 4 servants, 80 packages
396. E.J. Clark, 1 adult, 1 package
397. J.F. Trout, 2 adults and 5 children, 60 packages
398. Mrs. Solomon, 1 adult, 2 packages
399. M.A. McCaian, 1 adult and 2 children, 2 packages
400. Mrs. N. Wilder, 2 adults, 58 packages
401. Mrs. M.D. Wormack, 1 adult and 3 children, 22 packages
402. Mrs. C. Kill, 1 adult, 17 packages
403. Mrs. E. Sheirs, 1 adult and 3 children, 18 packages
404. J. Langston, 3 adults and 4 children, 50 packages
405. J.J. Jenkins, 2 adults and 7 children, 55 packages
406. Mrs. F.W. Flynn, 2 adult and 3 children, and 1 servant 20 packages
407. Mrs. C. Flynn, 1 adult, 10 packages
408. Mrs. C.M. Winn, 1 adult, 2 children, and 1 servant 30 packages
409. Mrs. C. Caldwell, 4 adults and 9 children, 20 packages and 1 cow
410. W.N. Kirkpatrick, 2 adults and 3 children, 40 packages
411. Mrs. F. Glave, 1 adult, 1 package
412. Mrs. M. Maddox, 1 adult, 5 children, and 1 servant, 20 packages
413. A.F. Morrison, 2 adults and 4 children, 10 packages
414. E. Monday, 2 adults and 6 children, 50 packages (did not go)
415. A.J. Blackham, 1 adult, 50 packages
416. Mrs. N.D. Wood, 2 adults, 25 packages

SEPTEMBER 18, 1864

417. Mrs. C. Wood, 2 adults, 20 packages
418. Mrs. L. Cox, 1 adult, no packages

419. Frank Berry, 2 adults and 2 children, 50 packages
420. James Turner, 1 adult, 1 package
421. Miss E. Simpson, 1 adult, 8 packages
422. A.D. Westmoreland, 1 adult and 1 servant, 20 packages
423. Mrs. L. Ross, 1 adult, 3 children, and 1 servant, 40 packages
424. Mrs. Morgan, 2 adults and 10 children, 12 packages
425. Mrs. M. Holnyd, 2 adults, 100 packages
426. Mrs. M.E. Clements, 1 adult, 3 children, and 1 servant, 50 packages
427. J.B. Colen, 1 adult, 1 package
428. Mrs. L.L. Grant, 1 adult, 2 children, and 1 servant, 50 packages
429. F.M. Jeffreys, 1 adult, no packages
430. J.J. Ford, 1 adult, no packages
431. Mrs. N. McDaniel, 1 adult and 5 children, 10 packages
432. E. Kennedy, 2 adults, 1 child, and 2 servants, 35 packages
433. Mrs. Kennedy, 3 adults, 22 packages
434. Mrs. V. Williams, 1 adult and 4 children, 20 packages
435. W. Terry, 1 adult, 20 packages
436. Mrs. Dolmon, 1 adult and 6 children, 10 packages
437. Mrs. Robbins, 1 adult and 1 child, 3 packages
438. Miss E. Johns, 2 adults, 10 packages
439. Mrs. Gilmore, 1 adult and 2 children, 20 packages
440. G.M. Barry, 1 adult, no packages

SEPTEMBER 20, 1864

441. Mrs. F. Carr, 1 adult, 10 packages
442. Mrs. J. Powell, 1 adult, 3 children, 12 packages
(A) Mrs. J. Dudley, 1 adult, 3 packages
(B) Mrs. A. Knight, 1 adult and 3 children, 4 packages
(C) Mrs. K. Bouls, Mrs. M. Bouls, 2 adults, 14 packages
(D) R.A. Davis, 1 adult, no package

Recapitulation

Adults	705
Children	860
Servants	86
Total	1,651

Packages of baggage 8,842

| Horses | 9 |
| Cows | 19 |

Appendix E. Civilians Forced to Evacuate Atlanta, September 1864

Calves	6
Wagons	2
Drays	2
Carriages	1
Buggies	1

Respectfully submitted
(signed) William G. Le Duc
Lieutenant-Colonel and Chief Quartermaster Twentieth Artillery

Appendix F

Some Civil War Atlantans

THE HISTORY AND LEGEND of Civil War Atlanta has generated mountains of scholarship that has turned up considerable amounts of personal information on Atlantans of the period. Two books illustrate the value of searching such historical works for genealogical and biographical data: Sarah Conley Clayton, *Requiem for a Lost City: A Memoir of Civil War Atlanta and the Old South* (Macon: Mercer University Press, 1999), the story from the view of a daughter of a wealthy slave-owning family and Thomas G. Dyer, *Secret Yankees: The Union Circle in Confederate Atlanta* (Baltimore: Johns Hopkins University Press, 1999), which discusses the war from the writings of a Unionist woman.

Below is a list of people with significant biographical information in those two works; also see Franklin M. Garrett, *Atlanta and Environs: A Chronicle of Its People and Events*, 2 vols. (New York: Lewis Publishing, 1954). Dozens of other persons have at least a mention in these two indexed books. For a similar work on Macon, see Richard W. Iobst, *Civil War Macon* (Macon: Mercer University Press, 1999).

Alston, Robert (Clayton)
Angier, Nedom L. (Dyer)
Austell, Alfred (Dyer)
Avery, Sallie (Clayton)
Baldwin, Lucy Hull (Clayton)
Barnard, Ann Morgan (Clayton)
Baylor, Eugene W. (Clayton)
Berry, Carrie (Dyer)
Berry, Madison (Dyer)
Betune, Blind Tom (Clayton)
Bohnefield, Charles (Dyer)
Bourlier, Emile (Dyer)
Bransford, John S. (Clayton)
Brantley, William T. (Clayton)
Briggs, George (Dyer)
Brown, Miss [Mariah S. Brown] (Clayton)
Calhoun, James M. (Dyer)
Cameron, Francina (Clayton)
Cassin, C.P. (Dyer)
Chaffee, Daniel (Dyer)
Chaffers, Edward (Clayton)
Clayton, Augustin Smith (1850–1916) (Clayton)
Clayton, Philip Augustin (Clayton)
Clayton, Thomas Andrew (Clayton)
Clayton, William Force (Clayton)
Clayton, William Harris (Clayton)
Clayton, William Wirt (Clayton)
Clift, William D. (Dyer)
Cogswell, William (Dyer)
Cole, Henry G. (Dyer)
Conley, Benjamin (Clayton)
Conley, Morris J. (Clayton)
Conley, Sarah Semmes (Clayton)
Conynham, David P. (Dyer)
Cooper, Mark Anthony (Clayton)
Cowart, Robert J. (Clayton) (Dyer)

Crane, Benjamin Elliot (Clayton)
Crew, James R. (Clayton) (Dyer)
Crussell, Thomas G.W. (Dyer)
Dabney, William H. (Clayton)
Davis, Thomas W. (Clayton)
Deake, C.T.C. (Dyer)
Delphy, Amans (Dyer)
Doile, Bridgett (Dyer)
Duncan, John W. (Dyer)
Dunning, B.E. (Dyer)
Dunning, James L. (Dyer)
Dyer, William (Dyer)
Edwards, George (Dyer)
Erskine, John (Dyer)
Farnsworth, Emily (Dyer)
Farnsworth, William (Dyer)
Faught, Luther (Dyer)
Ficken, John (Dyer)
Fishback, William G. (Clayton)
Fisher, W.H. (Clayton)
Fitch, Henry S. (Dyer)
Floyd, J.M. (Clayton)
Floyd, Lettie (Clayton)
Foard, Andrew Jackson (Clayton)
Foreacre, Greenberry Jones (Clayton)
Gartrell, Lucius Jeremiah (Dyer) (Clayton)
Gebhardt, Frederick William (Clayton)
Glenn, Luther J. (Dyer)
Goode, Anne E. (Clayton)
Goode, Eugenia (Clayton)
Goode, Lucy C. (Clayton)
Goulding, Charles Howard (Clayton)
Hambleton, James P. (Dyer)
Hamilton, A.E. Miss (Clayton)
Hanleiter, Josephine Etta (Clayton)
Harmsen, Ludwig (Clayton)
Harris, Caroline Yancey (Clayton)
Harris, Dennis B. (Clayton)
Hayden, Julius A. (Dyer)
Healey, Olive M. (Dyer)
Healey, Thomas G. (Dyer)
Herring, William F. (Dyer)
Hill, Benjamin H. (Dyer)
Hinton, Martin (Dyer)
Hinton, Mary (Dyer)
Holcombe, Henry C. (Dyer)
Holiday, Martha Anne (Clayton)
Howard, Rufus A. (Clayton)
Howard, W. Pinckney (Clayton)
Huge, Peter (Dyer)
Hunnicutt, E.T. (Dyer)
Hunnicutt, Henry (Dyer)
Huntington, Martha (Dyer)
Hurlburt, William H. (Dyer)
Hurt, Augustus F. (Clayton)
Jones, Edward L. (Dyer)
Jones, Oliver H. (Dyer)
Jordan, Thomas (Dyer)
Joyner, Mecca (Clayton)
Keely, John P. (Clayton)
Kile, Thomas (Dyer)
Kimbell, H.I. (Clayton)
King, Augusta Clayton (Clayton)
King, Carrie (Dyer)
Kontz, Christian (Clayton) (Dyer)
Le Duc, William G. (Dyer)
Lee, George Washington (Dyer)
Logan, James Payne (Clayton)
Lowry, Emma Markham (Dyer)
Lowry, Robert J. (Clayton) (Dyer)
Lynch, James (Dyer)
Lynch, John (Dyer)
Lynch, Michael (Dyer)
Maddox, Robert Foster (Clayton)
Manning, Jethro W. (Clayton)
Manning, William B. (Dyer)
Markham, Marcellus O. (Dyer)
Markham, William (Clayton) (Dyer)
Markley, Thomas C. (Clayton)
Marsh, Philip B. (Dyer)
Matthews, James R. (Dyer)
Mayes, Richard (Dyer)
Mayson, James R. (Clayton)

Appendix F. Some Civil War Atlantans

McCroskey, Robert H. (Dyer)
McIntire, Philip (Dyer)
McKeen, Georgia (Clayton)
Minor, James G. (Dyer)
Mitchell, Margaret (Clayton)
Morris, Elizabeth E. (Clayton)
Munday, E.W. (Dyer)
Neal, James Henry (Clayton)
Neal, John (Clayton)
Newcomb, D.S. (Dyer)
Newman, Thomas (Dyer)
Nisbet, James T. (Dyer)
Norcross, Jonathan (Dyer)
Oliver, Pliney R. (Dyer)
Orme, Aquilla J. (Clayton)
Ormond, James (Clayton)
Parker, Francis S. (Clayton)
Parson, Richard (Dyer)
Pattillo, William Pulaski (Clayton)
Peacock, L.P. (Dyer)
Peck, John C. (Dyer)
Peters, Richard (Clayton) (Dyer)
Peterson, Josiah S. (Dyer)
Pittman, Daniel N. (Clayton)
Pool, Margaret J. (Clayton)
Price, James (Clayton)
Purse, Isaiah (Clayton)
Quintard, Charles Todd (Clayton)
Rawson, E.E. (Dyer)
Rice, Frank (Dyer)
Rice, Z.A. (Clayton)
Richards, Samuel P. (Dyer)
Robson, Annie (Clayton)
Robson, Kate Hester (Clayton)
Root, Sidney (Clayton)
Rustin, William (Dyer)
Ryan, John (Dyer)
Schofield, Lewis (Clayton) (Dyer)
Scott, Anderson L. (Dyer)
Scrutchin, Thomas (Dyer)
Sells, H. Mrs. (Clayton)
Sells, Holmes (Dyer)
Semmes, Andrew Green (Clayton)
Semmes, Benedict Joseph (Clayton)
Semmes, Samuel Spencer (Clayton)
Semmes, Thomas Hemphill (Clayton)
Sharp, Jacob Hunter (Clayton)
Sharp, Thomas J. (Clayton)
Silvey, John (Dyer)
Smith, J. Henley (Dyer)
Snook, Peyton H. (Clayton)
Sterchi, Elizabeth (Clayton)
Stewart, James A. (Dyer)
Stone, Amherst (Dyer)
Stone, Cynthia (Dyer)
Summerlin, Mary (Dyer)
Thompson, George Harvey (Clayton)
Thompson, Joseph (Clayton)
Trout, Jeremiah (Clayton)
Turner, L.C. (Dyer)
Urquhart, David (Clayton)
Wallace, Alexander M. (Dyer)
Watterson, Henry (Clayton)
Way, Samuel (Clayton)
Webster, Robert (Dyer)
Westmoreland, Mariah Jourdan (Clayton)
Westmoreland, Willis Foreman (Clayton)
Whitaker, Jared I. (Dyer)
Whitney, Louisa (Dyer)
Williams, Frederick A. (Clayton)
Williams, James E. (Clayton)
Williams, Mary A. (Clayton)
Wilson, A.N. (Clayton)
Wilson, Alexander N. (Dyer)
Winship, Martha (Clayton)
Woodbury, Josephine (Dyer)
Wright, Austin (Dyer)
Yancey, Benjamin C. (Dyer)
Yancey, Benjamin Cudsworth (Clayton)
Yancey, Hamilton (Clayton)
Young, Davis (Dyer)

Appendix G

Research in Atlanta and the Atlanta Area

Background

Millions of Americans of very different backgrounds have family stories of ancestors who lived "near Atlanta" sometime in the past. The "Gate City" and the "Capital of the New South" always welcomed newcomers—except, generally, Sherman and his army in 1864!

Atlanta is also an important crossroads for families and individuals who moved on to build modern America. The area's research sources are plentiful, although "lived near Atlanta" means virtually anywhere within seventy-five miles of Five Points, the city's historical center, including west across the Georgia border into eastern Alabama.

Researchers can find Atlanta as confusing as its streets' illogical naming and arrangement. The area, allegedly Creek Indian lands occupied by the Cherokees, first appeared as a name on a map that shows a Native American community along the Chattahoochee River called Standing Peachtree. This mixed Cherokee-Creek settlement became the site of a military outpost in 1813 and is the origin of the name for the more than 60 "Peachtree" streets in the metro area today. Native Americans gave up the territory to the state of Georgia in 1821.[1]

The land was given away to white Georgia heads of families, and others, through pre-surveyed lots arranged in districts, by lottery, see Silas E. Lucas, Jr., *The 1820 and 1821 Land Lottery of Georgia* (Easley, SC: Southern Historical Press, 1973) and Paul G. Graham, *Georgia Land Lottery Records* (Atlanta: The Author, 2010). Unlike Brunswick, Columbus, Macon, and Milledgeville, the state of Georgia did not lay out or authorize the town lots in Atlanta.

The future Atlanta was included in what became DeKalb County in December 1822. Originally a crossroads community around a tavern called Whitehall, the settlement that would become Atlanta was first known as Terminus after the state of Georgia determined to make it the southern end of the proposed state-owned Western & Atlantic Railroad in 1837.[2] The W&A, however, never went to the West or the Atlantic! The records of the W&A are at the Georgia Archives in Morrow.

Other railroads joined the W&A at Terminus, four others by 1860, and fifteen by 1900. The city would eventually prosper on rail, highway, and air transportation but not as a port. Atlanta's Chattahoochee River is notoriously shallow that far north and made a poor defense against Sherman's armies.

Officially incorporated as Marthasville in 1843, the city began at that crossroads just before it had a permanent municipal government that kept records. On December 29, 1847, it became incorporated as Atlanta, a name invented by railroad superintendent J. Edgar Thomson (later a national transportation czar) from the Western & Atlantic Railroad that made this "Gate City" possible.[3]

Contrary to popular myth, General Sherman's soldiers did not burn Atlanta or its records during the Civil War. The city's buildings did suffer much damage from both armies during its 1864 siege, however, inspiring Atlanta's symbol of a phoenix rising from flames. That almost nothing survives from the Civil War city is due to fires in the early twentieth century and to the constant demolition and new construction that continues today.[4]

During the city's early years, as part of DeKalb County, its county seat was nearby Decatur. In December 1853, the Georgia legislature created Fulton County, with Atlanta as the site of its new courthouse. On January 1, 1928, the city acquired residential areas in western DeKalb County so that, while Atlanta is the county seat of Fulton County, its eastern neighborhoods are in DeKalb County and have Decatur as their county seat. In December 1932, the citizens of bankrupt Campbell and Milton counties voted to abolish and incorporate their counties (and records) into Fulton County.

Atlanta officially became the capital of the state of Georgia in 1868.

Libraries and Archives

Atlanta's historical documents are scattered among many research centers, not all within the seventy-five-mile radius of Five Points. Getting to them can be an adventure beyond research. Who would not want to pass up the chance to experience the city's infamous traffic and enigmatically twisted streets, what local writer Lewis Grizzard described as asphalt-covered buffalo tails and water runs?

The major research centers are listed below, but many local libraries, such as those of Decatur and Marietta, and archives such as the Roswell Historical Society and Kennesaw National Battlefield Park, also have valuable local resources. For Georgia as a whole:

Lists of Libraries: Georgia Library Service *https://georgialibraries.org/find-a-library/*

Lists of Archives: Georgia Society of Archivists *https://soga.wildapricot.org/resource/repositories*

Georgia Archives' Historical and Cultural Organizations Directory *https://www.georgiaarchives.org/ghrac/directory/*

The Kenan Research Center, Atlanta History Center, 130 West Paces Ferry

Road NW, Atlanta, GA 30305-1366, has extensive Atlanta-oriented private manuscript and photograph collections. The grounds include educational, entertaining, and extensive museums[5]: *http://www.atlantahistorycenter.com/cms/Kenan+Research+Center/185.html*

The Georgia Archives (formerly the Georgia Department of Archives and History) is now immediately southwest of Atlanta at 5800 Jonesboro Road, Morrow, GA 30260. It has extensive holdings of government, church, photographic, and manuscript materials for all of Georgia.[6]

Website: *http://www.sos.ga.gov/archives*.

The National Archives Atlanta Branch, the federal archives for court records, and much more for Atlanta, Georgia, the Southeastern United States, and Kentucky, shares a parking lot with the Georgia Archives, at 5780 Jonesboro Road, Morrow, GA 30260. Among its holdings of special interest to Atlanta researchers are federal court records, post–Civil War federal direct tax records, and the records of the Atlanta Federal Penitentiary. It has a number of valuable handouts on its specific holdings. Website: *http://www.archives.gov/southeast*

The Fulton County Public Library Central Branch has Special Collections, Central Library, One Margaret Mitchell Square, Atlanta, GA 30303: *https://www.fulcolibrary.org/central-library* and Auburn Avenue Research Library on African American Culture and History, 101 Auburn Avenue NE, Atlanta, GA 30303: *https://www.fulcolibrary.org/auburn-avenue-research-library*

The Stuart A. Rose Manuscript, Archives, and Rare Book Library, Emory University, 540 Asbury Circle, Atlanta, GA 30322-2870, has extensive Atlanta holdings but especially Civil War letters, diaries, etc., and the papers of some of the city's most famous citizens: *https://libraries.emory.edu/rose*

Just outside of the famous seventy-five-mile range of "near Atlanta" are two great libraries for Georgia research. The Hargrett Rare Book & Manuscripts Library, University of Georgia Libraries, 320 S. Jackson St., Athens, GA 30602-1641 (website: *http://www.libs.uga.edu/hargrett*), the most extensive holdings of historical Georgia non-government manuscript materials and books in the world as well as family, biographical, and other vertical files.[7] Georgia's great genealogical collection is the Genealogical & Historical Room, Washington Memorial Library, 1180 Washington Ave., Macon, GA 31201-1790 (website: *http://www.co.bibb.ga.us/library/GH.htm*), specializing in central Georgia, the eastern United States, and Great Britain.[8]

Many of Atlanta's early citizens came from, moved to, or passed back and forth from Troup County, Georgia, and the adjoining areas of Alabama and Georgia. A valuable resource for researching these sometimes Atlantans is the Troup County Archives, 136 Main Street, POB 1051, LaGrange, GA 30241 (website: *http://www.trouparchives.org*) for its local government records and genealogical collections for the families of the Georgia-Alabama border.[9]

The Southern History Department, Central Branch, Birmingham Public Library, 2100 Park Place, Birmingham, AL 35203-2744 (website: *www.bplonline.org/*

locations/central/southern), is two hours west of Atlanta. It is the one of the greatest collections of material for Southern genealogy and historical research ever assembled.

Local Government Records

For a detailed description of urban Georgia records most often preserved for Atlanta, see Paul K. Graham, "Historical Records of Urban Georgia," *Georgia Genealogical Society Quarterly* 43 (Summer 2007): 87–90. R. Michael Brubaker has used such records from the Kenan Research Center of the Atlanta History Center to publish articles on Atlanta's often forgotten or overlooked: "Atlanta Police Court Docket, May 1872–August 1872," *Georgia Genealogical Society Quarterly* 43 (Spring 2007): 17–57; "Some Residents of the Fulton County Almshouse," *ibid.*, 45 (Summer 2009): 149–152; and "Some Records from Atlanta's Home for the Friendless—1908–1909," *ibid.*, 46 (Spring 2010): 23–32.[10]

Georgia records, in general, are among the most extensive in the Southeastern United States. The Georgia Archives in nearby Morrow, Georgia, and the Genealogical Society of Utah have microfilm of almost all bound Georgia county records to at least 1900, including civil marriages, criminal and civil court minutes, estates, and tax digests. These records are also accessible from the free online site Familysearch.org.

County records for the Atlanta area usually survive except for those lost in the DeKalb County courthouse fire of 1842, the Ku Klux Klan's burning of the Gwinnett County courthouse in 1871, and the loss of the Cobb County civil archives in a misguided effort to save the records from approaching Federal troops in 1864. Fulton County deed books B, F, H, and mortgage book E were destroyed when thrown down the courthouse well around 1880. Many originals of the documents destroyed as copies in these books were recopied in later volumes of court records that have survived.[11]

Many records do survive, and some special sources are listed here. The Georgia Archives has an almost complete sets of original county tax digests (c 1872 to present) for the entire state, and many earlier ones for counties like Fulton. Many of those records are included on the online sites Ancestry.com and AncestryLibrary.com.[12] Ted O. Brooke has published Fulton County's first marriage books and a state-wide list of wills to 1900.[13]

Miscellaneous records of Campbell, Fulton, and Milton counties have been donated to the Kenan Research Center of the Atlanta History Center, although other important original manuscript county records for all three counties remain in the Fulton County Archives and Fulton County Court House, 141 Pryor Street SW, Atlanta, GA 30303-3444. Many of these records are on microfilm at the Georgia Archives.

Miscellaneous

The first Atlanta city directory appeared in 1859 and included the original of the several of the city's genealogically valuable histories, see *Williams' Atlanta Directory*,

City, Guide, or Business Mirror (Atlanta, GA: M. Lynch, 1859), available on the Internet from HathiTrust, *https://babel.hathitrust.org/cgi/pt?id=emu.10002331152&seq=1*, accessed May 24, 2024. Alternatively, see "Residents of Atlanta, Georgia, 1859–1860," *Georgia Genealogical Magazine* 36 (4) (1996): 285–293.

Other such works include the Pioneer Citizens' Society, *Pioneer Citizens' History of Atlanta, 1833–1902* (Atlanta: Byrd Printing, 1902) and Lucian Lamar Knight, *History of Fulton County, Georgia: Narrative and Biographical* (Atlanta: A.H. Cawston, 1930). The original volume three of Franklin Garrett, *Atlanta and Environs* (New York: Lewis Publishing, 1954) was a collection of biographical sketches of prominent Atlantans.

Most of these works have no index or have been poorly indexed. Researchers will find access better through the scanned copies online, including on the free Internet sources such as Archive.org, HathiTrust, and Google Books, including A.A. Hoehling, *The Last Train from Atlanta* (New York: Thomas Joseloff, 1958).

The Kenan Research Center of the Atlanta History Center has scanned the back issues of *Atlanta History* and its other historical publications. Access is free to everyone on the Kenan Research Center online site. The Atlanta History Center also has a card catalog index to these all now defunct historical journals.[14] Other Atlanta articles can be found on the free online sites for JSTOR: *https://www.jstor.org*.

Back issues of the *Georgia Genealogical Society Quarterly* have been scanned and are word searchable, for members of the Georgia Genealogical Society, on its site: *https://gagensociety.org/for-members-only*. Researchers can also learn of articles from genealogical journals through the Periodical Resource Index (PERSI): *https://www.genealogycenter.info/persi*

The *Atlanta Historical Bulletin* includes most of the text of what became Garrett's monumental two volume *Atlanta and Environs: A Chronicle of Its People and Events* 2 vols., (New York: Lewis Historical Publishing Company; 1954; facsimile reprint, Athens: University of Georgia Press, 1988), the great history of Fulton and surrounding counties. Those two volumes are very poorly indexed, however, making the above card catalogs of the *Atlanta Historical Bulletin* sometimes a better way of accessing its information than its own index (these two volumes have also been scanned onto and are word searchable on the Internet on Google Books).[15]

Many other unusual records for Atlanta and Fulton County have at least indexes in print, see for example, "Biographical Index to Some Early Atlantans," *Georgia Genealogical Society Quarterly* 30 (Winter 1994): 261–262; and "Civilians Held Prisoner in Atlanta, 1865–1866," *ibid.* 38 (Spring 2002): 36–38. Civil War widows and orphans who received benefits from Atlanta's Masonic Orphans Home Lottery, 1870–1876, appear in Robert S. Davis, *The Georgia Black Book II* (Easley, SC: Southern Historical Press, 1987), 159–190, while prison and asylum records are included in that volume and in *The Georgia Black Book: Morbid, Macabre, and Sometimes Disgusting Records of Genealogical Value* (Easley, SC: Southern Historical Press, 1982).

Members of the Fulton County militia in 1864 were recorded, with age, occupation, and place of birth for each man. These records are included in Nancy J. Cornell, *1864 Census for the Re-Organizing the Georgia Militia* (Baltimore: Genealogical Publishing Company, 2000), 252–265.

Many books have been written about Atlanta in the Civil War that include personal information on individuals. See, for example, Wendy Hamand Venet, *A Changing Wind: Commerce and Conflict in Civil War Atlanta* (New Haven, CT: Yale University Press, 2014).

Aside from the sources mentioned elsewhere, many other less well-known records for all of Georgia or the United States have great value. These works include Ted O. Brooke and Robert S. Davis, *Georgia Research: A Handbook for Genealogists, Historians, Archivists, Lawyers, Librarians, and Other Researchers* (2nd edition, Atlanta: Georgia Genealogical Society, 2012) and William Dollarhide, *Georgia Name Lists, 1733–2010* (Bountiful, UT: Family Roots, 2013).

Atlanta and Fulton County, along with what survives for the rest of Georgia, from Federal direct tax records for 1865–1866 (National Archives Microfilm 762); the extensive personal information on African Americans in Freedman's Bank Records for 1870–1874 (National Archives microfilm M816); and records of the field offices of the Freedmen's Bureau in Georgia (National Archives microfilm M1903) are all included on the subscription websites Ancestry.com and AncestryLibrary.com and can there be searched electronically.

Naturalizations

Atlanta has always had a significant foreign-born community, but finding naturalization and other citizenship records can be difficult. Before 1907, these records might be filed in the city court, county Superior Court, or federal court minutes.

Naturalization records from the federal court records are indexed in Linda Geiger and Meyer L. Frankel, *Index to Georgia's Naturalization Records to 1950* (Atlanta: Georgia Genealogical Society, 1996); also see "Alien Atlantans in 1864," *Georgia Genealogical Society Quarterly* 24 (Winter 1988): 110. Foreign place of birth is indicated in federal census records beginning in 1850.

Beyond those standard naturalization records, citizenship information on many of the foreign-born men appears in the 1867–1868 returns of qualified voters for Atlanta and the rest of Georgia at the Georgia Archives. The registered white men are included in John David Brandenburg and Rita Brinkley Worthy, *Index to Georgia's 1867–1868 Returns of Qualified Voters and Registration Oath Books* (Atlanta: The Authors, 1995), although these records also survive for African American men.[16]

Newspapers

No complete run of any Atlanta newspaper exists from before 1868 and the surviving issues are scattered among libraries across the eastern United States. A thorough bibliography of what has survived does not exist. Copies of previously thought lost issues are still being discovered.

A bibliography of known American newspapers is kept by the Library of Congress' Chronicling America: *https://chroniclingamerica.loc.gov/search/titles/*; also see Ruth Elaine Feldman, "A Checklist of Atlanta Newspapers, 1846-1948," (Master's Thesis, Emory University, 1948), a copy of which is in the Kenan Research Center. The American Antiquarian Society keeps records of originals of pre-1870s newspapers nationwide.

Not all of these newspapers have been microfilmed or scanned, and no single repository has copies of all of the microfilm. The Boston Anthenaeum, Kenan Research Center, the Georgia Archives, and the Woodruff Library of Emory University have different but significant collections of original and microfilm of the Atlanta newspapers beginning in the early 1850s.

Georgia Historic Newspapers of the Digital Library of Georgia offers free access online to many historical Atlanta (and Georgia) newspapers:. *https://gahistoricnewspapers.galileo.usg.edu*. The Georgia Newspaper Project of the University of Georgia Libraries has the largest collection of Georgia newspaper microfilm, although not all that is found in other repositories. The inventory of the GNP can be accessed over the Internet at: *http://www.libs.uga.edu/gnp/titlelist.html*

Many of the newspaper websites such as the Library of Congress' Chronicling America, Genealogybank, Newspapers.com, Newspaperarchive, and 19th Century Newspapers include Atlanta newspapers, especially the *Atlanta Constitution*, *Atlanta Georgian*, *Atlanta Journal*, and *Southern Confederacy*.

Chronicling America of the Library of Congress has online selected issues of the Atlanta Civil War *Memphis Daily Appeal*, a "refugee" newspaper. Also see Vicki Betts, "Memphis Appeal [Atlanta], June 1863-June 1864" (2016) accessed online June 12, 2024, *https://scholarworks.uttyler.edu/cw_newstitles/79* and other transcripts of the *Memphis Daily Appeal* online.

The Stuart A. Rose Library of Emory University has indexed scrapbooks of famed Atlanta journalist Henry Woodfin Grady (1850-1889), including articles from now lost newspapers. See the Henry Woodfin Grady Papers, Stuart A. Rose Manuscript, Archives, and Rare Book Library.

Religious Records

Mercer University and the Georgia Archives each have collections of microfilm of church records of many different Georgia faiths. For other faiths, see:

Queries about Baptist records in the Atlanta area should be made to Special Collections and University Archives, Mercer University: *https://ursa.mercer.edu/handle/10898/346*

For Atlanta's Jewish community, there is the William Breman Jewish Heritage Museum: *https://thebreman.org*. Also see Steven Hertzberg, *Strangers Within the*

Gate City: The Jews of Atlanta, 1845–1915 (Philadelphia, PA: Jewish Publication Society of America, 1978), accessed online June 17, 2024, at Archive.org: https://archive.org/details/strangerswithing0000hert/page/n7/mode/2up.

For the Methodist Episcopal Faith, see Brent H. Holcomb's published abstracts of marriages and deaths from the *Southern Christian Advocate*. Wofford College Library in South Carolina has abstracts of obituaries from that newspaper and some issues of the *Methodist Advocate*, 1869–1870s, that are also on the subscription site GenealogyBank. Original issues of Georgia's *Wesleyan Christian Advocate*, 1878–2008, are in the Pitt Theological Library, Emory University, Atlanta.

Presbyterian records for the Atlanta Area are kept by the C. Benton Kline, Jr., Special Collections & Archives, Columbia Theological Seminary, 701 S. Columbia Drive, Decatur, GA 30030: *https://www.ctsnet.edu/academics/c-benton-kline-jr-special-collection-archives*

The Archives of the Roman Catholic Archdiocese of Atlanta, 2401 Lake Park Drive S.E. Smyrna, GA 30080, has a website: https://archatl.com/offices/archives/

Vital Records

Vital records for the Gate City are confusing. Atlanta has city birth records beginning in 1887 and death records starting in 1896. Through 1918 these records should be requested from the Fulton County Health Department, 99 Butler Street, Atlanta, GA 30303. The state of Georgia began keeping vital records on January 1, 1919, although the law went largely ignored by many individual counties until ca. 1928. Death records for 1919–1927 are indexed and available online on the Georgia Archives' Virtual Vault. Death records for 1919–1943 are also indexed and available through Familysearch.org, as is the Social Security Death Index (1938–). The originals of the Georgia death certificates through 1943 are also available at the Georgia Archives. For death certificates from 1944 to the present, contact the Georgia Department of Public Health at Vital Records, 1680 Phoenix Blvd, Suite 100, Atlanta, GA 30349, Tel.: 404-679-4702:

These records are kept by the Vital Records Unit, Georgia Department of Human Resources, Room 217-H, 47 Trinity Avenue, Atlanta, GA 30334 and can be ordered through the VRU's website on the Internet: *http://health.state.ga.us/programs/vitalrecords/index.asp*

Other Death Records

For deaths before 1919, the most valuable single Atlanta specific source for research is the Atlanta or Garrett necrology of the Kenan Research Center of the Atlanta History Center. Franklin Miller Garrett (1906–2000), Atlanta's famed historian, compiled death information from cemetery records, death certificates, and obituaries on tens of thousands of white Atlantans for the 1840s to the 1920s.

Appendix G. Research in Atlanta and the Atlanta Area

From the post–Civil War painting *Cyclorama of the Battle of Atlanta* (1886) (Kenan Research Center at the Atlanta History Center).

The index exists as a computer database that refers the researcher to note books that are on microfilm and can be found in many genealogical libraries. It can be accessed from the Atlanta History Center's website: *http://garrett.atlanta historycenter.com/about.html* The Garrett Necrology has also been scanned and indexed, without its title on the subscription site Ancestry.com.

The online index of the Garrett Necrology at the Atlanta History Center's website does not include the records of Oakland Cemetery (the city's oldest public cemetery), Westview Cemetery (the second oldest public cemetery), the DeKalb County estates, and the Fulton County estates, as the entries on each of those rolls of the necrology microfilm are usually in alphabetical order.

The Georgia Archives has on microfilm an indexed scrapbook of Atlanta obituaries and funeral notices prepared by Mr. Garrett but not included in his necrology; see "Some Atlanta Obituaries, 1923–1932," *Georgia Genealogical Society Quarterly* 29 (Fall 1993): 166–173. Atlanta death notices are also found in Jeannette Holland Austin, *Atlanta Constitution* (1868–1884, 1887, 1890) (n. p.) and her *Georgia Obituaries* (1905–1910) (n.p.)

The Georgia Archives also has a microfilm copy of the original records of Atlanta's Oakland Cemetery, including information on the thousands of Confederate soldiers who died in the city's Civil War hospitals and battlefields. Names of these rebel dead are also found in volume two of Georgia Division United Daughters of the Confederacy, *Roster of Confederate Graves* (Atlanta: Georgia Division, UDC, 1995). Other records of Oakland Cemetery are at the cemetery and at the Kenan Research Center of the Atlanta History Center.

Most of the surviving records of the patients of Atlanta's Confederate hospitals are in the Stout Collection of the University of Texas in Austin and are not included in the compiled service records now on National Archives and Records Administration microfilm. The Stout Collection has not been indexed.[17]

Federal dead from the Atlanta campaign were buried in the Marietta National Cemetery. They are included with others buried there in volume three of Cobb County Genealogical Society, *Cobb County, Georgia, Cemeteries* (Marietta, GA: Cobb County, Georgia, Genealogical Society, 1994).

Chapter Notes

Acknowledgments

1. Materials in the collection were used in the controversial television documentary *The 1619 Project* and J.C. Hallman's *Say Anarcha: A Young Woman, a Devious Surgeon, and the Harrowing Birth of Modern Women's Health*. Shortly afterward, plans were announced to do away with the multi-million-dollar library, the most popular building with the students on campus. "Wallace State Library's Future in Question," *The Cullman (Alabama) Times*, June 17, 2023, and "Wallace State Shutters Genealogy Program, Terminates Longtime Instructor Robert Davis," ibid., July 1, 2023.

Preface

1. I dedicated my book *Ghosts and Shadows of Andersonville* to Ted Key. He introduced me to MacKinlay Kantor's *Andersonville*, the first big book I read, and my introduction to finding a book and interlibrary loan. *Ghosts and Shadows* is a non-fiction equivalent of what Kantor did in his Pulitzer Prize–winning novel telling the infamous prison's history through individuals.
2. The result of this internship was *Kettle Creek: The Battle of the Cane Brakes* (Atlanta, 1975), written with Kenneth H. Thomas, Jr., and reprinted in 2004.
3. "The Curious Civil War Career of James George Brown, Spy," *Prologue: The Quarterly of the National Archives* 26 (Spring 1994): 17–31.
4. "'Near Andersonville': An Historical Note on Civil War Legend and Reality," *Journal of African American History* 92 (Winter 2007): 96–105.
5. Thomas G. Dyer, *Secret Yankees: The Union Circle in Confederate Atlanta* (Baltimore, 2001).

Introduction

1. Dyer, *Secret Yankees*, 60–61. Other Southern cities such as Mobile also had such committees. See Jane Singer and John Stewart, *Lincoln's Secret Spy: The Civil War Case that Changed the Future of Espionage* (Guilford, CT, 2015).
2. Robert S. Davis, *Ghosts and Shadows of Andersonville: Essays on the Secret Social Histories of America's Deadliest Prison* (Macon, GA, 2006), 182–183.
3. Wendy Hamand Venet, *A Changing Wind: Commerce and Conflict in Civil War Atlanta* (New Haven, CT, 2014), 8–10. For Thomas Spalding see E. Merton Coulter, *Thomas Spalding of Sapelo* (Baton Rouge, LA, 1940).
4. Walter Johnson, *Soul by Soul: Life Inside the Antebellum Slave Market* (Cambridge, MA, 1999), 90.
5. R.S. Tharin, *Arbitrary Arrests in the South; Or, Scenes From the Experience of an Alabama Unionist* (New York, 1863), 58.
6. John T. Milner, *White Men Stand Together, 1860 and 1890* (Birmingham, AL, 1890), n. p. For Milner, see the autobiography of John T. Milner, Milner Family Papers, Collection 2420, Southern Historical Collection, University of North Carolina, Chapel Hill; and Dorothea Orr Warren, *The Practical Dreamer: A Story of John T. Milner* (Birmingham, AL, 1959).
7. Allen C. Guelzo, *Robert E. Lee: A Life* (New York, 2021), 145, 181–202, 426, 432–433.
8. James I. Robertson, "Names of the War," in Richard N. Current, Paul D. Escott, Lawrence N. Powell, James I. Robertson, Jr., and Emory M. Thomas, eds., *Encyclopedia of the Confederacy*, 4 vols. (New York, 1993), 1: 316.
9. Robert Strauss, *Worst President Ever: James Buchanan, the POTUS Rating Game, and the Legacy of the Least of the Lesser Presidents* (Guilford, CT, 2016), 152–153, 159–161.
10. John Rhodehamel, *America's Original Sin: White Supremacy, John Wilkes Booth, and the Lincoln Assassination* (Baltimore, MD, 2021), 16–17. For more on antebellum African Americans hiring out their professional services, see Jonathan D. Martin, *Divided Mastery: Slave Hiring in the American South* (Cambridge, MA, 2004).
11. Dr. Lewis T. Bullock, "Col. Robert Ashton Crawford," personality file, Atlanta History Center, Atlanta; Robert S. Davis, "Crawford, Frazer, & Company of Atlanta and Auburn," Dallas Genealogical Society, accessed online February 6, 2024: https://dallasgenealogy.org/crawford-frazer-company-of-atlanta-and-of-auburn; Sara Huff, *My 80 Years in Atlanta* (n. p., 1937), 11, 19–20; Reading, household 193/239, Middlesex County,

1865 State census, Massachusetts Hall of Records, Springfield, MA; Reading, Middlesex County, Massachusetts, p. 300A, *Ninth Census of the United States (1870)* (National Archives microfilm M593, roll 506); "Colonel Samuel D. Niles Is Claimed by Death" and "Mr. Niles Memory Honored by Friends," *Atlanta Journal*, November 13, 1907, p. 3, and November 17, 1907, p. 13; funeral notices, *Atlanta Constitution*, November 14, 1907, p. 2.

Chapter One

1. Crane Brinton, *The Anatomy of Revolution* (New York, 1965), 157–158.
2. "History," *Observer* (Fayetteville, NC), June 8, 1876; "Who Is General Lee?" *Commonwealth* (Atlanta), May 22, 1862. George Washington Lee has also been confused with Colonel G.W. Lee of the Twentieth South Carolina Militia Regiment, who served at the battle of Dingle's Mill, South Carolina, on April 9, 1865. No known connection exists between George W. Lee of Atlanta and the martyred African American Civil Rights leader George Washington Lee (1903–1955). George Alexander Sewell, *Mississippi Black History Makers* (Jackson, MS, 1984), 313–325.
3. Bible records, Lee/Huss Family Papers, AC 69-249, Georgia Archives (hereafter GAr), Morrow; Vivian Price, *The History of DeKalb County, Georgia 1822-1900* (Fernandina Beach, FL, 1997), 181–182.
4. Gordon B. Smith, *History of the Georgia Militia, 1783–1861*, 4 vols. (Milledgeville, GA, 2001), 1: 204, 209, 216-226; "Capt. Garmany's Company," *Weekly Gwinnett Herald* (Lawrenceville, GA), May 21, 1873.
5. Bible records, Lee/Huss Family Papers; Price, *The History of DeKalb County, Georgia 1822-1900*, 181–182; Pioneer Citizens' Society, *Pioneer Citizens' History of Atlanta 1833-1902* (Atlanta, 1902), 33; Atlanta, Fulton County, p. 873, *Eighth Census of the United States (1860)* (National Archives microfilm M653, roll 122), Records of the Bureau of the Census, Record Group (hereafter RG) 29, National Archives and Records Administration (hereafter NARA), Washington, D.C., available on the Internet on site FamilySearch.org, accessed May 24, 2024.
6. Robert S. Davis, "John Coffee's Search for the Lost History of the Cherokees," *Chattanooga Regional Historical Journal* 8 (December 2005): 143–164; William S. Irvine, ed., "Diary and Letters of Dr. William N. White, a Citizen of Atlanta Written 1847, 90 Years Ago," *Atlanta Historical Bulletin* 10 (July 1937): 39, 43, 47. Also see Mark Pifer, *Native Decatur: The Earliest History of the Decatur, Georgia Area from Its Bedrock Foundation to the Civil War* (Decatur, GA, 2012) and *Hidden History of Old Atlanta* (Charleston, SC, 2021).
7. Royce Singleton, *Richard Peters: Champion of the New South* (Macon, GA, 1985), 24; "Atlanta," *Southern Confederacy* (Atlanta), hereafter *SC*, July 13, 1862. Records in the National Archives of the United Kingdom identify many British ships named Atlanta, variations of *Atalante*, some infamous.
8. Robert S. Davis, "Georgia on the Eve of the Civil War: The Insurance Reports of C.C. Hine," *Atlanta History* 31 (spring-summer 1987): 51; "Atlanta," *SC*, July 13, 1862; Venet, *A Changing Wind*, 5, 7, 15. Other estimates of Atlanta's population run as high as 11,000 in 1859 to 15,000 in 1861. Sarah Conley Clayton, *Requiem for a Lost City: Sallie Clayton's Memoirs of Civil War Atlanta and the Old South*, Robert S. Davis, ed. (Macon, GA, 1999), 65. For a comparison to Chicago at that same time, see Toni Gilpin, *The Long Deep Grudge: A Story of Big Capital, Radical Labor, and Class War in the American Heartland* (Chicago, IL, 2020), 15. In the case of Atlanta, perhaps the Greek goddess Atalanta could have more appropriately chased golden peaches instead of apples!
9. Franklin M. Garrett, *Atlanta and Environs: A Chronicle of Its People and Events*, 2 vols. (New York, 1954), 1: 1–37; *Williams' Atlanta Directory, City Guide, and Business Mirror* (Atlanta, GA, 1859), 11–12. For more on the early development of Atlanta see Mark Pifer, *Hidden History of Old Atlanta* (Charleston, SC, 2021).
10. William Gibbs McAdoo diary, February 1, 1862, Floyd and McAdoo Families Papers, GHS 2689, Georgia Historical Society, Savannah.
11. "The New Railroad Enterprise," *Daily Intelligencer* (Atlanta, hereafter *ADI*), June 4, 1860. The only known surviving copy of that particular issue of the *Daily Intelligencer* is in the Beinecke Rare Book and Manuscript Library of Yale University.
12. Clarence H. Mohr, *On the Threshold of Freedom: Masters and Slaves in Civil War Georgia* (Athens, GA, 1986), 154.
13. Venet, *A Changing Wind*, 2, 8–9; William S. Irvine, "Diary and Letters of Dr. William N. White, a Citizen of Atlanta—Written 1847, 90 Years Ago," *Atlanta Historical Bulletin* 10 (July 1937): 40–41.
14. Venet, *A Changing Wind*, 2, 8–9; Stephen Davis, *What the Yankees Did to Us: Sherman's Bombardment and the Wrecking of Atlanta* (Macon, GA, 2012), 8.
15. Singer, "Confederate Atlanta," 15–19, 36.
16. Venet, *A Changing Wind*, 15–35; Ralph Betts Flanders, *Plantation Slavery in Georgia* (Chapel Hill, NC, 1933), 275; advertisements, Atlanta (Georgia) *Weekly Intelligencer*, November 11, 1858; Louis Fuller, *The Crusade Against Slavery* (New York, 1960), 28; Clarence Mohr, "Harrison Berry: A Black Pamphleteer in Georgia During Slavery and Freedom," *Georgia Historical Quarterly* (Summer 1983): 189–205.
17. Michael Beschloss, *Presidents of War* (New York, 2018), 164–165; Frederick B. Gates, "The Impact of the Western & Atlantic Railroad on the Development of the Georgia Upcountry, 1840–1860," *Georgia Historical Quarterly*, 91 (Summer, 2007): 169–184; W.K. Wood, "The Georgia Railroad

and Banking Company," *Georgia Historical Quarterly* 57 (winter 1973): 553; Eugene D. Genovese, *The Political Economy of Slavery* (New York, 1961), 269; David F. Weiman, "Urban Growth on the Periphery of the Antebellum Cotton Belt: Atlanta, 1847–1860," *Journal of Economic History* 48 (June 1988): 269; "Georgia Airline Railroad," *DI*, June 4, 1860; "Report of the Board," *Floridian and Journal* (Tallahassee), December 30, 1854; Keith S. Bohannon, "The Northeast Georgia Mountains During the Secession Crisis," (Ph.D. diss, Pennsylvania State University, 2001), 42–44; Edgar T. Thompson, *Plantation Societies, Race Relations, and the South: The Regimentation of Populations* (Durham, NC, 1975), 43–49, 222; Robert S. Davis, "Hysteria and Literature: Atlanta's First Execution and Its Legendary Ties to Organized Crime," *Georgia Historical Quarterly* 92 (fall 2008): 321–339; James Michael Russell, *Atlanta 1847–1890: City Building in the Old South and the New* (Baton Rouge, LA, 1988), 34–36.

18. Garrett, *Atlanta and Environs*, 1: 173, 304, 353–354; George W. Lee, credit report, Georgia, vol. 13, p. 11, R.G. Dun & Co. credit report volumes, Baker Library, Harvard Graduate School of Business Administration, Boston; *Rhodes v. Lee*, case A-03600, microfilm drawer 313 roll 67, 1857 and 1858 tax digests, Atlanta, Fulton County, microfilm drawer 70 roll 28, Fulton County Superior Court Minute Book C (1859–1860), pp. 159, 475, 577, microfilm drawer 105 roll 80, Deed Book D (1859–1860), pp. 139–143, microfilm drawer 100 roll 57, Deed Book E (1860–1861), microfilm drawer 100 roll 58, pp. 600–602, and Fulton County Superior Court Minutes Book D (1860–1866), pp. 84–85, 149, microfilm drawer 106 and roll 55, Georgia Archives (hereafter GAr), Morrow. Rhodes was later a foreman for the Confederate Nitre Bureau in Rome, Georgia. See Marion O. Smith, *Confederate Niter District Eight: Middle Tennessee and Northwest Georgia* (Cookeville, TN, 2011).

19. Atlanta, Fulton County, p. 873, *Eighth Census of the United States (1860)* (National Archives microfilm M653, roll 122), NARA; George W. Lee, credit report; "To the Public," *Daily Intelligencer* (Atlanta) (hereafter *ADI*), January 5, 1861; "An Officer" to James A. Seddon, January 26, 1864, 51 A 1864, *Letters Received by the Confederate Secretary of War, 1861–1865* (hereafter *SOW*) (National Archives microfilm M437, roll 118), War Department Collection of Confederate Records, RG 109, NARA.

20. Greg H. Williams, *Civil War Suits in the U.S. Court of Claims: Cases Involving Compensation to Northerners and Southerners for Wartime Losses* (Jefferson, NC, 2006), 120; "William Markham," *Sunny South* (Atlanta), November 22, 1890; "Marcellus O. Markham and Mrs. Robert J. Lowery" in "Cases Dismissed by the Court of Claims," Senate Documents, 64th Congress, 1st Session, United States Congressional Serial Set, issue 6954; Pioneer Citizens' Society of Atlanta, *Pioneer Citizens' History of Atlanta*, 313. For more on the Secret Yankees, see Thomas G. Dyer, *Secret Yankees: The Union Circle in Confederate Atlanta* (Baltimore, MD, 2001).

21. Robert S. Davis, "Hysteria and Literature: Atlanta's First Execution and Its Legendary Ties to Organized Crime," *Georgia Historical Quarterly* 92 (Fall 2008): 321–339.

22. Watson W. Jennison, *Cultivating Race: The Expansion of Slavery in Georgia, 1750–1860* (Lexington, KY, 2012), 266–273; R.S. Tharin, *Arbitrary Arrests in the South; Or, Scenes from the Experience of an Alabama Unionist* (New York, 1863), 60. The Native American Party had support across Georgia. Thomas W. Thomas to Alexander H. Stephens, May 5, 1855, Alexander Hamilton Stephens Collection, Ms 95, Series 1.1., Box 2, folder 5, Rose Library, Emory University, Atlanta.

23. Mark A. Lause, *A Secret Society History of the Civil War* (Urbana, IL, 2011), 57–58, 110–111, 116–117; Smith, *History of the Georgia Militia*, 4: 323, 331–332; "The Contemplated Revolution in Cuba," *Daily Morning News* (Savannah, Georgia), April 14, 1851; David C. Keehn, *Knights of the Golden Circle: Secret Empire Southern Secession, Civil War* (Baton Rouge, LA, 2013), 41, 47, 147, 208 n. 7.

24. A George Lee does appear in the San Francisco passenger lists of the early 1850s, but nothing can identify him as George W. Lee of Atlanta. Louis J. Rasmussen, *San Francisco Passenger Lists*, 4 vols. (Baltimore, MD, 1965), 2: 165, 3: 50.

25. Keri Leigh Merritt, *Masterless Men: Poor Whites and Slavery in the Antebellum South* (New York, 2017), 99–102, 288.

26. Davis, *Cotton, Fire, & Dreams*, 102–105; Singer, "Confederate Atlanta," 16–17; Garrett, *Atlanta and Environs*, 1: 511–52l; Venet, *A Changing Wind*, 8–10. For more on antebellum African Americans hiring out their professional services, see Jonathan D. Martin, *Divided Mastery: Slave Hiring in the American South* (Cambridge, MA, 2004). The site of Ponder's factory is now on the campus of the Georgia Institute of Technology. Venet, *A Changing Wind*, 8–10.

27. Thompson, *Plantation Societies*, 255; J. William Harris, *Plain Folk and Gentry in a Slave Society: White Liberty and Black Slavery in Augusta's Hinterlands* (Middletown, CT, 1985), 74–79; Eugene D. Genovese, *In Red and Black: Marxian Explorations in Southern and Afro-American History* (New York, 1968), 330–335. For discussions of class and the secession crisis see, among other works, John McCardell, *The Idea of a Southern Nation: Southern Nationalists and Southern Nationalism, 1830–1860* (New York, 1979); Raimondo Luraghi, *The Rise and Fall of the Plantation South* (New York, 1978); Paul D. Escott, *The Confederacy: The Slaveholders' Failed Venture* (Santa Barbara, CA, 2009); and David Williams, *Rich Man's War: Class, Caste, and Confederate Defeat in the Lower Chattahoochee Valley* (Athens, GA, 1998). For discussions of the issues of men of Lee's

class of artisans and middle-class merchants and their sympathies during the Civil War see J. William Harris, *Plain Folk and Gentry in a Slave Society: White Liberty and Black Slavery in Augusta's Hinterlands* (Baton Rouge, LA, 1998); Richard E. Beringer, Herman Hattaway, Archer Jones, and William N. Still, Jr., *Why the South Lost the Civil War* (Athens, GA, 1986); Stephanie McCurry, *Confederate Reckoning: Power and Politics in the Civil War South* (Cambridge, MA, 2010); and Eugene D. Genovese, *A Consuming Fire: The Fall of the Confederacy in the Mind of the White Christian South* (Athens, GA, 1998).

28. Robert Strauss, *Worst President Ever: James Buchanan, the POTUS Rating Game, and the Legacy of the Least of the Lesser Presidents* (Guilford, CT, 2016), 152–153, 159–161; Richard Clement Wade, *Slavery in the Cities: The South, 1820–1860* (London, 1967), 243–251; Davis, *What the Yankees Did to Us*, 188; Russell, *Atlanta*, 71; Singer, "Confederate Atlanta," 15–17; Venet, *A Changing Wind*, 9–10.

29. Venet, *A Changing Wind*, 8–9, 54; William A. Link, *Atlanta, Cradle of the New South: Race and Remembering in the Civil War's Aftermath* (Chapel Hill, NC, 2013), 204 n 62. For more on African Americans who hired out their skilled services see Jonathan D. Martin, *Divided Mastery: Slave Hiring in the American South* (Cambridge, MA, 2004).

30. "Return of Sims, the Fugitive Slave," *Detroit (Michigan) Free Press*, April 29, 1863; American Anti-Slavery Society, *Fugitive Slave Law and Its Victims* (revised and Enlarged Edition, New York, 1861), 12–13; Jacqueline Jones, *Saving Savannah: The City and the Civil War* (New York, 2008), 3–24; Garrett, *Atlanta and Environs*, 1: 379; Robert S. Davis, "The Celebrity Fugitive Slave Who Fought for Freedom," *Chattanooga Regional Historical Journal* 20 (2) (January 2018): 87–92. For more on this "free" Black labor, officially enslaved or not, see Joseph P. Reidy, *Illusions of Emancipation: The Pursuit of Freedom and Equality in the Twilight of Slavery* (Chapel Hill, NC, 2019).

31. Edgar T. Thompson, *Plantation Societies, Race Relations, and the South: The Regimentation of Populations* (Durham, NC, 1975), 43–49, 222; Russell, *Atlanta*, 58, 74–75.

32. Kathleen Diffey, "After Sumter: The Surge of War and Periodical Outcry" in Kathleen Diffey and Benjamin Fagan, eds., *Visions of Glory: The Civil War in Word and Image* (Athens, GA, 2019), 30.

33. Robert Strauss, *Worst President Ever: James Buchanan, the POTUS Rating Game, and the Legacy of the Least of the Lesser Presidents* (Guilford, CT, 2016), 152–153, 159–161. For more on the Panics of 1857 and 1859, see Brian P. Luskey, *Men Is Cheap: Exposing the Frauds of Free Labor in Civil War America* (Chapel Hill, NC, 2000).

34. Merritt, *Masterless Men*, 191; John Reeves, *Soldier of Destiny: Slavery, Secession, and the Redemption of Ulysses S. Grant* (New York, 2023), 61. For social definitions of "empire" beyond political boundaries see Charles S. Maier, *Among Empires: American Ascendancy and Its Predecessors* (Cambridge, MA, 2006) and for how it has been applied to American history see Dora L. Costa and Mathew E. Kahn, *Heroes and Cowards: The Social Face of War* (Princeton, NJ, 2008); Christopher Gelphi, Peter D. Feaver, and Jason Reifer, *Paying the Human Costs of War: American Public Opinion and Casualties in Military Conflicts* (Princeton, NJ, 2009); Fred Anderson and Andrew Cayton, *The Dominion of War: Empire and Liberty in North America, 1500–2000* (New York, 2005); and Niall Ferguson, *Colossus: The Price of America's Empire* (New York, 2004).

35. See Michael P. Johnson, *Toward a Patriarchal Republic: The Secession of Georgia* (Baton Rouge, LA, 1987).

36. Samuel Richards, *Sam Richards's Diary: A Chronicle of the Atlanta Home Front*, Wendy Hamand Venet, ed. (Athens, GA, 2009), 38–39.

37. George W. Lee to H.C. Wayne, January 5, 1860, G.W. Lee File, and E.P. Watkins to Henry Wayne, January 9, 1860, E.P. Watkins File, File II Names, Record Group 4-2-46, Fulton County election returns, Record Group 1-1-5 (DOC277), and Georgia Military Records Book 4 (1841–1862), 88, 117, 119, microfilm drawer 40 roll 17, GAr. Lee was commissioned as captain of the 1026th Georgia Militia District on February 6, 1861.

38. Wallace P. Reed, ed., *History of Atlanta, Georgia* (Syracuse, NY, 1889), 94–96; Walter G. Cooper, *Official History of Fulton County* (Atlanta, GA, 1934), 94–95; "Fulton Dragoons" and "Arms for the Fulton Dragoons," *ADI*, May 29 and December 21, 1860; Singer, "Confederate Atlanta," 39–49, 50; "Minute Men of '60" and "The City Under Siege," *Atlanta (Georgia) Constitution*, September 16, 1888, p. 5, c. 3, and July 20, 1898, p. 13, c. 7.

39. Lee to Brown, January 25, 1861, Executive Correspondence of Governor Joseph E. Brown, RG 1-1-5, and Lee to Wayne, January 31 and February 13, 1861, Letters Received by Adjutant General Henry C. Wayne, RG 22-1-17, GAr; Michael Johnston Kenan notebook 2, pp. 200–202, MS 948, Georgia Historical Society, Savannah; For the problems with understanding Brown, see Wallace T. Hettle, "An Ambitious Democrat: Joseph Brown and Georgia's Road to Secession," *Georgia Historical Quarterly* 81 (Fall 1997): 577–592 and G. Richard Wright and Kenneth H. Wheeler, "New Men in the Old South: Joseph E. Brown and His Associates in the Etowah River Valley," *Georgia Historical Quarterly* 93 (Winter 2009): 363–387.

40. James A. Riley, "Desertion and Disloyalty in Georgia during the Civil War" (Master's Thesis, University of Georgia, 1951), 7.

41. Smith, *History of the Georgia Militia*, 4: 298–301; "An Imposter—Major Lee," *ADI*, April 21, 1859; Barbara B. Canaday, David L. Canaday, and Donald R. McKinney, eds., *Georgia Freemasons, 1861–1865* (n. p., 2001), 54–57.

42. "Letters to the People. The First Confederate

Flag" in Flags, Confederate Miscellany, microfilm drawer 283 roll 51, GAr; Henry D. Capers, "At the Court of Jefferson Davis," and "Gate City Guard Not First to Leave," *Atlanta* (Georgia) *Journal*, January 26, 1901, p. 12, and August 3, 1901, p. 2; "Military," *ADI*, January 26, 1861.

43. Joseph E. Brown to L.P. Walker, April 15, 1861, Keith Read Collection, Box 3, folder 17, Mss 921, Hargrett Rare Book and Manuscript Library, University of Georgia Libraries, Athens; "Captain George Washington Lee's Company," "Atlanta Volunteers," and "Capt. G.W. Lee," *Southern Confederacy* (Atlanta, Georgia, hereafter as *SC*), March 19, March 21, and April 3, 1861; telegram to Governor Joseph E. Brown, April 29, 1861, Box 3 Folder 164, Vertical Files, Western Reserve Library, Cincinnati, Ohio. For the history of the siege of Pensacola, see John K. Driscoll, *The Civil War on Pensacola Bay, 1861–1862* (Jefferson, NC, 2007) and George F. Pearce, *Pensacola During the Civil War: A Thorn in the Side of the Confederacy* (Tallahassee, FL, 2000). Bruce W. Duncan has an undated manuscript from Pensacola that lists Lee and his officers with the words, "The first Confederate soldiers received by Pres Davis—for service in Confederate war 1861 to 1865 volunteers from Atlanta Ga." Duncan to author May 2, 2014.

44. Lee to L.P. Walker, June 14, 1861, 1609 1861, *SOW* (National Archives Microfilm M437, roll 4), NARA; Samuel Cooper to Bragg, March 19, 1861, *ORs*, Series I, vol. 1, p. 451; orders, April 5, 1861, Captain G.W. Lee Collection, Kentucky Historical Society, Frankfort; "By the Arrival of a Gentleman," *Commonwealth* (Atlanta), May 17, 1861; "Captain George W. Lee," "Lee's Volunteers," "Captain Lee's Volunteer Company," and "Note of Explanation," *SC*, March 6, 18, 19, and 22, April 27, 1861; "Letter from Captain Geo. W. Lee," *ADI*, April 2, 1861; Horace Randall Williams, ed., *The Alabama Guide: Our People, Resources, and Government* (Montgomery, AL, 2009), 75.

45. Michael Jason Spurr, "'The Latent Enmity of Georgia': Sherman's March and Its Effects on the Social Division of Georgia" (Ph. D. diss., University of Las Vegas Nevada, 2009), 29; Lee to W.H. Bassford, March 26, 1861, in Janet B. Hewett, ed., *Supplement to the Official Records of the Union and Confederate Armies*, 100 vols. (Wilmington, NC, 1999), Serial 93, pp. 114–118, 120, and Record of Events, Company D, 36th (Villepique's) Regiment, Ser. 18, pp. 666–667, 672; "Correspondence," *Chronicle & Sentinel* (Augusta, GA), February 24, 1861; "First Independent Georgia Battalion," *Daily Constitutionalist* (Augusta, Georgia), June 16, 1861; Joseph T. Derry, *Georgia*, vol. 7 of Clement A. Evans, comp., *Confederate Military History*, 17 vols. (1898; extended edition, Wilmington, NC, 1987), 7: 23, 79–80; "The Southern Congress," *New York Herald*, March 2, 1861; "First Independent Georgia Battalion," and "Captain Jabez R. Rhodes," *ADI*, June 18, 1861 and March 19, 1862; W. David Lewis, *Sloss Furnace and the Rise of the Birmingham District: an Industrial Epic* (Tuscaloosa, AL, 1994), 22, 32; *Journal of the Senate at Extra Session* (Milledgeville, GA, 1863), 160. Lee's original company became Company D of the 36th (Villepigue's) Georgia Infantry Regiment in November 1861 and a part of the First Georgia Confederate Infantry Regiment on January 31, 1862, commanded by John Bordenave Villepigue, before becoming parts of Company A and C of the First Confederate Infantry Battalion. These companies served in Mississippi and Tennessee. Many of these soldiers had returned to Atlanta by July 2, 1862, to serve under Lee again. Janet B. Hewett, ed., *Supplement to the Official Records of the Union and Confederate Armies*, 100 vols. (Wilmington, NC, 1995), Serial 18, 557, 665, 667–668, 671–672. Information on these soldiers appears in Lillian B. Wood Henderson, comp., *Roster of Confederate Soldiers of Georgia, 1861–1865* 6 vols. (Atlanta, GA, 1959–1964), 1: 35–52. Also see Confederate Pensions and Records, Georgia Soldier Roster Commission, Roster compiled by the Commission, 1861–1865, Record Group 58-2-26, Georgia Archives, Morrow.

46. Stephen Davis and Bill Hendrick, *The Atlanta Intelligencer Covers the Civil War* (Knoxville, TN, 2022), 150.

47. Augustus R. Wright to Walker, August 27, 1861, 3609 1861, *SOW* (National Archives microfilm M437, roll 8), and Special Orders 134, 158, and 185, Headquarters of the Army of Pensacola, Entry 83, and General Order 71, Confederate Manuscripts, RG 109, NARA; photographs, Lee/Huss Family Papers; "Captain G.W. Lee," *ADI*, August 8 and 18, 1861; "Lee's Volunteers," and "The Fight at Santa Rosa Island," *SC*, October 13 and October 15, 1861. Stewart Sifakis, *Compendium of Confederate Armies: South Carolina and Georgia* (New York, 1995), 248.

Chapter Two

1. Wright to Jefferson Davis, October 10, 1861, 6722 1861, Wright to Walker, August 27, 3609 1861, and Lewis J. Parr to Davis, November 4, 1861, 7394 1861, *SOW* (National Archives microfilm M437, rolls 12 and 14), NARA; "The Sumner Rifled Gun," *Augusta* (Georgia) *Chronicle*, October 29, 1861. The Rushton Company, like so many other such small efforts, found itself excluded from making artillery for the new nation because of the inferior quality of its products. The company only seems to have further furnished the Confederate government with a set of scales. Two of the large Rushton cannons that traveled with Wright's Legion proved to be useless. Lee had them returned to Atlanta. Eventually the artillery companies received new heavy guns made in Rome, Georgia, by the Noble Company, which itself would eventually be banned from making artillery because of its inferior product. Many companies experimented with making artillery for the Confederacy without becoming regular manufacturers. See Rushton & Company file, *Confederate Papers Relating to Citizens or Business Firms*

(National Archives microfilm M346, roll 892), RG 109, NARA; Cornelius Hanleiter diaries, vol. 1 (1861–1862), February 11, 1862, folder 12, vol. 2 (1862), April 12 and 13, 1862, folder 13, Cornelius Hanleiter Papers, Mss 109, Kenan Research Center, Atlanta History Center; James C. Hazlett, Edwin Olmstead, and M. Hume Parks, *Field Artillery Weapons of the Civil War* (2nd ed., Newark, NJ, 1983), 87.

2. David T. Dixon, "Augustus R. Wright and the Loyalty of the Heart," *Georgia Historical Quarterly* 94 (Fall 2010): 342–371.

3. Cornelius Hanleiter diaries, vol. 1 (1861–1862), November 6, 11, and 16, 1861; "Recruits Wanted," *Savannah* (Georgia) *Republican*, August 7, 1862.

4. George Anderson Mercer diary, March 3, 1862–September 14, 1863, entry of June 15, 1862, folder 3B volume 3, MS 00503, Southern Historical Collection, University of North Carolina, Chapel Hill.

5. G. Dale Nichols, *Hurrah for Georgia! The History of the Thirty-eighth Georgia Regiment* (Nashville, TN, 2015), 7–9; Cornelius Hanleiter diaries, volume 1 (1861–1862), January 2, 3, and 11, February 1, March 14, 1862, volume 2 (1862), May 3, 1862; Mercer diary, entry of March 3, 1862. For Hanleiter's biography, see Smith, *History of the Georgia Militia*, 4: 299–300 and Pioneer Citizens' Society, *Pioneer Citizens' History of Atlanta 1833–1902* (Atlanta, GA, 1902), 364. A map of the defenses of Savannah shows Camp Lee. William S. Smedlund, *Camp Fires of Georgia Troops, 1861–1865* (Sharpsburg, GA, 1994), 186.

6. Cornelius Hanleiter diaries, vol. 1 (1861–1862), December 19, 1861.

7. Cornelius Hanleiter diaries, vol. 3 (1862–1863), July 1, 1862.

8. Wright to Davis, October 10, 1861, 6722 1861, and petition, Isle of Hope Georgia, no date, from officers of Wright's Legion to General H.W. Mercer, 172 L 1862, *SOW* (National Archives microfilm M437, rolls 12 and 57), and compiled service record of Augustus R. Wright, *Compiled Service Records of Confederate Soldiers Who Served in Organizations from the State of Georgia* (National Archives microfilm M266, roll 441), RG 109, NARA; Cornelius Hanleiter diaries, vol. 1 (1861–1862), February 14 and 23, March 4, 1862, vol. 2 (1862), May 7, 1862; Record of Events, Twenty-fifth Georgia Provost Battalion, in Hewett, *Supplement to the Official Records*, Serial 18, p. 696; Nichols, *Hurrah for Georgia!*, 8. Wright's descendants claimed that he resigned his commission because of his advanced age. He remained on good terms with the men of his former legion. After the war, Wright claimed to have always supported the Union. Derry, *Georgia*, 1060; Cornelius Hanleiter diaries, vol. 2 (1862), June 4, 1862; "A Card from the Hon. A.R. Wright of Rome," *North Georgia Citizen* (Dalton), August 6, 1868. For a history of Wright's Legion and the Thirty-eighth Georgia Infantry see "The Thirty-eighth Georgia, Or Wright's Legion," *DI*, October 22, 1862; "Wright's Legion," *Sunny South* (Atlanta), January 10, 1891; and G. Dale Nichols, *Hurrah for Georgia! The History of the Thirty-eighth Georgia Regiment* (Nashville, TN, 2015). A roster of Wright's Legion/Thirty-eighth Georgia Infantry is in Lillian B. Henderson, comp., *Roster of Confederate Soldiers of Georgia, 1861–1865* 6 vols. (Atlanta, 1959–1964), 4: 116–149, and Janet B. Hewett, comp., *Georgia Confederate Soldiers* 4 vols. (Wilmington, NC, 1998), 4: 636–645. Also see Confederate pensions and records, Georgia Soldier Roster Commission, Roster compiled by the Commission, 1861–1865, Record Group 58-2-26, Georgia Archives, Morrow.

9. For more on the shortages of salt, saltpeter, etc., see Clarence R. Mohr, *On the Threshold of Freedom: Masters and Slaves in Civil War Georgia* (Athens, GA, 1986), 155–157.

10. Mercer diary, entries of April 24, May 2, and June 15, 1862. The state of Georgia had invested heavily in the large guns of Fort Pulaski, made by the Tredegar Iron Works of Richmond, Virginia, despite the fort's isolated location. An argument could have been made for abandoning and destroying Fort Pulaski rather than expending scarce resources, in a hopeless effort of defending it. Joseph E. Brown to L.P. Walker, April 15, 1861, Keith Read Collection, Box 3, folder 17, Ms921, Hargrett Rare Book and Manuscript Library, University of Georgia Libraries, Athens.

11. David G. Surdam, *Northern Naval Superiority and the Economics of the American Civil War* (Columbia, SC, 2001), 13–33, 24–25, 42–50, 73, 83–84; Scott R. Nelson, *Iron Confederacies: Southern Railways, Klan Violence, and Reconstruction* (Chapel Hill, NC, 1999), 2, 27–45. For a discussion of these operations failures of the Confederate national politicians and its military, see David J. Eicher, *Dixie Betrayed: How the South Really Lost the Civil War* (New York, 2006); and for the systems set up for the commissary and ordnance needs of the army see Jerrold N. Moore, *Confederate Commissary General: Lucius Bellinger Northrop and the Subsistence Bureau of the Southern Army* (Shippensburg, PA, 1996) and Frank E. Vandiver, *Ploughshares into Swords: Josiah Gorgas and Confederate Ordnance* (College Station, TX, 1952).

12. [no title], *DI*, April 3, 1862; return of May 1862, compiled service record of George W. Lee in *Compiled Service Records of Confederate Soldiers who Served in Organizations From the State of Georgia* (National Archives microfilm M266, roll 437), RG 109, NARA; Record of Events, Thirty-eighth Georgia Infantry, in Hewett, *Supplement to the Official Records*, Part 1, Reports, volume 1, Serial 18, pp. 687–688, 693, 695; Cornelius Hanleiter diaries, vol. 2 (1862), May 12, 1862. Hanleiter, however, would initiate the successful capture of the federal warship *Water Witch* in 1864. Smith, *History of the Georgia Militia, 1783–1861*, 4: 300.

13. "Large Fire," "Fire in Atlanta," and "Destructive Fire," *SC*, May 13 and 15, 1862 and June 30,

1863; "The Fire on Sunday," and "Still Another Fire," *DI*, May 13 and 18, 1862; Richards, *Sam Richards's Civil War Diary*, 110.

14. "Explosion of a Locomotive," "The Collision on the State Road," "Accident on the State Road," and "No More Cotton to Go to the Yankees, *SC*, June 16, 1861, June 12, 1862, April 27, 1863, and March 22, 1862; William S. Hoole, *Lawley Covers the Confederacy* (Tuscaloosa, 1964), 75; Russell S. Bonds, *Stealing the General: The Great Locomotive Chase and the First Medal of Honor* (Yardley, PA, 2007), 92–93; "The Engineer's Story," *Georgia Journal and Messenger* (Macon), July 13, 1853.

15. Paul D. Lack, "Law and Disorder in Confederate Atlanta," *Georgia Historical Quarterly* 66 (Summer 1982): 185; Venet, *A Changing Wind*, 98–100, 144.

16. Lee to Secretary of War G.W. Randolph, October 18, 1862, 651 L 1862, *SOW* (National Archives microfilm M437, roll 58); "Speculation Again" and "Are They Incendiaries or Spies," *SC*, April 5 and May 15, 1861; Clayton, *Requiem for a Lost City*, 13.

17. List of intelligence depositions and reports, Department of the Cumberland, October 1863–May 1865, Entry 92, Records of the Continental Commands, pt. i, RG 393, NARA.

18. James O. Hall, "A Modern Hunt for a Fabled Agent: The Spy Harrison," *Civil War Times Illustrated*, 24 (10) (1986): 18–25; Ferdinand L. Sarmiento, *Life of Pauline Cushman: The Celebrated Union Spy and Scout* (Philadelphia, PA, 1865), 155, 186.

19. Robert S. Davis, "The Eyes of Chickamauga: General George H. Thomas as a Civil War Spy Master," *Chattanooga Regional Historical Journal* 5 (July 2004): 73–92.

20. Deposition of Carrie King, April 27, 1864, entry 36, RG 110, NARA.

21. Deposition and receipt of Samuel Wilson, entry 36, RG 110, NARA.

22. Lida Poynter, "Dr. Mary Walker: The Forgotten Woman," Lida Poyster Manuscripts, Archives and Special Collections, Allegheny University of Health Sciences, Philadelphia, PA; pay receipt, April 8, 1864, entry 95, RG 110, NARA.

23. Emile Bourlier file, Entry 36, Box 2, RG 110, NARA; Chancery Court Minutes, Book 47, p. 81, Clerk of Court, Jefferson County, Louisville, Kentucky; Alan D. Murray, comp., *Death Notices for Jefferson County, Kentucky* 1 vol. to date (Wyanclotte, OK, 2005), 1: 15.

24. Depositions of James C. Moore, entry 36, RG 110, NARA.

25. Lists of payments made to spies and scouts, however, do survive in Dodge's papers in the State Historical Society of Iowa. Brent Hamilton Ponsford, "Major General Grenville M. Dodge's Military Intelligence Operations During the Civil War," (M.A. thesis, Iowa State University, 1976), 21–22. For Dodge's work as Grant's spymaster, see William B. Feis, *Grant's Secret Service: The Intelligence War from Belmont to Appomattox* (Omaha: University of Nebraska Press, 2002).

26. For examples of spies captured and executed by the Confederacy see *Fayetteville* (North Carolina) *Observer*, April 25, 1864; *Southern Confederacy* (Atlanta, Georgia), March 18, 1864; *Augusta* (Georgia) *Daily Constitutionalist*, March 31, 1864; and *Montgomery* (Georgia) *Monitor*, April 29, 1886.

27. *Montgomery* (Georgia) *Monitor*, January 30, 1896, p. 2, c. 2–3; History Commission, *Official History of Whitfield County, Georgia* (Dalton, GA, 1936), 59.

28. Statement of John Vantye, April 3, 1864, and deposition of Mirom Hetchum, February 11, 1865, entry 36, RG 110, NARA.

29. "The Story of a Spy," *Macon* (Georgia) *Telegraph*, March 24, 1897; pension file of Samuel W. Kenney, certificate 441,670, Civil War pension claims, Department of Veterans Affairs, Record Group 15, NARA.

30. John Fitch, *Annals of the Army of the Cumberland* (Philadelphia, PA, 1864), 626.

31. Wilbur Kurtz, "A Federal Spy in Atlanta," *Atlanta Historical Bulletin* 10 (December 1957): 20; C.B. Kinsey, "The Man Found Hanging at Vining's Station," *National Tribune* (Washington, D.C.), February 7, 1864, May 15, 1884; *Biographical and Historical Memoirs of Western Arkansas* (Chicago, IL, 1891), 405; claim of Milton J. Glass, Quartermaster Claims, Records of the Quartermaster General, RG 92, NARA. In his diary, William King identified the hanging man as one Smith, a waggoneer from the Roswell Mills and a Unionist. A paper in the man's pocket was a pass from D.P. Duncan of the Georgia militia. Earl J. Hess, *Kennesaw Mountain: Sherman, Johnson, and the Atlanta Campaign* (Chapel Hill, NC, 2013), 212–213; Michael Jason Spear, "'The Latent Enmity of Georgia': Sherman's March and Its Effects on the Social Division of Georgia" (Ph.D. diss., University of Las Vegas Nevada, 2009), 71–72.

32. See Miles Harvey, *The King of Confidence: A Tale of Utopian Dreamers, Frontier Swindlers, True Believers, False Prophets, and the Murder of an American Monarch* (New York, 2020); Karen Halttunen, *Confidence Men and Painted Women: A Study of the Middle-class Culture in America, 1830–1870* (New Haven, CT, 1982); and Mark W. Summers, *The Plundering Generation: Corruption and the Crisis of the Union, 1849–1861* (New York, 1987) and *The Era of Good Stealings* (New York, 1993).

33. Harvey, *The King of Confidence*, 11.

34. This other Robert C. Crawford (sometimes misidentified as Robert A. Crawford in the records) lived a life that represents another example of the adventures of the middle-class entrepreneur in Civil War era Atlanta. He worked in the Atlanta Arsenal and, although a crippled veteran, and as a private in the hospitals. A bookkeeper born ca. 1824–1830 in South Carolina, he married Adelia Thurmond of Chesterfield District, South Carolina, in Dekalb County, Georgia, on December 29, 1846. He was an Atlanta grocer in 1853; ran for

public office unsuccessfully in the Native American or "Know Nothing" Party in 1855; served on the Atlanta City Council in 1863–1866 and some county government positions by 1867. A M.C. Crawford (b. 1788), his mother, died in Atlanta on April 9, 1867, and was interred in Oakland Cemetery. After spending time in the state mental hospital near Milledgeville in 1877, likely to escape his creditors, Robert returned home and disappeared shortly afterwards. Pension of Robert Crawford, Fulton County, Georgia Confederate pensions, microfilm 273 roll 26, Georgia Archives, Morrow; Garrett, *Atlanta and Environments*, 1: 387–388, 563, 669, 702, 703, 733; legal notices, *Weekly Republican & Discipline* (Atlanta) March 28, 1856; G.W. Lee to Henry C. Wayne, October 3, 1863, Robert Crawford file, Defense-Adjutant General–Incoming, Record Group 22-1-17, DOC 452, GAr; Fulton County, 789, *Eighth Census of the United States (1860)* (National Archives microfilm M653, roll 122), Robert Crawford file, *Confederate Papers Relating to Citizens or Business Firms* (National Archives microfilm M346, roll 206), Record Group RG 109, War Department Collection of Confederate Records, NARA; internment records, Oakland Cemetery, Atlanta History Center, Atlanta; Central State Hospital records, Georgia Archives, Morrow, Adelia Windsor Thurmond, Family trees, online Familysearch.org.

35. In an application for a pardon for his Civil War service, Robert A. Crawford stated that he was born in Virginia in 1811–1812. William Aduston Rogers Crawford was reportedly born in Gloucester County, Virginia, on February 11, 1812, to Samuel and Rosa Lily Rogers Crawford. Robert A. Crawford named his oldest daughter Rosa and his youngest daughter Lillian. Forty years after his death, Robert A. Crawford's grave was marked with a tombstone with his middle name as "Ashton," which would be easily confused in memory or misread from some records, instead of as "Aduston." Robert A. Crawford's descendants have a story that he was one of five siblings, three of whom died in an epidemic, leaving only him and a brother. William A.R. Crawford was reportedly one of nine children, six of whom died in 1832 and whom all but one brother he had outlived by 1867. Another family story tells of a connection to a slave ship named the *Ajax*, what could have been the infamous vessel that ran between Crawford's native Virginia and New Orleans, where he resided in 1835. Robert A. Crawford, *Case Files of Applications from Former Confederates for Presidential Pardons ("Amnesty Papers"), 1865–1867* (National Archives microfilm M1003), Record Group (hereafter RG) 94 Records of the Adjutant General's Office, 1865–1867, National Archives and Records Administration (hereafter NARA), College Park, MD; Robert A. Crawford and William Adustin Rogers Crawford family group sheets, Family trees, Ancestry.com, accessed on May 24, 2024; Bullock, "Col. Robert Ashton Crawford."

36. "Richard Crawford the Forger," *Tarboro Press* (Tarboro, North Carolina), February 10, 1838; petition of Job Stanbery, December 5, 1839, Legislative Petitions Digital Collection, Library of Virginia, Richmond; William Moseley Brown, *Blandford Lodge No. 3 A.F. & A.M., Petersburg, VA, A Bicentennial History* (Petersburg, VA, 1957), 141, 181, 184–185, 229, 241, 276; Moses Crawford and Samuel Crawford, Craftsman Database, Museum of Early Southern Decorative Arts, Winston Salem, North Carolina; Samuel Crawford, October 8, 1857, Deaths and Burials 1853–1912, Library of Virginia, Richmond; "Funeral of Samuel Crawford," *Richmond* (Virginia) *Enquirer*, October 13, 1857; A.C. Wood, 1837, Register of Prisoners, Kentucky State Department of Libraries and Archives, Frankfort.

37. John Le Carré, *The Pigeon Tunnel: Stories from My Life* (New York, 2016), 283.

38. Bullock, "Col. Robert Ashton Crawford"; Brent H. Holcomb, comp., *Marriage and Death Notices from the Southern Christian Advocate* 2 vols. (Easley, SC, 1979–1980), 1: 206; Mrs. W.B. [Mary B.] Frazer, *Early History of Auburn* (Auburn, AL, 1920), 6; R.A. Crawford to Matthew Turner, August 5, 1851, and same to John W.W. Drake et al., August 10, 1852, Macon County deed book H (1851–1852), 142, 636, LGM rolls 23–24, Alabama Department of Archives and History, Montgomery; Tad Evans, comp., *Georgia Newspaper Clippings Harris County Extracts 1828–1888* (Savannah, 2005), 250, 266; Houston Sheriff Sale, "Houston April Sheriff's Sales," *Georgia Telegraph* (Macon, GA), March 2, 1858, *Weekly Georgia Telegraph* (Macon, Georgia), May 10, 1859; Elizabeth Evans Kilbourne, comp., *Columbus, Georgia Newspaper Clippings (Columbus Enquirer)*, 12 vols. (Savannah, 2010), 10: 115; Gordon B. Smith, *History of the Georgia Militia 1783–1861*, 4 vols. (Milledgeville, GA, 2001), 4: 325, 328–332; "The K.G.C.," *Daily Dispatch* (Richmond, VA), April 18, 1860.

39. Robert A. Crawford file, *Case Files of Applications from Former Confederates for Presidential Pardons ("Amnesty Papers"), 1865–1867* (National Archives microfilm M1003), Record Group 94 Records of the Adjutant General's Office, 1865–1867, NARA; Bullock, "Col. Robert Ashton Crawford"; Holcomb, *Marriage and Death Notices from the Southern Christian Advocate*, 1: 206; Mrs. W.B. [Mary B.] Frazer, *Early History of Auburn* (Auburn, AL, 1920), 6; R.A. Crawford to Matthew Turner, August 5, 1851, and same to John W.W. Drake et al., August 10, 1852, Macon County deed book H (1851–1852), 142, 636, LGM rolls 23–24, Alabama Department of Archives and History, Montgomery; Tad Evans, comp., *Georgia Newspaper Clippings Harris County Extracts 1828–1888* (Savannah, 2005), 250, 266; Houston Sheriff Sale, "Houston April Sheriff's Sales," *Georgia Telegraph* (Macon, Georgia), March 2, 1858, *Weekly Georgia Telegraph* (Macon, Georgia), May 10, 1859; Elizabeth Evans Kilbourne, comp., *Columbus, Georgia Newspaper Clippings (Columbus Enquirer)*, 12

vols. (Savannah, Georgia, 2010), 10: 115; Gordon B. Smith, *History of the Georgia Militia 1783–1861*, 4 vols. (Milledgeville, GA, 2001), 4: 325, 328–332; "The K.G.C.," *Daily Dispatch* (Richmond, Virginia), April 18, 1860.

40. Robert A. Crawford file, *Case Files of Applications from Former Confederates for Presidential Pardons ("Amnesty Papers")*, 1865–1867 (National Archives microfilm M1003), Record Group 94 Records of the Adjutant General's Office, 1865–1867, NARA; Pension of R.A. Crawford, Fulton County, Georgia Confederate pensions, microfilm drawer 273 roll 26, Georgia Archives, Morrow; "An Old Soldier Was Laid to Rest Yesterday," *Atlanta* (Georgia) *Constitution*, May 14, 1892; Bullock, "Col. Robert Ashton Crawford"; Robert S. Davis, "Crawford, Frazer & Company of Atlanta and Auburn," Dallas Genealogical Society eNews Articles https://dallasgenealogy.com/dgs/category/enews/.

41. Crawford, Confederate Service Cards, microfilm drawer 255 roll 45, and pension of R.A. Crawford, Fulton County, Georgia Confederate pensions, microfilm drawer 273 roll 26, Georgia Archives, Morrow; "From the Front," *Weekly Chronicle & Sentinel* (Augusta, GA), June 1, 1864; "The Fall of Lieutenant General Polk," *Southern Confederacy* (Atlanta), June 16, 1864.

42. No title, *Rome* (Georgia) *Tri-Weekly Courier*, November 13, 1879, and *Henry County Weekly* (Hampton, Georgia), November 14, 1879; "An Old Soldier Was Laid to Rest Yesterday," *Atlanta* (Georgia) *Constitution*, May 14, 1892.

43. Richards, "'We Live Under a Constitution,'" 28–29; "Atlanta," *Georgia Weekly Telegraph* (Macon), May 23, 1862; Clarence L. Mohr, "The Atlanta Campaign and the African American Experience in Civil War Georgia," in Lesley G. Gordon and John C. Inscoe, eds., *Inside the Confederate Nation: Essays in Honor of Emory M. Thomas* (Baton Rouge, LA, 2005), 276; "Headquarters, Military Post Atlanta," *Banner and Baptist* (Atlanta), June 21, 1862. A pass signed by Lee for Jerry Cowles, on September 1, 1862, is in the Jerry Cowles Papers, Ms. 178, Georgia Historical Society, Savannah. For restrictions placed on travel by African Americans in Georgia before and during the Civil War, see Clarence L. Mohr, *On the Threshold of Freedom: Masters and Slaves in Civil War Georgia* (Athens, GA, 1986), 14–17, 44–46, 52, 184–186, 197–199. At least two important African Americans in the Civil Rights movement would have the name George Washington Lee although neither had any known connection to the provost marshal of Atlanta.

44. Michael K. Shaffer, *Day by Day: Through the Civil War in Georgia* (Macon, GA, 2022), 109–110; Randolph to Braxton Bragg, August 12, 1862, *ORs*, Series 2, vol. 4, 844.

45. Clifford Dowdey, *The Seven Days: The Emergence of Robert E. Lee and the Dawn of a Legend* (New York, 2012), 13, 73–75.

46. "Colonel G.W. Lee," *DI*, June 3, 1862; "The News," *Georgia Weekly Telegraph* (Macon, Georgia), June 3, 1862; "From Wright's Brigade," *SC*, July 5, 1862; compiled service record of H.W. Mercer in *Confederate General Staff Officers and Non-Regimental Enlisted Men* (National Archives microfilm M331, roll 176), RG 109, NARA; [no title], *Macon* (Georgia) *Daily Telegraph*, June 2, 1862; Shaffer, *Day by Day Through the Civil War in Georgia*, 110; "Reinforcements to Stonewall Jackson," *Georgia Weekly Telegraph* (Macon), June 20, 1862; Gregory C. White, *"This Most Bloody & Cruel Drama": A History of the 31st Georgia Volunteer Infantry* (Baltimore, MD, 1997), 24; Alton J. Murray, *South Georgia Rebels: The True Wartime Experiences of the 26th Regiment, Georgia Volunteer Infantry* (St. Mary's, GA, 1976), 42–44; Sifakis, *Compendium*, 249; report of Captain W.H. Battey, July 27, 1862, and Samuel Cooper to Lee, June 10, 1862, in *ORs*, Series I, vol. 11, part ii, p. 648, part iii, p. 585; Cornelius Hanleiter diaries, volume 3 (1862), June 5 and 7, July 1, 1862. Captain William H. Battey died at the Battle of Antietam on September 17, 1862. "The Thirty-eighth Georgia, Or Wright's Legion," *DI*, October 22, 1862.

47. Brown to Lee, February 14, 1863, Governor's Letter book (1861–1865), 427, microfilm drawer 61 roll 79, GAr; [no title], *SC*, April 7, 1863; L.H. Briscoe to J.J. Hall, March 29, 1864, Adjutant General's Letter Book no. 22 (February 2-Aptil 4, 1864), p. 483, GAr; Dyer, *Secret Yankees*, 102–103, 201; "Provost Marshals," *Army Argus and Crisis* (Mobile, AL), November 19, 1864.

48. Compiled service record of George W. Lee, *Confederate General Staff Officers and Non-Regimental Enlisted Men* (National Archives microfilm M331, roll 155), RG 109, NARA; Organization of the Troops in the Department of East Tennessee, December 27, 1862, in Robert N. Scott, comp., *The War of the Rebellion: A Compilation of the Official Records of the Union and Confederate Armies*, 128 vols. (Washington, D.C., 1890–1904, hereafter *ORs*), Series I, vol. 20, part ii, p. 466; Sifakis, *Compendium*, 249; Derry, *Georgia*, 116; "Headquarters Military Post" and "Colonel G.W. Lee," *DI*, May 20 and June 3, 1862.

49. W.L. Hubbard to Randolph, October 18, 1862, 1145 H 1862, WD 3413 1862, August 9, 1862, *SOW* (National Archives microfilm M437, roll 53), NARA; Lack, "Law and Disorder in Confederate Atlanta," 171, 180, 187; Kenneth Radley, *Rebel Watchdog: The Confederate States Army Provost Guard* (Baton Rouge, LA, 1989), 85–86, 195; William A. Richards, "'We Live Under a Constitution': Confederate Martial law in Atlanta," *Atlanta History* 33 (2) (Summer 1989): 28; Randolph to Bragg, August 12, 1862, *ORs*, Series II, vol. 4, p. 844; "Meeting of Citizens," *Memphis Daily Appeal* (Atlanta, Georgia), August 19, 1863; Lee to Randolph, July 23, 1862, telegraph 109, endorsement book, p. 9, *Telegraphs Received by the Confederate Secretary of War, 1861–1865* (National Archives microfilm M618, roll 11), War Department Collection of Confederate Records, RG 109,

and Robert Crawford to Randolph, August 9, 1862, *Compiled Service Records of Confederate Soldiers who Served in Organizations From the State of Georgia* (National Archives microfilm M266, roll 606), NARA. Green J. Foreacre (1828–1886) would return to Atlanta after the war and, as a revered citizen, is buried in the city's historic Oakland Cemetery. Garrett, *Atlanta and Environs*, 1: 486–487.

50. Robert S. Davis, "Hysteria and Literature: Atlanta's First Execution and Its Legendary Ties to Organized Crime," Georgia Historical Quarterly 92 (fall 2008): 321–339.

51. Lack, "Law and Disorder in Confederate Atlanta," 185; Venet, *A Changing Wind*, 94–97; Lee to Randolph, May 22, 1862, 268 L 1862, *SOW* (National Archives microfilm M437, roll 57); Garrett, *Atlanta and Environs*, 1: 526, 548; [notices], *SC*, June 5, 15, and 19, August 3 and 9, and October 28, 1862, January 25, 1863; Clayton, *Requiem for a Lost City*, 61 note 15, 87 note 25; Pioneer Citizens' Society, *Pioneer Citizens' History of Atlanta*, 176; Lee to Brown, January 21, 1864, Executive Correspondence of Governor Joseph E. Brown, RG 1-1-5, and Markham v. Powell, et al., 33 Georgia Reports 509–10, case file 33–508, Supreme Court Case Files, Record Group 92-1-1, GAr; Lee to James A. Seddon, February 20, 1863, 98 L 1863, *SOW* (National Archives microfilm M437, roll 99), NARA; Royce Singleton, *Richard Peters: Champion of the New South* (Macon, 1985), 90; "Atlanta Correspondence of the Charleston Courier," *SC*, March 24, 1863.

52. Lee to Randolph, August 11 and 19, 1862, telegram 117 and 223, endorsement book, pp. 14 and 18, *Telegraphs Received by the Confederate Secretary of War, 1861–1865* (National Archives microfilm M618, roll 11), Compiled service record of George W. Lee, *Confederate General Staff Officers and Non-Regimental Enlisted Men* (National Archives microfilm M331, roll 155) and Lee to Thomas Jordan, November 15, 1862, Number 1286 L 1862, Leonidas Polk to Joseph E. Johnston, March 5, 1864, Number 525 P 1864, *Letters Received by the Confederate Adjutant and Inspector General, 1861–1865* (hereafter *CSAAG*) (National Archives microfilm M474, rolls 31 and 135), RG 109, NARA; "The Yankee Raid in N.E. Alabama and Northwest Georgia," *SC*, May 5, 1863; Record of Events, Twenty-fifth Georgia Provost Battalion, in Hewett, *Supplement to the Official Records*, Serial No. 18, p. 557; Davis to Lee, January 16, 1863, in Dunbar Rowland, ed., *Jefferson Davis Constitutionalist; His Letters, Papers, and Speeches*, 10 vols. (Jackson, MS, 1923) 5: 418.

53. Record of Events, Twenty-fifth Georgia Provost Battalion, in Hewett, *Supplement to the Official Records*, Part III Records of Events, Serial 18, p. 558–59. The quote comes from Caldwell v. Georgia, 34 GA 10, A-0320, Georgia State Supreme Court Case Reports, RG 92-1-1, GAr. Camp Preston most likely would be the Camp Lee in Smedlund, *Camp Fires of Georgia's Troops*, 185. Rosters of the Twenty-fifth Georgia Provost Battalion are in Janet B. Hewett, comp., *Georgia Confederate Soldiers* 4 vols. (Wilmington, NC, 1998), 4: 546–555 and John C. Rigdon, *Historical Sketch and Roster of the Twenty-fifth Infantry Battalion Provost Guards* (Cartersville, GA, 2019). Also see Confederate Pensions and Records Georgia Soldier Roster Commission, Roster compiled by the Commission, 1861–1865, Record Group 58-2-26, Georgia Archives, Morrow.

54. "A Serenade," *DI*, October 27, 1863.

55. Lee to Randolph, October 22, 1862, telegraph 674, *Telegraphs Received by the Confederate Secretary of War, 1861–1865* (National Archives microfilm M618, roll 11), and Lee to Randolph, July 24, 1862, Number 437 L 1862, *SOW* (National Archives microfilm M437, roll 57), NARA; J.A. Garrison, "Interesting Letter," *Christian Index* (Macon, Georgia), October 16, 1863.

56. "Burglars," *SC*, February 8 and 10, 1863; State vs. James Rowlings et al, Fulton County Superior Court Minute Book D (1860–1865), pp. 539–546, microfilm drawer 106 roll 55, and Caldwell v. Georgia, 34 GA 10, A-0320, Georgia State Supreme Court Case Reports, RG 92-1-1, GAr; Lee to Randolph, October 22, 1862, telegraph 674, *Telegraphs Received by the Confederate Secretary of War, 1861–1865* (National Archives microfilm M618, roll 12), NARA.

57. Cornelius Hanleiter diaries, April 14, 1862, Cornelius Hanleiter Collection, folder 13, Mss 109, Atlanta History Center; Lee to Randolph, August 1, 1862, and September 19, 1862, telegrams 136 and 482, endorsement book, pp. 11 and 32, *Telegraphs Received by the Confederate Secretary of War, 1861–1865* (National Archives microfilm M618, roll 11), NARA; Bohannon, "The Northeast Georgia Mountains," 86–92; Radley, *Rebel Watchdog*, 55–59; Singleton, *Richard Peters*, 90; Garrett, *Atlanta and Environs*, 1: 526; General Orders, Hewett, *Supplement to the Official Records*, Serial 94, pp. 288–289, 499–500; Cornelius Hanleiter diaries, vol. 1 (1861–1862), November 17, December 7 and 11, 1861, vol. 2 (1862), April 2 and 26, 1862.

58. "More of the Fruits of Retailing Liquor," *Weekly Constitutionalist* (Augusta, Georgia), October 29, 1862.

59. Cornelius Hanleiter diaries, vol. 2 (1862), April 14, 1862; Brown to Lee, May 26 and June 5, 1863, Letter book, pp. 1256 and 1279, Brown to Lee, May 28, 1863, and no date, copy book 1860–1863, pp. 307 and 330, Joseph E. Brown Papers, Ms. 95, Hargrett Rare Books and Manuscripts Library, University of Georgia Libraries, Athens; "Doomed Spirits," *DI*, May 18, 1862; [no title], and "Whiskey Speculator," *SC*, April 9, 1863, and October 17, 1862; [no title], *DI*, March 25, 1864; Lee to G.W. Randolph, November 11, 1862, 704 L 1862, John A. Rowland, supt. W&A. Railroad, to Randolph, October 20, 1862, 661 R 1862, J. Sullivan to Randolph, September 20, 1862, 930 S 1862, Lee to Randolph, October 2, 1862, 1043 S 1862, J.S. Smith to Randolph, October 3, 1862, 996 S 1862, William Bacon to Seddon, May 7, 1863, 376 B 1863, *SOW*

(National Archives microfilm M437, rolls 58, 69, 73, 79, 82), NARA.

60. "A Wild Career," *Weekly Constitution* (Atlanta), June 23, 1885; "Grand Army Stealing," and "Editorial Correspondence," *SC*, November 18 and 20, 1862; "Swindling by Government Officers," *State Gazette* (Austin, TX), December 31, 1862; James M. McPherson, *Battle Cry of Freedom* (New York, 1988), 854; Williams, *Rich Man's War*, 5; J.J. Harris to Randolph, October 7, 1862, *Telegraphs Received by the Confederate Secretary of War, 1861–1865* (National Archives microfilm M618, roll 12), NARA.

61. Gregory P. Downs, *After Appomattox: Military Occupation and the Ends of War* (Cambridge, MA, 2005), 187; George Gordon Meade, *Major General Meade's Report on the Ashburn Murder* (Atlanta, GA, 1868), 51, 52, 55, 61, 66, 78, 83; Robert S. Davis, *A History of Montgomery County, Georgia to 1918* (Roswell, GA, 1992), 165–166.

62. "Memorandum of My Life by Sidney Root," Mss 908f, Atlanta History Center. For the Confederate draft see David Williams, *Bitterly Divided: The South's Inner Civil War* (New York, 2008).

63. Jennifer Lund, "Conscription," in Richard N. Current, ed. *Encyclopedia of the Confederacy*, 4 vols. (New York, 1993), 1: 396–399.

64. John F. Andrews to Wayne, August 5, 1863, John F. Andrews File, Letters Received by Adjutant General Henry C. Wayne, RG 22-1-17, and "Adjutant General's Letter book number 16 June 15–July 24, 1863," (typescript, 1941–1942), p. 16, GAr.

65. Radley, *Rebel Watchdog*, 204–5; T. Conn Bryan, *Confederate Georgia* (Athens, GA, 1959), 143; Sidney Andrews, *The South Since the Civil War* (Boston, MA, 1866), 344.

66. Petition to James A. Seddon, July 25, 1863, compiled service record of George W. Lee, *Confederate General Staff Officers and Non-Regimental Enlisted Men* (National Archives microfilm M331, roll 155); "Georgia Items," *Daily Constitutionalist* (Augusta) August 6, 1863; James P. Hambleton to Lieutenant Colonel John B. Weems, November 17, 1862, 1243 H 1862, SOW (National Archives microfilm M437, roll 53), NARA; Richards, *Sam Richards's Civil War Diary*, 194; Wayne to J.C. Garlington, October 19, 1863, Outgoing Correspondence from Adjutant General Henry C. Wayne and Executive Minutes (1860–1866), May 26, 1863, p. 207, GAr; Riley, "Desertion and Disloyalty in Georgia During the Civil War," 4, 18, 20, 27–28, 87–88. For more on desertion and draft evasion, see Kenneth W. Noe, *Reluctant Rebels: The Confederates Who Joined the Army after 1861* (Chapel Hill, NC, 2015).

67. Singer, *Confederate Atlanta*, 212; Atlanta Fire Department, *History of Service* (Atlanta, GA, 2000), 4–5; "The Fire Battalion," *SC*, February 8, 1864; Greg H. Williams, *Civil War Suits in the U.S. Court of Claims: Cases Involving Compensation to Northerners and Southerners for Wartime Losses* (Jefferson, NC, 2006), 112. Rosters of the Third Battalion State Guards are in Janet B. Hewett, comp., *Georgia Confederate Soldiers* 4 vols. (Wilmington, NC, 1998), 3: 320–322. Also see the few names found in Confederate Pensions and records, Georgia Soldier Roster Commission, Roster compiled by the Commission, 1861–1865, Record Group 58-2-26, Georgia Archives, Morrow.

68. Judith L. Hallock and Grady McWhiney, *Braxton Bragg and Confederate Defeat*, 2 vols. (Tuscaloosa, AL, 1969, 1991), 2: 38; John F. Andrews to Wayne, August 5, 1863, John F. Andrews File, Letters Received by Adjutant General Henry C. Wayne, RG 22-1-17, and "Adjutant General's Letter book number 16 June 15–July 24, 1863," (typescript, 1941–1942), p. 16, GAr; "An Officer" to Seddon, January 26, 1864, 51 A 1864, SOW (National Archives microfilm M437, roll 118), and Lee to Samuel S. Cooper, December 1, 1862, 1244 L 1862, and Brigadier General John K. Jackson to Major Kinlock Falconer, October 7, 1863, 1628 B 1863, CSAAG (National Archives microfilm M474, rolls 31 and 58), NARA; Joseph Jones, "Roster of the Medical Officers of the Army of Tennessee," *Southern Historical Society Papers*, 29 (1901): 239.

69. Some lists of prisoners sent by Lee to Richmond from Streight's Raid appear in Lee to J.H. Winder, July 31, 1863, George W. Lee file, Department of Henrico Papers, Mss 3 C7604a, Confederate Military Manuscripts Series A, Section 3, a14–253, microfilm roll 8, frames 30–45, Virginia Historical Society, Richmond. For Streight's Raid see Brandon H. Beck, *Streight's Foiled Raid on the Western & Atlantic Railroad* (Charleston, SC, 2016).

70. "Col. G.W. Lee, of Atlanta," *Rome* (Georgia) *Tri-Weekly Courier*, September 12, 1863; Charles W. Sanders, Jr., *While in the Hands of the Enemy: Military Prisons of the Civil War* (Baton Rouge, LA, 2005), 145; John M. Dullum, "Unremitting Vigilance: Naval Intelligence and the Union Blockade During the American Civil War," (Master's Thesis, U.S. Army Command and General Staff College, 2000), 101; Spurr, "'The Latent Enmity of Georgia,'" 104; "Return of Sims, the Fugitive Slave," *Detroit* (Michigan) *Free Press*, April 29, 1863; *Guide to Civil War Maps in the National Archives* (Washington, D.C., 1986), 84. Sherman's armies also carried copies of Edward Arista Vincent's 1853 street map of Atlanta, see Paul K. Graham, "Edward Arista Vincent: Antebellum Immigrant, Cartographer, and Architect," *Georgia Historical Quarterly* 95 (Fall 2011): 391–407.

71. Davis, *Inventing Loreta Velasquez*, 5–21; Davis, *Ghosts and Shadows of Andersonville*, 163–178.

72. "Atlanta Correspondence of the Charleston Courier," *SC*, March 24, 1863; Lack, "Law and Disorder in Confederate Atlanta," 181.

73. "Atlanta Correspondence of the Charleston Courier," *SC*, March 24, 1863; William G. McAdoo diaries, January 13 and March 6, 1863; Genovese, *A Consuming Fire*, 47–49; Clayton, *Requiem for a Lost City*, 18–19; "Atlanta Correspondence of the Charleston Courier," *SC*, April 24, 1864; Fair, *The*

Tifts of Georgia, 74–75; Michael K. Shaffer, *Day by Day Through the Civil War in Georgia* (Macon, GA, 2022), 135. For another negative report on the business practices of the owners of the Roswell factory, see Georgia, vol. 7, 283, R.G. Dun & Co. credit report volumes, Baker Library.

74. Harold S. Wilson, *Confederate Industry and Quartermasters During the Civil War* (Jackson, MS, 2002), 99–100.

75. Edward J. Wood to Mary Augusta Williams Wood, August 9, 1864, in Edward J. Wood, *A Fierce, Wild Joy: The Civil War Letters of Colonel Edward J. Wood, 48th Indiana Volunteers Infantry Regiment*, ed. Stephen E. Towns (Knoxville, TN, 2007), 197.

76. G.S. Plumley, "In Dixie," *Harper's New Monthly Magazine* 29 (July 1864): 233–234; "Silver and Gold for Bacon," *SC*, May 1, 1864.

77. Spurr, "'The Latent Enmity of Georgia,'" 53–54, 58; Cornelius Hanleiter diaries, vol. 1 (1861–1862), Cornelius Hanleiter Papers, folder 12, pp. 40, 44–45, 171, Mss 109, Kenan Research Center, Atlanta History Center; untitled manuscript, Telamon Cuyler Collection, Box 164, folder 8, Mss 1170, and Howell Cobb to Jefferson Davis, July 18, 1864, Keith Read Collection, Box 5, folder 9, Mss 921, Hargrett Rare Book and Manuscript Library, University of Georgia Libraries, Athens; "Plowing Milch Cows," *Columbus* (Georgia) *Times*, March 4, 1865.

78. "Rioting Women," *SC*, March 21, 1863; Spurr, "'The Latent Enmity of Georgia,'" 93–96; Michael B. Chesson, "Harlots or Heroines? A New Look at the Richmond Bread Riot," *Virginia Magazine of History and Biography* 92 (April 1984): 136–137.

79. Clayton, *Requiem for a Lost City*, 15–16; "Memorandum of My Life by Sidney Root," Mss 908f, Atlanta History Center; Robert S. Davis, comp., *The Georgia Black Book*, 2 vols. (Easley, SC, 1987), 2: 157–190. See James Marten, *The Children's Civil War* (Chapel Hill, NC, 1998).

Chapter Three

1. George W. Lee file, *Confederate Papers Relating to Citizens or Business Firms* (National Archives microfilm M346, roll 577), NARA.

2. "Late from Georgia," *Chicago* (Illinois) *Daily Tribune*, January 12, 1863; advertisement, *DI*, September 10 and 13, 1863, *Augusta* (Georgia) *Chronicle*, June 6 and September 1, 1863.

3. Shaffer, *Day by Day Through the Civil War in Georgia*, 127–128; Ben Tarnoff, *A Counterfeiter's Paradise: The Wicked Lives and Surprising Adventures of Three Early American Moneymakers* (New York, 2012), 176–261.

4. General orders, *SC*, September 16, 1863; "Counterfeit Money," *Hampshire Gazette* (Northampton, MA), December 11, 1862; Richard M. McMurry, "Rebels, Extortionists and Counterfeiters: A Note on Confederate Judaeophobia," *Atlanta History* 22 (Fall-Winter 1978): 46–47; Lynn Glaser, *Counterfeiting in America: The History of an American Way to Wealth* (Philadelphia, PA, 1960), 149–150; George B. Tremmel, *Counterfeit Currency of the Confederate States of America* (Jefferson, NC, 2003), 21–22.

5. "Counterfeiters Arrested," "We Won't Take Them," and "A Discrete Boy," *SC*, July 29, 1862, November 16, 1862, and April 25, 1863; Richards, *Sam Richards's Civil War Diary*, 125–126; G.H. Gilbert to Lee, January 16, 1863, 865 M 1863, *SOW* (National Archives microfilm M437, roll 105), and C.G. Memminger to Lee, May 4, 1863, Entry 144, Letters Received Secretary of Treasury and the Treasurer, 1861–1865, RG 109, NARA. Ironically, when the United States later created the modern Secret Service, the first agent paid would be the previously mentioned federal spy James George Brown. James G. Brown File, *Union Provost Marshal's Files* (National Archives microfilm M345, roll 37), Record Group 110 Records of the Provost Marshal, NARA.

6. Lee to Lucius Jeremiah Gartrell, September 5, 1862, 596 G 1862, Lee to Seddon, July 10, 1863, 536 B 1863, *SOW* (National Archives microfilm M437, rolls 49 and 83), and George McGinneley file, *Confederate Papers Relating to Citizens or Business Firms* (National Archives microfilm M346, roll 630), RG 109, NARA; Venet, *A Changing Wind*, 71; J.G.M. Ramsey, *Dr. J.G.M. Ramsey: Autobiography and Letters*, William B. Hesseltine, ed. (Nashville, TN, 1954), 103–104; Judith Benner, *Fraudulent Finance: Counterfeiting and the Confederate States, 1861–1865* (Hillsboro, TX, 1970), 38–39.

7. Lee to A. Fullarton, December 1, 1862, and to H. Pinckney, June 17, 1863, Box 1, folders 3 and 4, British Consulate papers, 1859–1866, MSS 15, Rose Library, Emory University, Atlanta; Charges and Specifications Against Captain W.K. Bradford, August 12, 1864, folder 12, box 68, Howell Cobb Papers, Mss 1376, Hargrett Rare Book and Manuscripts Library, University of Georgia Libraries, Athens; Robert S. Davis, "Georgians in Confederate Government Private Files," *Georgia Genealogical Society Quarterly* 41 (Fall 2005): 218–221.

8. Stephen Davis and Bill Hendrick, *The Atlanta Intelligencer Covers the Civil War* (Knoxville, TN, 2022), 288; "President Davis and General Joseph E. Johnston," *DI*, December 17, 1863.

9. Lee to Randolph, July 27, 1863, telegraph 1915, *Telegraphs Received by the Confederate Secretary of War, 1861–1865* (National Archives microfilm M618, roll 14), and Lee to Cooper (telegraph) July 27, 1863, 1221 C 1863, CSAAG (National Archives microfilm M474, roll 61), NARA; Clayton, *Requiem for a Lost City*, 92–95; Frank Moore, ed., *The Rebellion Record*, 11 vols. (New York, 1864), vol. 6, "Documents," p. 78; "Executive Department," *Macon* (Georgia) *Daily Telegraph*, May 27, 1863; Special Order 197, August 19, 1863, *ORs*, Series II, vol. 6, pp. 218–219; William Gibbes McAdoo diary, September 5, 1863.

10. Cornelius Hanleiter diaries, April 16, 1862, Cornelius Hanleiter Collection, folder 13, Mss 109, Atlanta History Center.

11. Davis and Hendrick, *The Atlanta Intelligencer*, 248; Venet, *A Changing Wind*, 91–92.
12. Radley, *Rebel Watchdog*, 208–209; Clayton, *Requiem for a Lost City*, 89–91; "The City," *SC*, November 29, 1863.
13. Clayton, *Requiem for a Lost City*, 18–19.
14. Clayton, *Requiem for a Lost City*, 89.
15. Clayton, *Requiem for a Lost City*, 18–19.
16. "Office Soldiers' Executive Aid Association for the Relief of the Army of Tennessee" and "Meeting of Citizens," *Memphis Daily Appeal* (Atlanta), August 19, 1863 and July 3, 1864; advertisements, *SC*, September 27 and November 20, 1863; "To the Rescue" and public notices, *DI*, September 25 and October 2, 1863; [no title], *DI*, September 16, October 12, December 25, 1862, October 2, 1863, January 19, 1864, and June 3, 1864, January 13, 1863, September 27, 1863, November 20, 1863. Charles and Napoleon Bonaparte "Boney" Tank received a wound in the hip and lost an eye at the Battle of First Manassas. As the first wounded Confederate to reach Atlanta, he would complain that Atlantans nearly killed him with kindness. Robert S. Davis, "Lumpkin County Folk Hero: The Legend (and Truth) of Boney Tank," *North Georgia Journal* 10 (4) (Winter 1993): 42–46.
17. [no title], *Macon* (Georgia) *Telegraph*, May 4, 1865; "Executive Aid Association," *Memphis Daily Appeal* (Atlanta) July 1, 1864.
18. Frederick A. Eiserman, "Longstreet's Corps at Chickamauga: Lessons in Inter-Theater Deployment," (Master's Thesis, U.S. Army Command and General Staff College, 1985), 3, 27, 38, 49, 61, 110, 113.
19. Wayne to Lee, September 1 and Wayne to Galt, September 13, 1863, Outgoing Correspondence from Adjutant General Henry C. Wayne, DOC2-553, Record Group 22-1-1, GAr.
20. "Will the Army be Fed," *SC*, May 1, 1864.
21. Spurr, "'The Latent Enmity of Georgia,'" 49–51, 96.
22. George Gilman Smith, Jr., Reminiscence, Mss3141, and Garrett Necrology, roll 7, frame 10, Kenan Research Center, Atlanta History Center, Atlanta, GA; "Segar Manufactory," "Atlanta Fire Company Fortified," and "The Grape Culture," *Atlanta Weekly Intelligencer* (Atlanta, GA), December 9, 1858, January 13, 1859, January 20, 1859; A.B. Pruitt, comp., *Abstracts of Deeds: DeKalb County, GA Books M & N (1850–1854)* (Whitakers, NC, 2015), 5, 17, 88, 89, 120–121; Pioneer Citizens' Society of Atlanta, *Pioneer Citizens' History of Atlanta, 1833 to 1902* (Atlanta, GA, 1902), 34, 157, 165; "Vines, Wines, and Woes," *Four Centuries & More* (2021), September-October 2021, n. p.
23. "A Supplement to a Letter from Atlanta," *Georgia Citizen* (Macon), August 23, 1850; Robert S. Davis, *Cotton, Fire, & Dreams: The Robert Findlay Iron Works and Heavy Industry in Macon, Georgia, 1839-1912* (Macon, GA, 1998), 108–110; John E. Talmadge, "Georgia Tests the Fugitive Slave Law," *Georgia Historical Quarterly* 49 (2) (April 1965): 57–64; Singer, "Confederate Atlanta," 36–37.
24. Ruth Scarborough, *Opposition to Slavery in Georgia to 1860* (Nashville, TN, 1933), 121.
25. Russell, *Atlanta*, 72; Frederick Bancroft, *Slave-Trading in the Old South* (Baltimore, MD, 1931), 248; Ulrich Bonnell Phillips, *American Negro Slavery* (New York, 1928), 190; Scarborough, *Opposition to Slavery in Georgia to 1860*, 121; Fulton County, Georgia, p. 748, *Eighth Census of the United States (1860)* (National Archives microfilm M653, roll 122), Record Group 29 Records of the Bureau of the Census, National Archives and Records Administration (hereafter NARA), Washington, D.C.; ad for Robert E. Clarke and "Great Sale of Negroes," *Southern Confederacy* (Atlanta), October 18, 1862; John Allen Wyeth, *Life of General Nathan Bedford Forrest* (New York, 1899), 20–21, 36.
26. Deyle, *Carry Me Back*, 151.
27. Venet, *A Changing Wind*, 96–97; advertisements, *Atlanta Daily Intelligencer*, May 15, September 11, October 2, 1863, and January 20, 1864. For a description of slave markets, see Michael Tadman, *Speculators and Slaves: Masters, Traders, and Slaves in the Old South* (Madison, WI, 1989), 97–102.
28. J.C. Hallman, *Say Anarcha: A Young Woman, a Devious Surgeon, and the Harrowing Birth of Modern Women's Health* (New York, 2023), 70; Ken Denney to author, December 9, 2019, and May 15, 2024, in the author's possession; Garrett, *Atlanta and Environs*, 1: 418; Venet, *A Changing Wind*, 97.
29. Sara Huff, *My 80 Years in Atlanta* (n. p., 1937?), 11, 19–20.
30. Fulton County tax digest, 1026th District, 1862/1863, p. 44, microfilm drawer 70 roll 28, 1864, p. 59, microfilm drawer 70 roll 29, Georgia Archives, Morrow.
31. Russell, *Atlanta*, 72; Frederick Bancroft, *Slave-Trading in the Old South* (Baltimore, MD, 1931), 248; Ulrich Bonnell Phillips, *American Negro Slavery* (New York, 1928), 190; Scarborough, *Opposition to Slavery in Georgia to 1860*, 121.
32. "Reminiscences of an Old Atlanta by Newsboy of the Sixties," *Atlanta Constitution Sunday Magazine*, November 7, 1937.
33. Walter Johnson, *Soul by Soul: Life Inside the Antebellum Slave Market* (Cambridge, MA, 1999), 5, 7; Deyle, *Carry Me Back*, 117–118, 138, 143, 149, 153–154, 157, 169–170, 175–176, 184–186; George B. Halstead, *Report of Cases Determined in the Court of Chancery and in the Prerogative Court, and, on Appeal in the Court of Error and Appeals State of New Jersey* (Newark, NJ, 1854), 4: 356, 370, 375–376, 379, 470; "The Forgery at Louisville," *Public Ledger* (Philadelphia, PA), December 1, 1837.
34. Calvin Schermerhorn, *The Business of Slavery and the Rise of American Capitalism, 1815-1860* (New Haven, CT, 2015), 150. Also see Robert H. Gudmestad, *A Troublesome Commerce: The Transformation of the Interstate Slave Trade* (Baton Rouge, LA, 2003).

35. Deyle, *Carry Me Back*, 159–160, 162–164, 231; Johnson, *Soul by Soul*, 167–168.

36. Calvin Schermerhorn, *Money Over Mastery, Family Over Freedom: Slavery in the Antebellum Upper South* (Baltimore, MD, 2011), 102–104; Edward E. Baptist, "'Cuffy,' 'Fancy Maids,' and 'One-Eyed Men': Rape Commodification and the Domestic Slave Trade in the United States," in Walter Johnson, ed., *Chattel Principle: Internal Slave Trades in the Americas* (New Haven, CT, 2004), 165–202; Deyle, *Carry Me Back*, 159–160, 162–164, 231; Johnson, *Soul by Soul*, 2–3, 62–63, 136–140, 168–175, 190.

37. Receipt to John P. Hurst, May 2, 1863, ahc. MSS561f, Kenan Research Center, Atlanta History Center, Atlanta; "The Peculiar Institution," *Daily Evansville* (Indiana) *Journal*, July 1, 1864; "The Atlanta Markets," *Daily Evening Traveler* (Boston, MA), March 21, 1863; *Macon* (Georgia) *Telegraph*, February 7, 1865, advertisement; Russell, *Atlanta*, 72. This slave market also symbolizes the wrongs of slavery in William Rattle Plum's novel *The Sword and the Soul: A Romance of the Civil War* (New York, 1917), 320. For "fancy maids" see Baptist, "'Cuffy,' 'Fancy Maids,' and 'One-Eyed Men,'" 126, 165, 166, 176, 180, 182–189.

38. "The Atlanta Markets," *Daily Evening Traveler* (Boston, MA), March 21, 1863; Venet, *A Changing Wind*, 97–98. William A.R. Crawford (aka Robert A. Crawford) was raised in Petersburg, and Northern Virginia was important in his lifetime for supplying New Orleans, where Crawford began working in 1835, with enslaved people to sell. The auction in the antebellum print "Slave Auction in the American South" likely inspired the auctioneer in John Rogers' controversial statuette *The Slave Auction* (1859). The auctioneer resembles Crawford. George B. Halstead, *Report of Cases Determined in the Court of Chancery and in the Prerogative Court, and, on Appeal in the Court of Error and Appeals State of New Jersey* (Newark, NJ, 1854), 4: 356, 370, 375–376, 379, 470; Paul and Meta Bleier, *John Rogers Statuary* (West Chester, PA, 2001).

39. "Something Racy," *Columbus* (Georgia) *Times*, February 15, 1865.

40. "$500 Reward," *DI*, January 5, 1865.

41. Lack, "Law and Disorder in Confederate Atlanta," 174.

42. Garrett, *Atlanta and Environs*, 1: 418; Venet, *A Changing Wind*, 97; advertisements, *Atlanta* (Georgia) *Daily Intelligencer*, September 17, 1863.

Chapter Four

1. R.S. Tharin, *Arbitrary Arrests in the South; or, Scenes from the Experience of an Alabama Unionist* (New York, 1863), 60; David Williams, *Bitterly Divided: The South's Inner Civil War* (New York, 2016), 43, 109, 137–140; Michael W. Fitzgerald, *Reconstruction in Alabama: From Civil War to Redemption in the Cotton South* (Baton Rouge, LA, 2017), 58; Marilyn David Barefield, *Historical Records of Randolph County, Alabama 1832-1900* (Easley, SC, 1985), 61–62. For Atlanta's so-called secret Yankees, see Thomas G. Dyer, *Secret Yankees: The Union Circle in Confederate Atlanta* (Baltimore, MD, 1999).

2. Walter Johnson, *Soul by Soul: Life Inside the Antebellum Slave Market* (Cambridge, MA, 1999), 90. For more on the attitudes of Southern workers about competition with African American labor see Clifton Ellis, *Slavery in the City: Architecture and Landscapes in North America* (Charlottesville, VA, 2017); Claudia Dale Goldin, *Urban Slavery in the American South, 1820-1860: A Quantitative History* (Chicago, IL, 1970); Jonathan D. Martin, *Divided Mastery: Slave Hiring in the American South* (Cambridge, MA, 2004); and Keri Leigh Merritt, *Masterless Men: Poor Whites and Slavery in the Antebellum South* (New York, 2017).

3. Steven Hahn, *The Roots of Southern Populism: Yeoman Farmers and the Transformation of the Georgia Upcountry, 1850-1890* (New York, 1983), 16–18, 20; Jones, *The Dispossessed*, 55, 57; Charles C. Bolton, *Poor Whites and the Antebellum South: Tenants and Laborers in Central North Carolina and Northeast Mississippi* (Durham, NC, 1994), 52–53, 66–68, 70–71, 75, 77–78; Eugene D. Genovese, *Roll, Jordan, Roll: The World the Slaveholders Made: Two Essays in Interpretation* (New York, 1969), 208–209; Douglas C. North, "The Economic Structure of the South," and Morton Rothstein, "The Antebellum South as a Dual Economy," in Eugene D. Genovese, ed., *The Slave Economics*, 2 vols. (New York, 1973), 2: 143–156, 157–169.

4. For homesteading lands see Michael L. Lanza, *Agrarianism and Reconstruction Politics: The Southern Homestead Act* (Baton Rouge, LA, 1999) and Neil Irvin Pinter, *Exodusters: Black Migration to Kansas after Reconstruction* (New York, 1992).

5. For more on guerrillas in the Civil War, see Gerald W. Flinchum, *The Devil's Time: Georgia's Guerrilla War 1861-1865* (Columbia, SC, 2020); Matthew C. Hulbert, *The Ghosts of Guerrilla Memory: How Civil War Bushwhackers Became Gunslingers in the American West* (Athens, GA, 2016); Matthew C. Hulbert and Joseph M. Beilein, Jr., eds., *The Civil War Guerrilla: Unfolding the Black Flag in History, Memory, and Myth* (Lexington, KY, 2015); Clay Mountcastle, *Punitive War: Confederate Guerrillas and Union Reprisals* (Lawrence, KS, 2009); and Daniel E. Sutherland, *A Savage Conflict: The Decisive Role of Guerrillas in the American Civil War* (Chapel Hill, NC, 2009).

6. For how white Southerners felt about the Civil War, see J. William Harris, *Plain Folk and Gentry in a Slave Society: White Liberty and Black Slavery in Augusta's Hinterlands* (Baton Rouge, LA, 1998); Richard E. Beringer, Herman Hattaway, Archer Jones, and William N. Still, Jr., *Why the South Lost the Civil War* (Athens, GA, 1986); Stephanie McCurry, *Confederate Reckoning: Power and Politics in the Civil War South* (Cambridge,

MA, 2010); and Eugene D. Genovese, *A Consuming Fire: The Fall of the Confederacy in the Mind of the White Christian South* (Athens, GA, 1998).

7. See Stephen E. Towne, *Surveillance and Spies in the Civil War: Exposing Confederate Conspiracies in America's Heartland* (Athens, OH, 2014).

8. Spurr, "The latent enmity of Georgia," 34, 42. As early as 1861, rumors spread through Atlanta of plots to burn the railroad bridges. At that time, only the two most important trestles had any security at all and that consisted of only two old men each, none of whom had guns. G.D. Phillips to Joseph E. Brown, June 7, 1861, Telamon Cuyler Collection, Ms. 1170, Box 56, folder 2, Hargrett Rare Books and Manuscripts Library, University of Georgia, Athens. For more information on the significance of this railroad in Civil War Georgia see Robert S. Davis, "White and Black in Blue: The Recruitment of Federal Units in Civil War North Georgia," *Georgia Historical Quarterly* 85 (Fall 2001): 348–374.

9. Venet, *A Changing Wind*, 92. For the Tennessee bridge burners, see Confederate States of America prison (Madison, GA) records, 1862, Ms. 455, Hargrett Rare Books and Manuscripts Library, University of Georgia Libraries, Athens, published as "East Tennesseans as Confederate Political Prisoners (1862)," *Tennessee Ancestors* 22 (December 2006): 164–178; T.T. Crittenden to Andrew Johnson, December 29, 1862, in Leroy P. Graf, Ralph W. Haskins, and Paul H. Bergeron, eds., *The Papers of Andrew Johnson*, 16 vols. (Knoxville, TN, 1967–2000), 6: 105–106; Cameron Judd, *The Bridge Burners: A True Adventure of East Tennessee's Underground Civil War* (Johnson City, TN, 1996); and Tate Greene, "Dissidents of Rebellion: The Hidden Stand and Sacrifice of the East Tennessee Bridge Burners" (accessed September 23, 2023): http://www.tennesseehistory.org/wp-content/uploads/jr-ind-doc-greene.pdf.

10. "Statement of Colonel Jefferson Falkner and Mr. A.R. Hill, of Randolph County, Ala." *ORs*, Series IV, vol. 2, pp. 396–398; R.H. Thrasher, et al., to Alexander H. Stephens, July 18, 1860, Alexander Hamilton Stephens Papers, Series I, Rose Library, Emory University, Atlanta, Georgia.

11. R.S. Tharin, *Arbitrary Arrests in the South; or, Scenes from the Experience of an Alabama Unionist* (New York, 1863), 60; David Williams, *Bitterly Divided: The South's Inner Civil War* (New York, 2016), 43, 109, 137–140; Michael W. Fitzgerald, *Reconstruction in Alabama: From Civil War to Redemption in the Cotton South* (Baton Rouge, LA, 2017), 58; Marilyn David Barefield, *Historical Records of Randolph County, Alabama 1832–1900* (Easley, SC, 1985), 61–62; W.H. Walker to Braxton Bragg, May 8, 1864, *ORs*, Series IV, vol. 3, pp. 393–398.

12. For the memoirs of one such Southern Unionist, see J.R. Phillips, "My Life's Story," (1923), Family vertical files, Genealogy Collection, Library, Wallace State Community College, Hanceville, Alabama.

13. Emily Burke, *Pleasure and Pain: Reminiscences of Georgia in the 1840s*, introduction by Felicity Calhoun (1850; rep. ed. Savannah, GA, 1978), 77. For more on African Americans in Appalachia see Wilma A. Dunaway, *Slavery in the Mountain South* (New York, 2003).

14. David Williams, *Georgia's Civil War: Conflict on the Home Front* (Macon, GA, 2017), 50–51; Spurr, "The Latent Enmity of Georgia," 24–26, 45.

15. William Gibbes McAdoo diary, November 17–21, December 8–9, 1862, June 22, July 8 and 12, September 3, October 7, 1863.

16. Robert S. Davis, "A Soldier's Story: The Records of Hubbard Pryor, Forty-Fourth United States Colored Troops," *Prologue: The Quarterly of the National Archives* 31 (1999): 266–272 and "White and Black in Blue: The Recruitment of Federal Units in Civil War North Georgia," *Georgia Historical Quarterly* 85 (Fall 2001): 348–374; Mohr, *On the Threshold of Freedom*, 84–96.

17. Robert S. Davis, "War on the Edge: Civil War Era Politics and Its Legacy in an Appalachian County" in John D. Fowler and David B. Parker, eds., *Breaking the Heartland: The Civil War in Georgia* (Macon, GA, 2011), 1–18.

18. "Ludville Family Split by Civil War," Marble Valley Historical Society *newsletter*, 2 (January 1998): 1; Pickens County Heritage Book Committee, *Pickens County Heritage Book 1853–1998* (Jasper: the author, 1998), 120–122.

19. George Washington Lee, Family trees, Ancestry.com, online accessed on May 17, 2024; Glenda McWhirter Todd, *Unionists in the Heart of Dixie: 1st Alabama Cavalry, USV*, 3 vols. (Westminster, MD, 2012), 2: 243–244, 3: 240–245.

20. Robert M. Sandow, "'Grudges and Loyalties Die Slowly': Contested Memories of the Civil War in Pennsylvania's Appalachia," in Andrew L. Slap, ed., *Reconstructing Appalachia: The Civil War's Aftermath* (Lexington, KY, 2010), 269–292; Jennison, *Cultivating Race*, 239, 307, 311; "Remarkable Escape." *Memphis Appeal* (Atlanta), July 1, 1864; Daniel E. Sutherland, *A Savage Conflict: The Decisive Role of Guerrillas in the American Civil War* (Chapel Hill, NC, 2009), 45; John Van Houten Dippel, *Race to the Frontier: "White Flight" and Western Expansion* (New York, 2005), 39–64; Hahn, *The Roots of Southern Populism*, 108–111; Gerald W. Flinchum, *The Devil's Time: Georgia's Guerrilla War 1861–1865* (Columbia, SC, 2020), 10–14, 33. For more on the attitudes of these people with regards to race and the Civil War see John C. Inscoe, *Race, War, and Remembrance in the Appalachian South* (Lexington, KY, 2008), 13–64; and Richard B. Drake, "Slavery and Antislavery in Appalachia," in John C. Inscoe, ed., *Appalachians and Race: The Mountain South from Slavery to Segregation* (Lexington, KY, 2001), 16–26.

21. For the Northern draft see Paul Taylor, *'Tis Not Our War: Avoiding Military Service in the Civil War North* (Kent, OH, 2009).

22. Lack, "Law and Disorder in Confederate Atlanta," 173–174; Spurr, "The Latent Enmity of

Georgia," 42; Jefferson Davis speech, September 24, 1864, in Lynda L. Crist, Mary S. Dix, and Kenneth H. Williams, eds., *The Papers of Jefferson Davis*, 14 vols. to date (Baton Rouge, LA, 1997–2015), 11: 61–63; William Gibbs McAdoo diary, October 5, 1863.

23. Robert S. Davis, "Civil War Guerrilla Fighter John P. Gatewood," *North Georgia Journal* 17 (3) (Autumn 2000): 56–58. For more on Gatewood see Larry Stephens, *John T. Gatewood: Confederate Bushwhacker* (Gretna, LA, 2012), and Thurman Sensins, *Champ Ferguson: Confederate Guerrilla* (Nashville, TN, 1942).

24. Lee to Randolph, March 26, 1863, telegram 1364, *Telegraphs Received by the Confederate Secretary of War, 1861–1865* (National Archives microfilm M618, roll 13), NARA; Jonathan D. Sarris, "'Hellish Deeds ... in a Christian Land': Southern Mountain Communities at War, 1861–1865," (Ph.D. diss., University of Georgia, 1998), 86, 95–100, 118–119; Isaac W. Avery, *The History of the State of Georgia from 1850 to 1881* (New York, 1881), 189; "Colonel Lee's Expedition to N.E. Georgia" and "Tories and Bushwhackers," *SC*, February 4, 1863, and April 30, 1864; "A Gloomy Prospect for North Georgia and East Tennessee," *The Soldier's Friend* (Atlanta), November 5, 1863; McCurry, *Confederate Reckoning*, 59; Riley, "Desertion and Disloyalty," 14, 31, 40; David Williams, *Bitterly Divided: The South's Inner Civil War* (New York, 2016), 138–140. For more on the problems of the Confederate draft and desertion in Georgia, see Mark A. Weitz, *A Higher Duty: Desertion Among Georgia Troops During the Civil War* (Lincoln, NB, 2000).

25. Gerald W. Flinchum, *The Devil's Time: Georgia's Guerrilla War 1861–1865* (Columbia, SC, 2020), 51–52.

26. [untitled articles on James G. Brown and George W. Ashburn], *Daily Gazette* (Chattanooga), October 26 and 28, 1864; George W. Ashburn credit reports, Georgia vol. 3 (Bibb County), p. 176, vol. 20 (Monroe County), p. 68, vol. 23 (Columbus), p. 96, R.G. Dun & Co. credit report volumes; Robert S. Davis, "A Spy's Story: The Civil War of James George Brown," *Chattanooga Regional Historical Journal* 12 (2) (Winter 2009): 19–68; "North Georgia Glimpses," *Springfield* (Illinois) *Republican*, September 11, 1882.

27. For Joseph E. Brown's background, see Ulrich Bonnell Phillips, *Georgia and States Rights: A Study of the Political History of Georgia from the Revolution to the Civil War* (Washington, D.C., 1902), 180–181.

28. Lee to Jefferson Davis, January 13, 1863, in Lynda L. Crist, Mary S. Dix, and Kenneth H. Williams, eds., *The Papers of Jefferson Davis*, 14 vols. to date (Baton Rouge, LA, 1997–2015), 9: 23; Lee to Randolph, January 13, 1863, telegraph 998, *Telegraphs Received by the Confederate Secretary of War, 1861–1865* (National Archives microfilm M618, roll 12), NARA.

29. Brown to Davis, August 25, 1863, in Crist, et al., *The Papers of Jefferson Davis*, 9: 355; William Gibbs McAdoo diary, September 5, 1863; Keith S. Bohannon, "The Northeast Georgia Mountains During the Secession Crisis and Civil War," (Ph.D. diss., Pennsylvania State University, 2001), 139–140, 180–185; William Harris Bragg, *Joe Brown's Army: The Georgia State Line, 1862–1865* (Macon, GA, 1987), 18–19; Sean M. O'Brien, *Mountain Partisans: Guerrilla Warfare in the Southern Appalachians, 1861–1865* (Westport, CT, 1999), 141–143. Governor Joseph E, Brown was accused of organizing a political party to oppose Jefferson Davis' administration, a charge he denied. Brown to Jefferson Davis, April 4, 1862, Keith Read Collection, Box 3, folder 18, Mss 921, Hargrett Rare Book and Manuscript Library, University of Georgia Libraries, Athens.

30. Bragg, *Joe Brown's Army*, 18–21, 49; Jonathan D. Sarris, *A Separate Civil War: Communities in Conflict in the Mountain South* (Charlottesville, VA, 2006), 91–97, and "'Shot for Being Bushwhackers': Guerrilla War and Extralegal Violence in a North Georgia Community, 1862–1865" in Daniel E. Sutherland, ed., *Guerrillas, Unionists, and Violence on the Confederate Home Front* (Fayetteville, NC, 1999), 39–42; "The Ladies of Dahlonega," *SC*, February 10, 1863; O'Brien, *Mountain Partisans*, 143–44. For an account of Lee's men coming to a house in search of deserters see Keith S. Bohannon, "They Had Determined to Root Us Out: Dual Memoirs by a Unionist Couple in Blue Ridge Georgia," in John C. Inscoe and Robert C. Kenzer, eds., *Enemies of the Country: New Perspectives on Unionists in the Civil War South* (Athens, GA, 2001), 106–109.

31. Quote from Frank C. Barnes, "What a glorious time for men to harden themselves," *Georgia Backroads* 12 (Winter 2013): 10.

32. Lee to Brown, January 27 and February 3, 1863, Executive Correspondence, RG 1-1-5, GAr; telegrams, January 1863, folder 5, box 58, Mss 1170 Telamon Cuyler Collection, Hargrett Rare Book and Manuscripts Library, University of Georgia Libraries, Athens; "Desperate Efforts of the Rebels," *New York Herald*, February 6, 1863; "Colonel Lee's Battalion," *DI*, October 10 and 21, 1863; "The Troubles of North East Georgia" and "The Troops," *SC*, February 12, 1863; 'State Defense," May 28, 1863, *Daily Constitutionalist* (Augusta) October 4, 1863.

33. Sutherland, *A Savage Conflict*, 186; "Rebellion Among the Rebels of Georgia," *Bangor* (Maine) *Daily Whig*, February 14, 1863; "Colonel Lee's Expedition to N.E. Georgia," *SC*, February 4, 1863; Brown to Lee, February 6, 1863, Letter books, p. 1179, Joseph E. Brown Papers; H.H. Walker to E.M. Galt, April 14, 1863, H.H. Walker file, Letters Received by Adjutant General Henry C. Wayne, RG 22-1-17, GAr.

34. Williams, *Georgia's Civil War*, 50; Thomas S. Kidd, *Thomas Jefferson: A Biography of Spirit and Flesh* (New Haven, CT, 2022), 196; Faye Stone Poss, comp., *The Southern Watchman, Athens,*

Georgia Civil War Home Front Coverage 1861-1865 (Snellville, GA, 2008), 344; "Mr. Aldred of Pickens County," *DI*, March 2, 1865; Heritage of Cherokee County, Georgia, Book Committee, *The Heritage of Cherokee County Georgia 1831-1998* (Waynesville, NC, 1998), 481-482; Andrew W. Cain, *History of Lumpkin County for the First Hundred Years 1832-1932* (Atlanta, 1932), 348-349; John W. Latty, *A Fine Body of Athletic Soldiers: A History of the 11th Georgia Cavalry Regiment* (Gainesville, GA, 2007), 34. For Georgia Baptists and the politics of the Civil War in general, see Bruce T. Gourley, *Diverging Loyalties: Baptists in Middle Georgia During the Civil War* (Macon, GA, 2011).

35. Williams, *Georgia's Civil War*, 138; William Gibbs McAdoo diary, July 8, August 22-27, 1863.

36. "Major Lee's Expedition into North Georgia," *Southern Banner* (Athens, Georgia), October 14, 1863.

37. "Expedition into North Georgia" and "Maj. Lee," *DI*, October 9, 15, and 21, 1863; Poss, *The Southern Watchman*, 263.

38. "Expedition into North Georgia," *Confederate Union* (Milledgeville, Georgia), October 27, 1863; "Col. G.W. Lee, of Atlanta," *Rome* (Georgia) *Tri-Weekly Courier*, September 12, 1863; "Hunting Deserters," *Charleston* (South Carolina) *Mercury*, October 14, 1863; "To the People of Georgia," and "Lieut. Col. G.W. Lee's Expedition," *Daily Constitutionalist* (Augusta), September 9 and October 4, 1863; "Major Lee's Expedition into North Georgia," *Southern Banner* (Athens, GA), October 14, 1863. The Colonel Busty could be Unionist partisan David C. "Tinker Dave" Beatty of Fentress County, Tennessee, the nemesis of the notorious Confederate Partisan Champ Ferguson (1821-1865). Beatty was accused of murdering prisoners and stealing bounty enlistment money intended for his soldiers. He testified at Ferguson's trial where the court found the Confederate guilty and had him executed. "Tinker Dave," *Knoxville* (Tennessee) *Daily Chronicle*, February 17, 1872; "A Race for Life," *Nashville* (Tennessee) *Union and American*, January 5, 1872; Williams, *Bitterly Divided*, 149-50. Books have been written about Champ Ferguson, one of the few people of the Civil War tried for war crimes and only one of two executed. Coincidently, the Captain Jacob V. Ferguson of White County, Georgia, killed for being a Unionist, was the son of Unionist Champion Ferguson (1813-1881) of no known relation to the Confederate partisan of the same name! For White County during this time see Gerald W. Flinchum, *The Devil's Time: Georgia's Guerrilla War 1861-1865* (Columbia, SC, 2020), 11-12.

39. Sutherland, *A Savage Conflict*, 44-45, 187; Sarris, *A Separate Civil War*, 99; John C. Inscoe and Gordon B. McKinney, *The Heart of Confederate Appalachia: Western North Carolina in the Civil War* (Chapel Hill, NC, 2000), 120, 143, 150; William Gibbs McAdoo diary, September 1 and September 5, 1863; Riley, "Desertion and Disloyalty," 31-32; Derry, *Georgia*, 7: 719-720.

40. "Col. Lee's Battalion," *DI*, October 10, 1863; "Expedition into North Georgia," *Confederate Union* (Milledgeville, Georgia), October 27, 1863.

41. "Expedition into North Georgia" and "Maj. Lee," *DI*, September 5, October 9, 15, and 21, 1863; Poss, *The Southern Watchman*, 263. For other accounts of this second expedition, see the entries of September 9, October 7 and 16, 1863, William G. McAdoo diaries; Michael Parrish and Robert M. Willingham, Jr., comps., *Confederate Imprints: A Bibliography of Southern Publications from Secession to Surrender* (Austin, TX, 1987), 130; Sarris, "Hellish 'Deeds,'" 120-121; O'Brien, *Mountain Partisans*, 145; Brown to Lee, June 13 and September 5, 1863, Governor's Letter book (1861-1865), 492, 643, GAr; "Lieut. Colonel G.W. Lee," *Daily Columbus* (Georgia) *Observer*, October 8, 1863; "The Troubles in North-East Georgia" and "Major Lee's Expedition into North Georgia," *SC*, October 14, 1863.

42. Zebulon B. Vance to Davis, March 3, 1864, *ORs*, Series I, vol. 51, p. 832; Auman, *Civil War in the North Carolina Quaker Belt*, 54-71, 180. Later in the war, however, Governor Vance called for a meeting of the Confederacy's remaining governors to coordinate efforts against desertion. Spurr, "The Latent Enmity of Georgia," 75.

43. Latty, *A Fine Body of Athletic Soldiers*, 1, 9, 90, 98, 248; Poss, *The Southern Watchman*, 283, 336-338; "After a Spy," *Atlanta Constitution*, August 31, 1883; Lee to Randolph, October 3, 1862 and March 2, 1863, telegraph 569, endorsement book 39, telegram 11094, *Telegraphs Received by the Confederate Secretary of War, 1861-1865* (National Archives microfilm M618, rolls 11 and 13), NARA; "Arrival of Gold," *DI*, October 5, 1862; M.H. Wright to G.W. Rains, October 14, 1863, *ORs*, Series I, vol. 30, pt. iv, p. 748; Inscoe and McKinney, *The Heart of Confederate Appalachia*, 123. A report that Bryson's efforts to raise 1,000 men had failed appeared in the same article as an account that Coot Rhea led a fourteen-man death squad that killed two bandit brothers named Orr in Polk County, Tennessee. "Letter from North Georgia," *Southern Banner* (Athens, Georgia), July 9, 1864. For information on William Clayton Fain, one of the Georgia Unionist guerrilla leaders, see Travis H. McDaniel, "The Last Ride of North Georgia Unionist William Clayton Fain," *Georgia Backroads* 10 (August 2011): 8-12; Sarris, "Hellish 'Deeds,'" 30, 99, 159-362; and "Tories and Bushwhackers," *SC*, April 30, 1864. Also see Robert S. Davis, "Into the Wilderness: John Kellogg's Journey through Civil War North Georgia," *Chattanooga Regional Historical Journal* 7 (December 2004): 215-232.

44. For the Qualla settlement and the Eastern Cherokees, see John R. Finger, *The Eastern Band of Cherokees, 1819-1900* (Knoxville, TN, 1984), 16-59; and Charles Lanman, *Letters from the Alleghany Mountains* (New York, 1849), 94-115. Also see Lance Greene, *Their Determination to Remain: A Cherokee Community's Resistance to the Trail of Tears in North Carolina* (Chapel Hill, NC, 2022).

45. "From the Upcountry," "Goldman Bryson," and "Goldman Bryson Dead," *Southern Watchman* (Athens, Georgia), September 30, October 7, and November 11, 1863; [no title], *Early County* (Georgia) *News*, November 18, 1863.

46. Lee to Cooper, December 25, 1863, 1442 L 1863, CSAAG (National Archives microfilm M474, roll 72), NARA; M.H. Wright to G.W. Rains, October 14, 1863, *ORs*, Series I, vol. 30, pt. iv, p. 748; O'Brien, *Mountain Partisans*, 15–18, 145; "Affair About Ellijay," "Major Lee's Expedition into N.E. Georgia," and "Death of Bryson the NC Tory," *DI*, September 16, October 9, October 21, and November 14, 1863; Finger, *The Eastern Band of Cherokees*, 66, 94. Lieutenant Campbell H. Taylor of Colonel William H. Thomas North Carolina Legion claimed to have personally killed Bryson on October 28, 1863. C.H. Taylor to Lieutenant Colonel Walker, November 1, 1863, *ORs*, Series I, vol. 31, pt. 1, 235; Vernon H. Crow, *Storm in the Mountains: Thomas Confederate Legion of Cherokee Indians and Mountaineers* (Cherokee, NC, 1982), 51, 161, 234.

47. The quote comes from Vicki Betts, *Memphis Appeal [Atlanta and Montgomery], June 28, 1865–November 3, 1864* (Tyler, TX, 2016), [*Memphis Daily Appeal*, July 1, 1864].

48. Poss, *The Southern Watchman*, 234; "The Campbell Resistance," *The Central Georgian* (Sandersville, GA), July 8, 1863; Lee to Brown, October 9, 1863, folder 14, box 58, Mss 1170, Telamon Cuyler Collection; Bohannon, "'They Had Determined to Root Us Out,'" 106–108, 116 n. 14.

49. Wayne to J.J. Findley and Wayne to Lee, January 23, 1864, Adjutant General's Letter Book no. 21 (January 6 to February 6, 1864), p. 249–250, GAr; Congressman Hiram P. Bell to Seddon, October 7, 1864, 307 L 1864, SOW (National Archives microfilm M437, roll 133), NARA.

50. J.F. Belton to E.P. Watkins, June 13, 1862, and Geo. William Brent to C.J. Polignac, June 17, 1862, *ORs*, Series II, vol. 4, pp. 772–773, 777–778.

51. Venet, *A Changing Wind*, 128, 146–147; David Brion Davis, *The Problem of Slavery in the Age of Emancipation* (New York, 1988), 193–225.

52. For more on the African American struggle for freedom during the Civil War, see David Williams, *I Freed Myself: African American Self-Emancipation during the Civil War* (New York, 2014).

53. David Williams, "'The Faithful Slave Is About Played Out': Civil War Slave Resistance in the Lower Chattahoochee Valley," *Alabama Review* 52 (April 1999): 98–100; Harris, *Plain Folk and Gentry*, 167–170; "A Slave Revolt in Georgia," *Daily State Gazette* (Trenton, NJ), October 29, 1863; "Georgia Items," *Daily Telegraph* (Macon), October 10, 1863; Kent Anderson Leslie, *Woman of Color, Daughter of Privilege: Amanda America Dickson, 1849–1893* (Athens, GA, 1995), 53–54. African Americans also had secret organizations like that of the Freemasons and the Knights of the Golden Circle, including some dedicated to general emancipation. Mark A. Lause, *A Secret Society History of the Civil War* (Urbana, IL, 2011), 69–85.

54. Dyer, *Secret Yankees*, 101–102; David Williams, *I Freed Myself: African American Self-Emancipation during the Civil War* (New York, 2014), 166. For the incidents in Texas, see Richard B. McCashin, *Tainted Breeze: The Great Hanging at Gainesville, Texas 1862* (Baton Rouge, LA, 1997).

55. Dyer, *Secret Yankees*, 108–111.

56. Venet, *A Changing Wind*, 92; Dyer, *Secret Yankees*, 72–73, 94, 101–113 and "Half Slave, Half Free: Unionist Robert Webster in Confederate Atlanta," in Gordon and Inscoe, *Inside the Confederate Nation*, 298–300; Lee to Winder, May 11, 1863, W.N. Stark to same, May 26, 1863, George W. Lee file, Department of Henrico Papers, microfilm roll 8, frames 30–45, Virginia Historical Society, Richmond; report on money stolen from Colonel Streight, November 13, 1863, file C(WD) 1048, Correspondence Relating to Civilian Prisoners, Entry 131, Records of the Commissary of Prisoners, RG 249, NARA; "Financial," *SC*, August 3, 1862.

57. Lee to Randolph, September 17, 1862, and enclosed petition of August 17, 1862, 708 L 1862, SOW (National Archives microfilm M437, roll 58), NARA; Bonds, *Stealing the General*, 278–284, 310; Don Carlos Buell to Lorenzo Thomas, August 5, 1862, and endorsement by G.W.R., G.J. Foreacre to Randolph, September 16, 1862, and Lee to Clifton H. Smith, November 18, 1862, *ORs*, Series I, vol. 10, pt. i, 534–535, 638–639; testimony of William Pittenger, April 7–12, 1862, in Hewett, *Supplement to the Official Records*, Part 1 Reports, Volume 1, Seral 1, pp. 670–671; "Escape of Bridge-Burners," *SC*, October 10, 19, and 25, 1862; William Pittenger, *Daring and Suffering: A History of the Andrews Railroad Raid in 1862* (New York, 1887), 309, 312, 323, 360, 369; "'Another Nancy Hart,'" *Augusta* (Georgia) *Constitutionalist*, October 22, 1862; "Engine Thieves," *National Tribune* (Washington, D.C.), April 2, 1885, p. 2. The federal government later hanged Ned Edwards of Whitfield County as a spy and guerrilla. "A Noted Spy and Guerrilla Hung," *Nashville* (Tennessee) *Dispatch*, July 12, 1864. Jacob Moorland escaped from execution on a desertion charge by a court under Lee's command. Moorland's commander saved him. "A Story of the War," *Weekly Constitution* (Atlanta), June 23, 1885.

58. "The Difference," *SC*, March 1, 1863.

Chapter Five

1. "Letter From St. Louis," *Sunny South* (Atlanta), January 24, 1876; "The Outraged South," *The Sunny South* (Atlanta), February 28, 1880.

2. For discussions on the effects of the war upon the Southern population see James L. Roark, "Behind the Lines: Confederate Economy and Society" in McPherson and Cooper, *Writing the Civil War*, 201–227; "Our Importations–Trading

with the Yankees," *DI*, October 29, 1862; Elizabeth Ann Regosin, *Freedom's Promise: Ex-Slave Families and Citizens in the Age of Emancipation* (Charlottesville, VA, 2002); and Armstead L. Robinson, *Bitter Fruits of Bondage: The Demise of Slavery and the Collapse of Slavery, 1861-1865* (Charlottesville, VA, 2005).

3. Brown to Randolph, July 4, 1863, in compiled service record of George W. Lee, *Confederate General Staff Officers and Non-Regimental Enlisted Men* (National Archives microfilm M331, roll 155), RG 109, NARA; [no title], *SC*, October 31, 1862.

4. Hubbard to Randolph, October 18, 1862, 1145 H 1862, *SOW* (National Archives microfilm M437, roll 53), NARA.

5. Clayton, *Requiem*, 15; Wayne to Samuel Jones, November 20, 1862, Adjutant General's Letter Book no. 12 (September 11-December 31, 1862), p. 350, GAr; "Southern," *Frank Leslie's Illustrated Newspaper* (New York), April 18, 1863; "An Officer" to Seddon, January 26, 1864, 51 A 1864, *SOW* (National Archives microfilm M437, roll 118); [no title], *Daily Telegraph and Confederate* (Macon), November 29, 1864.

6. "Attempted Assassination," "John Kershaw," and "Roswell Factory," *SC*, August 20, 1862, August 22, 1862, and June 19, 1864; "From the Front," *Charleston* (South Carolina) *Mercury*, June 17, 1864; "Daring Assault," *Daily Constitutionalist* (Augusta), April 22, 1865. Nothing in the service records of the Kershaws mentions the attack on Lee.

7. "Atrocious Act of Incendiarism," *DI* (October 15, 1863.

8. Brown to Jefferson Davis, April 4, 1862, Keith Read Collection, Box 3, folder 18, Mss 921, Hargrett Rare Book and Manuscript Library, University of Georgia Libraries, Athens; "Martial Law," *SC*, September 20, 1862; Richards, "'We Live Under a Constitution,'" 30-34.

9. Bragg to Joseph E. Johnson, March 2, 1863, and same to "General," July 22, 1863, and Randolph to Braxton Bragg, August 12, 1862, *ORs*, Series I, vol. 23, part ii, pp. 656-657, 924-925, Series 2, vol. 4, 844.

10. G.W. Lee to Seddon, February 27, 1863, 108 L 1863, *SOW* (National Archives microfilm M437, roll 100), and Lee to H.L. Clay, July 20, 1863, compiled service record of George W. Lee, *Confederate General and Staff Officers and Non-Enlisted Men* (National Archives Microfilm M331, roll 155), RG 109, NARA; Moses H. Wright to W.W. Mackall, July 28, 1863, *ORs*, Series I, vol. 23, part ii, p. 935. For a description of the Atlanta munitions works see "The Government Works at Atlanta," *Nashville* (Tennessee) *Daily Times & True Union*, August 3, 1864.

11. General Order 13, in Hewett, *Supplement to the War of the Rebellion*, Serial 93, p. 120; Dyer, *Secret Yankees*, 99, 346 n. 6; "Captain G.W. Lee," *DI*, July 24, 1864; deposition of William McConnell, September 8, 1862, 545 L 1862, *SOW* (National Archives microfilm M437, rolls 26 and 58) and Bragg to B.S. Ewell, March 1, 1863, compiled service record of George W. Lee, *Confederate General and Staff Officers and Non-Enlisted Men* (National Archives Microfilm M331, roll 155), RG 109, NARA; Bragg to Joseph E. Johnson, March 2, 1863, and same to "General," July 22, 1863, *ORs*, Series I, vol. 23, part ii, pp. 656-657, 924-925; Crist, et al., *The Papers of Jefferson Davis*, 9: 274 n. 10; Inscoe and McKinney, *The Heart of Confederate Appalachia*, 123.

12. Frances Thomas Howard, *In and Out of the Lines: An Accurate Account of Incidents during 1865* (Cartersville, GA, 1997), 40. In 1862, Lee signed and read a speech written for him at a flag presentation to Wright's Legion. His friend and constant critic Cornelius Hanleiter did not mention Lee being illiterate. Hanleiter diaries, vol. 3 (1862-1863), June 5, 1862.

13. Compiled service record of Jabez R. Rhodes, *Confederate Soldiers Who Served in Organizations Raised Directly by the Confederate Government* (National Archives Microfilm M258, roll 57), RG 109, and Wright to Davis, August 14, 1863, 1474 W 1863, *CSAAG* (National Archives microfilm M474, roll 88), NARA; "From Tennessee-Military Execution," *Daily Dispatch* (Richmond), September 7, 1863. A native of South Carolina, John Bodenave Villepique had seven years' experience in the United States Army and would later serve as colonel of the Thirty-eighth Georgia Infantry and as a brigadier general before his death from pneumonia on November 9, 1862. Ezra J. Warner, *Generals in Gray: Lives of the Confederate Commanders* (Baton Rouge, LA, 1959), 317-318.

14. Anonymous to Brown, October 4, 1861, Anonymous File, Letters Received by Governor Joseph E. Brown, Record Group 1-1-5, GAr.

15. Hallock and McWhiney, *Braxton Bragg*, 1: 31-32, 2: 36-39; Steven E. Woodworth, *No Band of Brothers: Problems in the Rebel High Command* (Columbia, MO, 1999), 70-80; Clayton, *Requiem for a Lost City*, 105-106. For more on Bragg and his relations with other officers, see Earl J. Hess, *Braxton Bragg: The Most Hated Man of the Confederacy* (Chapel Hill, NC, 2021) and Samuel J. Martin, *General Braxton Bragg, C.S.A.* (Jeffersonville, NC, 2011).

16. Radley, *Rebel Watchdog*, 238.

17. Genovese, *Roll, Jordan, Roll*, 140-145; Jay W. Simson, *Naval Strategies of the Civil War: Confederate Innovation and Federal Opportunism* (Nashville, TN, 2001), 12.

18. "Late News from Chattanooga and the North," *Memphis Daily Appeal* (Atlanta, GA), July 1, 1864; "The City Under Siege," *Atlanta* (Georgia) *Constitution*, July 20, 1898.

19. Dyer, *Secret Yankees*, 14-15, 72-73, 77-79, 197; William Gibbs McAdoo diary, November 6, 1863. The Atlanta Rolling Mill (aka the Gate City Rolling Mill), erected in 1858, had been Atlanta's most sought-after and significant manufactory before the war. It stood near the later Confederate Arsenal. The original owners, Lewis Schofield,

James Blake, and William Markham, sold the company to the South Carolina Railroad Company for $600,000 for the buildings and equipment, plus $75,000 for the mill's 100 enslaved workers. The company also employed 100 white workers. Trenholm, Fraser & Company of Charleston, South Carolina, came to own the Atlanta Rolling Mill. When Sherman's armies threatened Atlanta, the machinery of the plant was moved to Columbia, South Carolina. The rolling mill's buildings were at least damaged when eighty-one ammunition cars were detonated by the retreating Confederate army on the morning of September 2, 1864. Researcher Ken Denney believes, however, that the building was likely fully demolished by Sherman's engineers. An 1864 photograph of the ruins of the rolling mill is one of the most often reproduced images of the Civil War. "Southern Commercial Convention," *Charleston* (South Carolina) *Mercury*, May 16, 1858; "The Atlanta Rolling Mill," *Albany* (Georgia) *Patriot*, December 15, 1859; [no title], *Nashville* (Tennessee) *Daily Times & True Union*, August 3, 1864; B.C. Trumond, "The Works of the Rebel Government," *Buffalo* (New York) *Commercial*, September 17, 1864; Garrett, *Atlanta and Environs*, 1: 427, 633–634; Clayton, *Requiem for a Lost City*, 180; Mohr, *On the Threshold of Freedom*, 154.

20. William Gibbes McAdoo diaries, November 6, 1863; Wallace P. Reed, *History of Atlanta, Georgia* (Syracuse, NY, 1889), 93–95; Confederate States of America vs. George W. Lee (case file 868), Records of the Confederate District Court of North Georgia, Records of the United States District Courts, Record Group 21, National Archives at Atlanta, Morrow, GA. For more on Atlanta entrepreneurs profiting from the war, see Mary A. DeCredico, *Patriotism for Profit: Georgia's Urban Entrepreneurs and the Confederate War Effort* (Chapel Hill, NC, 1990).

21. "Meeting of Loyal Georgians," *DI*, March 17, 1865; Russell, *Atlanta 1847–1890*, 95; "Sherman in Atlanta," *Atlanta Constitution*, September 30, 1888; testimony of George W. Lee, February 5, 1868, Markham v. United States (case file 11137), Records of the United States Court of Claims, RG 123, NARA.

22. "Outlawry" and "Sherman's Order of Outlawry," *Daily Intelligencer* (Macon), October 22 and 27, 1864; "Outlawed," *Confederate Union* (Milledgeville), November 1, 1864; "Civilians Held Prisoner in Atlanta, 1865–1866," *Georgia Genealogical Society Quarterly* 38 (2002): 36–38. Sherman likely acted in response to Jefferson Davis declaring federal General Benjamin F. Butler an outlaw to suffer execution without trial for having executed a Confederate sympathizer in New Orleans in December 1862. Sanders, *While in the Hands of the Enemy*, 145.

23. Dyer, *Secret Yankees*, 103–105, 113–114, 201–202; credit reports, Georgia, vol. 13, pp. 14, 402, R.G. Dun & Co. credit report volumes, Baker Library; "Post Mortem Examination of Michael Myers" and "The Late Michael Myers," *DI*, September 3 and 4, 1862; "Death of Michael Myers," *SC*, August 30, 1862.

24. Dyer, *Secret Yankees*, 21, 68–69; Confederate States of America vs. George W. Lee, case 868, Records of the Confederate District Court of North Georgia, Records of the United States District Courts, Record Group 21, National Archives Atlanta Region, Morrow, GA.

25. Lee to Secretary of War G.W. Randolph, October 18, 1862, 651 L 1862, *SOW* (National Archives microfilm M437, roll 58), NARA; William Gibbes McAdoo diary, January 27, February 26, 1864. William Gibbs McAdoo's son and namesake, born in Marietta, Georgia, on October 31, 1863, grew up to become son-in-law to President Woodrow Wilson, Secretary of Treasury, creator/first chairman of the Federal Reserve, director of the national railroads during World War I, candidate for president of the United States, and United States Senator. See William Gibbs McAdoo, *Crowded Years: The Reminiscences of William G. McAdoo* (New York, 1931). The Floyd-McAdoo Papers are in the collections of the Georgia Historical Society in Savannah although the Library of Congress has a microfilm copy.

26. Dyer, *Secret Yankees*, 116–17, 200, 260–261, and "Atlanta's Other Civil War Novel: Fictional Unionists in a Confederate City," *Georgia Historical Quarterly* 79 (Spring 1995): 161; Lee to Seddon, December 23, 1863, 14 L 1864, and Wm. G. McAdoo to Seddon, February 2, 1864, 90 M 1864, *SOW* (National Archives microfilm M437, rolls 132 and 134), NARA; William Gibbes McAdoo diaries, January 27, 1864; Russell, *Atlanta 1847–1890*, 96; deposition of Jonathan Dunwoody, April 8, 1869, and Moses Cole, January 23, 1868, Markham v. United States (case file 11137), Records of the United States Court of Claims, RG 123, NARA.

27. Dyer, "Atlanta's Other Civil War Novel," 147–168.

28. Advertisements, *Atlanta Daily Intelligencer*, September 10 and September 13, 1863; Dyer, *Secret Yankees*, 116–119, 122, 126; *Augusta* (Georgia) *Chronicle*, June 6 and September 1, 1863, advertisements.

29. See John D. Fair, *The Tifts of Georgia: Connecticut Yankees in King Cotton's Court* (Macon, GA, 2010) and June Hall McCash, *A Titanic Love Story: Ida and Isidor Straus* (Macon, GA, 2012). Straus' observation on Southern anti–Semitism is in McCash, *A Titanic Love Story*, 44–45.

30. "Atlanta," *Nashville* (Tennessee) *Daily Times & Press*, June 28, 1864; Venet, *A Changing Wind*, 70.

31. "A Shadow of Atlanta," *SC*, June 25, 1864.

32. Castel, *Decision in the West*, 71; Mills Lane, comp., *The People of Georgia* (Savannah, 1992), 159–160.

33. G.S. Plumley, "In Dixie," *Harper's New Monthly Magazine* 29 (July 1864): 233–34; deposition of William Whipple, July 26, 1864, "Statements of Escaped Union Prisoners, Refugees, and

Rebel Deserters," entry 4294, p. 26, RG 393, pt. i, NARA. For a different view of Civil War Macon, see "A Jaunt to Macon," *SC*, March 16, 1864.

34. See, for example, the Lost Friends Advertisements in *Southeastern Christian Advocate* (accessed on September 27, 2023): https://www.hnoc.org/database/lost-friends/index.html.

35. Samantha Seeley, *Removal and the Right to Remain: Migration and the Making of the United States* (Chapel Hill, NC, 2001), 265, 267, 276–277, 281, 309.

36. Bruce Levine, *Confederate Emancipation: Southern Plans to Free and Arm Slaves During the Civil War* (New York, 2006), 61–63; also see Jamie Amanda Martinez, *Confederate Slave Impressment in the Upper South* (Chapel Hill, NC: 2013). Numerous books have been published on the controversial African American service in the Confederate military, as labor and soldiers.

37. See Dudley Taylor Cornish, *The Sable Arm: Black Troops in the Union Army, 1861–1865* (Lawrence, KS, 1987); William A. Dobak, *Freedom by the Sword: The U.S. Colored Troops, 1862–1867* (Washington, D.C., 2011); Margaret Humphreys, *Intensely Human: The Health of the Black Soldier in the Civil War* (Baltimore, MD, 2008); James G. Mendez, *A Great Sacrifice: Northern Black Soldiers, Their Families, and the Experience of Civil War* (New York, 2019); and Holly A. Pinheiro, Jr., *The Families' Civil War: Black Soldiers and the Fight for Racial Justice* (Athens, GA, 2022). For the Georgia African American soldiers see Robert S. Davis, "A Soldier's Story: The Records of Hubbard Pryor, Forty-Fourth United States Colored Troops," *Prologue: The Quarterly of the National Archives* 31 (1999): 266–272, and "A Story of Two Soldiers: Colonel Lewis Johnson and Private Hubbard Pryor of the Forty-Fourth United States Colored Troops in Chattanooga, Dalton, and Nashville," *Chattanooga Regional Historical Journal* 15 (Winter, 2012): 7–24.

38. See David Williams, *I Found Myself: African American Self-Emancipation in the Civil War Era* (New York, 2004); and Kris Manjapra, *Black Ghost of Empire: The Long Death of Slavery and the Failure of Emancipation* (New York, 2022).

39. Huff, *My 80 Years in Atlanta*, 11, 19–20. For Robert A. Crawford and the Atlanta trade in the enslaved during the Civil War, see Bullock, "Col. Robert Ashton Crawford"; Venet, *The Changing Wind*, 97–100, 144; and Albert Castel, *Decision in the West: The Atlanta Campaign of 1864* (Lawrence, KS, 1992), 70, 212.

40. Crawford, Frazer & Company, *Confederate Papers Relating to Citizens or Business Firms* (National Archives microfilm M346, rolls 206), Record Group RG 109, War Department Collection of Confederate Records, NARA; untitled news story, *SC*, March 7, 1863.

41. Steven M. Stowe, *Keep the Days: Reading the Civil War Diaries of Southern Women* (Chapel Hill, NC, 2018), 47.

42. For homesteading lands see Michael L. Lanza, *Agrarianism and Reconstruction Politics: The Southern Homestead Act* (Baton Rouge, 1999) and Neil Irvin Pinter, *Exodusters: Black Migration to Kansas after Reconstruction* (New York, 1992).

43. Peter S. Carmichael, *The War for the Common Soldier: How Men Fought, Thought, and Survived the Civil War* (Chapel Hill, NC, 2018), 7.

44. "What the Government Might Have Done," *The Soldier's Friend* (Atlanta), June 30, 1864; William Shaw Paludan, "What Did the Winners Win?" in James M. McPherson and William J. Cooper, Jr., *Writing the Civil War: The Quest to Understand* (Columbia, SC, 1998), 207; Stanley Lebergott, "Why the South Lost: Commercial Purpose in the Confederacy, 1861–1865," *Journal of American History* 70 (June 1983): 58–74; Anne Farrow, Joel Lang, and Jenifer Frank, *Complicity: How the North Promoted, Prolonged, and Profited from Slavery* (New York, 2005), 121–133; Cotton, Captured, and Abandoned Property, 1872–1890, Entry 371, Record Group 56 Records of the Treasury, NARA (index in Entry 366).

Chapter Six

1. "Col. G.W. Lee—Important Appointment," *Columbus* (Georgia) *Enquirer*, September 6, 1863.

2. Lack, "Law and Disorder in Confederate Atlanta," 180–181, 184–187.

3. Colonel M.H. Wright to Cooper, September 8, 1863, 1633 W 1863, *CSAAG* (National Archives microfilm M474, roll 88), NARA.

4. "Atlanta Matters," *SC*, March 1, 1863.

5. See Thomas Weber, *The Northern Railroads in the Civil War, 1861–1865* (Bloomington, IN, 1999).

6. See, for example, Robert S. Davis, "The Eyes of Chickamauga: General George H. Thomas as a Civil War Spy Master," *Chattanooga Regional Historical Journal* 5 (July 2004): 73–92.

7. Lee to Lucius Jeremiah Gartrell, June 6, 1863, in compiled service record of George W. Lee, *Confederate General Staff Officers and Non-Regimental Enlisted Men* (National Archives microfilm M331, roll 155), RG 109, NARA; Wayne to Galt, September 10, 1863, Outgoing Correspondence from Adjutant General Henry C. Wayne; "Col. G.W. Lee-Important Appointment," *Columbus* (Georgia) *Daily Enquirer*, September 6, 1863; "Report of Bureau of Volunteer and Conscript Bureau for Month of October 1863," *ORs*, Series IV, vol. 2, pp. 963–964. For the origins of home guard units in the South see Salley E. Hadden, *Slave Patrols: Law and Violence in Virginia and the Carolinas* (Boston, MA, 2003).

8. Wallace P. Reed, *History of Atlanta, Georgia: With Illustrations and Biographical Sketches of Some of Its Prominent Pioneers* (Syracuse, NY, 1889), 126; Flinchum, *The Devil's Time*, 19–22.

9. Henry Wayne to E.M. Galt, September 13, 1863, Adjutant General Outgoing Correspondence, Record Group 22-1-1, DOC 2-553, Georgia Archives, Morrow; Robert S. Davis, "A Partial Roster of the Georgia Confederate Home Guards,"

Georgia Genealogical Society Quarterly 31 (Fall 1995): 146–155.

10. Horace Montgomery, *Howell Cobb's Confederate Career* (Tuscaloosa, AL, 1959), 117; Robert S. Davis, "Notes on the Confederate Home Guards of North Georgia," *Northwest Georgia Historical and Genealogical Society Quarterly* 27 (2) (June 1995): 2–4; "Wholesale Butchery," *Chronicle Union* (Bridgeport, CA), October 8, 1891. Lee's men served with a state equivalent of his Provost Guard Battalion in the form of Georgia home guard battalions like those commanded by Benjamin McCollum in Cherokee County and the one led by James J. Findley in Lumpkin County that reportedly included deserters from both armies in their ranks. "Tom Polk Edmundson," *Atlanta Constitution*, May 1, 1888. For biographical information on the leaders of the most notorious of Georgia's various local defense units, see O'Brien, *Mountain Partisans*.

11. Sutherland, *A Savage Conflict*, 252; David Williams, Teresa Crisp Williams, and David Carlson, *Plain Folk in a Rich Man's War: Class and Dissent in Confederate Georgia* (Gainesville, FL, 2002), 172; "A Horrid Report," *SC*, December 5, 1862; David Carlson, "'The Loanly Runagee': Draft Evaders in South Georgia," *Georgia Historical Quarterly* 84 (Winter 2000): 589–615.

12. Seddon to Cooper, July 14, 1863, *ORs*, Series I, vol. 23, pt. ii, p. 910; "Colonel G.W. Lee," *Memphis Daily Appeal* (Atlanta), September 4, 1863; Derry, *Georgia*, 7: 720; "Colonel G.W. Lee— Important Appointment," *Daily Enquirer* (Columbus), September 6, 1863; Carlson, "'The Loanly Runagee,'" 604–606; Lois Barefield Mays and Richard H. Mays, *Queen of the Okefenokee* (Folkston, GA, 2003), 92; Williams, *Georgia's Civil War*, 167; Flinchum, *The Devil's Time*, 65–80; Williams, *Bitterly Divided*, 143; William Gibbs McAdoo diary, September 19, 1863.

13. Davis, *Ghosts and Shadows of Andersonville*, 61–64, 210.

14. Williams, *I Freed Myself*, 167; Michael W. Fitzgerald. "'He was always preaching the Union': The Wartime Origins of Republicanism During Reconstruction," in Kenneth W. Noe, ed., *The Yellowhammer War: The Civil War and Reconstruction in Alabama* (Tuscaloosa, AL, 2013), 228–233; Robert S. Davis, "Some Unforgotten Alabama Union Soldiers," *Alabama Family History and Genealogy News* 17 (2) (1996): 12–19.

15. Spurr, "The Latent Enmity of Georgia," 68, 71, 74, 78, 81–82.

16. McCurry, *Confederate Reckoning*, 100 182; A.J. Glen to Brown, August 7, 1863, folder 12, box 58, Telamon Cuyler Collection.

17. W.W. Mackall to General G.W. Smith, June 12, 1864, Orders of the Secretary of War, June 24, 1864, *ORs*, Series I, vol. 38, pt. iv, pp. 770, 789, vol. 39, pt. ii, p. 663; John S. Preston to Seddon, December 31, 1863, and Howell Cobb to Cooper, April 19, 1864, *ORs*, Series IV, vol. 2, p. 1071, vol. 3, p. 311; Record of Events, Twenty-fifth Georgia Provost Battalion, in Hewett, *Supplement to the Official Records*, Ser. 18, pp. 555; "Expedition into North Georgia," *DI*, October 9 and 21, 1863.

18. Lee to Wright, April 30, 1864, compiled service record of George W. Lee, *Confederate General and Staff Officers and Non-Enlisted Men* (National Archives Microfilm M331, roll 155), RG 109, NARA; "The Guns Are Ready—Who Will Use Them," *DI*, March 20, 1863; "Come out! Come out!," *Memphis Daily Appeal* (Atlanta), July 14, 1863; "To the People of Georgia," *Tri-Weekly Courier* (Rome), September 10, 1863; "From Roswell," *SC*, June 17, 1864; "Interesting Letter," *DI*, June 22, 1864.

19. Katherine Brackett, "Remembering the Nancy Harts: A Female Militia, Gender, and Memory," *Georgia Historical Quarterly* 102 (Winter, 2008): 303–338. Also see Thomas P. Lowry, *The Story the Soldiers Wouldn't Tell: Sex in the Civil War* (Danver, MA, 2013) and *Confederate Heroines: 120 Southern Women Convicted by Union Military Junto* (Baton Rouge, LA, 2006).

20. Some lists of prisoners sent by Lee to Richmond from Streight's Raid appear in Lee to J.H. Winder, July 31, 1863, George W. Lee file, Department of Henrico Papers, Mss 3 C7604a, Confederate Military Manuscripts Series A, Section 3, a14-253, microfilm roll 8, frames 30–45, Virginia Historical Society, Richmond.

21. Stephen Davis, *What the Yankees Did to Us: Sherman's Bombardment and Wrecking of Atlanta* (Macon, GA, 2012), 54–56. For the militia census, see Nancy J. Cornell, *1864 Census for Reorganizing the Georgia Militia* (Baltimore, MD, 2000), and for the cotton purchases made from the Confederacy, see Philip Leigh, *Trading with the Enemy: The Covert Economy During the American Civil War* (Yardley, PA, 2014).

22. Diary, July-September 1864, William King Papers, #2985-z, Southern Historical Collection, The Wilson Library, University of North Carolina at Chapel Hill.

23. Venet, *A Changing Wind*, 170.

24. "Martin's Landing … a Brief History" at the web page http://ivic02.residentinteractive.com/programs/download.pdf?xinput=41183677; Garrett, *Atlanta and Environs*, 1: 567–69; [no title], *Daily Columbus* (Georgia) *Enquirer*, June 3, 1864; "From the Front," *Weekly Chronicle & Sentinel* (Augusta, Georgia), June 1, 1864; Wayne to Lee, March 4, 12, and 14, 1864, Adjutant General's Letter books no. 24 (April 29–June 5, 1864), pp. 127, 225, 258, GAr; W.W. Lowe to D.F. How, July 14, 1864, John P. Cummings to E.H. Murray, July 31, 1864, and Green B. Raun to S.B. Moe, July 29, 1864, *ORs*, Series 1, vol. 53, p. 867, vol. 52, pt. i, p. 107, vol. 38, pt. v, p. 299; "Note Book and Skraps [sic] from a Diary Kept by M.H. Brown," *Civil War Times Illustrated* Collection, U.S. Army Military History Institute, Carlisle, PA; "Federal Raid in Pickens County," *Columbus* (Georgia) *Ledger Enquirer*, June 12, 1864; "Disloyalty," *Southern Watchman* (Athens), August 17, 1864; Robert Winn to "Dear

Sister," July 27, 1864, Winn-Cook Family Papers, Mss A W776 8, Filson Club, Louisville, Kentucky.

25. Lee to Howell Cobb, July 31, 1864, folder 10, August 4, 1864, folder 11, August 7, 1864, folder 12, box 68, Mss 1376, Howell Cobb Papers; W.W. Mackall to G.W. Smith, June 12, 1864, *ORs*, Series I, vol. 38, pt. iv, p. 771; Lee to Wayne, July 24, July 25, and August 29, 1864, George W. Lee file, Letters Received by Adjutant General Henry C. Wayne, RG 22-1-17, and Wayne to Lee, August 15, 1864, Adjutant General's Letter books no. 25 (June 10-August 24, 1864), p. 351, GAr; David Evans, *Sherman's Horsemen: Union Cavalry Operations in the Atlanta Campaign* (Bloomington, IL, 1996), 300, 311-317; Richard W. Iobst, *Civil War Macon: The History of a Confederate City* (Macon, GA,1999), 142; "Communicated," *Daily Intelligencer* (Macon, Georgia), August 3, 1864; [no title], *Macon* (Georgia) *Telegraph*, August 6, 1864.

26. Wayne to Lee, August 18, 1864, Adjutant General's Letter books no. 25 (June 10-August 24, 1864), p. 424, Lee to Wayne, August 18 and September 20, 1864, George W. Lee file, Letters Received by Adjutant General Henry C. Wayne, RG 22-1-17, G.W. Lee file, Courts of Enquiry, RG 22-1-65, L.H. Briscoe to ?, August 17, 1864, and Adjutant General's Letter books no. 25 (June 10-August 24, 1864), 384, GAr.

27. William Gibbes McAdoo diaries, November 19, 21, 23, and 26, 1864; Gustavus Smith to Charles C. Jones, October 3, 1867, Charles C. Jones Jr. Papers, 1757-1926, Collection RL 00642, David M. Rubenstein Rare Book and Manuscript Library, Duke University, Durham; Keith Bohannon, "Ambrose Ransom Wright" in William C. Davis, ed., *The Confederate General*, 6 vols. (Washington, D.C., 1991), 6: 160-163. Lee had only limited success in removing the state records from Milledgeville. Sherman's men littered the streets with historical official records of the state. The soldiers collected some of these documents as souvenirs. Lee's train likely also carried Fleming Grieve and the records of the Georgia Supreme Court. "Restored to Archives," *Valdosta* (Georgia) *Times*, July 23, 1887; "Letter Bearing Signature of Washington in Atlanta," *Atlanta* (Georgia) *Journal*, July 25, 1943, 16-C; Robert S. Davis, "One Man's Civil War: The Curious Adventures of Flem Grieve and the *Georgia Reports*," *Georgia Historical Quarterly* 69 (Summer 1985): 231, and "William A. Fuller, the Western & Atlantic Railroad, and the Other Great Locomotive Chase," *Chattanooga Regional Historical Journal* 10 (July 2007): 71-80.

28. "The Siege of Atlanta" and "Interesting Letter from Atlanta," *Nashville* (Tennessee) *Daily Times & True Union*, August 30 and September 17, 1864; "Col. G.W. Lee," *Augusta* (Georgia) *Chronicle*, November 22, 1864; Brown to Lee, December 5, 1864, in Allen D. Candler, ed., *The Confederate Records of the State of Georgia*, 3 vols. (Atlanta, 1909), 809; Ira H. Foster to Lee, April 25, 1865, Ira H. Foster Collection, Kentucky Historical Society, Frankfort; "To Whom It May Concern," SC (Macon), January 20, 1865; Lee to Brown, report on the Western & Atlantic Railroad, March 25, 1865, Brown Family Papers, Ms 785, Hargrett Rare Books and Manuscripts Library, University of Georgia Libraries, Athens; "Resigned," *Chattanooga* (Tennessee) *Daily Gazette*, July 7, 1864.

29. "Atlanta—Her past, Her Present, and Her Future," *Columbus* (Georgia) *Times*, December 24, 1864.

30. "Atlanta—Her past, Her Present, and Her Future." Also see Stephen Davis, *What the Yankees Did to Us: Sherman's Bombardment and the Wrecking of Atlanta* (Macon, GA, 2012).

31. See, for example, "Some North Georgians During the Civil War," *Northwest Georgia Historical and Genealogical Society Quarterly* 26 (Winter 1994): 2-3. A list of families allowed to remain within three miles of the federal railroad in Northwest Georgia in 1864 appears in Entry 2671, Record Group 393, at the National Archives in Washington, D.C. Federal soldiers sent some civilians north as "political prisoners." Their records are found in the Louisville, Kentucky, prison camp on roll 95 of National Archives microcopy M598— *Selected Records of the War Department Relating to Confederate Prisoners of War*. Information on the reason for the arrest of some of these individuals can be found in The National Archives micrococopy M345— *Union Provost Marshal's File of Papers Relating to Individual Civilians* indexes by every name thousands of miscellaneous records of all sorts on Southern soldiers and civilians found in that file and in M416—*Union Provost Marshal's File of Papers Relating to Two or More Civilians*. For the fate of the Roswell women and the other textile workers sent from Roswell and Sweetwater, see Mary D. Petite, *The Women Will Howl: The Union Army Capture of Roswell and New Manchester* (Jefferson, NC, 2008) and Michael D. Hitt, *Charged with Treason: Ordeal of 400 Mill Workers During Military Operations in Roswell, Georgia, 1864-1865* (Monroe, NY, 1991). A list of soldiers and civilians held by the Union Army in Georgia after the war and before the restoration of civil authority is in Entry 2671, Record Group 393 Records of U.S. Continental Commands, Part 1, at the National Archives in Washington, DC, see "Civilians Held Prisoner in Atlanta, 1865-1866," *Georgia Genealogical Society Quarterly* 38 (January 2002): 36-38.

32. Robert S. Davis, "The General Sherman Census of Atlanta, September 1864," *Georgia Genealogical Magazine* 31 (Winter-Spring 1991): 132.

33. Freeman Cleaves, *Rock of Chickamauga*, 279, 283.

34. Lucy Josephine Cunyus, *History of Bartow County* (1934; reprinted expanded edition, Easley, SC, 2017), 248.

35. Headquarters diary, May 25, 1865, April 1, 1863-May 25, 1865, George H. Thomas Papers, Generals Papers, Records of the Adjutant General, Record Group 94, National Archives and Records Administration, Washington, DC; also see the

order of May 25, 1865, in Robert N. Scott, comp., *The War of the Rebellion: A Compilation of the Official Records of the Union and Confederate Armies*, 128 vols. (Washington, D.C., 1890–1904), Series I, vol. 49, pt. ii, p. 905.

36. H.W. Brands, *The Last Campaign: Sherman, Geronimo and the War for America* (New York, 2022), 40; W.P. Howard, "Atlanta as Left by the Enemy," *Daily Constitutionalist* (Augusta), December 17, 1864; Robert Gibbons, "Life at the Crossroads of the Confederacy: Atlanta, 1861–1865," *Atlanta Historical Journal* 23 (Summer 1979): 56–57; William Gibbes McAdoo diaries, November 19, 1864; Major General Howell Cobb to James A. Seddon, December 22, 1864, *ORs*, Series I, vol. 44, p. 977; "Atlanta—Her past, Her Present, and Her Future."

37. Chris Hedges, interview, January 1, 2011, *In depth*, C-Span2, on the Internet: http://www.c-span.org/Events/In-Depth-with-Author-and-Journalist-Chris-Hedges/10737426679/.

38. Executive Minutes (1860–1866), December 5, 1864, p. 340, GAr; [no title], *Macon (Georgia) Telegraph*, January 9, 1865; "To the People of Georgia," *SC* (Macon) February 7, 1865; Lee and Farrow correspondence, *DI*, April 12, 1865; Luther J. Glenn to "Genl." [Howell Cobb?], December 29, 1864, Box 58, Telamon Cuyler Collection.

39. Lucian L. Knight, *History of Fulton County, Georgia* (Atlanta, 1930), 111; Dyer, *Secret Yankees*, 201, 214. For the damage inflicted on Civil War Atlanta see Stephen Davis, *What the Yankees Did to Us: Sherman's Bombardment and Wrecking of Atlanta* (Macon, GA, 2012).

40. Walter Lynnwood Fleming, *Civil War and Reconstruction in Alabama* (New York, 1905), 302–304; Cotton, Captured, and Abandoned Property, 1872–1890, Entry 371, Record Group 56 Records of the Treasury, NARA (index in Entry 366).

41. For Southern attitudes about the Confederate defeat, see Elizabeth Varon, *Appomattox: Victory, Defeat, and Freedom at the End of the Civil War* (New York, 2013).

42. Nick Tabor, *Africatown: America's Last Slave Ship and the Community It Created* (New York, 2023), 88–89. The United States had a large trade in exporting enslaved Americans to Brazil and Cuba, even before the Civil War. Joseph P. Reidy, *Illusions of Emancipation: The Pursuit of Freedom and Equity in the Twilight of Slavery* (Chapel Hill, NC, 2019), 27, 109, 339; Don E. Fehrenbacher, *The Slaveholding Republic: An Account of the United States Government's Relations to Slavery*, ed. Ward M. McAfee (New York, 2001), 150.

43. See, among other works, Michael L. Conniff and Cyrus B. Dawsey, eds., *The Confederados: Old South Immigrants* (Tuscaloosa, AL, 1998).

44. Whitelaw Reid, *After the War: A Tour of the Southern States, 1865–1866* (Cincinnati, OH, 1866), 355–357; Garrett, *Atlanta and Environs*, 1: 679–699, 729–730; James H. Tate, *Keeper of the Flame: The Story of Atlanta Gas Light Company, 1856–1985* (Atlanta, 1985), 11, 17. For attempts at kidnapping emancipated African Americans to sell in other countries that still had slavery, see Carol Wilson, *Freedom at Risk: The Kidnapping of Free Blacks in America, 1780–1865* (Lexington, KY, 1994).

45. John Richard Dennett, *The South as It Is: 1865–1866* (New York, 1965), 264–269; Andrews, *The South Since the Civil War*, 339–342.

46. Martin Ruef, *Between Slavery and Capitalism: The Legacy of Emancipation in the American South* (Princeton, NJ, 2014), 15, 95, 97, 157, 161.

47. Elizabeth Ott Daniell, "The Ashburn Murder Case in Georgia Reconstruction," *Georgia Historical Quarterly* 59 (Fall 1975): 296–312; Russell Duncan, *Entrepreneur of Equality: Governor Rufus Bullock, Commerce, and Race in Post-Civil War Georgia* (Athens, GA, 1994), 29, 47–48.

48. See Daniel E. Sutherland, *The Confederate Carpetbaggers* (Baton Rouge, LA, 1988) and Stephen M. Hood, *Patriots Twice: Former Confederates and the Building of America After the Civil War* (El Dorado Hills, CA, 2020).

49. "Savannah, Griffin & North Alabama Railroad," *Weekly Atlanta Intelligencer*, October 17, 1866; "Georgia and North Alabama," *Newnan (Georgia) Herald*, March 9, 1867; "The Press Convention," *Georgia Enterprise* (Covington), August 27, 1869; "Report on the Survey of the North Georgia & Ducktown Railway," *Standard & Express* (Cartersville), August 27, 1869; "The Georgia Bonds," *Bainbridge (Georgia) Democrat*, June 18, 1885; "Holders of State Bonds," *New York Tribune*, January 30, 1883; Bullock, "Col. Robert Ashton Crawford."

50. Robert A. Crawford, *Case Files of Applications from Former Confederates for Presidential Pardons ("Amnesty Papers"), 1865–1867* (National Archives microfilm M1003), Record Group 94 Records of the Adjutant General's Office, 1865–1867, National Archives and Records Administration, NARA; "An Old Soldier Was Laid to Rest Yesterday," *Atlanta (Georgia) Constitution*, May 14, 1892; Dr. Lewis T. Bullock's notes in the possession of James Bullock; Bullock, "Col. Robert Ashton Crawford."

51. [no title], *Macon (Georgia) Weekly Telegraph*, April 15, 1879.

52. Credit report, Georgia, vol. 13, 385, R.G. Dun & Co. credit report volumes.

53. "Meeting of Lumbermen," *Chronicle and Sentinel* (Augusta), May 23, 1866; Fulton County deed book K (1868–1870), pp. 604–608, microfilm drawer 100 roll 64, and deed book I (1866–1867), pp. 393–394, microfilm drawer 100 roll 61, GAr; Singleton, *Richard Peters*, 89; Jeffrey N. Lash, *Destroyer of the Iron Horse: General Joseph E. Johnston and Confederate Rail Transport, 1861–1865* (Kent, OH, 1991), 116–124.

54. *Acts of the General Assembly of the State of Georgia, Passed in Milledgeville, at an Annual Session in December 1865, and January, February, and March, 1866*, 2 vols. (Milledgeville, GA, 1866), 1: 149–150; "Theater," *DI*, April 13, 1866; Monthly and Special Lists, District 4, 1867, p. 197, *Internal*

Assessment Lists for Georgia, 1865-1866 (National Archives microfilm M762, roll 8), Record Group 68 Records of the Internal Revenue Service, NARA; "Hotel Arrivals" and legal notices, *DI*, August 28, 1866, September 11, 1867; [no title], *Tri-Weekly Courier* (Rome), April 22, 1869; "The Cartersville Foundry and Machine Shop," *Weekly Express* (Cartersville, GA), June 23, July 28, and October 30, 1870; "Bartow House," *Atlanta* (Georgia) *Constitution*, June 5, 1870; photograph, folder 4, Lee/Huss Family Papers.

55. "Report on the Auditing Committee of the State Road," *Atlanta Constitution*, July 27, 1872; claims 6 and 504, Western and Atlantic Railroad Report of Committee, vol. 1-3011, testimony of G.W. Lee, Testimony Before Special Committee, vol. 2-12385, p. 150, and claim 740, vol. 2-12832, pp. 154-155, Legislature-Commissions and Committees, Reports and Investigations, 1871-1872, Record Group 37-8-4, Box 1992-3056A, Georgia Archives, Morrow; Alan Conway, *The Reconstruction of Georgia* (Minneapolis, MN, 1966), 187; Garrett, *Atlanta and Environs*, 1: 772; "Former Editor of the Age Dead," *Democratic Standard* (Coshocton, OH), January 31, 1896; *The Evidence Taken by a Joint Committee of the Legislature of the State of Georgia Appointed to Investigate the Management of R.B. Bullock and Foster Blodgett* (Atlanta, 1872), 43-44.

56. Fourth District, Bartow County, p. 363, *Ninth Census of the United States (1870)* (National Archives microfilm M593, roll 135), RG 29, NARA; Bartow County Marriage Book F (1869-1876), 92, Probate Court, Cartersville, GA; death certificate of Kathron Lee Howard, June 24, 1929, Illinois Vital Records, Springfield; wedding announcement, George Anne Howard, *Chicago Tribune*, July 2, 1922, p. 77. Joseph Robert Rawlins had remarried and moved to Texas by 1884. Nancy Lee is mentioned in the Gwinnett County will of her father Hiram Hornbuckle Dean, signed September 21, 1896, as is her daughter Anna Rawlins. Joseph Robert Rawlins abandoned his wife and children in 1881. Indiana/Anna married Isadore Adler in Birmingham, Alabama, in 1899 and is listed as a widow in Chicago, Illinois, by 1920. As Annie Adler, she died there in 1934.

57. "Steam Road Wagon Comp'y," *Atlanta* (Georgia) *Daily Sun*, February 16, 1872; "History," *Observer* (Fayetteville, NC), June 8, 1876; "City Council," *Daily Sun* (Atlanta), March 8, 1873; legal notices, *Atlanta Constitution*, February 1, 1878; credit report, Georgia, vol. 13, 385, R.G. Dun & Co. credit report volumes, Baker Library.

58. "Samuel D. Niles Claimed by Death," *Atlanta Georgian and News*, November 13, 1907, p. 12; Samuel Dexter Niles and Flora Niles Carr, Family trees; Ancestry.com, online accessed on May 17, 2024; "Married," *New England Farmer* (Boston, MA), December 23, 1854.

59. "Colonel Samuel D. Niles is Claimed by Death," *Atlanta Constitution*, November 13, 1907, p. 2; Atlanta, Fulton County, p. 707B, *Eighth Census of the United States (1860)* (National Archives microfilm M653, roll 122); *Williams' Atlanta Directory, City, Guide, or Business Mirror* (Atlanta, GA, 1859), 123; Fulton County tax digest, 1026th District, 1862/1863, p. 44, microfilm drawer 70 roll 28, Georgia Archives, Morrow; Rev. S.D. Niles, credit report, Georgia, vol. 13, p. 80, R.G. Dun & Co. credit report volumes, Baker Library; "Another Fire," *Gate City Guardian* (Atlanta), February 23, 1861; advertisement, *Southern Confederacy* (Atlanta), November 27, 1862.

60. Fulton County tax digest, 1026th District, 1862/1863, p. 44, microfilm drawer 70 roll 28, 1864, p. 59, microfilm drawer 70 roll 29, Georgia Archives, Morrow; Dyer, Secret Yankees, 60-61; Huff, *My 80 Years in Atlanta*, 11, 19-20; Sifakis, *Compendium*, 151; Singer, *Confederate Atlanta*, 212; Atlanta Fire Department, *History of Service* (Atlanta, GA, 2000), 4-5; "The Fire Battalion," *SC*, February 8, 1864. Davis, *What the Yankees Did to Us*, 63.

61. Wilbur G. Kurtz, Sr., "At the Dexter House," Wilbur G. Kurtz, Sr. Papers, Mss 130, Box 46, folder 18, Kenan Research Center, Atlanta History Center, Atlanta, GA; Davis, *What the Yankees Did to Us*, 113-114. Because of the historical significance of the long-lost Niles house, described by Huff to Wilbur Kutz, the site has a strange history of its historical markers. *Georgia Battlefields*, January 2018, on the Internet, May 17, 2024: accessed online June 12, 2024, Georgiabattlefields.org; Kurtz, "At the Dexter House."

62. Reading, household 193/239, Middlesex County, 1865 State census, Massachusetts Hall of Records, Springfield, MA; Reading, Middlesex County, Massachusetts, p. 300A, *Ninth Census of the United States (1870)* (National Archives microfilm M593, roll 506).

63. *Shoales Directory of the City of Atlanta* (Atlanta, GA, 1882), 154; Fulton County tax digest, 1885, Georgia Archives, Morrow, GA; "Colonel Samuel D. Niles Is Claimed by Death" and "Mr. Niles Memory Honored by Friends," *Atlanta Journal*, November 13, 1907, p. 3, and November 17, 1907, p. 13; funeral notices, *Atlanta Constitution*, November 14, 1907, p. 2.

64. Williams, *Civil War Suits in the U.S. Court of Claims*, 120; "William Markham," *Sunny South* (Atlanta), November 22, 1890; "Marcellus O. Markham and Mrs. Robert J. Lowery" in "Cases Dismissed by the Court of Claims," Senate Documents, 64th Congress, 1st Session, United States Congressional Serial Set, issue 6954; Pioneer Citizens' Society of Atlanta, *Pioneer Citizens' History of Atlanta*, 313.

65. Tad Evans, comp., *Baldwin County, Georgia Newspaper Clippings (Union Recorder) Volume XI 1878-1882* (Savannah, GA, 1997), 97; Shirley F. and James P. Kinney, Jr., *Myrtle Hill Cemetery Obituaries and Internments: Annotated Genealogical Abstracts Rome Floyd County, Georgia Volume XI* (Rome, GA, 1997), 244; Sextant's records, Myrtle Hill Cemetery, Rome, Georgia; [no title], *Daily*

Constitution (Atlanta), April 6, 1879. Lee Street in Atlanta, created over Whitehall or the oldest intersection in Atlanta, may take its name from George Washington Lee in 1871 as local developers, and Lee contemporaries, G.W. Adair and Richard Peters, citizens in Civil War Atlanta, gave other streets in the West End area names from locally prominent Confederates.

66. Alexander H. Stephens, *Recollections of Alexander H. Stephens: His Diary Kept When a Prisoner at Fort Warren, Boston Harbor, 1865*, ed. Mary L. Avery (New York, 1971), 104. The Stephens' quote comes from Eudora Ramsey Richardson, *Little Aleck: A Life of Alexander H. Stephens, the Fighting Vice President of the Confederacy* (Indianapolis, 1932), 195.

67. William Shaw Paludan, "What Did the Winners Win?," in James M. McPherson and William J. Cooper, Jr., *Writing the Civil War: The Quest to Understand* (Columbia, SC, 1998), 207; Stanley Lebergott, "Why the South Lost: Commercial Purpose in the Confederacy, 1861–1865," *Journal of American History* 70 (June 1983): 58–74; "What the Government Might Have Done," *The Soldier's Friend* (Atlanta), June 30, 1864; Anne Farrow, Joel Lang, and Jenifer Frank, *Complicity: How the North Promoted, Prolonged, and Profited from Slavery* (New York, 2005), 121–133.

68. Among other works, see James Ronald Kennedy and Walter Donald Kennedy, *The South was Right!* (New Orleans 2011) and Karen L. Cox, *Dreaming of Dixie: How the South Was Created in American Popular Culture* (Chapel Hill, NC, 2011).

69. See, for example, the arguments in Richard E. Beringer, Herman Hattaway, Archer Jones, and William N. Still Jr., *Why the South Lost the Civil War* (Athens, GA, 1986).

Appendix C

1. This appendix is an updated version of "William A. Fuller, the Western & Atlantic Railroad, and the Other Great Locomotive Chase," *Chattanooga Regional Historical Journal* 10 (July 2007): 71–80. For the history of the Western & Atlantic Railroad, see Ulrich B. Phillips, *An American State-owned Railroad: The Western and Atlantic* (n. p., 1906) and James H. Johnston, *Western and Atlantic Railroad of the State of Georgia* (Atlanta, GA, 1931); and for its significance in the Civil War see Robert S. Davis, "White and Black in Blue: The Recruitment of Federal Units in Civil War North Georgia," *Georgia Historical Quarterly* 85 (Fall 2001): 348–374.

2. Henry T. Kurtz, Jr., "Hijack of a Locomotive: The Andrews Raid Revisited," *Atlanta History* 34 (3) (Fall 1990): 5–14. A list of these "bridge burners" is found in Confederate States of America Prison (Madison, GA) Records, Mss 455, Hargrett Rare Books and Manuscripts Library, University of Georgia Libraries, Athens. For an in-depth history of the Great Locomotive Chase, see Russell S. Bonds, *Stealing the General: The Great Locomotive Chase and the First Medal of Honor* (Yardley, PA, 2007).

3. Stephen Davis, "The Conductor Versus the Foreman: William Fuller, Anthony Murphy, and the Pursuit of the Andrews Raiders," *Atlanta History* 34 (4) (Winter 1990–1991): 41–42.

4. James G. Bogle, "The General's Long Road Home," *Blue & Gray Magazine* 4 (July 1987): 62–63.

5. Davis, "The Conductor Versus the Foreman," 38–55.

6. Theodore A. Fuller and Kay F. Mitchell, *Early Southern Fullers* (Laske Wylies, SC, 2003), 706–709; and Robert S. Davis, "A Note on the Fuller Family of Camden District," *South Carolina Magazine of Ancestral Research* 44 (Fall 2016): 190–192.

7. Joseph T. Derry, "Georgia," in Clement A. Evans, *Confederate Military History*, 19 vols. (1899; rep. expanded edition, Wilmington, NC, 1987), 6: 667.

8. Fuller to Allen D. Candler, April 20, 1903, Local Defense Troops—Captain Fuller's Company, Records of the Georgia Civil War Roster Commission, Record Group 58-2-26, Georgia Archives, Morrow.

9. The papers of William A. Fuller (Mss. Collection 92) and his son-in-law, Civil War historian Wilbur Kurtz (Mss. Collection 130), are in the Kenan Research Center of the Atlanta History Center but contain no information on Fuller saving the rolling stock of the Western & Atlantic.

10. I.W. Avery, *The History of the State of Georgia* (New York: Brown & Derby, 1881), 306–311; *Journal of the Senate of the State of Georgia … 1864* (Milledgeville, GA, 1864), 22; Herbert Fielder, *A Sketch of the Life and Times and Speeches of Joseph E. Brown* (Springfield, MA, 1883), 312–317; *Confederate Union* (Milledgeville), December 6, 1864; memoirs of T.C. Warthen, n.d., Howell's Battery, Civil War Miscellany Collection, Record Group 57-1-2, Georgia Archives, Morrow. At least five locomotives and 150 to 200 freight cars were destroyed in the fighting around Atlanta. "The Raid on the Central Railroad," *Southern Recorder* (Milledgeville), August 9, 1864, and *Augusta (Georgia) Constitutionist*, September 10, 1864.

11. Johnston, *Western and Atlantic Railroad*, 59; Josiah Sherman to Joseph E. Brown, November 4, 1871, Records of the Western & Atlantic Railroad, Record Group 18-5-8, Georgia Archives, Morrow; James G. Bogle, "Civil War Railroads—Georgia and Tennessee," *Atlanta Historical Bulletin* 12 (3) (September 1967): 23–37. The Western & Atlantic Railroad purchased eight locomotives, 152 box cars, fifty-three flat cars, and three passenger cars from the federal government after the war. Robert C. Black III, *The Railroads of the Confederacy* (Chapel Hill, NC, 1952), 343 n 20.

12. *Reports of Committees of the House of Representatives for the Second Session of the Fortieth Congress, 1867–'68* 2 vols. (Washington, D.C., 1868) (Congressional Serial no, 1357), 1: 63–64; pay

entries for M.H. Dooley, Auditer's Book, Records of the Western & Atlantic Railroad, Record Group 18-5-22, Georgia Archives, Morrow; "Martin H. Dooley—A Merited Compliment," *North Georgia Citizen* (Dalton, GA), September 17, 1868.

13. Pioneer Citizens' Society, *Pioneer Citizens' History of Atlanta* (Atlanta, GA, 1902), 349; Bragg, *Joe Brown's Army*, 73, n 55; Roster of Captain Fuller's company, August 3, 1863, microfilm box 279, roll 93, and William A. Fuller file, State Troops Pay Records, Record Group 22-10, GAr; William A. Fuller to General Henry Wayne, August 19, 1863, Telamon Cuyler Collection, Mss 1170, box 17 (August-November 1863), Hargrett Rare Books and Manuscripts Library, University of Georgia Libraries, Athens; Fuller to Wilbur Kurtz, May 30, 1904, Wilbur Kurtz Papers, Mss 132, Kenan Research Center.

14. William Gibbes McAdoo diary, November 19, 1864, Savannah; "Restored to Archives," *Valdosta* (Georgia) *Times*, July 23, 1887; "Letter Bearing Signature of Washington in Atlanta," *Atlanta* (Georgia) *Journal*, July 25, 1943, 16-C. Fleming Grieve, on this train, saved the records of the Georgia Supreme Court. Robert S. Davis, "One Man's Civil War: The Curious Adventures of Flem Grieve and the *Georgia Reports*," *Georgia Historical Quarterly* 69 (Summer 1985): 231.

15. *Report of Bvt. Brig. Gen. D.C. McCallum* (Washington, D.C., 1866), pt. 1, pp. 32-33. The records of the USMRR are in Record Group 92, Records of the Quartermaster General, National Archives and Records Administration, Washington, D.C.

16. Fuller to Wilbur Kurtz, May 30, 1904, Wilbur Kurtz Papers, Mss 132, Kenan Research Center; James G. Bogle to author, April 18, 1990, in the author's possession.

Appendix G

1. See Robert S, Davis, "John Coffee's Search for the Lost History of the Cherokees," *Chattanooga Regional Historical Journal* 8 (December 2005): 143-64.

2. Garrett. *Atlanta and Environs*, 1: 1-37; Robert S. Davis, "John Coffee's Search for the Lost History of the Cherokees," *Chattanooga Regional Historical Journal* 8 (December 2005): 143-64.

3. Marthasville and Atlanta were both officially named for Martha Atalanta Wilson, the daughter of Georgia transportation promoter and governor Wilson Lumpkin. The governor had roughly chosen the site for the southern terminus of the W&A.

4. Clayton, *Requiem for a Lost City*, 19.

5. See Mike Brubaker, "Genealogy Resources at the James G. Kenan Research Center," *Georgia Genealogical Society Quarterly* 43 (Spring 2007): 3-6.

6. For information on its holdings and those of other Georgia libraries see Ted O. Brooke and Robert S. Davis, *Georgia Research* (Atlanta, GA, 2001) and Joanne Smalley, "Research at the Georgia Archives," *Georgia Genealogical Society Quarterly* 43 (Fall 2007): 151-58.

7. See Linda Aaron, "Research at the University of Georgia Libraries," *Georgia Genealogical Society Quarterly* (Winter 2007): 215-18.

8. See Amanda J. Cook, "Genealogical Resources in Washington Memorial Library, Macon, Georgia," *Georgia Genealogical Society Quarterly* 43 (Summer 2007): 91-94.

9. See Ann L. Sherman and Jane L. Splawn, "Libraries in Georgia with Genealogical Holdings: Atlanta-Fulton Public Library, Atlanta, Georgia," *Georgia Genealogical Society Quarterly* 36 (Fall 2000): 237-40.

10. Mr. Brubaker also serialized the Atlanta Police Court Docket for the 1870s, beginning in *Georgia Genealogical Society Quarterly* 41 (Winter 2005): 230-237.

11. Paul K. Graham, "The Search for Fulton County's Stolen Records," *Georgia Genealogical Society Quarterly* 45 (Fall 2009): 217-222.

12. Joanne Smalley, "Georgia County Records: An Overview of Some Genealogically Significant Records," *Georgia Genealogical Society Quarterly* 45 (Winter 2009): 301-310.

13. Ted O. Brooke, *Fulton County, Georgia, Marriage Records 1854-1902* (Cumming, GA: The Author, 2002); *Fulton County, Georgia, Marriage Records 1866-1902* ("Colored Books" A-G) (Cumming, GA, 2003); and *In the Name of God, Amen: Georgia Wills 1733–1860* (Atlanta, GA, 1976).

14. The *Georgia Historical Quarterly*, in the last two decades, has published a great deal on Atlanta history. It is indexed annually and has an annual but bibliography of history articles about Georgia.

15. *Atlanta and Environs* originally had a third volume of biographical sketches of then (1954) locally prominent men and, in 1987, a new third volume by Harold Martin in 1987 to bring the series up to 1976.

16. Also see "The South's 1867 Returns of Qualified Voters & Their Value in Genealogical Research," *Heritage Quest* no. 54 (November/December 1994): 62-63.

17. Most of the Stout Collection has been microfilmed and is available at such libraries as the Genealogy Collection, Wallace State Community College, Hanceville, Alabama.

Bibliography

I. Manuscript Collections

Baker Library, Harvard University, Cambridge, MA
  R. G. Dun & Co. credit report volumes.
Georgia Archives (abbreviated GAr), Morrow
  Adjutant General's Letter Books
  Correspondence, Adjutant General, Record Group 22-1-17
  Executive Correspondence, Record Group 1-1-5
  File II Names, Record Group 4-2-46
  Fulton County Records, Microfilm Library
  Lee/Huss Family Papers, AC 69-249
  Rosters, Adjutant General, Record Group 22-1-64
  Soldier Roster Commission, Record Group 58-2-26
  State Supreme Court Case Files, Record Group 92-1-1
Georgia Historical Society, Savannah
  Floyd and McAdoo Families Papers, Ms 2689
  Jerry Cowles Papers, MS 178
  Michael Johnston Kenan notebooks, MS 948
Hargrett Rare Books and Manuscripts Library, University of Georgia Libraries, Athens
  Brown Family Papers, Mss 785
  E. Merton Coulter Collection, Mss 998
  Howell Cobb Papers, Mss 1376
  Joseph E. Brown Papers, Mss 95
  Keith Read Collection, Mss 921
  Telamon Cuyler Collection, Mss 1170
Iowa State Department of Archives and History, Des Moines
  Grenville M. Dodge Papers
Kenan Research Center, Atlanta History Center
  Cornelius Hanleiter Papers, Mss 109
  Robert A. Crawford, Personality Files
  Sidney Root Memoirs, Mss 908f
  Wilbur G. Kurtz, Sr. Papers, Mss 130
Kentucky Historical Society, Frankfort
  Ira H. Foster Collection
Manuscripts Division, Library of Congress, Washington, DC
  Floyd McAdoo Family Papers (microfilm)
Southern Historical Collection, Chapel Hill, NC
  George Anderson Mercer Diary, 00503
  William King Papers, 02985-z
Stuart A. Rose Library, Emory University, Atlanta
  British Consulate Papers, 1859–1866, MSS 15
Virginia Historical Society, Richmond
  Department of Henrico Collection, Mss. 3C7604a.

II. National Archives and Records Administration (NARA), College Park, MD, and Washington, DC

Barred and Disallowed Claims. National Archives microfilm M1407. Records of the United States House of Representatives, Record Group 233.

Compiled Service Records of Confederate Soldiers Who Served in Organizations from the State of Georgia. National Archives microfilm M266. War Department Collection of Confederate Records. Record Group 109.

Confederate General Staff Officers and Non-Regimental Enlisted Men, National Archives microfilm M331. War Department Collection of Confederate Records. Record Group 109.

Confederate Papers Relating to Citizens or Business Firms. National Archives microfilm M346. War Department Collection of Confederate Records. Record Group 109.

Confederate Soldiers Who Served in Organizations Raised Directly by the Confederate Government. National Archives Microfilm M258. War Department Collection of Confederate Records. Record Group 109.

Eighth Census of the United States (1860). National Archives microfilm M653. Records of the Bureau of the Census. Record Group 29.

Internal Assessment Lists for Georgia, 1865–1866. National Archives microfilm M762. Records of the Internal Revenue Service. Record Group 58.

Letters Received by the Confederate Adjutant and Inspector General, 1861–1865 (abbreviated as *CSAAG*). National Archives microfilm M474. War Department Collection of Confederate Records. Record Group 109.

Letters Received by the Confederate Secretary of War, 1861–1865 (abbreviated as *SOW*). National Archives microfilm M437. War Department Collection of Confederate Records. Record Group 109.

Ninth Census of the United States (1870). National Archives microfilm M593. Records of the Bureau of the Census. Record Group 29.

Records of the Confederate District Court of North Georgia. Records of the United States District

Courts. Record Group 21. (National Archives at Atlanta, Morrow, GA).
Records of the Provost Marshal. Record Group 110.
Selected Records of the War Department Commissary General of Prisoners of War Confined at Andersonville, Georgia, 1864–65. National Archives Microfilm Publication M1303. Record Group 249.
Southern Claims Commission Approved Claims, 1871–1880: Georgia. National Archives microfilm M658. Records of the Accounting Officers of the Department of the Treasury. Record Group 217.
Records of the Secretary of the Treasury. Record Group 56.
Records of the United States Court of Claims. Record Group 123.
Records of the U.S. Army Continental Commands, 1821–1920. Record Group 393, pt. i.
Telegraphs Received by the Confederate Secretary of War, 1861–1865. National Archives microfilm M618. War Department Collection of Confederate Records, Record Group 109.
Union Provost Marshal's File of Papers Relating to Individual Civilians. National Archives microfilm M345. Records of the Provost Marshal General, Record Group 110.
War Department Collection of Confederate Records. Record Group 109.

III. Newspapers

Some of the newspapers below were found or searched through Chronicling America, Library of Congress; Digital Library of Georgia Newspapers; Genealogybank.com; Newspaperarchive.com; Newspapers.com; and 19th Century Newspapers.

Army Argus and Crisis (Mobile, AL). The only copies of this newspaper are in the Alabama Department of Archives and History.
Atlanta (Georgia) *Constitution*.
Atlanta (Georgia) *Daily Sun*.
Atlanta (Georgia) *Journal*.
Augusta (Georgia) *Constitutionalist*.
Augusta (Georgia) *Weekly Chronicle Sentinel*.
Banner and Baptist (Atlanta).
Chronicle and Sentinel (Augusta).
Commonwealth (Atlanta). Copies only found in the original at the Boston Athenaeum.
Confederate Union (Milledgeville).
Daily Columbus (Georgia) *Observer*.
Daily Constitutionalist (Augusta).
Daily Dispatch (Richmond).
Daily Enquirer (Columbus).
Daily Intelligencer (abbreviated as *DI*) (Atlanta). Some copies survive only in the original at the Atlanta History Center.
Daily Intelligencer (Macon).
Daily State Gazette (Trenton, NJ).
Daily Telegraph and Confederate (Macon).
Floridian and Journal (Tallahassee, FL).
Georgia Journal and Messenger (Macon).
Georgia Weekly Telegraph (abbreviated as *GWT*) (Macon).
Hampshire Gazette (Northampton, MA).
Macon (Georgia) *Daily Telegraph* (abbreviated as *MDT*).
Memphis Daily Appeal (Atlanta). Available online as part of the Library of Congress' Chronicling America: http://chroniclingamerica.loc.gov/lccn/sn83045160/.
North Georgia Citizen (Dalton).
Observer (Fayetteville, NC).
Savannah (Georgia) *Republican*.
Selma (Alabama) *Morning Reporter*.
The Soldier's Friend (Atlanta). Copies at the Atlanta History Center.
Southern Banner (Athens, GA).
Southern Confederacy (abbreviated as *SC*) (Atlanta).
State Gazette (Austin, TX).
Sunny South (Atlanta).
Tri-Weekly Courier (Rome).
Valdosta (Georgia) *Times*.
Weekly Columbus (Georgia) *Enquirer*.
Weekly Constitution (Atlanta).
Weekly Express (Cartersville, GA).

IV. Articles, Books, Dissertations, Other Printed Sources, and Theses

Alvarez, Eugene. *Travel on Southern Antebellum Railroads, 1828–1860*. Tuscaloosa: University of Alabama Press, 1974.
Andrews, Sidney. *The South Since the Civil War*. Boston: Ticknor & Fields, 1866.
Auman, William T. *Civil War in the North Carolina Quaker Belt: The Confederate Campaign Against Peace Agitators, Deserters, and Draft Dodgers*. Jefferson, NC: McFarland, 2013.
Avery, Isaac W. *The History of the State of Georgia from 1850 to 1881*. New York: Derby Publishers, 1881.
Baptist, Edward E. "'Cuffy,' 'Fancy Maids,' and 'One-Eyed Men': Rape Commodification and the Domestic Slave Trade in the United States." In Walter Johnson, ed., *Chattel Principle: Internal Slave Trades in the Americas* (New Haven, CT: Yale University, 2004), 165–202.
_____. *The Half Has Never Been Told: Slavery and the Making of American Capitalism*. New York: Basic Books, 2014.
Beck, Brandon H. *Streight's Foiled Raid on the Western & Atlantic Railroad*. Charleston, SC: History Press, 2016.
Beckert, Sven. *Empire of Cotton: A Global History*. New York: Vintage Books, 2014.
Beers, Henry Putney, and Kenneth W. Munden. *The Union: A Guide to Federal Archives Relating to the Civil War*. 1962; renamed reprint, Washington, DC: National Archives Trust Fund Board, 1986.

Bell, Hiram P. *Men and Things*. Atlanta: Foote & Davies, 1907.

Bellamy, Donnie D. "Macon, Georgia, 1823-1860: A Study in Urban Slavery." *Phylon* 45 (December 1984): 298-310.

Benner, Judith. *Fraudulent Finance: Counterfeiting and the Confederate States, 1861-1865*. Hillsboro, TX: Hill Junior College Press, 1970.

Beringer, Richard E., Herman Hattaway, Archer Jones, and William N. Still, Jr. *Why the South Lost the Civil War*. Athens: University of Georgia Press, 1986.

Birdsall, Clair M. *The United States Branch Mint at Dahlonega, Georgia: Its History and Coinage*. Easley, SC: Southern Historical Press, 1984.

Black, Robert C., III. *The Railroads of the Confederacy*. Chapel Hill: University of North Carolina Press, 1952.

Blanton, DeAnne, and Lauren M. Cook. *They Fought Like Demons: Women Soldiers in the American Civil War*. Baton Rouge: Louisiana State University Press, 2002.

Bohannon, Keith S. "The Northeast Georgia Mountains During the Secession Crisis." Ph.D. diss., Pennsylvania State University, 2001.

Bolton, Charles C. *Poor Whites and the Antebellum South: Tenants and Laborers in Central North Carolina and Northeast Mississippi*. Durham: Duke University Press, 1994.

Bonds, Russell S. *Stealing the General: The Great Locomotive Chase and the First Medal of Honor*. Yardley, PA: Westholme, 2007.

Bragg, William Harris. *Joe Brown's Army*. Macon, GA: Mercer University Press, 1987.

_____. *Joe Brown's Pets: The Georgia Militia, 1861-1865*. Macon, GA: Mercer University Press, 2004.

Brands, H.W. *The Last Campaign: Sherman, Geronimo and the War for America*. New York: Doubleday, 2022.

Brinton, Crane. *The Anatomy of Revolution*. New York: Vintage, 1965.

Bryan, Thomas Conn. *Confederate Georgia*. Athens: University of Georgia Press, 1953.

Butler, John Campbell. *Historical Record of Macon and Central Georgia*. Macon, GA: J.W. Burke, 1879.

Candler, Allen D., comp., *The Confederate Records of the State of Georgia*. 3 vols. Atlanta: Chas. F. Byrd, 1909.

Carey, Anthony G. *Parties, Slavery, and the Union in Antebellum Georgia*. Athens: University of Georgia Press, 1997.

Casstevens, Frances H. *George W. Alexander and Castle Thunder: A Confederate Prison and Its Commandant*. Jefferson, NC: McFarland, 2004.

Castel, Albert. *Decision in the West: The Atlanta Campaign of 1864*. Lawrence: University of Kansas Press, 1992.

_____. "Mary Walker: A Samaritan or a Charlatan?" *Civil War Times Illustrated*. 33 (May/June 1994): 40-43.

Charles River Editors. *The Knights of the Golden Circle: The History and Legacy of 19th Century America's Most Notorious Secret Societies*. Coppell, TX: CreateSpace, 2001.

Cheesman, Clive, and Jonathan Williams. *Rebels, Pretenders, & Imposters*. New York: St. Martin's Press, 2000.

Chesnut, Mary. *The Private Mary Chesnut: The Unpublished Civil War Diaries*, eds. C. Vann Woodward and Elisabeth Muhlenfeld. New York: Oxford University Press, 1984.

Clark, John Elwood, Jr. "'To Strain Every Energy': Civil War Railroads: A Comparison of Union and Confederate War Management." Ph.D. diss., Princeton University, 1997.

Clayton, Sarah Conley. *Requiem for a Lost City: Sallie Clayton's Memoirs of Civil War Atlanta and the Old South*, ed. Robert S. Davis. Macon, GA: Mercer University Press, 1999.

Coulter, E. Merton. *Thomas Spalding of Sapelo*. Baton Rouge, LA: Louisiana State University Press, 1940.

_____. comp. *Travels in the Confederate States: A Bibliography*. Baton Rouge: Louisiana State University Press, 1994.

Crow, Vernon H. *Storm in the Mountains: Thomas Confederate Legion of Cherokee Indians and Mountaineers*. Cherokee, NC: Press of the Museum of the Cherokee Indian, 1982.

Crute, Joseph H., Jr., *Units of the Confederate States Army*. Midlothian, VA: Derwent Books, 1987.

Current, Richard N., Paul D. Escott, Lawrence N. Powell, James I. Robertson, and Emory M. Thomas, eds. *Encyclopedia of the Confederacy*. New York: Simon & Schuster, 1993.

Curry, Stephanie. *Confederate Reckoning: Power and Politics in the Civil War South*. Cambridge: Harvard University Press, 2010.

Davis, David Brion. *The Problem of Slavery in Western Culture*. New York: Oxford University Press, 1988.

Davis, Jefferson. *Jefferson Davis Constitutionalist: His Letters, Papers, and Speeches*, ed. Rowland Dunbar. 10 vols. Jackson: Mississippi Department of Archives and History, 1923.

_____. *The Papers of Jefferson Davis*, eds. Lynda L. Crist, Mary S. Dix, and Kenneth H. Williams, 11 vols. to date. Baton Rouge: Louisiana State University Press, 2011.

Davis, Robert S. *Cotton, Fire, & Dreams: The Robert Findlay Iron Works and Heavy Industry in Macon, Georgia, 1839-1912*. Macon, GA: Mercer University Press, 1998.

_____. "The Eyes of Chickamauga: General George H. Thomas as a Civil War Spy Master." *Chattanooga Regional Historical Journal* 5 (July 2004): 73-92.

_____. "Forgotten Union Guerrilla Fighters from the North Georgia Mountains." *North Georgia Journal* 5 (2) (Summer 1988): 30-40.

_____. *Ghosts and Shadows of Andersonville: Essays on the Social Histories of America's Deadliest Prison*. Macon, GA: Mercer University Press, 2006.

_____. "Hysteria and Literature: Atlanta's First Execution and Its Legendary Ties to Organized

Crime." *Georgia Historical Quarterly* 92 (Fall 2008): 321–339.

_____. "Into the Wilderness: John Kellogg's Journey Through Civil War North Georgia." *Chattanooga Regional Historical Journal* 7 (December 2004): 215–232.

_____. "Some Unforgotten Alabama Union Soldiers." *Alabama Family History and Genealogy News* 17 (2) (1996): 12–19.

_____. "War on the Edge: Civil War Era Politics and Its Legacy in an Appalachian County." pp. 1–18 of John D. Fowler and David B. Parker, eds., *Breaking the Heartland: The Civil War in Georgia* (Macon: Mercer University Press, 2011).

Davis, Stephen. *What the Yankees Did to Us: Sherman's Bombardment and Wrecking of Atlanta.* Macon, GA: Mercer University Press, 2012.

_____, and Bill Hendrick, *The Atlanta Intelligencer Covers the Civil War.* Knoxville: University of Tennessee Press, TN, 2022.

Davis, William C. *An Honorable Defeat: The Last Days of the Confederate Government.* New York: Harcourt, 2001.

_____. *Inventing Loreta Velasquez: Confederate Soldier Impersonator, Media Celebrity, and Con Artist.* Carbondale: Southern University Press, 2016.

DeCredico, Mary A. *Patriotism for Profit: Georgia's Entrepreneurs and Confederate War Effort.* Chapel Hill: University of North Carolina Press, 1990.

De Grave, Kathleen. *Swindler, Spy, Rebel: The Confidence Woman in Nineteenth-Century America.* Columbia: University of Missouri Press, 2002.

Delblanco, Andrew. *The War Before the War: Fugitive Slaves and the Struggle for America's Soul from the Revolution to the Civil War.* New York: Penguin Press, 2018.

Dennett, John Richard. *The South as It Is: 1865–1866.* Henry M. Christman, ed. New York: Viking, 1965.

De Pauw, Linda Grant. *Battles Cries and Lullabies: Women in War from Prehistory to the Present.* Norman: University of Oklahoma Press, 1998.

Derry, Joseph T. *Georgia,* vol. 7 of Clement A. Evans, comp., *Confederate Military History,* 17 vols. 1898; extended edition, Wilmington, NC: Broadfoot, 1987.

deTreville, John R. "The Little New South: Origins of Industry in Georgia's Fall-Line Cities." Ph.D. diss., University of North Carolina, 1985.

Dew, Charles B. *Ironmaker to the Confederacy: Joseph R. Anderson and the Tredegar Iron Works.* New Haven: Yale University Press, 1966.

Diffey, Kathleen. "After Sumter: The Surge of War and Periodical Outcry" in Kathleen Diffey and Benjamin Fagan, eds., *Visions of Glory: The Civil War in Word and Image* (Athens, GA: University of Georgia Press, 2019.

Dippel, John Van Houten. *Race to the Frontier: "White Flight" and Western Expansion.* New York: Algora, 2005.

Dixon, David T. "Augustus R. Wright and the Loyalty of the Heart." *Georgia Historical Quarterly* 94 (Fall 2010): 342–371.

Dowdey, Clifford. *The Seven Days: The Emergence of Robert E. Lee and the Dawn of a Legend.* New York: Skyhorse, 2012

Driscoll, John K. *The Civil War on Pensacola Bay, 1861–1862.* Jefferson, NC: McFarland 2007.

Dubose, Beverly M., III. "The Manufacture of Confederate Ordnance in Georgia." *Atlanta Historical Bulletin* 12 (December 1967): 8–21.

Dyer, Thomas G. "Atlanta's Other Civil War Novel: Fictional Unionists in a Confederate City." *Georgia Historical Quarterly* 79 (Spring 1995): 147–168.

_____. *Secret Yankees: The Union Circle in Confederate Atlanta.* Baltimore: Johns Hopkins University Press, 1999.

Eaton, Clement. *A History of the Southern Confederacy.* New York: Macmillan, 1954.

Eicher, David J. *Dixie Betrayed: How the South Really Lost the Civil War.* New York: Little Brown, 2006.

Elam, Mark. "The Road to Atlanta: The Role of Geography in Command and Decision Making During the Atlanta Campaign." Ph.D. diss, Florida State University, 1996.

Escott, Paul D. *The Confederacy: The Slaveholders' Failed Venture.* Santa Barbara, CA: Praeger, 2010.

Evans, Clement A., comp. *Confederate Military History,* 17 vols. 1898; extended edition, Wilmington, NC: Broadfoot, 1987.

Evans, David. *Sherman's Horsemen: Union Cavalry Operations in the Atlanta Campaign.* Bloomington: Indiana University Press, 1996.

Fair, John D. *The Tifts of Georgia; Connecticut Yankees in King Cotton's Court.* Macon: Mercer University Press, 2010.

Farrow, Anne, Joel Lang, and Jenifer Frank. *Complicity: How the North Promoted, Prolonged, and Profited from Slavery.* New York: Ballantine Books, 2005.

Faust, Drew Gilpin. *The Creation of Confederate Nationalism: Ideology and Identity in the Civil War South.* Baton Rouge: Louisiana State University Press, 1988.

Finger, John R. *The Eastern Band of Cherokees, 1819–1900* Knoxville, TN: University of Tennessee Press, 1984.

Fishel, Noel C. *War at Every Door: Partisan Political and Guerrilla Violence in East Tennessee, 1860–1869.* Chapel Hill: University of North Carolina Press, 1997.

Flanders, Ralph Betts. *Plantation Slavery in Georgia.* Chapel Hill: University of North Carolina Press, 1933.

Fletchum, Gerald W. *The Devil's Time: Georgia's Guerrilla War 1861–1865.* Columbia, SC: The Author, 2020.

Franklin, John Hope, and Loren Schweninger. *Runaway Slaves: Rebels on the Plantation.* New York: Oxford University Press, 1999.

Frederickson, George M. *Why the Confederacy Did*

Not Fight a Guerilla War After the Fall of Richmond: A Comparative View. Gettysburg: Gettysburg College, 1996.

Freehling, William W. *The South vs. The South: How Anti-Confederate Southerners Shaped the Course of the Civil War*. New York: Oxford University Press, 2000.

Fuller, Louis. *The Crusade Against Slavery*. New York: Harpers, 1960.

Furgurson, Ernest B. *Ashes of Glory: Richmond at War*. New York: Alfred A. Knopf, 1996.

Garrett, Franklin M. *Atlanta and Environs: A Chronicle of Its People and Events*. 2 vols. New York: Lewis Historical Publishing, 1954.

Gates, Frederick B. "The Impact of the Western & Atlantic Railroad on the Development of the Georgia Upcountry, 1840–1860." *Georgia Historical Quarterly* 91 (Summer, 2007): 169–184.

Genovese, Eugene D. *A Consuming Fire: The Fall of the Confederacy in the Mind of the White Christian South*. Athens: University of Georgia Press, 1998.

_____. *In Red and Black: Marxian Explorations in Southern and Afro-American History*. New York: Vintage, 1968.

_____. *The Political Economy of Slavery*. New York: Pantheon Press, 1965.

_____, ed. *The Slave Economics*. 2 vols. New York: Wiley, 1973.

_____. *The World the Slaveholders Made: Two Essays in Interpretation*. New York: Pantheon Books, 1969.

Georgia Division United Daughters of the Confederacy, comp. *Confederate Reminiscences and Letters*. 20 vols. Atlanta: The Author, 1997–2006.

Gibbons, Robert. "Life at the Crossroads of the Confederacy: Atlanta, 1861–1865." *Atlanta Historical Journal* 23 (Summer 1979): 11–72.

Gilpin, Toni. *The Long Deep Grudge: A Story of Big Capital, Radical Labor, and Class War in the American Heartland*. Chicago: University of Chicago Press, 2020.

Glaser, Lynn. *Counterfeiting in America: The History of an American Way to Wealth*. Philadelphia: Clarkson N. Potter, 1960.

Goff, Richard D. *Confederate Supply*. Durham: Duke University Press, 1969.

Golden, Alan Lawrence. "The Confederate Provost Marshal's Prison, 1862–1865." Master's Thesis, University of Richmond, 1980.

Goldin, Claudia Dale. *Urban Slavery in the American South, 1820–1860: A Quantitative History*. Chicago: University of Chicago Press, 1970.

Goldstein, Joshua S. *War and Gender: How Gender Shapes the War System and Vice Versa*. New York: Cambridge University, 2001.

Gordon, Lesley H., and John C. Inscoe, eds., *Inside the Confederate Nation: Essays in Honor of Emory M. Thomas*. Baton Rouge: Louisiana State University Press, 2005.

Graham, Paul K. "Edward Arista Vincent: Antebellum Immigrant, Cartographer, and Architect." *Georgia Historical Quarterly* 95 (Fall 2011): 391–407.

_____. *Georgia Land Lottery Records*, Atlanta: The Author, 2010.

_____. "Historical Records of Urban Georgia." *Georgia Genealogical Society Quarterly* 43 (Summer 2007): 87–90.

_____. "The Search for Fulton County's Stolen Records." *Georgia Genealogical Society Quarterly* 45 (Fall 2009): 217–222.

Grenier, John. *The First Way of War: American War Making on the Frontier*. Cambridge: Harvard University Press, 2005.

Grimsley, Mark. *The Hard Hand of War: Union Military Policy Towards Southern Civilians, 1861–1865*. New York: Cambridge University Press, 1995.

Gudmestad, Robert H. *A Troublesome Commerce: The Transformation of the Interstate Slave Trade*. Baton Rouge, LA: Louisiana State University Press, 2003.

Guelzo, Allen C. *Robert E. Lee: A Life*. New York: Knopf, 2021.

Guttridge, Leonard F., and Ray A. Neff. *Dark Union: The Secret Web of Profiteers, Politicians, and Booth Conspirators That Led to Lincoln's Death*. Hoboken, NJ: John Wiley & Sons, 2003.

Hadden, Salley E. *Slave Patrols: Law and Violence in Virginia and the Carolinas*. Boston, MA: Harvard University Press, 2003.

Hahn, Steven. *The Roots of Southern Populism: Yeoman Farmers and the Transformation of the Georgia Upcountry, 1850–1890*. New York: Oxford University Press, 1983.

Hall, Richard. *Patriots in Disguise: Women Warriors of the Civil War*. New York: Paragon House, 1993.

Hallman, J.C. *Say Anarcha: A Young Woman, a Devious Surgeon, and the Harrowing Birth of Modern Women's Health*. New York: Henry Holt and Company, 2023.

Hallock, Judith L., and Grady McWhiney. *Braxton Bragg and Confederate Defeat*. 2 vols. Tuscaloosa: University of Alabama Press, 1969, 1991.

Halttunen, Karen. *Confidence Men and Painted Women: A Study of the Middle-class Culture in America, 1830–1870*. New Haven: Yale University Press, 1982.

Harris, J. William. *Plain Folk and Gentry in a Slave Society: White Liberty and Black Slavery in Augusta's Hinterlands*. Middletown, CT: Wesleyan University Press, 1985.

Harrold, Stanley. *The Abolitionists and the South, 1831–1861*. Lexington: University of Kentucky Press, 1995.

Harvey, Miles. *The King of Confidence: A Tale of Utopian Dreamers, Frontier Swindlers, True Believers, False Prophets, and the Murder of an American Monarch*. New York: Little, Brown, 2020.

Hazlett, James C., Edwin Olmstead and M. Hume Parks. *Field Artillery Weapons of the Civil War*. Newark: University of Delaware Press, 1983.

Head, Sylvia Gailey, and Elizabeth W. Etheridge. *The Neighborhood Mint: Dahlonega in the Age of Jackson.* Dahlonega, GA: The Author, 2000.

Hess, Earl J. *Kennesaw Mountain: Sherman, Johnson, and the Atlanta Campaign.* Chapel Hill, NC: University of North Carolina Press, 2013.

Hettle, Wallace T. "An Ambitious Democrat: Joseph Brown and Georgia's Road to Secession." *Georgia Historical Quarterly* 81 (Fall 1997): 577–592.

Hewett, Janet B., comp. *Supplement to the Official Records of the Union and Confederate Armies,* 100 vols. Wilmington, NC: Broadfoot, 1999.

Hine, C.C. "Georgia on the Eve of the Civil War: The Insurance Reports of C.C. Hine." Robert S. Davis, ed. *Atlanta History* 31 (Spring-Summer 1987): 48–56.

Hitt, Michael D. *Charged with Treason: Ordeal of 400 Mill Workers During Military Operations in Roswell, Georgia, 1864–1865.* Monroe, NY: Library Research Associates, 1991.

Hoole, William Stanley. *Lawley Covers the Confederacy.* Tuscaloosa: Confederate Publishing Company, 1964.

Howard, Frances Thomas. *In and Out of the Lines: An Accurate Account of Incidents During 1865.* New York: Neale, 1905.

Huff, Sara. *My 80 Years in Atlanta*: n.p., 1937.

Inscoe, John C., ed. *Appalachians and Race: The Mountain South from Slavery to Segregation.* Lexington: University of Kentucky Press, 2001.

———. *Race, War, and Remembrance in the Appalachian South.* Lexington: University of Kentucky Press, 2008.

———, and Gordon B. McKinney. *The Heart of Confederate Appalachia: Western North Carolina in the Civil War.* Chapel Hill: University of North Carolina Press, 2000.

———, and Robert C. Kenzer, eds. *Enemies of the Country: New Perspectives on Unionists in the Civil War South.* Athens: University of Georgia Press, 2001.

Jennison, Watson W. *Cultivating Race: The Expansion of Slavery in Georgia, 1750–1860.* Lexington: University of Kentucky Press, 2012.

Johnson, Ludwell H. "Northern Profit and Profiteers: The Cotton Rings of 1864–1865." *Civil War History* 12 (March 1966): 101–115.

Johnson, Michael P. "A New Look at the Popular Vote for Delegates to the Georgia Secession Convention." *Georgia Historical Quarterly* 56 (Summer 1972): 259–275.

———. *Toward a Patriarchal Republic: The Secession of Georgia.* Baton Rouge: Louisiana State University Press, 1987.

Johnson, Walter. *River of Dark Dreams: Slavery and Empire in the Cotton Kingdom.* Cambridge, MA: Harvard University Press, 2013.

———. *Soul by Soul: Life Inside the Antebellum Slave Market.* Cambridge, MA: Harvard University Press, 1999.

Jones, Jacqueline. *The Dispossessed: America's Underclasses from the Civil War to the Present.* New York: HarperCollins, 1992.

Judd, Cameron. *The Bridge Burners: A True Adventure of East Tennessee's Underground Civil War.* Johnson City, TN: Nolichuckey Press, 1996.

Karp, Matthew. *This Vast Southern Empire: Slaveholders at the Helm of American Foreign Policy.* Cambridge, MA: Harvard University Press, 2016.

Keehn, David C. *Knights of the Golden Circle: Secret Empire Southern Secession, Civil War.* Baton Rouge: Louisiana State University, Press. 2013.

Kennett, Lee. *Marching Through Georgia: The Story of the Soldiers and Civilians During Sherman's Campaign.* New York: HarperCollins, 1995.

Kurtz, Henry H., Jr. "Hijack of a Locomotive: The Andrews Raid Revised." *Atlanta History* 34 (Fall 1990): 5–14.

Lack, Paul D. "Law and Disorder in Civil War Atlanta." *Georgia Historical Quarterly* 66 (Summer 1982): 171–195.

Lash, Jeffrey N. *Destroyer of the Iron Horse: General Joseph E. Johnston and Confederate Rail Transport, 1861–1865.* Kent, OH: Kent State University Press, 1991.

Lebergott, Stanley. "Why the South Lost: Commercial Purpose in the Confederacy, 1861–1865." *Journal of American History* 70 (June 1983): 58–74.

Leigh, Philip. *Trading with the Enemy: The Covert Economy During the American Civil War.* Yardley, PA: Westholme, 2014.

Leonard, Elizabeth D. *All the Daring of the Soldier: Women of the Civil War Armies.* New York: W.W. Norton, 1999.

Levine, Bruce. *Confederate Emancipation: Southern Plans to Free and Arm Slaves During the Civil War.* New York: Oxford University Press, 2006.

Lowenstein, Roger. *Ways and Means: Lincoln and His Cabinet in the Financing of the Civil War.* New York: Penguin, 2022.

Lowry, Thomas P. *Confederate Heroines: 120 Southern Women Convicted by Union Military Justice.* Baton Rouge: Louisiana State University Press, 2006.

Lupold, John S., and Thomas L. French *Bridging Deep South Rivers: The Life and Legend of Horace King.* Athens, GA: University of Georgia Press, 2004.

Luraghi, Raimondo. *The Rise and Fall of the Plantation South.* New York: New Viewpoints, 1978.

Martin, Jonathan D. *Divided Mastery: Slave Hiring in the American South.* Cambridge, MA: Harvard University Press, 2004.

McCardell, John. *The Idea of a Southern Nation: Southern Nationalists and Southern Nationalism, 1830–1860.* New York: W.W. Norton, 1979.

McKinney, Donald R. *Georgia Freemasons, 1861–1865.* Macon, GA: Georgia Lodge of Research, 2001.

McMurry, Richard M. "Rebels, Extortionists and Counterfeiters: A Note on Confederate Judaeophobia." *Atlanta History* 22 (Fall-Winter 1978): 45–52.

McPherson, James M. *Battle Cry of Freedom: The Civil War Era*. New York: Ballentine Books, 1992.

_____, and William J. Cooper, Jr. *Writing the Civil War: The Quest to Understand*. Columbia: University of South Carolina Press, 1998.

Merritt, Keri Leigh. *Masterless Men: Poor Whites and Slavery in the Antebellum South*. New York: Cambridge University Press, 2017.

Milner, John T. *White Men Stand Together, 1860 and 1890*. Birmingham, AL: McDavid Publishing, 1890.

Mohr, Clarence L. "The Atlanta Campaign and the African American Experience in Civil War Georgia," in Lesley G. Gordon and John C. Inscoe, eds., *Inside the Confederate Nation: Essays in Honor of Emory M. Thomas*. Baton Rouge: Louisiana State University Press, 2005. 272–294.

_____. "Harrison Berry: A Black Pamphleteer in Georgia During Slavery and Freedom." *Georgia Historical Quarterly* (Summer 1983): 189–205.

_____. *On the Threshold of Freedom: Masters and Slaves in Civil War Georgia*. Athens: University of Georgia, 1986.

Moore, Frank, ed. *The Rebellion Record*, 11 vols. New York: D. Van Nostrand, 1864.

Moore, Jerrold N. *Confederate Commissary General: Lucius Bellinger Northrop and the Subsistence Bureau of the Southern Army*. Shippensburg, PA: White Mane, 1996.

Morgan, Chad. *Planters' Progress: Modernizing Confederate Georgia*. Gainesville: University of Florida Press, 2005.

Morgan, James F. *Graybacks and Gold: Confederate Monetary Policy*. Pensacola: Perdido Press, 1985.

Murray, Alton J. *South Georgia Rebels: The True Wartime Experiences of the 26th Regiment, Georgia Volunteer Infantry*. St. Mary's, GA: The Author 1976.

Neely, Mark E., Jr. *Southern Rights: Political Prisoners*. Charlottesville: University of Virginia Press, 1999.

Nelson, R. Scott. "The Confederacy Serves the Southern: The Construction of the Southern Railway Network, 1861–1865." *Civil War History* 41 (September 1995): 227–243.

_____. *Iron Confederacies: Southern Railways, Klan Violence, and Reconstruction*. Chapel Hill: University of North Carolina Press, 1999.

Nichols, G. Dale. *Hurrah for Georgia! The History of the Thirty-eighth Georgia Regiment*. Nashville, TN: A15 Publishing, 2015.

Noe, Kenneth W. *Reluctant Rebels: The Confederates Who Joined the Army after 1861*. Chapel Hill, NC: University of North Carolina Press, 2010.

_____, ed. *The Yellowhammer War: The Civil War and Reconstruction in Alabama*. Tuscaloosa, AL: University of Alabama Press, 2013.

O'Brien, Sean Michael. *Mountain Partisans: Guerilla Warfare in the Southern Appalachians, 1861–1865*. Westport, CT: Praeger, 1999.

O'Connor, Thomas H. "Lincoln and the Cotton Trade." *Civil War History* 7 (March 1961): 20–35.

O'Neill, Charles. *Wild Train: The Story of the Andrews Raiders*. New York: Random House, 1956.

Parker, Ernest. *Days Gone By: Early Gilmer County, Georgia*. Ellijay: Gilmer County Genealogical Society, 1999.

Parrish, T. Michael, and Robert M. Willingham, Jr. *Confederate Imprints: A Bibliography of Southern Publications from Secession to Surrender*. Austin, TX: Jenkins Publishing, 1987.

Pearce, George F. *Pensacola During the Civil War: A Thorn in the Side of the Confederacy*. Gainesville: University of Florida Press, 2000.

Petite, Mary D. *The Women Will Howl: The Union Army Capture of Roswell and New Manchester*. Jefferson, NC: McFarland, 2008.

Phillips, Ulrich Bonnell. *Georgia and State Rights: A Study of the Political History of Georgia from the Revolution to the Civil War*. Washington, [DC]: Government Printing Office, 1902.

Pifer, Mark. *Hidden History of Old Atlanta*. Charleston, SC: The History Press, 2021.

_____. *Native Decatur: The Earliest History of the Decatur, Georgia Area from Its Bedrock Foundation to the Civil War* Decatur, GA: Downriver Books, 2012.

Pioneer Citizens' Society. *Pioneer Citizens' History of Atlanta 1833–1902*. Atlanta: Byrd, 1902.

Pittenger, William. *Capturing a Locomotive: A History of the Secret Service in the Late War*. Washington, DC: The National Tribune, 1905.

_____. *Daring and Suffering: A History of the Andrews Railroad Raid in 1862*. Philadelphia: J.H. Daughaday, 1887.

Ponsford, Brent Hamilton. "Major-General Grenville M. Dodge's Military Intelligence Operations During the Civil War." Master's Thesis, Iowa State University, 1976.

Poss, Faye Stone, comp. *The Southern Watchman, Athens, Georgia Civil War Home Front Coverage 1861–1865*. Snellville, GA: The Author, 2008.

Price, Vivian. *The History of DeKalb County, Georgia 1822–1900*. Fernandina Beach, FL: Wolfe Publishing, 1997.

Radley, Kenneth. *Rebel Watchdog: The Confederate States Army Provost Guard*. Baton Rouge: Louisiana State University Press, 1989.

Ramsdell, Charles W. *Behind the Lines in the Southern Confederacy*. Baton Rouge: Louisiana State University, 1944.

Reed, Wallace P. *History of Atlanta, Georgia: With Illustrations and Biographical Sketches of Some of Its Prominent Pioneers*. Syracuse, NY: D. Mason & Co., 1889.

Regosin, Elizabeth Ann. *Freedom's Promise: Ex-Slave Families and Citizens in the Age of Emancipation*. Charlottesville, VA: University of Virginia Press, 2002.

_____, and Donald R. Shaffer, eds. *Voices of Emancipation: Understanding Slavery, the Civil War, and Reconstruction Through the U.S. Pension Bureau Files*. New York: New York University Press, 2008.

Reid, Whitelaw. *After the War: A Tour of the Southern States, 1865-1866*. Cincinnati: Moore, Wilstach & Baldwin, 1866.
Reidy, Joseph P. *Illusions of Emancipation: The Pursuit of Freedom and Equality in the Twilight of Slavery*. Chapel Hill, NC: University of North Carolina Press, 2019.
Rhoades, Priscilla. "The Women of Castle Thunder." *The Kudzu Monthly* 2 (August 2002): 8-17. Internet journal accessed on May 1, 2024, http://www.kudzumonthly.com/kudzu/aug02/CastleThunder.html
Rhodehamel, John. *America's Original Sin: White Supremacy, John Wilkes Booth, and the Lincoln Assassination*. Baltimore, MD: Johns Hopkins University Press, 2021.
Richards, Samuel. *Sam Richards's Civil War Diary: A Chronicle of the Atlanta Home Front*. Wendy Hamand Venet, ed. Athens: University of Georgia, 2009.
Richards, William A. "'We Live under a Constitution': Confederate Martial Law in Atlanta." *Atlanta History* 33 (Summer 1989): 25-33.
Richardson, William M., Jr. *Justice in Grey: A History of the Judicial System of the Confederate States of America*. Cambridge: Harvard University Press, 1941.
Riley, James A. "Desertion and Disloyalty in Georgia during the Civil War." Master's Thesis, University of Georgia, 1951.
Robinson, Armstead L. *Bitter Fruits of Bondage: The Demise of Slavery and the Collapse of the Confederacy, 1861-1865*. Charlottesville: University of Virginia Press, 2005.
Ruef, Martin. *Between Slavery and Capitalism: The Legacy of Emancipation in the American South*. Princeton: Princeton University Press, 2014.
Russell, James Michael. *Atlanta 1847-1890: City Building in the Old South and the New*. Baton Rouge: Louisiana State University Press, 1988.
Sanders, Charles W., Jr., *While in the Hands of the Enemy: Military Prisons of the Civil War*. Baton Rouge, LA: Louisiana State University Press, 2005.
Sarris, Jonathan D. "'Hellish Deeds ... in a Christian Land': Southern Mountain Communities at War, 1861-1865." Ph.D. diss., University of Georgia, 1998.
_____. *A Separate Civil War: Communities in Conflict in the Mountain South*. Charlottesville, VA: University of Virginia Press, 2006.
Savas, Theodore P., and David A. Woodbury, eds. *The Campaign for Atlanta and Sherman's March to the Sea*. Campbell, CA: Savas Woodbury Publishers, 1994.
Scarborough, Ruth. *Opposition to Slavery in Georgia to 1860*. Nashville, TN: George Peabody College for Teachers, 1933.
Schermerhorn, Calvin. *The Business of Slavery and the Rise of American Capitalism, 1815-1860*. New Haven, CT: Yale University Press, 2015.
_____. *Money Over Mastery, Family Over Freedom: Slavery in the Antebellum Upper South*. Baltimore, MD: Johns Hopkins University Press, 2011.
Seeley, Samantha. *Removal and the Right to Remain: Migration and the Making of the United States*. Chapel Hill, NC: University of North Carolina Press, 2001.
Sensins, Thurman. *Champ Ferguson: Confederate Guerrilla*. Nashville: Vanderbilt University Press, 1942.
Sewell, George Alexander. *Mississippi Black History Makers*. Jackson, MS: University Press of Mississippi, 1984.
Shaffer, Michael K. *Day by Day Through the Civil War in Georgia*. Macon, GA: Mercer University Press, 2022.
Sifakis, Stewart. *Compendium of Confederate Armies: South Carolina and Georgia*. New York: Facts on File, 1995.
Simson, Jay W. *Naval Strategies of the Civil War: Confederate Innovation and Federal Opportunism*. Nashville, TN: Cumberland House, 2001.
Singer, Jane. *The Confederate Dirty War: Arson, Bombings, Assassinations and Plots for Chemical and Germ Attacks on the Union*. Jefferson, NC: McFarland, 2005.
_____, and John Stewart. *Lincoln's Secret Spy: The Civil War Case That Changed the Future of Espionage*. Guilford, CT: Lyons Press, 2015.
Singer, Ralph B. "Confederate Atlanta." Ph.D. diss., University of Georgia, 1973.
Singleton, Royce G. *Richard Peters: Champion of the New South*. Macon, GA: Mercer University Press, 1985.
Smedlund, William S. *Camp Fires of Georgia Troops, 1861-1865*. Sharpsburg, GA: The Author, 1994.
Smith, Gordon B. *History of the Georgia Militia, 1783-1861*. 4 vols. Milledgeville: Boyd Publishing, 2001.
Smith, Marion O. *Confederate Niter District Eight: Middle Tennessee & Northwest Georgia*. Cookeville, TN: The Author, 2011.
Spurr, Michael Jason. "'The Latent Enmity of Georgia': Sherman's March and Its Effects on the Social Division of Georgia," Ph.D. diss., University of Las Vegas, 2009.
Stephens, Larry. *John T. Gatewood: Confederate Bushwhacker*. Gretna, LA: Pelican Publishing, 2012.
Stewart, John. *Pinkertons, Prostitutes and Spies: The Civil War Adventures of Secret Agents Timothy Webster and Hattie Lawton*. Jefferson, NC: McFarland, 2019.
Strauss, Robert. *Worst President Ever: James Buchanan, the POTUS Rating Game, and the Legacy of the Least of the Lesser Presidents*. Guilford, CT: Lyons Press, 2016.
Summers, Mark W. *The Era of Good Stealings*. New York: Oxford University Press, 1993.
_____. *The Plundering Generation: Corruption and the Crisis of the Union, 1849-1861*. New York: Oxford University Press, 1987.
Sumner, Ellen Louise. "Unionism in Georgia, 1860-1861." Master's Thesis, University of Georgia, 1960.

Surdam, David G. *Northern Naval Superiority and the Economics of the American Civil War.* Columbia: University of South Carolina Press, 2001.

_____. "Traders or Traitors: Northern Cotton Trading During the Civil War." *Business and Economic History* 28 (Winter 1999): 301–312.

Sutherland, Daniel E. *The Confederate Carpetbaggers.* Baton Rouge: Louisiana State University Press, 1988.

_____. *A Savage Conflict: The Decisive Role of Guerrillas in the American Civil War.* Chapel Hill: University of North Carolina Press, 2009.

Tabor, Nick. *Africatown: America's Last Slave Ship and the Community It Created.* New York: St. Martin's Press, 2023.

Tadman, Michael. *Speculators and Slaves: Masters, Traders, and Slaves in the Old South.* Madison: University of Wisconsin Press, 1989.

Tatum, Georgia Lee. *Disloyalty in the Confederacy.* Chapel Hill: University of North Carolina Press, 1934.

Taylor, Charles E. *The Signal and Secret Service of the Confederate States.* 1903; special reprint, Harmans, MD: Toomey Press, 1986.

Tharin, R.T. *Arbitrary Arrests in the South; Or, Scenes From the Experience of an Alabama Unionist.* New York: John Bradburn, 1863.

Thompson, Edgar T. *Plantation Societies, Race Relations, and the South: The Regimentation of Populations.* Durham: Duke University Press, 1975.

Todd, Glenda McWhirter. *Unionists in the Heart of Dixie.* 3 vols. Westminster, MD: Heritage Books, 2012.

Towne, Stephen E. *Surveillance and Spies in the Civil War: Exposing Confederate Conspiracies in America's Heartland.* Athens: Ohio University Press, 2014.

Tremmel, George B. *Counterfeit Currency of the Confederate States of America.* Jefferson, NC: McFarland, 2003.

The Union Army. 9 vols. 1908; rep. ed., Wilmington, NC: Broadfoot Publishing Company, 1998.

United States Congress. Joint Select Committee on the Condition of Affairs in the Late Insurrectionary States. *Testimony Taken by the Joint Select Committee to Enquire into the Conditions in the Late Insurrectionary States.* Washington, DC: Government Printing Office, 1872.

United States War Department. (Robert N. Scott, compiler) *The War of the Rebellion: A Compilation of the Official Records of the Union and Confederate Armies.* 128 books. Washington, DC: Government Printing Office, 1880–1901. (Abbreviated as *ORs*) Free access to these volumes is available online and word searchable: collections.library.cornell.edu/moa_new/waro.html and on the subscription site Ancestry.com. The *ORs* have also been microfilmed, with special indexes and finding aids, as *Correspondence of Military Commands Utilized in The War of the Rebellion: a Compilation of the Official Records of the Union and Confederate Armies, 1861–1865* (National Archives microfilm P2282; available on the subscription site Fold3), Record Group 94 Records of the Adjutant General's Office, 1780s-1917; *Official Records of the Union and Confederate Armies, 1861–1865* (National Archives microfilm M262, 128 rolls); and *Military Operations of the Civil War: a Guide Index to Official Records of the Union and Confederate Armies, 1861–1865* (National Archives microfilm M1815 and M1858), Records of the Adjutant General's Office 1917-, Record Group 407, National Archives and Records Administration. An atlas and several other works supplement the *ORs*.

Vandiver, Frank E. *Ploughshares into Swords: Josiah Gorgas and Confederate Ordnance.* College Station: Texas A & M, 1952.

Venet, Wendy Hamand. *A Changing Wind: Commerce and Conflict in Civil War Atlanta.* New Haven: Yale University Press, 2014.

Warner, Ezra J. *Generals in Gray: Lives of Confederate Commanders.* Baton Rouge: Louisiana State University Press, 1959.

Warren, Dorothea Orr. *The Practical Dreamer: A Story of John T. Milner.* Birmingham, AL: Southern Family Press, 1959.

Weber, Thomas. *The Northern Railroads in the Civil War, 1861–1865.* Bloomington, IN: Indiana University Press, 1999.

Weiman. David F. "The Economic Emancipation of the Non-Slaveholding Class: Upcountry Farmers in the Georgia Cotton Economy." *Journal of Economic History* 45 (March 1985): 71–93.

_____. "Urban Growth on the Periphery of the Antebellum Cotton Belt: Atlanta, 1847–1860." *Journal of Economic History* 48 (June 1988): 259–272.

Weitz, Mark A. *A Higher Duty: Desertion Among Georgia Troops During the Civil War.* Lincoln: University of Nebraska Press, 2000.

White, Gregory C. *"This Most Bloody & Cruel Drama": A History of the 31st Georgia Volunteer Infantry.* Baltimore: Genealogical Publishing Company, 1997.

White, William N. "Diary and Letters of Dr. William N. White, a Citizen of Atlanta—Written 1847, 90 Years Ago." William S. Irvine, ed., *Atlanta Historical Bulletin* 10 (July 1937): 35–50.

Williams, David. "'The Faithful Slave Is About Played Out': Civil War Slave Resistance in the Lower Chattahoochee Valley." *Alabama Review* 52 (April 1999): 83–104.

_____. *Georgia's Civil War: Conflict on the Home Front.* Macon, GA: Mercer University Press, 2017.

_____. *I Freed Myself: African American Self-Emancipation During the Civil War.* New York: Cambridge University Press, 2014.

_____. *Rich Man's War: Class, Caste, and Confederate Defeat in the Lower Chattahoochee Valley.* Athens: University of Georgia Press, 1998.

_____, Teresa Crisp, and David Carlson. *Plain Folk in a Rich Man's War: Class and Dissent in Confederate Georgia.* Gainesville: University of Florida Press, 2002.

Williams, Greg H. *Civil War Suits in the U.S. Court of Claims: Cases Involving Compensation to Northerners and Southerners for Wartime Losses*. Jefferson, NC: McFarland, 2006.

Williams' Atlanta Directory, City Guide, and Business Mirror. Atlanta: M. Lynch, 1859, available on the Internet, https://babel.hathitrust.org/cgi/pt?id=emu.10002331152&seq=1, accessed May 24, 2024

Wilson, Carol. *Freedom at Risk: The Kidnapping of Free Blacks in America, 1780–1865*. Lexington: University of Kentucky Press, 1994.

Wise, Stephen R. *Lifeline of the Confederacy: Blockade Running During the Civil War*. Columbia: University of South Carolina Press, 1988.

Wood, W.K. "The Georgia Railroad and Banking Company." *Georgia Historical Quarterly* 57 (Winter 1973): 544–561.

Woods, Michael E. *Arguing Until Doomsday: Stephen Douglas, Jefferson Davis, and the Struggle for Democracy*. Chapel Hill: University of North Carolina Press, 2020.

Woodworth, Steven E. *No Band of Brothers: Problems in the Rebel High Command*. Columbia: University of Missouri Press, 1999.

Wright, Richard G., and Kenneth H. Wheeler. "New Men in the Old South: Joseph E. Brown and His Associates in the Etowah River Valley." *Georgia Historical Quarterly* 93 (Winter 2009): 363–387.

Index

Adair, George W. 63, 66, 145
Adler, Isadore 195n56
African Americans 11, 20–21, 35, 42, 49, 60, 61, 63–65, 74, 76, 88–90,103–104, 124–126, 132, 188n53
Aikin, James 75
Air Line Railroad 16
Alabama (eastern counties) 74
Alabama Street 53
Allred, Elias W. 83
Amos, Ligon & Company 65
Anderson, G. Whit 99
Anderson, John 82
Andersonville (Camp Sumter) 8, 53, 110, 171n1
Andrews, Dr. Lewis Feuilleteau Wilson Andrews 63
Andrews Raiders 35, 90–91, 137
Anglin, Dr. N.L. 133
Athenaeum 35
Appalachia 74, 78, 80
artillery 29, 175n1
Ashburn, George W. 79–80, 119
assassination attempts 93–94
Atalanta and Atlantis 14, 16
Atlanta 2, 14–17, 34–35, 42–45, 50–51, 55, 102, 107, 112,114–115, 116, 117, 119, 127, 160–169
Atlanta Advanced Guards 27
Atlanta Grays 23
Atlanta Ladies Hospital Association 52
Atlanta Machine Works 99
Atlanta Medical College 60, 135, 136
Atlanta munitions works 89
Atlanta Press Guards 50, 122
Atlanta Rolling Mill 17, 59, 99, 116, 117, 136, 189n19
Atlanta Rolling Mill (second) 121, 123
Augusta 16
Austell, A. 133
Avery family 76
Axe (Cherokee warrior) 87

Bagby, William K. 65
Ball Ground 113
banking 18
Baptists 82–83
Barker, J.J. 143
Barker, John Barker 143
Barlow, G.D. 143
Barnes & Campbell 133
Bartow County 122
Bassett, S.P. 122
battlefields 117
Batty, William H. 42, 44
Beach & Root 65
Beatty, David C. 83, 187n38
Beaufort (SC) 33
Bell, Hiram P. 88
Bensinger, W. 143
Berch & Root 132
Berry, Harrison 18
Berry, J.H. 142
Berry & Wood 133
Bethow, J.W. 142
Bickley, George W.L. 20 24
Biggors, Dr. Stephen T. 58
Bird, Boyd 76
Blackjack Island 110
Blairsville 84
Blake, Colonel 76
Blake, Scofield & Markham see Atlanta Rolling Mill
blockade of Southern harbors 53, 101
Booth, John Wilkes 49
Bourlier, Emile 38
Bragg, Braxton 26, 28, 38, 39, 49, 94–95, 98, 123–124
Brazil 118, 194n42
bridge burners 35, 137–138, 196n2
broken leg company 84
Brown, James George 39, 76, 79, 83, 119, 182n5
Brown, John 18
Brown, Joseph E. 24, 50, 79–80, 82, 117, 119
Brown, Wilson 143
Brown, W.W. 143
Bryson, Goldman 83, 84, 85–86, 87, 187n43, 188n46

Buell, Don Carlos 35
Buffins, Robt. 143
Bufman, R. 143
Burchett, N.C. 142
bureaucracy 33–34, 107
Burleson, William Washington 79
Burleson family 76
Burton, James A. 58
businesses 16, 18–19, 34, 40, 54, 58, 62–66, 101, 119, 131–136
Busty, Colonel 83, 85, 187n38
Butler, Lemuel C. 66, 67
Butts County 40

Calhoun, James M. 35, 83, 92
Camden, Marvel J. 48
Camp McDonald 43
Camp Oglethorpe 113
Campbell, W.H. 143
Campbell County 88
Canton 78, 79
Cartersville 121
Cassville 78, 79
Castle Thunder (Richmond, VA) 38, 88
Catawba tribe 86–87
Cayce, M.C. 65
Centre & Treadwell 135
Chattanooga (TN) 14, 16, 35, 36, 52, 58, 74, 80, 88, 105–106
Cherokee County (AL) 78–79
Cherokee County (GA) 82, 85
Cherokee County (NC) 85
Cherokees 86–87
Chestatee Artillery 31
Chicago and Atlanta 74, 172n8
Chickamauga battle 51, 61, 106
children and orphans 45, 55–56
Chisholm, William 65
Churchwell, Wm. M. 143
Civil War 105, 108–109, 111
civilians 193n31
Clark & Lewis 133
Clarke, Robert M. 63, 65
Clarke & Grubbs 63
Cobb, Howell 116

Index

coffee 55
Cohan, Solomon 66
Collier, Wesley G. 46
Columbus (GA) 16, 38, 58
Confederate military 50, 52, 105–106, 108
Confederate States Court 99
confidence criminals 39–40
Conscription Act 74, 77–78, 109
conspiracies 19–20, 45
cotton 11, 20–21, 22–23, 53, 62, 106, 118, 124, 126, 127
Coulter, E. Merton 1–2
counterfeiting 57–58
Crawford, Elisha 48
Crawford, John Calhoun 69
Crawford, M.C. 178n34
Crawford, Robert A. 20, 39–42, 60–61, 66, 92, 104, 120, 178n35
Crawford, Robert C. 40, 44, 177n34
Crawford, William Adulston Rogers 40, 66–67, 178n35, 184 n. 38
Crawford, Frazer & Company 57, 63–65, 68–70, 101, 104
credit reports 131
crime (Atlanta) 19, 45, 46–49, 118
Cuba 20, 118, 194n42
Cyclorama of the Battle of Atlanta 6, 168

Dahlonega 80–82, 83, 86
Dalton 16, 39, 109
dancing 53
Davies, J.C. 133
Davis, Jefferson 24–25, 59, 71, 83, 85
Dawson County 31, 88
Dean, Hiram Hornbuckle 14, 195 56
Dean, Sarah Hudson 14
Dean Merchant Mill 94
Decatur *see* DeKalb County
Decatur Street 18, 53, 66
DeKalb County 14, 16, 91
Democratic Party 19
Denney, Ken 65, 67, 99, 135
desertions 52, 79, 82, 110
Dobson, Dan 88
Dodge, Grenville 39
Dooly, Martin H. 121, 139
Dority, P. 142
Dorsey, D.A. 143
draft evasion 46, 49–51, 74–75, 81
D.S. Myer & Co. 133
Ducktown (TN) 85
Duffell, Thos. L. 142
Dun, R.G. (credit reports) 131
Dunning, James L. 99, 123
Dyer, Thomas G. 3

East Alabama 74
Eberhart, E.B. 84
Echol's Battery 46
Edwards, Ned 90, 188n57
Edwards, W.A. 80
Elbert County 84
Ellijay 83

Fagin, J.T. 82
Fain, William C. 85
Fairburn 88
fancy girls 69
Fannin County 81
Farrow, Henry P. 117
Federal Road 16
Ferguson, Champ 38, 187n38
Field, Gresham & Company 65, 68
Fields, L. 65
financing 18
Finch, John 39
Findlay Iron Works 63
Findley, James J. 192n10
Finn, J.H. 133
fire and fire companies 35, 51
First Alabama Cavalry Regiment (USA) 77
First Georgia Cavalry Battalion (USA) 76, 79
First Georgia Infantry Battalion (USA) 76
First Georgia Regiment State Troops (CSA) 88
Fitzhugh, George 72
Five Points 14, 68
flag 24, 31, 117
Florida 110–111
Ford, John J. 65
Foreacre, Green Jones 24, 44, 90, 158, 180n49
foreign nationals 59
Forrest, Nathan Bedford 51, 63
Forsythe County 88
Fort McPherson 56
Fort McRae 26
Fort Pickens *see* Pensacola
Fort Pulaski 31, 176n10
Fort Sumter 25, 26
Foster, Ira A. 139
Franklin & Armfield 66
Franklin County 14
Frazer, Addison D. 63
Frazer, Thomas Lafayette 63
Fred Gresham & Company 65
Fry, David 143
Fugitive Slave Act of 1850 22
Fuller, William Allen 137–141
Fulton County Probate Court 45
Fulton Dragoons 24

Gaines Mill battle 44
Galt, Edward F. 80, 81

galvanized Yankees 49
Gasaway, Jas. 142
Gate City *see* Atlanta
Gate City Guards 15
Gatewood, John 45, 78–79
General (locomotive) 137, 138, 140–141
Gentleman George 49, 97
Georgia Railroad Bank 87
Georgia records 114, 162, 163, 165
Georgia state records 193n27
Georgia Volunteers *see* Lee's Volunteers
Gilbert, G.H. 58
Glass, John Milton 39
Glenn, Luther 116
gold (Dahlonega Mint) 85–86
Gone With the Wind 3, 8, 60, 117
Goodan Shields & Co. 134
Gout, J.M. 79
Grant, Lemuel P. 112
Grant, Ulysses S. 51–52
Graves, Frank N. 49
Green, John 143
Griffin (GA) 40
Griffin, S.H. 65
guerrillas 184n5
Guild, L.A. 18
Gwinnett County 14

Hall, J.J. 47
Hammond, A.W. 133
Hammontree family 76
Hancock County 89
Hanleiter, Cornelius Redding 30, 35, 59–60, 63, 176n5
Harford, Joseph 48, 100
Hargrove James Spurlock 46
Harpers Ferry 18
Harrington, Mrs. 48
Harris, Asa L. 121
Hawkins, M.J. 143
Healy & Berry 133
Henderson, Captain 84
Henderson, James 55
Henderson, W.H. 66
Hendricks, Bradford 39
Hendrix, John C. 83, 94
Herald, A.J. 142
Hicks, J. 142
Hillyard, George 140
Hines, Charles Cole 131
Hoganville 26
Holmes, Ryland F. 82, 84, 85
home guards 109–110, 115, 192n10
hospitals (Atlanta) 60–61, 183n6
hotels 17
Houston County 40
Howard, Kathron Stewart 122

Index

Hubbard & Chisolm 135
Huff, Sarah 12, 66, 104, 122
hunger 47, 55–56, 62, 78, 114, 117
Hunnicutt, Eli Tellinger 89, 99

Immell, P.J. 135
Independent State Guards 140
Ingram, J.J. 142
Inman & Cole 65
Insurance 131–132
Ironton 122

Jackson, John K. 48, 51
Jackson, Thomas 43
Jackson & Bro. 133
Jacobin Club *see* Secret Yankees
Jasper County (GA) 55
Jewish merchants 9, 36, 101, 167
J.L. Winter & Company 65
Jo. Thompson Artillery 31
Johnson, J.H. 134
Johnson, M.J. 134
Johnson, Myrtle Burkett 122
Johnston, Joseph E. 43, 59, 123
Jones, Oliver H. 89
Jones & McLandon 133
Jordan, Benjamin F. 83

Kay, William 17–18
Kenan, Michael Johnston 24
Kenny, Samuel W. 39
Kidd, W. 133
Kile, Thomas 14
King, Carrie 38
Knight, Wm. 143
Knights of the Golden Circle 20
Ku Klux Klan 80, 109, 119
Kuhrt, H.G. 16, 133
Kyle, T.O. 48

labor and class 10–11, 13, 19–23, 62, 124–125
LaGrange 26
Lamshee, L. 135
Lamshee & Purell 134
land grants (federal) 72–75, 105
Lawton, Alexander Robert 30, 35
Lawton, John William 39
Lawton, Winburn J. 44
Lawton-Gordon-Evans Brigade 43
Laxley, L.C. 79
Leary, Major 28
Lee, Barnett 14
Lee, Barney Drury 14
Lee, Cynthia Ann Jordan 14
Lee, George Washington 13–15, 18–19, 23–24, 26–27, 29, 31, 57–59, 61–62, 84–85, 92–97, 104, 105, 107, 109, 111, 113, 114, 116, 117, 119, 120, 121–122, 123, 125, 126, 127, 129–130, 141
Lee, George Washington (Civil Rights leaders) 171n2, 179n43
Lee, George Washington (cousin) 76–77
Lee, George Washington Custis 85
Lee, G.W. (South Carolina) 172n2
Lee, Indiana "Anna" F. 14, 30, 122, 195n56
Lee, Major 24
Lee, Marcus D. 46, 48, 121
Lee, Nancy Catherine Dean 14, 30
Lee, Robert E. 10–11, 30, 34, 43, 53, 71
Lee, Sarah 14
Lee family 19, 115, 145, 146
Lee Street 196n65
Lee's Volunteers 24, 25, 26, 46, 95–97
Lester, W.H. 134, 135
Leyton, Austin 44
Ligon, W.C. 142
Long, Henry 22
Longstreet, James 61
Loomis, John Q. 95
Loudon (TN) 84
Lowe, Thomas J. 46
Lumpkin, Martha Atalanta 14
Lumpkin County 80–81
Lynch, J. & J. 133
Lynch, Jno. 133

Macon (GA) 16, 55, 63, 102, 113–114
Madison (GA) 74
Majors, F.G. 142
Malone, Milton 49
Malvern Hill battle 44
Mangum, Nathanael 81
manufacturing 33–34, 55, 62, 68
Marietta Paper Mill 57
Markham, William O. 19, 45, 99, 100–101
Marthasville 14
Martin, B. 142
Martin, J. 142
Mason, E.H. 143
Masonic Orphans Home 56
Mayer, Jacobe D. 65
McAdoo, William Gibbs 16–17, 54, 83, 100, 140–141
McAdoo, William Gibbs, Jr. 190n25
McClelland, J.D. 79
McCollum, Benjamin F. 192n10
McCoy, Thos. 143
McGinnely, George 58
McGready, James Getty 58
McMillen & Fleming 135
McNaught, Ormon & Co. 134
Mercer, George Anderson 30, 33
Mercer, Hugh Weeden 30, 31, 43
Mexico 20, 41
Meyer, D. 132
Meyers, Michael 100, 134
Miller, Henry 143
Mills, H. 143
Milner, John T. 10, 25
Minutemen of Fulton County 23
Missionary Ridge 74
Mitchell, David Y. 124
Mitchell, Ormsby Macknight 137
Moore, James C. 38
Moorland, Jacob 188n57
Morgan, John H. 59
Morganton 83, 84
Mühlenbrinck, Hancke C. 63
munitions works 189n10
Murphy (NC) 85
Murphy, Andrew 137
Myers, M. 134
Myrtle Hill Cemetery 124, 125

Native American "Know Nothing" Party 19, 173n22
Nelson, Allison 20
Nesbit, E.A. 116
New Orleans 21, 28, 34, 41, 66, 67, 85, 108, 178n35, 184n38, 190n22
New York 17, 18, 42, 74, 101, 120, 121, 122
Newcomb, D.S. 18
Niles, Samuel Dexter 50, 66, 122–123
Niter and Mining Bureau 117
Noble Iron Works 175n1
Norcross, Jonathan 100–101
North Georgia 74, 112–113, 117

Oakland Cemetery 60, 160
Ocmulgee Indian Mounds 113
Okefenokee Swamp 110
Opposition *see* resistance to secession or war

Palmetto 91
Panic of 1857 and 1859 11, 16, 18, 22
Parr, Lewis J. 29, 30
Parrott, J. 143
Patrick, John R. 88
Peace Society 52, 71, 74
Peachtree Street 14, 46, 48, 53, 65–66, 160
Pensacola (FL) 25–27, 96–97

Pettinger, Wm. 143
Pickens County (GA) 50, 56, 76, 83, 113
Pierce, Peter 143
police force (Atlanta) 44–45
Polk, Leonidas 42
Pollin, Mrs. 38
Ponder, Ephraim 10, 20–21
population of Atlanta 16, 36, 102
Porter, J.K. 143
Power, S.F. 69
Powers, Bennet 143
prisoners of war 88, 113, 142–143
profiteers 36, 53, 101, 190n20
prostitution 53, 67, 69
Provost Marshal 44

Qualla Boundary 87

Railroad Battalion 140–141
railroads 15, 16, 18, 33, 47, 61–62
Ramson, Gilbert & Burr 132
Randolph County (AL) 74
Rattle (Cherokee warrior) 87
Rawlins, Joseph Robert 122, 195n56
Reddick, W. 143
Reed, Jas. 142
refugees 35–37, 66, 73, 93
Relly, W.H. 142
resistance to secession or war 71, 81–88
Reynolds, Alexander Reynolds 42
Rhea, H. Blount 86
Rhea, John H. "Coot" 86, 187n43
Rhodes, Jabez 96
Rhodes, Twiggs L.W. 19
Rhodes, V.W. 19, 173n18
Richards, Jabez 58
Richards, John 83
Richards, Samuel 21
Richmond (VA) 43, 48, 51, 88
rioting 55–56
Ripley, Roswell Sabine 43
Ripley, T.R. 133
Roane County (NC) 76
Roark, W.W. 134
Robinson, S. 143
Rome (GA) 38, 51, 121
Root, Sidney 49, 56
Rosecrans, William R. 39, 89
Ross, Marion 143
Roswell 113
Roswell textile factory 54–55, 114, 115, 183n73
Rothchild family 101
Rushton Company 29, 175n1
Ryan, J. 134

Salmans Mathews & Co. 134
salt 18, 33, 55, 57, 101
saltpeter 33
Savannah 16, 29–30, 31, 33
Scott, Dr. Anderson L. 47
Scott, John Scott 143
Seago, A.K. 66
Secret Service 58
Secret Yankees 19, 89–90, 100
Selma (AL) 88
Sequestration Act 99
Seven Pines Campaign 43
Shackleford, S.J. 65
Shadrach, Perry G. 143
Sheets, Charles Christopher Columbus 77
Shehan Jas. 142
Shepard's Plantation battle 14
Sherman, William Tecumseh 99, 116
Shropshire & Thomas 69
sickness 30, 45, 60, 65
Sims, C. 142
Skidaway Island 30
Slavens Samuel 143
slavery 17–18, 42, 60, 62–70, 71–72, 103–104, 118
smallpox see sickness
Smith, B.D. 66
Smith, Charlotte 99
Smith, Edmund Kirby 91
Smith, Horace 99
Smith, L.W. 132
Smith, William Duncan 30, 43
Soldiers Executive Aid Association 60
South Georgia 109–110
Southern Confederacy (newspaper) 41, 58, 93, 94
Southern Insurance Company 122
speculators see profiteers
Spencer, Ambrose 53
spies 36, 38–39, 177n25
Standing Peachtree 14
Steam Road Wagon Company 122
Stephens, Alexander H. 17, 49, 94, 124
Sterne, Simon 58
Stiles, Joseph C. 18
Stone, Amherst W. 100, 101
Stone, Cyrena 90, 98, 100, 101, 123, 126
Stone Mountain (New Gibraltar) 8, 14, 18, 121, 122
Strauss, Isidor 101
Streight, Abel 51, 90, 112

Tank, Charles 183n6
Tank, Napoleon 183n6
Tate, William 82
Taylor, Campbell H. 188n46

Taylor, C.W. 142
Tennessee 31
Texas 89, 103
Texas (locomotive) 137, 138
Thirty-eighth Georgia Regiment 31, 43–44, 176n8, 189n13
Thomas, George Henry 38
Thomas Legion 86
Thompkins, John 143
Thompson, W.H. 142
Thompson, Wm. 143
Thomson, J. Edgar 14
Thrasher, J.J. 133
Thurman, Benjamin 66
Tift family 101
Timson, John 87
Tomlinson & Barnes 133
Tompkins, J. 143
transportation (Atlanta) 17
Trout House Hotel 17, 58, 134
tuberculosis 7, 13, 24, 28, 31, 43–44, 123
Tullahoma (TN) 39
Turner, J.A. 69
Turner, Winguit H. 65
Tuscaloosa (AL) 88
Twenty-fifth Infantry Battalion 46–48, 83–84, 111–112

Union Circle 98
Unionists see resistance to secession or war
United States Military Railroad 141
Upham, Samuel C. 57
Upson County 60

Valentino, L. 134
Vance, Zebulon 85
Van Dorn, Earl 59
Vaughn, Mr. 47
Vaughn, Nancy 91
Velásquez, Loreta Janeta 53
Vicksburg soldiers 51, 52, 61, 74
Villepique, John Bodenave 96, 189n13
Vincent, Edward Arista 181n70

W. Herring & Son 132
wagoning 18
Walker, H.H. 82
Walker, Dr. Mary 38
Wallace, Alex M. 99
Wallace, C.H. 134
Wallace, J.R. 134
Walls, John 143
Washburn, W.P. 76
Washington Hall Hotel 65, 67, 124
Wassaw Island 30
Watkins, Elihu P. 23, 24, 43, 44

Wayne, Henry Constantine 61, 88, 93, 94, 95, 113
Welborn, Taylor, & Co. 65
Western & Atlantic Railroad 16, 35, 48, 80, 83, 94, 112–113, 114, 117, 121, 137, 139, 160, 185n8, 196n1
Westmoreland, Willis Foreman 23
whiskey 46–47
Whitaker, Thomas E. 65
Whitaker & Turner 67
White, Ransom 143
White, William N. 17
White County 84, 88
Whitehall Street 53, 65–66
Wiggin, B.F. 19
Williams, F.A. 133
Wilson, A. 143
Wilson, G.D. 143
Wilson, James H. 114
Wilson, T.C.H. 135
Winder, John H. 110
Wirz, Henry 8
Wollam, John 143
women 55–56, 60, 144–155
Wood, A.C. 41
Wood, Edward J. 55
Wood, M. 143
workers 20
Worth County 110
Wright, Augustus Romaldus 27, 29, 96, 176n8
Wright, Moses Hannibal 95, 99, 107
Wright's Legion 29, 30–31, 47, 176n8

Yonah (locomotive) 137

www.ingramcontent.com/pod-product-compliance
Lightning Source LLC
Chambersburg PA
CBHW060342010526
44117CB00017B/2939